ELIMINATING WASTE IN BUSINESS

RUN LEAN, BOOST PROFITABILITY

Linda M. Orr
Dave J. Orr

apress®

Eliminating Waste in Business: Run Lean, Boost Profitability

Copyright © 2014 by Linda M. Orr and Dave J. Orr

This work is subject to copyright. All rights are reserved by the Publisher, whether the whole or part of the material is concerned, specifically the rights of translation, reprinting, reuse of illustrations, recitation, broadcasting, reproduction on microfilms or in any other physical way, and transmission or information storage and retrieval, electronic adaptation, computer software, or by similar or dissimilar methodology now known or hereafter developed. Exempted from this legal reservation are brief excerpts in connection with reviews or scholarly analysis or material supplied specifically for the purpose of being entered and executed on a computer system, for exclusive use by the purchaser of the work. Duplication of this publication or parts thereof is permitted only under the provisions of the Copyright Law of the Publisher's location, in its current version, and permission for use must always be obtained from Springer. Permissions for use may be obtained through RightsLink at the Copyright Clearance Center. Violations are liable to prosecution under the respective Copyright Law.

ISBN-13 (pbk): 978-1-4302-6088-2

ISBN-13 (electronic): 978-1-4302-6089-9

Trademarked names, logos, and images may appear in this book. Rather than use a trademark symbol with every occurrence of a trademarked name, logo, or image we use the names, logos, and images only in an editorial fashion and to the benefit of the trademark owner, with no intention of infringement of the trademark.

The use in this publication of trade names, trademarks, service marks, and similar terms, even if they are not identified as such, is not to be taken as an expression of opinion as to whether or not they are subject to proprietary rights.

While the advice and information in this book are believed to be true and accurate at the date of publication, neither the authors nor the editors nor the publisher can accept any legal responsibility for any errors or omissions that may be made. The publisher makes no warranty, express or implied, with respect to the material contained herein.

> President and Publisher: Paul Manning
> Acquisitions Editor: Jeff Olson
> Developmental Editor: Jennifer Lynn
> Editorial Board: Steve Anglin, Mark Beckner, Ewan Buckingham, Gary Cornell, Louise Corrigan, James DeWolf, Jonathan Gennick, Jonathan Hassell, Robert Hutchinson, Michelle Lowman, James Markham, Matthew Moodie, Jeff Olson, Jeffrey Pepper, Douglas Pundick, Ben Renow-Clarke, Dominic Shakeshaft, Gwenan Spearing, Matt Wade, Steve Weiss, Tom Welsh
> Coordinating Editor: Rita Fernando
> Copy Editor: Kezia Endsley
> Compositor: SPi Global
> Indexer: SPi Global
> Cover Designer: Anna Ishchenko

Distributed to the book trade worldwide by Springer Science+Business Media New York, 233 Spring Street, 6th Floor, New York, NY 10013. Phone 1-800-SPRINGER, fax (201) 348-4505, e-mail orders-ny@springer-sbm.com, or visit www.springeronline.com. Apress Media, LLC is a California LLC and the sole member (owner) is Springer Science + Business Media Finance Inc (SSBM Finance Inc). SSBM Finance Inc is a Delaware corporation.

For information on translations, please e-mail rights@apress.com, or visit www.apress.com.

Apress and friends of ED books may be purchased in bulk for academic, corporate, or promotional use. eBook versions and licenses are also available for most titles. For more information, reference our Special Bulk Sales–eBook Licensing web page at www.apress.com/bulk-sales.

Any source code or other supplementary materials referenced by the author in this text is available to readers at www.apress.com. For detailed information about how to locate your book's source code, go to www.apress.com/source-code/.

Apress Business: The Unbiased Source of Business Information

Apress business books provide essential information and practical advice, each written for practitioners by recognized experts. Busy managers and professionals in all areas of the business world—and at all levels of technical sophistication—look to our books for the actionable ideas and tools they need to solve problems, update and enhance their professional skills, make their work lives easier, and capitalize on opportunity.

Whatever the topic on the business spectrum—entrepreneurship, finance, sales, marketing, management, regulation, information technology, among others—Apress has been praised for providing the objective information and unbiased advice you need to excel in your daily work life. Our authors have no axes to grind; they understand they have one job only—to deliver up-to-date, accurate information simply, concisely, and with deep insight that addresses the real needs of our readers.

It is increasingly hard to find information—whether in the news media, on the Internet, and now all too often in books—that is even-handed and has your best interests at heart. We therefore hope that you enjoy this book, which has been carefully crafted to meet our standards of quality and unbiased coverage.

We are always interested in your feedback or ideas for new titles. Perhaps you'd even like to write a book yourself. Whatever the case, reach out to us at editorial@apress.com and an editor will respond swiftly. Incidentally, at the back of this book, you will find a list of useful related titles. Please visit us at www.apress.com to sign up for newsletters and discounts on future purchases.

The Apress Business Team

To Makayla, Isabella, Victoria, and Christian.

Contents

About the Authors...ix
Introduction xi

Chapter 1: Areas of Waste ··1
Chapter 2: Strategy of Waste 23
Chapter 3: Marketing...69
Chapter 4: Sales 131
Chapter 5: Human Resources 167
Chapter 6: Technology 201
Chapter 7: Finance 241
Chapter 8: Business Operations 263
Appendix: Tools to Eliminate Waste.............................303

Index 329

About the Authors

Linda M. Orr, Ph.D., is an Associate Professor of Marketing at the University of Akron. Her specialties are sales, sales management, and data analytics. She is the author of *When to Hire—or Not Hire–a Consultant, Advanced Sales Management Handbook and Cases: Analytical, Applied, and Relevant,* and a co-editor of two other books: *Direct Marketing in Action: Cutting Edge Strategies for Finding and Keeping your Best Customers,* finalist for the American Marketing Association's Berry Book Prize for the Best Book in Marketing (2009), and *Marketing in the 21st Century: Volume 3: Company and Customer Relations.* Dr. Orr has also published in several refereed journals. In addition, Dr. Orr served as assistant marketing director for Warner Bros. Records in Nashville, and in a variety of managerial capacities in the restaurant and finance industries. She has served as a consultant in numerous Fortune 500 companies and smaller companies in many industries.

Dave J. Orr is the System Director of Business Intelligence at Summa Health System. He has worked in process improvement, technical sales, engineering, product development, operations management, business analysis, and quality roles for over 15 years. He has served the healthcare, automotive, appliance, military, consumer product, and aerospace industries. Dave is a certified Six Sigma Master Black Belt from Kent State University. He earned his MBA from Robert Morris University and has a BS in Plastics Engineering Technology from Penn State University. Dave is an author of *When to Hire—or Not Hire–a Consultant and Advanced Sales Management Handbook and Cases: Analytical, Applied, and Relevant.* In addition to his work in healthcare, Dave is a lecturer in the EMBA program at Kent State University.

Introduction

Many of us have heard the stories of the infamous ways that large businesses waste their money. Typical examples abound, such as Mercedes-Benz buying Chrysler in 1998 for a whopping $20 billion. Adjusted for inflation in today's dollar that would be $26.6 billion.[1] Less than 10 years later, in 2007, Mercedes sold Chrysler Cerberus Capital Management for $7 billion—that's a 19.6 billion-dollar loss! Then, there are failures like New Coke and the numerous cross-cultural marketing blunders like "Nothing sucks like an Electrolux." And, of course, there are ginormous examples of waste in government, like the fact that Washington spends $25 billion annually maintaining unused or vacant federal properties.[2]

Too, we often hear statistics like, out of the 30,000 new products that are introduced into the market each year, 95 percent of them fail,[3] and about one in four restaurants closes or changes ownership within their first year of business. Over three years, that number rises to three in five. This equates to about a 60 percent failure rate, which is equivalent to cross-industry averages for every new business.[4] These are the prominent business statistics we hear all the time.

Because of examples such as these, there are numerous books and resources available to help business leaders avoid these mistakes that are, unfortunately, all too common. However, this book is not about avoiding huge, disastrous failures. The topics covered in this book certainly address these enormous disasters, but also covers the tiny, day-to-day activities that cost small businesses and large corporations billions every day.

---

[1] Goldman, Leah and Gus Lubin, "The 25 Worst Mistakes In History," http://www.businessinsider.com/worst-mistakes-in-history-2011-4?op=1 4/1/2013, April 26, 2011.
[2] Office of Senator Tom Coburn (R-OK), "Subcommittee Oversight Efforts Identify $1.1 Trillion in Waste or Questionable Spending," October 19, 2006, at http://coburn.senate.gov/oversight/?FuseAction=OversightAction.Home&ContentRecord_id=611f1f4c-802a-23ad-475d-223d6490f308.
[3] Christensen, Clay, "Clay Christensen's Milkshake Marketing," http://hbswk.hbs.edu/item/6496.html?wknews=02142011, February 14, 2011.
[4] Miller, Kelly, "The Restaurant Failure Myth," http://www.businessweek.com/stories/2007-04-16/the-restaurant-failure-mythbusinessweek-business-news-stock-market-and-financial-advice, April 16, 2007.

Some of these wastes we never think about: meeting after meeting with no agenda or measurable outcomes; excessive business travel; unnecessary motivators; redundant employees; office space and more office space; storerooms full of extra stock "in case we need it;" marketing money sprayed in all directions in the vain hope it will create customers; paper, paper, and more wasted paper; HR policies that fatten the corporate waistline rather than keeping it trim; software and hardware expenditures for systems that are never used or never used fully; consultants; and companies exercising budgeting practices that result in "more of the same, plus 2 percent."

More or less, we see the business world as stuck at an important crossroad. On one hand, they keep repeating the same ridiculous practices because it is simply "the way things have always been done." It's as if they are stuck in 1950, spending all day in meetings and spending every last dime on marketing. On the other hand, companies dive into new practices, like cloud computing, social media presence, and ERP and CRM systems without a clue how to effectively and efficiently use the tools or without knowing why they are even pursuing them.

Waste, Waste, and More Waste

Take something as simple as paper. In the days before the copy machine, workers had their secretary type one perfect copy of a report. Then, this report was passed around from person to person in the conference room during a meeting. This was a waste of time and money. True, you didn't have enormous paper and supply costs, but you had the cost of the secretary who did the typing and the cost of all the managers who had to sit there in the meeting individually reading the report.

Then, the copy machine was invented. Now every employee in the meeting could have a copy of a report. We didn't need the secretaries to type it up, and we could save time by having everyone have their own copy. Now, without even thinking about things, we think we have to make a copy for everyone to hold in their hands and review. Have we changed anything? Have we actually saved any money? It's doubtful. As we will show in this book, we are spending more time in meetings and more time managing and reading paper, even though we have electronic means to need make meetings and paper practically, if not totally, obsolete.

While the details are covered later in the book, no one probably even realized that they were creating a massive black hole of money waste when the copier came out. The average office worker uses 10,000 sheets of paper a year.

This cost is roughly 10–11 percent of the total cost of the paper.[5] Some of the other costs of the paper include the copy machine itself, the ink, the paper storage fees, and the trash disposal fees. For a small company of 100 employees, that's $100,000 in paper costs! For a larger company of 10,000 employees, that's $10 million dollars!!! From paper!!!

> **Note** The average small business company wastes $100,000 a year in paper costs. The average large company wastes more than $10 million in paper costs a year!!!

Trapped by a Mindset

Even today, with the enormous surges in technology, we still utilize the 1980s thinking. How many times have you printed something that someone e-mailed to you? How many times have you even considered who needs a copy of the document? It seems now, we actually send documents to more people because we can, because it is so easy to send a mass e-mail. Then, everyone who got the e-mail, at a minimum, wastes the time it takes to read it. It's so easy to set up meetings and invite anyone to the meeting with the click of a mouse. So we do it, without even thinking about the time it wastes.

Just imagine if that company in the paper waste example, of 10,000 employees, purchased an iPad or tablet for every employee so that everyone could save and view all documents electronically. That action would reduce the $10 million in paper costs to $5 million the first year. Then, just to be fair, there would be a few more million in IT costs to implement all the necessary software and get every employee proper trained on the software. So, for the first year, becoming a paperless office might net the company only a small amount of money. But, then, forever, the company has a $10 million dollar surplus, minus any hardware, network, and software upgrade costs.

So, why is every office in America not paperless? Are business leaders seriously that dumb? Of course not.

We have a similar example from our personal lives. For the longest time, just as many business leaders are hung up on the, "I *have* to buy paper" mindset, we thought we "had" to buy laundry detergent. Yes, that's right, a couple of years ago, we were shocked when we learned that our family of 6, who does at least one load of laundry per day, didn't actually need to be

---

[5] McCorry, K.J., "The Cost of Managing Paper: A Great Incentive to Go Paperless!" http://www.informit.com/articles/printerfriendly.aspx?p=1393497, September 16, 2009.

spending $20–$30 a month on commercial detergent. We are sure all the executives reading this book are thinking you just *have* to buy paper, just as we were thinking, "We *have* to buy laundry detergent." How do you think people washed clothes before Procter & Gamble? We'll spare you the details because this is a business book (if you're interested, Google homemade laundry detergent), but we can remember how mad and happy we were at the same time when we realized that homemade laundry detergents are all natural, irritant free, work better, and about 1/25 the cost of the brand-name detergents. Then there's vinegar to clean floors at about 1/100 the price of floor cleaners. The marketers (maybe you?) have convinced us that we need all these things.

We have become so trapped in these mindsets that we don't know how to think any other way. We've come so far, with so much technology and innovation, and we do not seem to be using it properly. In our personal and professional lives, we have actually increased our daily costs and made our lives less efficient.

We all are working more hours now than ever before. In fact, almost 40 percent of professionals are expected to work more than 50 hours a week.[6] Likewise, as you can see in Figure FM-1, a survey of employed e-mail users finds that 22 percent of employees are expected to respond to work e-mail when they're not at work, 50 percent check work e-mail on the weekends, 46 percent check work e-mail on sick days, and 34 percent of employees check work e-mail while on vacation.[7] These statistics mean that businesses have integrated technologies, but have made no attempt to integrate the technologies in a manner that makes employees more productive.

---

[6]Williams, Joan C. and Heather Boushey, "The Three Faces of Work-Family Conflict: The Poor, the Professionals, and the Missing Middle," http://www.americanprogress.org/issues/2010/01/pdf/threefaces.pdf, January 2010.
[7]Pew Internet and American Life Project, "Networked Workers," http://www.pewinternet.org/~/media//Files/Reports/2008/PIP_Networked_Workers_FINAL.pdf.pdf, September 2008.

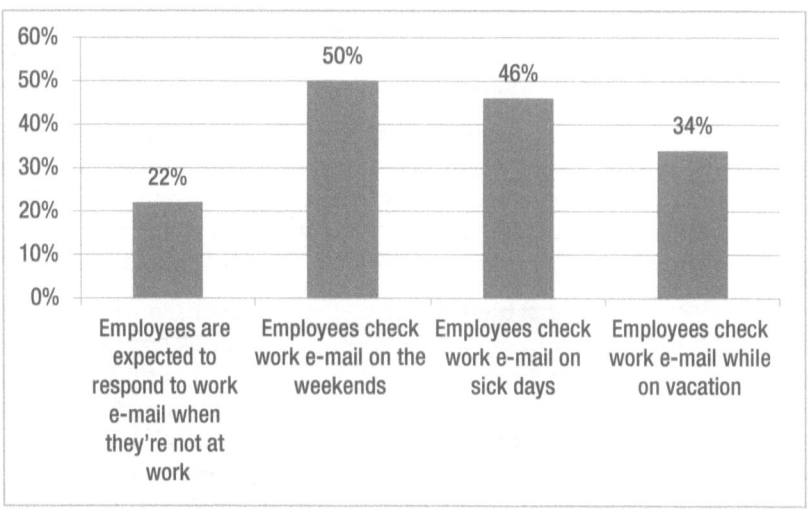

Figure FM-1. Overworked America. (*Source*: Pew Internet and American Life Project, "Networked Workers," http://www.pewinternet.org/~/media//Files/Reports/2008/PIP_Networked_Workers_FINAL.pdf.pdf, September 2008.)

Note Technology has actually caused us to work more. Few people take the time to integrate technologies with the purpose of making employees more efficient. Fewer people track post-implementation efficiency gains.

A New Way of Thinking

We used the laundry detergent and cleaning products example because most of us can identify with how much we pay for cleaning products. If you own a small personal business, you probably look at every bottle of window cleaner and every staple and think about how to get it cheaper. For you, this book is about a radically new way of thinking. Don't think, "where can I buy the cheapest window cleaner?" Instead think, "do I need to buy window cleaner at all?" (And no, we're not suggesting becoming slobs.) For the biggest companies, the example is probably more like the following. You might not think about your cleaning product expense if you pay a maid every week to clean your home. You might be thinking if someone can afford a maid, why do they care? That's exactly the wrong logic.

Even if you "outsource" your cleaning, there is still a significant difference between Windex ($3 a bottle or $40 for a box of commercial powdered Windex) and pennies for natural cleaners. If the cleaning person saved the $5 a week needed for commercial cleaning fluids, by retirement in 40 years, that savings would amount to $140,288.86! How could anyone turn down that kind of money? That's just one person making one small change. Multiply that by all the tiny areas of waste on a personal level. Now multiply all those areas of waste by the number of employees.

Just imagine all that waste across thousands of people in a large corporation! That's when you start seeing $50,000 granite tables, $10,000 office furniture, and Keurig machines in every corner. Managers fail to think about the real reasons purchases are made. Does a Keurig machine increase employee satisfaction and productivity? How many have measured that assumption?

Nearly every corner of most businesses, small and large, harbors this pointless waste—wasted money, time, effort, or all three. This book highlights common ways that businesses across all industries waste money without realizing it. We're not talking about the equivalent of cutting out gourmet coffee from your personal budget. We hope everyone knows that $50,000 granite tables, $10,000 office furniture, and Keurig machines are wasteful, just like the individual stopping for a $5 coffee every morning. However, if you are still hosting lavish affairs like the former CEO of Tyco, Leonard Dennis Kozlowski, you have to know people are only thinking negative thoughts about you. Instead, we are referring to more minor, more mundane, everyday types of activities that every business does and doesn't think about.

What You'll Get Out of This Book

Taking an analytical and practical view, this book challenges universally accepted business practices—many taught in business schools—by pointing out how these practices drive waste, and then shows how to eliminate them and reap the benefits. It challenges you to rethink the way you have always done things. It challenges you to use technology and innovativeness, not because it is the thing to do, but because you want to save time and money. When you chose to implement new processes or technologies, you must thoroughly analyze how to use them to make people and processes more efficient (not less).

As you'll see, Lean Six Sigma and other methods are helpful in improving operations, inventory management, and more. However, this book goes beyond these concepts and covers such areas as marketing spending, personnel administration, and the many categories that make up what is in most companies a bloated monster: overhead and day-to-day waste. We will tackle some of the obvious and easy-to-get-rid-of organizational fat that, for whatever reason, many managers are blind to.

This is not another *Lean* book and not another, "look how stupid some business leaders are" book. In short, this book takes a comprehensive view of the broad spectrum of money- and time-wasters and shows you how to get rid of them once and for all. It is practical and provides actual templates for calculating and eliminating waste.

CHAPTER 1

Areas of Waste
Where Does All the Money Go?

> *I am not a teacher, but an awakener.*
>
> —Robert Frost

In order to look at waste, you first need to develop an understanding of where the waste is created. As described in this book's introduction, we are not referring to big, grandiose sources of waste like that of Mercedes-Benz or the federal government. Instead, we focus on the ways you might be wasting money on a daily basis—like printing unnecessary meeting agendas and reports, attending meetings, or sending mass emails—without even realizing it. These smaller wastes typically occur because you are doing things the way you have always done them. Only once you begin to realize where you're wasting money in your organization—be it on processes or on personnel—can you begin to stop the waste.

Where Do Businesses Spend Money?

So, just where do businesses actually spend their money? A snapshot of where "the average" business spends its money is a bit irrelevant because all business are so radically different. A manufacturer or retailer, for example, will have a lot more inventory on hand than an accounting firm or hospital. In turn, a hospital or accounting firm may incur more in labor costs than a manufacturer or retailer. By the same token, large corporations spend their money in radically different ways than small businesses.

While it is obvious that a manufacturer will have more inventory than an accounting firm, it makes no sense that large companies tend to be more wasteful than small companies. For the individual consumer and businesses, it seems that the more you have, the more you waste. It is easy to find an example of the small business owner using an old folding table as a desk or even buying thrift shop furniture, but this is rare in large corporations. Likewise, corporations have expenses that small businesses would never incur: political lobbying, dividend payouts, and different tax and benefit expenses and deductions. Nevertheless, in all businesses there are some common themes about where money is spent.

> **Note** As we will discuss later, we are not fans of benchmarking. We do not want you to look at Figure 1-1 as an example that you should follow. It is our position that all businesses are doing some things well and some things very poorly. Averages tend to lump that all together and provide a fuzzy picture.

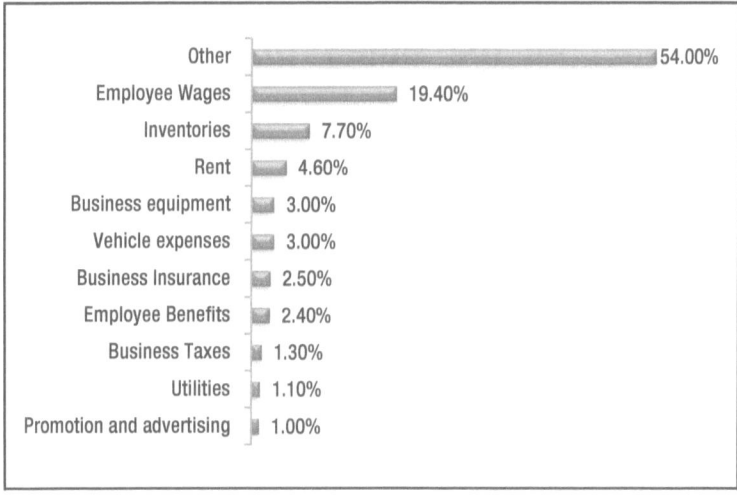

Figure 1-1. Average Small Business Expenses[1]

Figure 1-1 looks at the way the average small business in America spends its money. (These are figures from small businesses. Large businesses have radically different spending patterns.)

As you can see from Figure 1-1, roughly 20 percent of income is typically spent on employees (not including benefits). This doesn't mean that this is what expenses necessarily should be; it is simply what is being spent now. No one should *ever* look at another company, even in the same industry, and base their hiring and firing decisions based upon that benchmark. Every person, resource, and company is different. Inventories, while averaging 7.7 percent, could be 0 percent in a pure service business or as high as 20–30 percent for a manufacturer or retailer.

---

[1] Jason Del Rey, "Infographic: How Small Businesses Spend Their Money," http://www.openforum.com/articles/infographic-how-small-businesses-spend-their-money/, July 19, 2011.

> **Note** No company should ever base major decisions, such as hiring or firing, on what another company, even in the same industry, does.

WAGES ACROSS THE BOARD

Some extremely labor-heavy service-type businesses will have much higher wage percentages than shown in Figure 1-1. Industries with the highest median percentage of operating expenses devoted to salaries, according to the Society of Human Resource Management, include health care services (52 percent), for-profit services (50 percent), educational services (50 percent), durable goods manufacturing (22 percent), and construction/mining and oil/gas (22 percent). Retail/wholesale trade (18 percent) has the lowest median percentages of salaries as a percentage of operating expense.[2]

Note in Figure 1-1 that the Other category is enormous (54 percent). This is of course due to the extreme diversity of business and its varying needs. While there is obviously a large amount of waste in this category, the point is that you can reduce expenses in every category. It is not just about paper and cleaning supplies. Instead, this book is about every little microbe of waste. In what ways are you wasting money or time just because you are doing things the way you have always done them? In what ways are you wasting money or time because you don't understand how to use new technologies and analytical tools? In what ways are you creating waste because you have yet to adopt new technologies and analytical tools?

The Seven Areas of Waste

We have outlined this book based on the functional areas within companies, almost like departments. These "departments," or areas of waste, include:

- Management and corporate strategy
- Marketing and advertising
- Sales
- Human resources

---

[2]Society of Human Resource Management, "Salaries as a Percentage of Operating Expense" http://www.shrm.org/Research/Articles/Articles/Pages/MetricoftheMonthSalariesasPercentageofOperatingExpense.aspx, November 1, 2008.

- Technology
- Finance and accounting
- Business operations

It's important to understand that the areas discussed here and in the following chapters are by no means departmental issues. In fact, departmentalization, or creating silos, is often a tremendous cause of waste. Whether you are the president of a company or a middle manager of a single department, these seven departments represent waste that is company-wide and should affect every decision you make. For example, if you are in marketing, don't read the marketing chapter and skip everything else. You might have tremendously efficient marketing strategies and execution tactics, but have tremendous waste by having twice the necessary employees. Likewise, as an HR manager, you can't accurately determine many employees to cut if you do not understand any of the strategies and objectives of each functional level.

Note Departmentalization itself creates waste.

Let's look at each of these areas of waste in more detail.

Management and Corporate Strategy

Chapter 2 focuses on waste from management and strategy. The way many strategies are set up today leads companies to be inefficient. Typically, companies develop fluffy, unattainable strategies, such as "to be the best in class." Then, managers communicate these ideas to the workforce. Employees on the front lines are left staring at each other, with no idea what to do. What does the frontline employee do to be "best in class"? When employees cannot achieve this "goal," sales go down. Then, management realizes the problem through some lagging indicator, such as sales, and holds a strategic planning session at the country club. The employees feel demotivated by this waste at the Country Club when sales are down, so they work less, causing sales to decline further. Eventually, layoffs are necessary. The employees feel even more upset than they did before. Management is even more upset. This time, they have a strategic planning session in Napa Valley. After all, they seriously need to get away from it all. They spend $34,000 on benchmarks to review during the retreat. Management comes back from this retreat with extremely forceful goals for the employees to follow, based on what the competition is doing. They put up banners throughout the building with sayings about how everyone should "strive for excellence." Employees feel belittled and burned out. Service decreases. Can you see where this is going? Does it sound familiar?

> **Note** Enormous waste is created by the strategic planning process.

So much waste is created by the strategic plan. Waste because the strategic plan is not measurable, and waste from the process of actually creating the strategic plan.

A lot of waste is created because of a misguided desire to grow. Business schools teach us to be concerned with growth. By the way we fund organizations, we are incentivized to grow in order to increase the value of the company. Private equity firms or large investment groups evaluate companies to determine the equity they can build in order to sell the companies for a higher price—when, in fact, there is a point in any business where the business is big enough, and further growth can actually harm it. We all know inherently that greed is destructive, but we seem to forget this when running businesses.

Common growth strategies include mergers and acquisitions (M&As) and price wars, among others, which also result in waste. As we show in Chapter 2, M&As, on average, cost more money than they make. In most M&As, management assumes that $1 + 1 = 3$, when in reality $1 + 1 = 0$, wasting company resources and time. Leaders need to think twice every time they consider a growth strategy that includes a merger or acquisition and evaluate other options, such as joint ventures or development of new competencies.

Additionally, the work that executive management does around product development and strategy may cause work and expenses that are in excess of the benefits. Because of the desire to grow and the inability to be happy with what the company does well, leaders may decide to create new core competencies. Sometimes, this is a necessary strategy, but at other times, it will only drive mediocrity and cause the organization to lose its identity. In Chapter 2, we discuss when it is time to diversify your skills and when it is time to exploit your current skills to their maximum potential.

> **Note** The perverse desire to grow, especially through strategies like M&As and new product development, creates waste.

Another cause of managerial waste are the boundaries that companies put between departments. In efforts to perform well against budget expectations and get positive performance reviews, department managers tend to focus on the success of their individual department instead of the success of the organization as a whole. Managers may add to administrative expense by charging other departments for services provided in order to account for the activities they perform. Also, in order to show improvements, the managers may make process changes or stop offering services to other areas in the organization, which cause additional expenses in other areas that are greater than the savings incurred by their group. Building measurement systems and business processes that span across the organization and that focus on the overall health of the organization will reduce the waste.

In addition to all these areas, Chapter 2 also discusses strategy metrics—or rather the fact that there actually shouldn't be any. While every other chapter of this book strongly professes the need for metrics, Chapter 2 warns against them. You should not be looking at overall, strategic-level indicators, such as profit and return on assets, as a guide to the health of your organization. Instead, you should be looking at all the other metrics that measure each individual process that the company is doing. The manager's job is to incorporate these metrics and make decisions from them. It is not until these activities are mapped out that overall lagging indicators like profitability will make any kind of sense.

The source of strategic waste is described in Chapter 2 and shown in Figure 1-2.

Management and Strategy Waste Areas	Ever-changing or unattainable strategic plans
	Strategy based on fluffy outcomes (not what drives your business)
	The strategic planning process
	Too much leadership
	Commitment-stuck leaders
	Too much benchmarking
	The growth trap
	Mergers and acquisitions (M&As)
	Bad R&D
	Organizational silos

Figure 1-2. Waste from Strategy

In Chapter 3, we focus on how waste is generated from marketing and advertising. Most companies do some kind of market research, but few do it well. Marketing professionals tend to shoot from the hip when doing market research. Whether it is a basic lack of knowledge of the statistical skills or sheer laziness, this haphazard methodology usually leads to poor decision making and lost opportunities. We talk about the many mistakes that we have seen and how you can conduct effective research that has real meaning.

In a similar vein, faulty research leads to faulty product decisions. Having poor or no product-development processes, along with faulty research, leads to waste within product development. We cover this in Chapter 3, along with the extremely valuable concept of brand loyalty. If managers do not take the time to develop and nurture brand loyalty, they will spend way too much time and money on unnecessary promotional efforts.

On that note, while watching the morning news last week, we saw an advertisement for selling bone marrow. It was running at 5:45 A.M. The question that we had was, "How many people who might give bone marrow are watching TV right now?" Chances are, the biggest portion of this target market is college students, who likely aren't watching the news in the morning. Then, following the bone marrow commercial, we saw several back-to-back ads for local car dealerships. Again, this shows no understanding of the target market. The huge majority of people make their car-buying decisions today by doing research online.

■ **Note** Traditional market research techniques and advertising are hugely wasteful. Marketers should consider big data options for market research, customer satisfaction, and word of mouth before they think about advertising.

Companies assume that certain marketing and advertising methods are necessary because that is what everyone else is doing, or once again, because they have always done things that way. In our last book, *When to Hire or Not Hire a Consultant: Getting Your Money's Worth from Consulting Relationships*,[3] we discussed a restaurant owner who wanted to increase his presence on Facebook to get a younger crowd in his restaurant, when all he needed to do was modernize his menu. In this example, as with many business misconceptions, the owner did not understand his target market. Rather than research what the real issue was and fix the root cause, he chose to do what everyone else was doing. We not only talk about the mistakes that people make when considering advertising methods, but also how to calculate the effectiveness of advertising so that you can learn from your mistakes. Of course, there are times when it makes sense to jump on the social media and mobile bandwagons. We also discuss how to measure the effectiveness of these tools.

---

[3]Linda M. Orr and Dave J. Orr, *When to Hire or Not Hire a Consultant: Getting Your Money's Worth from Consulting Relationships* (New York, NY: Apress, 2013). p. 82–83.

The issues examined in Chapter 3 are shown in Figure 1-3.

Marketing Waste	Research	• Wrong market research technique • Weak statistical and analytical capabilities • Trying to rationalize irrational consumer behavior • Marketing silos • Outsourcing research
	Product	• New product planning • Misguided innovation • Over-paying for branding • Packaging
	Promotion and Advertising	• Too much advertising • Spending on the wrong media • Not understanding the impact of brand loyalty and word of mouth • Not focusing on brand loyalty and word of mouth
	Price	• Pricing too low • Discounting too much
	Place	• Bad supply relationships • Logistics • Warehousing
	Bad Metric Usage	• Which to use • How to interpret

Figure 1-3. Waste from Marketing and Advertising

Sales

In Chapter 4, we discuss sales productivity and waste in sales cycles. Sales has a long history of being filled with people with "good personalities." There was seldom any science to sales, let alone much use of analytics. These mindsets need to go. The sales processes should be mapped using value stream mapping just like in manufacturing. Likewise, you must examine productivity and other measures. Sales needs processes, metrics, and analytics as much as any of the departments in the business. Without these, the entire sales department becomes a source of waste.

■ **Note** Everyone in sales should use value-stream mapping. Likewise, productivity metrics should be used.

We also talk about other antiquated sales activities, such as golfing with clients or high-entertainment expenses, and how these are wasteful. Even though there is a natural reciprocity phenomenon when these activities occur, studies show that high-entertainment spending and spending more time with the client actually produces lower sales. We discuss what sales professionals should actually be doing to maximize their value and drive sales. This includes spending more time planning for sales and serving current customers and less time "just stopping by to check in." As company budgets get tighter, it is necessary to focus our travel expenses on trips that provide real value. There is no success in being on the road all of the time. Instead, resources should be aimed at the company, and they should provide real value. Sales are made by strategizing and being analytical about accounts, not by how much time you spend with the clients.

■ **Note** The *less* time you spend with clients, the *higher* your sales will be!!! Strategy is what's important, not golf.

The topics covered in Chapter 4 are summarized in Figure 1-4.

Sales Waste	
	No value-stream mapping of sales processes
	Not calculating productivity
	Retaining ineffective sales people and/or managers
	Sales expenses/entertainment and travel
	Trade shows
	Bad territory alignment
	Third-party lead generating, prospecting, and appointment setting firms
	No metrics, bad metrics, or no understanding of how to use metrics

Figure 1-4. Waste from Sales

Human Resources

Human resources (HR) is, in theory, a department whose primary function is to provide services to the entire organization. Even though as a support function it should help everyone, the processes implemented by human resource professionals are typically enormous sources of waste.

Recently we heard from a friend about someone applying for a finance position in a local company that employed a few hundred people. This person's resume never made it to the hiring manager because she was flagged by human resources. The obvious initial reaction is that she must have some kind of issue that would keep her from functioning in this job. This applicant was a vice president at a national bank with an exceptional record. She was perfectly qualified. Her resume was removed from the pool of applicants because she had no experience in the company's specific industry. This qualification had been determined by someone in HR. This is a reasonable requirement for engineering or some direct contributor role, but it seems like a bizarre one for a finance director.

We chose this example because it gets to the root of the problem. At some point in the last few decades, human resources forgot that its job is to advise and help management. Now it operates like its job is to control management. Whether or not this is true in your firm, the lesson is still the same. Any time a manager makes decisions without proper understanding, analysis, and relevant data on which to base them, you have inherent waste. Employees in a different department than yours rarely have the proper data to make good decisions for your department, at least not without your input.

Note Every decision made in every company should be made with accurate and relevant data analysis.

Beyond poor decision making and lack of understanding, the human resources role creates waste within the hiring process. Much of this waste is because, like so many other things, they do things the way they have always done them.

Consider this example. In academia, hiring takes place once a year. We send two-three professors to a once-a-year conference. This costs a few thousand dollars for rooms, food, travel, and conference registrations. During this conference, about 50-75 interviews take place. So, comparing the expenses to the number of interviews, this might be an efficient use of resources. However, after meeting face-to-face with all of these candidates, the top three or four are invited back to campus for "campus visits." During these visits, each candidate spends two or three days in town. The university pays for their airfare, local travel, hotels, and food. And it's not just food for the candidate. Every meal is planned with the candidate and several other faculty members. All totaled, these visits cost a few thousand dollars each. Also, there is paperwork, faculty members' time, and committee meetings. Each search ends up costing the university tens of thousands of dollars.

We mention this scenario because this is an obvious case where the existing processes create thousands of dollars of waste for each position that is filled. You could argue that hiring the wrong employee creates even more waste, so the process needs to be done right. However, this expensive process doesn't guarantee better hiring decisions. It happens, once again, because this is the way things have always been done. With all of these expenses—all the steak dinners for four and breakfasts that no one wants—we can still make major hiring mistakes. These particular expenses do not enhance the hiring process. There are no metrics in place to determine the added value of any part of the process and really no post-hire reassessments. Likewise, new technologies are not even considered. There are opportunities to improve practices like these. For example, many companies use tools like Skype to reduce interviewing costs.

> **Note** *Every* expense should have an associated ROI analysis.

Once they hire new employees, companies seem to have remarkably little idea how to motivate them to increase performance. The ubiquitous pizza party or fancy banquet for a job well done is a common business practice, although there is no proof that they actually increase performance. In fact, most people dread the obligatory need to attend such events. Another common motivator is the idea of casual or blue jean Friday as a motivation. Do these things actually motivate employees to perform better? By the same token, team and organizational-based bonuses that don't tie to individual performance, don't incentivize performance. Once again, where was the measurement and analysis? When were employees asked what they wanted? We discuss real motivators in Chapter 5.

The best companies are ones that invest in their employees. We have worked for organizations where many people chose to work there for lower than market wages because of the attractive benefits package. These employees tended to be more conscientious and loyal because their focus was less on the weekly paycheck and more on the overall relationship with the company. Some students graduating from undergraduate degree programs will not consider working for companies without reimbursement programs for earning a master's degree. Yet, benefits such as healthcare, retirement, tuition reimbursement, and paid time off are frequently looked upon as areas where money can be saved with little or no productivity loss. This is a faulty assumption.

Making the decision not to support employees who care about their health, future, or work-life balance is making the decision to lose those employees. Aren't these the employees you want? We have heard business leaders claim that they pay for employee education, only to have those employees leave the business. This is a risk worth taking. Not only do you have a motivated employee while she is working on improving her education, you also have the benefit of the education while she is working on her degree. We will talk about these and other decisions that human resource leaders make. They might look good on paper, but they cost the company money.

Note Managers must *truly* understand what motivates their employees.

Additionally, with technological advancements, employees have more flexible work schedules and outcome-based work processes. We also have workforce models where we can use part time or contingent workers to minimize costs. We know workers are 12 percent more productive when working from home.[4] Employees who work from home report higher job satisfaction and have 50 percent lower attrition.[5] So, it is a shock to see more and more office buildings popping up all over the place. There are also more ways to automate processes and measure efficiencies. We talk about why some of these improvements are good, whereas others are hurting the companies that use them.

The sources of human resource waste are shown in Figure 1-5.

---

[4]Steve Cooper, "Boost Productivity by Working from Home, Really!" http://www.forbes.com/sites/stevecooper/2012/08/31/boost-productivity-by-working-from-home-really/, August 31, 2012.
[5]Ibid.

Human Resources Waste	Hiring: Bad hiring decisions, ineffective hiring processes, too much reliance on benchmarks
	Motivation: Ineffective "motivators," not investing in your people
	Training: Too much training/not enough training
	Flex time: Not using cloudsourcing, outsourcing, and interns, not utilizing work-from-home policies, lack of automation
	Management and evaluation: Poor workforce management, poor employee evaluation processes
	Lack of metrics

Figure 1-5. Waste from Human Resources

Technology

Technology can be a good way to increase efficiency and effectiveness when it's used properly. It can also be a tremendous source of waste. We have seen companies without good information technology systems and companies with hundreds of software packages that are not integrated. We have also seen companies that still do most things by hand, using simple Word documents and Excel spreadsheets, instead of learning how to automate processes. There is no magic formula for the correct way to manage your technology, but there are some good tips to follow that will reduce the risk of misusing it.

Software can serve multiple purposes and be a key piece of any company's success. Whether it is an Enterprise Resource Planning (ERP) system or Microsoft Office, the software expense should have a return on investment. Companies often have a base software suite, such as Microsoft Office (Word, Excel, PowerPoint, and Outlook), Lotus Symphony, or Google Docs to perform routine tasks such as word processing and basic computing. In addition to this base software, there are other software needs that are unique to each business. Each piece of software should have a specific purpose.

Companies should also understand how to use social media effectively, and not just be trying to follow the latest fad. Technology advancements are not limited to Facebook and Twitter. We discuss many aspects of social media usage. Also, companies should understand how to use social media and other technologies to help the sales force's efforts. In Chapter 6, we discuss how to utilize big data to identify opportunities. We also show how sales force automation and customer relationship management software can increase the capacity of each sales person.

> **Note** Every software and hardware expense must have an ROI.

Another technology is the use of reports. I (Dave) once worked with an IT manager who questioned the necessity of all of the reports that his team created and managed. He decided to move all of the reports to a different area on the company's network to see what would happen. After about two weeks, he had received four phone calls about missing reports, which he addressed by replacing the reports for those users. In the following two months, he heard from seven other employees who were looking for their reports. In the end, his experiment showed that less than 10 percent of the reports that his department created were actually used. Reports can be a huge source of waste. The strategies of some organizations are to push reports to employees in order to ensure that nothing is missed. When this strategy is used, the reports are deleted before many of those users read them. Another strategy is to teach users how to run reports as needed. In this case, if the method to run reports is simple, the method may be effective, although the learning curve may keep many users from ever running reports. We discuss how to create, use, analyze, and kill reports.

Data access is an ongoing issue in most organizations. Most people agree that salary and personal information should be kept secure. In the banking industry, specific customer information must be kept secure. The government has regulated the use of healthcare information to keep private information secure. But what is the right data access policy? We have found that companies either use too loose of a strategy, relying on worker ignorance of the IT systems to secure data, or too stringent of a strategy, keeping workers from accessing the information they need to do their jobs effectively. We discuss the benefits and issues with both strategies, so you can formulate a strategy that will keep your data secure without causing waste or inadvertently making the data less secure in the process.

A couple of common jokes in the information technology field are the concepts of P.I.C.N.I.C. (*problem in chair, not in computer*) or I.D.10T (*idiot*) errors. This is not the fault of the individual workers but rather those techno-savvy workers who set up software and policies without training users on how to use the software. I will never forget hearing in my early career about a vice president who was told by the IT manager to "go to My Computer" while on a phone call. This vice president left his office and walked to the IT manager's office. The IT manager meant to have the vice president click on the "My Computer" desktop icon in order to help troubleshoot the problem, but his lack of basic computer knowledge made this a long-standing joke about how poorly some people understand technology. Implementation of any software must include effective training for its users.

Any office-based role must have a minimum computer knowledge requirement for employment. We cannot leverage the potential efficiencies from technology without this knowledge. There are tenured college professors teaching students today who still use overhead projectors with materials that were created in the 1980s or earlier. There are business executives who have their administrative assistant print all of their e-mails because the executive cannot use the computer. We know people in VP roles who do not know how to use PowerPoint, so they must have an assistant create presentations for them. Most businesses use technology, so your expectation of your employees and leaders must include knowledge of that technology. We talk in Chapter 6 about how to create gap analyses and formulate capability build training for the use of software. These two tools can help overcome some of the large source of waste involved with technology implementations.

When implementing technology, IT leaders often tend to take one of two approaches: customize nothing or customize everything. There is normally no focus on understanding the best process and either selecting the software based upon the process needs or customizing the software to fit the best process. When businesses choose to implement new technology, the IT team usually selects the technology before they truly understand the business's needs. We talk about the right process to ensure that technology purchases actually improve your work.

When companies choose to implement new technology, it is likely because they are replacing outdated technology and hoping for improvements in operations. Unfortunately, business leaders often choose new technology that mimics the technology they are replacing. We discuss how to access current technology and how to decide if new technology is necessary. We also focus on how to maximize the effective use of any new technology. This discussion explores the use of cloud technology, including SaaS (Software as a Service). As we show, organizations can save over 90 percent of IT operating costs by utilizing the "cloud."

The topics discussed in Chapter 6 are shown in Figure 1-6.

Technology Wastes	Social media
	Mobile marketing
	Salesforce automation
	Too much or too little software
	Not the right software
	Not utlizing the full potential of software
	Expecting software to be the solution
	Too many reports
	Not the right reports
	Inadequate data access and distribution
	Failure to conduct a gap analysis/ ineffective technolgy training
	Lack of using the cloud
	Still using outdated technologies, espcially phones

Figure 1-6. Waste from Technology

Finance and Accounting

The processes of finance and accounting include managing investments, obtaining capital, accurate reporting in accordance with regulatory requirements, and controlling expenses. Unfortunately, these processes can cause waste. When business owners think they are controlling waste by managing it better, they are, in reality, creating waste.

With the goal of controlling expenses, we have seen ridiculous approval processes put in place by leaders. A division president of a very large manufacturing organization with over 150 employees enacted a policy whereby every expense over $25 needed his approval. This added waste and demotivated employees by instilling a sense of mistrust. Other organizations we have seen required that routine purchases for supplies needed up to four signatures to be approved and an employee reimbursement needed three signatures, regardless of the size of the expense. The adage, "when multiple people are responsible for something, no one is" holds true here. We talk about how to improve these expense-control methods in an effort to reduce administrative expense and improve accountability.

Travel policies may also drive up expenses. We once worked with a person who remodeled his basement with the money he accrued by renting a car for all long road trips and then charging the company mileage for the distance traveled. The expense versus reimbursement for him ended up being quite profitable. Likewise, as we explain in other chapters, travel on the whole is quite unnecessary today, so sometimes the whole category can be wasteful. We look at how to not only improve the process for capturing travel expenses, but also how to reduce actual travel expenses.

Additionally, the budgeting processes used in many companies are ineffective and costly. The basis for the new budget cycle is often the prior year's performance, with some modification based upon the new sales projections. This process encourages managers to spend their budget so that they can get an equivalent budget the following year. We have witnessed this many times and heard from other managers who will admit to this process. It can be further proven by looking at the expenses throughout the course of the year. We talk in Chapter 7 about how to implement a zero-based budget strategy to eliminate this wasteful spend-and-budget process.

■ **Note** Implement a zero-based budget strategy to reduce waste caused by faulty budgeting practices.

Budgeting is not limited to the annual budget. New projects, products, and services often include a pro forma with a list of projected revenues and expenses. We have frequently noticed a trend across multiple companies where the projections on the revenues don't come to fruition while the expenses are equal to or greater than projections. We discuss how to identify and avoid being trapped by fake projections or other fake numbers through accurate forecasting.

Traditional cost-accounting methods make it difficult to manage expenses and drive real improvement in an organization. We discuss how to implement activity-based costing for a better view of the cost drivers in the organization and to see movement from improvement efforts.

As part of the purchasing discussion, we explore capital expenses. One key decision around capital expenses is the lease versus buy question. Once reserved for equipment and building purchases, this decision has been expanded to other purchases, such as software. As with any decision, there are reasons to adopt either method. We explore those reasons and identify the potential wastes they cause.

If you've spent any time watching the *Hoarders: Buried Alive* show on A&E, you are familiar with some of the personal issues that people face when they cannot let go of possessions due to personal attachments. This happens within organizations as well. Brad Pitt said in *Fight Club* that "The things you own, own you." This applies to businesses. We discuss how holding onto unneeded assets can be detrimental to an organization. These often-unlooked issues can be a large source of waste for companies. We highlight some of these in Figure 1-7.

Finance Wastes	Expense control policies
	Budgeting methods
	Cost-accounting methods
	Money-management methods
	Asset management
	Insurance costs
	Tax management
	Credit policies

Figure 1-7. Waste from Finance

Business Operations

It may sound too obvious to say, but every business needs to operate. However, when many people hear "operations management" or "process improvement," they might think those terms apply only to very large businesses or to manufacturers. That is absolutely wrong. Every business has operational needs.

In the early stages of a business, only critical functions are created and supported. Large-scale operational efficiencies are never really considered, thought about, or maybe not even needed at this phase of the business. When survival is the name of the game, normally people are quite frugal. As the business grows, more processes are created to support this growth. At some point, these processes become redundant and less effective. This happens due to lack of a grand design of what the business should look like at various phases. We discuss how to address these wastes through business process analysis. In these analyses, we look at the work environment and use Lean Six Sigma techniques to identify root causes of waste. This kind of waste is often due to redundant or inefficient processes, resources, facilities, equipment, and inventory. Many of these processes deal with the mundane, everyday processes that every employee gets trapped doing.

For instance, most professional workers attend almost 62 meetings a month.[6] If you account for travel time of 15 minutes between each meeting, this is over 50 percent of the working time. Over 50 percent of the meeting time is wasted,[7] which means that more than 25 percent of a professional worker's time is wasted in meetings. The average small business owner's time is worth over $250.[8] If you assume a 50-hour work week, the average business owner wastes over $162,000 a year in meetings! In Chapter 8, we demonstrate how much money is wasted in meetings based on different types of employees and their average salaries.

Note The average small business owner wastes $162,000 a year in meetings.

As we have said it many times, we have these meetings because it is what we have always done. We buy into business "myths." One of these myths, brainstorming, is as rampant as an urban legend. The concept was originally created by an advertising executive trying to sell books. It has never been proven to be effective and, in fact, has been shown to be detrimental to group success, in terms of quality and the number of ideas generated.

For this reason, managing time and prioritizing task work are important skills to have in a business. We talk about meeting-management techniques that can help maximize the productivity of meetings, as well as limit the number of them. We also discuss how to manage your time and prioritize tasks to ensure that the time when you are not in meetings is well spent.

Additionally, one fundamental issue in business operations is the concept of process management. Process management combines relevant metrics that show operational performance, all in a time frame that allows managers to react to variations in performance.

Lord Kelvin, a British physicist from the late 19th Century, has two famous quotations that deal with measurement. The first is, "to measure is to know." This deals with the fact that most people have opinions, but only those with data to support their opinions can be sure of the validity of their opinions. The second quote is, "if you cannot measure it, you cannot improve it." This is a fundamental characteristic of Six Sigma process improvement; in order

---

[6]A Network MCI Conferencing White Paper, "Meetings in America: A Study of Trends, Costs, and Attitudes Toward Business Travel, Teleconferencing, and Their Impact on Productivity," INFOCOMM, Greenwich, CT: 1998.
[7]Robert B. Nelson and Peter Economy, *Better Business Meetings* (Burr Ridge, IL: Irwin, Inc. 1995). p. 5.
[8]David Mielach, "What's a Small Business Owner's Most Valuable Assest?" http://www.businessnewsdaily.com/2942-business-owner-time.html, August 2, 2012.

to show improvement, you must have a measureable baseline and a post-improvement measurement, and then be able to show a statistical difference between the two. Lord Kelvin is correct on both accounts, which is why the process-management portion of this book is important.

Although this section of the business operations chapter focuses on process management, we talk about process management throughout all of the chapters. When we talk about process management, we explore how to identify what measurements help you see process changes before they affect the outcome. In each chapter, we review which key performance indicators show how successful you are in each area of your business.

As we explain throughout Chapter 2, we all learned in high school algebra that $Y=f(X)$. This states that the output (Y) is a function of the inputs (Xs). This simple formula holds true for business processes as well, and we look at how to identify which inputs drive the outputs you desire. These will become the key process metrics that you will monitor on an hourly, daily, or weekly basis to help drive monthly or quarterly performance. By using a combination of these process metrics and visual cues of performance gaps, you will be able to identify where process improvement or redesign is necessary.

With the effective process management that we discuss throughout the book, you will identify performance gaps that you will need to improve. In the process-improvement portion of this chapter, we explain various process-improvement techniques and how to apply them to business situations. These process-improvement techniques include Six Sigma (improve quality and process effectiveness), lean management (improve process efficiency), and the theory of constraints (remove process bottlenecks).

Additionally, we discuss how simple items such as paper, Post-It notes, filing cabinets, and printers drive cost inefficiencies. Along with identifying these wastes, we show you how a change in business processes and effectively leveraging technology can eliminate these wastes and provide a real return on investment. Inventory is one of the eight wastes identified in lean manufacturing. This is because this money is tied up and can't be used to meet the customers' needs. Inventory also hides problems. Therefore, effective management of inventory is a key step in managing a company. If you carry too much inventory, problems that you need to solve may hide from you.

Along with justifying which supplies are used in the business, we discuss warehousing and distribution methods. This includes how to choose the right methods for different types of businesses. We explore common mistakes in distribution and inventory-control decisions so that you can avoid them.

Every company needs to purchase products and services, yet so many companies create waste through its purchasing practices. The old way of purchasing was to focus only on price when making a purchasing decision. After the product or service specifications were created, the purchasing professionals would look for a supplier to provide that service. As long as the supplier was able to provide what was needed, the cheapest option was pursued. As part of this decision-making process, transportation fees or taxes are added to the base cost of the item. Unfortunately, this basic practice is still in use and drives waste. We discuss more effective practices, which consider the total cost of purchasing with the aim of driving down not only purchasing costs but also operational expenses. The summary of the topics discussed in Chapter 8 is provided in Figure 1-8.

Operations Waste	
	Poor time management
	Poor or lacking process management
	Poor or lacking measurement of processes
	Poor or lacking process improvement
	Poor project management
	Unneeded supplies and expenses
	Ineffective inventory-management processes
	Ineffective supply chain management processes
	Poor purchasing processes

Figure 1-8. Waste from Operations

Appendix

In the final section of this book, you'll find the appendix. When we initially came up with the idea to write a book about business waste that is different from the thousands of waste books on the market, we had a few areas of business in mind (ones where we consistently see egregious waste). As we worked on this project, researched information on waste, and brainstormed waste we had seen or experienced, we realized that this book could be more of an encyclopedia of business waste rather than a simple book outlining some specific wastes. For this reason, the appendix of this book serves as a key resource for our readers.

Because process management is a key and often poorly executed area of business, we have decided to incorporate elements of process management throughout this book. Although process-improvement techniques are used throughout this book, we intend this book to be a reference guide. We outline various process-improvement techniques and templates in the appendix for you to use.

Conclusion

We designed this book to be different from other waste books available on the market. The book is organized into traditional functional areas, but we show how waste in some areas causes waste in other areas. By examining the common business functions and their fundamental process wastes, we show why you should question all of the processes. We hope that you adopt the mindset, "if you can't measure it, don't do it." Every resource, process, and activity should produce a positive ROI. We hope that this is an eye-opener to the enormous amount of waste that exists in all organizations. There are formulas, tools, and questions to help you work through the waste in your organization and realize the overall benefits that you can achieve.

CHAPTER 2

Strategy of Waste

Waste at the Strategic Level Creates Waste Everywhere

There's only one growth strategy: work hard.

—William Hague

In the business world, we tend to equate growth with success. In both the business and academic worlds, we seem to be obsessed with the fastest growing companies, the largest companies, and the companies that have the most rapid increases in stock price. In fact, public companies traditionally receive high praise and recommendations for investment possibilities because of their capability to deliver rapid earnings growth, along with quickly rising stock prices, despite any real qualitative factors about the true well being of the company.

However, in one of the seminal books on strategy, George Day, in 1990, warned of overcapacity. He stated that all markets/industries in America suffered from chronic overcapacity by 15–40 percent, depending on the industry.[1] We've known this for over two decades. We think most people have grown tired of the whole "hyper-competition" subject, the idea of "saturated markets," and

---

[1] George Day, *Market Driven Strategy: Processes for Creating Value* (New York, NY: The Free Press, 1990).

concepts like "how to stand apart from the clutter." Now, overproduction has reached China as well, to the point at which more than 1,400 companies in 19 industries in China have been asked to reduce their production due to overcapacity.[2] So, why more than two decades after being warned about excess, and now experiencing international excess, are we still obsessed with growth? Why is growth still our number one goal and the foremost indicator of a sound strategy?

Note Long-term growth is not always profitable or sustainable. Only grow when it makes sense, based on the market conditions. When it doesn't make sense, be satisfied with profitability.

We believe that this whole growth mindset is skewed in the wrong direction. It has set the template for how businesses are managed and how strategies are created. But growth should never be the goal by itself. Growth is not a goal. It is a consequence of meeting other goals.

In fact, we believe that a goal of growth leads to downward spirals. It leads to generating innovation for the wrong reasons and cheapening quality for the sake of growth. It leads to a desire to expand without considering the market or the industry factors. It leads to managers constantly trying to revamp and update the strategy. It leads to excessive, misunderstood, and pointless benchmarking, as everyone is always trying to "keep up with the Joneses." It leads to unnecessary innovation and financially unsound mergers and acquisitions.

Having growth as a strategy often leads to internal excess and waste. This chapter focuses on how to make strategy more efficient and effective, how to take strategy away from what everyone has likely heard in business schools, and how to focus on key factors other than growth. It is only through a focus on efficiency and on the customer that a company can see long-term growth.

---

[2]Stanway, Dan, Reuters, "China faces test over plans to cut industrial capacity," http://www.reuters.com/article/2013/06/26/china-industry-overcapacity-idUSL3N0EU28B20130626, June 26, 2013.

CREATING A LEAN ENTERPRISE

In the words of George Day in 1990, winners are focused on two things: a shared strategic vision and responsiveness to marketplace/customer desires. This is still true today. Managers must create a stable, common-sense strategy that everyone in the company can implement and that is based on customer desires. The only thing that has changed in the last decades is an additional emphasis on efficiency and quality, because markets are now even more saturated. Using these principles, managers need to work to create a lean enterprise.

Prime Areas of Waste

We organized this book to focus on waste in the typical functional areas of business, so there is overlap between chapters. In this chapter on strategy waste, the primary source of waste is the creation of the strategic plan itself—and, unfortunately, the creation of this plan seems to be a *tremendous* source of waste. But we will also focus on other areas of waste created by strategy. Some of these are ineffective leadership, lack of tangible outcomes in a strategic plan, benchmarking, and pointless growth. (Many of the specifics about these areas of waste are discussed later in this book in their respective chapter. For example, if you feel you have waste caused by ineffective leadership, refer to Chapter 5 on human resources.)

Waste from an Ever-Changing or Unattainable Strategic Plan

Every company needs to have a strategic plan, but the frequency and level of planning that companies undertake is often much too extensive. For the small to midsized companies, for example, a strategic plan should last for several years and sometimes even decades or longer. In a larger organization, there should be an overarching strategic plan that lasts just as long. For instance, a company like General Electric would have a General Electric strategic plan and plans for each division, such as GE Financial, GE Transportation, and GE Appliance. This is due to the breadth of the organization and the differences between the business units. Even in these large organizations, planning too frequently can be counterproductive and wasteful.

But before we can get into how strategy is wasteful, we need to focus on what strategy is—or more importantly, what it should be.

What Is Strategy?

We have heard many times in our careers that strategies should be ever changing, innovative, and hard for competitors to predict. Many times, strategy is described as a maneuver on a battlefield or a football field. Anyone who says this doesn't understand strategy. Strategy is constant. Tactics change.

Think of Amazon.com. They have had the same basic strategy for almost two decades. They amazingly have no innovative products or services, no great technological geniuses, nothing extraordinarily remarkable, and nothing that can't be readily copied. Their success flies in the face of everything we learn in business schools about competitive advantages and the resource theory.

■ **Note** Strategy is constant. Tactics change.

One of the first theories about strategy and competitive advantage was the *resources-based view*. In that view, in order for a firm to have and maintain a competitive advantage, it needed to possess resources that were rare, valuable, imperfectly imitable, and non-substitutable. The *capabilities view* of the firm came out shortly thereafter and essentially said the same thing, but in regard to processes instead of resources. More or less, the company had to do or possess something that competitors could not easily have, do, and copy in the near future.

Then, a wave of business school research came out touting the advantages of the *learning* organization. In this view, firms should collect information, process it, disseminate it, and ultimately learn from it. This was all done in order to innovate and change. The company would always be changing and adapting to customer trends, with the goal of outpacing the competitor by keeping up with the customers' ever-changing needs. Figure 2-1 shows the evolution of strategy.

Implicit Strategy View 1970-1980	Sustainable Competitive Advantage (1990-early 2000's)	Micro Strategy for Today
• One ideal competitive position in the industry	• Unique competitive position for the company	• Unique competitive position for the customer
• Benchmarking of all activities to achieve best practice	• Activities tailored to strategy	• Activities tailored to strategy, which revolves around customer satisfaction
• Aggressive outsourcing and partnering to gain efficiencies	• Clear trade-offs	• Clear trade-offs. Use best method for customer satisfaction and cost effectiveness (cannot take one without the other)
• Advantages from a few key success factors, critical resources, and core competencies	• Competitive advantage arises from fit across activities	• Competitive advantage arises from superior customer satisfaction, brand equity, and word of mouth
• Flexibility and rapid response to all compotitive market changes	• Sustainability comes from processes, not the parts. Operational effectiveness is a given	• Efficiency equals agility. Everything is customizable at a low cost

Figure 2-1. The evolution of strategy. Source: Heavily adapted from Porter, Michael, "What Is Strategy?" *Harvard Business Review,* November/December 1996, pp. 61-78

Let's go back to the Amazon.com example. Why are they obviously winning and killing everyone else around in numerous categories (Borders Books and Best Buy)? They have no rare, valuable, imperfectly imitable, and non-substitutable resources or capabilities, and they sure aren't making any mass moves. You could argue that they have had some changes, like those with the Kindle, but let's go back to what strategy is. We looked around and found the definition we liked best, of all places, from ehow:

> "Organizational strategy is the creation, implementation, and evaluation of decisions within an organization that enables it to achieve its long-term objectives. Organizational strategy specifies the organization's mission, vision, and objectives and develops policies and plans, often in terms of projects and programs, created to achieve the organization's objectives. It also allocates resources to implement them."[3]

That's it. An organization needs to figure out what it does, make sure it is feasible, and do it the best they possibly can. They need to do it with a complete customer focus in mind, at the most broad level. Sure, things have changed in 20 years for Amazon.com. Customers now expect free shipping, and they want to read reviews before buying products. But, the basics are still there. Where can a customer go to buy anything, in the most convenient way? There's nothing terribly secret about that. It's just that everyone else seems to be more focused on finding something rare or learning and innovating toward the next greatest thing.

STRATEGY: IT'S EASIER THAN YOU THINK

We cannot make this any simpler. Stop reading all those books on strategy and holding strategic planning sessions. First, figure out a feasible plan of action for what you do best. Make sure there is a customer need. Note that we're not even saying unmet need. Because there really aren't many unmet needs left to be fulfilled. The key is that you are going to find something you do well, and you are going to do it well. At least good enough to have exceptional customer satisfaction, which will lead to brand loyalty and word of mouth. You will not change it or modify it because your strategy is going to be specific enough to provide direction, but not so specific that it does not allow for change. Amazon.com did not out set out to be the best paper book distributor (or they would not have called themselves Amazon.com, they would be "Book-A-Plenty.com"). Instead, they set out to be a massive online distributor. This implies that Amazon.com must have exceptional warehousing and Internet systems, but does not lock them into any particular product. All of their most valuable metrics and analysis tools should involve things like speed of delivery, user search functions, ease of buying for the customer, and other similar metrics. They need to make sure that customers go to Amazon.com when they're thinking about shopping online and they need to understand why. They will not change unless people stop buying online. This is all there is to strategy. Stop wasting resources by making it more complicated than that.

---

[3] ehow.com/Christine Meyer, "Definition of Organizational Strategy," http://www.ehow.com/about_6689983_definition-_organization-strategy_.html#ixzz2h3mUcMM3, 2013.

> **Note** Stop overcomplicating strategy. Figure out what you do best and do it the best.

Developing a Strategic Plan

The process of determining the strategic plan includes compiling data on yourself and your competitors. After the data is analyzed, you must identify any gaps and develop strategies to address these gaps. Once you develop a good plan and set good metrics, you should use the Hoshin Kanri process (see Figure 2-2). This process eliminates the need to do special data analysis projects, since these metrics are likely ongoing measures used in the business. It also makes sure that when the strategy is initially created, all the proper groups have a say. This will lead to a stronger strategy and more consensus in the long term. Finally, this process includes the implementation plan and the metrics as part of the strategy. Waste is reduced by setting up a lean structure in the beginning.

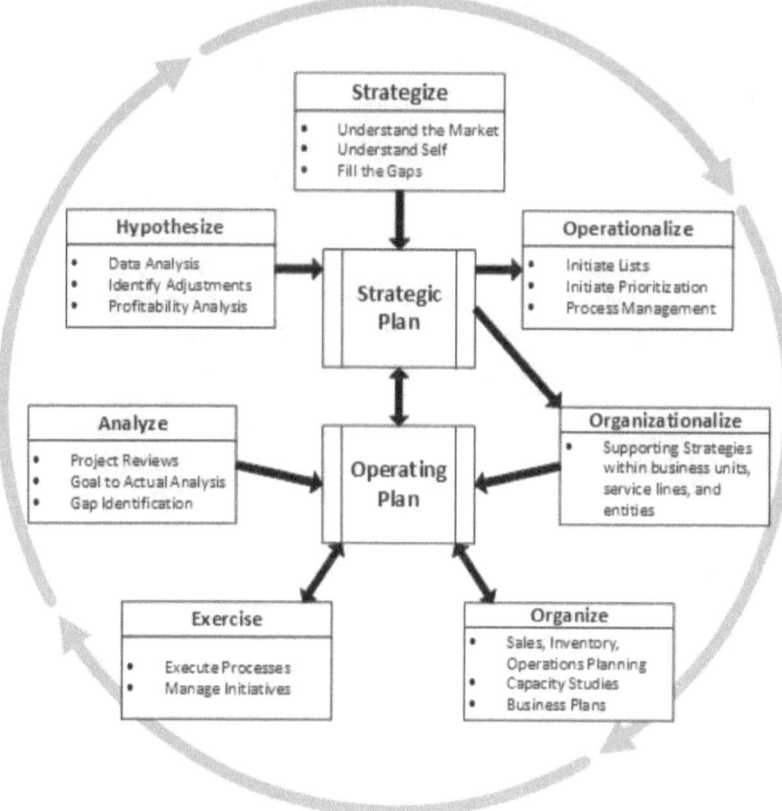

Figure 2-2. Hoshin Kanri Process

Understanding What You're Good At

If you are going to develop a strategy that does not cause waste, you first need to understand what you are good at. You can start with a SWOT analysis, taught in all MBA programs. Keep in mind that SWOT analyses should not be done every year. We are assuming that you are either starting with a new company or at a loss in terms of what you are good at. The elements of SWOT are simple:

- **Strengths:** What are you good at?
- **Weaknesses:** What aren't you good at?
- **Opportunities:** Where can you take advantage of the market?
- **Threats**: What are you at risk of losing to your competitors?

Please realize that SWOT should only be used to organize your research. It is not an analysis tool. You also have to remember the adage, garbage in, garbage out. Your information will be incorrect if you are not basing it on sound data collected from relevant departments in your company using the right metrics.

Understanding Your Market

Understanding yourself is the first step to developing a strategy. The second step is to understand your market. (These steps are intertwined.) You must understand these both in order to determine if you have something to offer that you are not currently offering, or if you can expand what you already do well. You need to understand yourself first, because otherwise, you may be tempted to try to be something that you cannot do and waste resources on failure. After you understand your company, you can focus on your customers' needs. This understanding of market needs comes from market research (covered in Chapter 3).

Developing the Strategy

Once you have identified opportunities that match your capabilities, it is time to develop a strategy. The shortest distance between two points is a straight line (see Figure 2-3). Strategy is the method you use to plot that straight line.

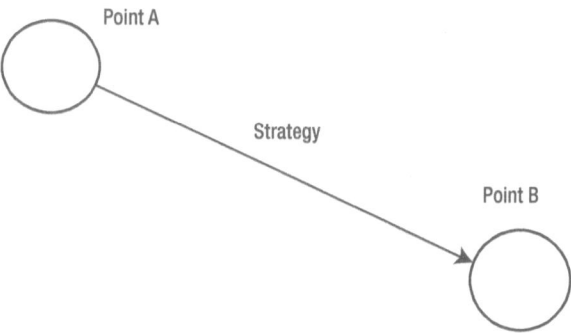

Figure 2-3. Strategy as the Straight Line

Too often, companies develop mission and vision statements and set up immeasurable goals without a real plan to reach those goals. See Figure 2-4 on these differences. This is often *called* strategy. This is *not* strategy. Strategy is the roadmap between where you are now and where you want to be. Therefore, there are probably turns that you need to take on the path to meet your goals. This is strategy.

Figure 2-4. Measurable and Immeasurable Strategies

From there, you start to develop tactics. In order to build these tactics, you identify gaps between the current and future state of the business. The steps to fill these gaps can be placed on a timeline, with clear, measureable goals assigned to each phase. Each phase may represent six to twelve months. Once this plan is assembled, you assign tasks to implement the first phase and track each action to show progress toward that phase's goals. Every three years, you should revisit the strategy (not necessarily to re-create it). You do this because, as the company matures, different long-term goals may be necessary or outside forces affect the current plan. But again, we want to urge you to use consistency in your strategic planning. You can see how you should track the initiatives associated with each strategy in Figure 2-5.

Indicator	Strategy	Initiative	Metric	Value	Accountable	End Date
▼	Grow to 55% Market Share				Jones, Amy	12/31/2016
▼			Market Share	43%		
▲		Analyze Gaps in Service Offering			Cooper, John	12/15/2014
		Develop New Services			Maleski, Kim	6/1/2015
▼		Increase Primary Service to 65%			Cooper, John	3/31/2015
▼			Market Share	58%		

Figure 2-5. Initiative Tracking

Note Strategy is based upon a series of tactics. In this way, it is a roadmap, not a destination.

OUTSIDE FORCES: A REASON TO CHANGE STRATEGY

In 2010, when the Patient Protection and Affordable Care Act was signed into law, healthcare providers were forced to revisit current strategic plans. This is an example of why it is important to continue to revise strategies as outside forces change. In this case, failure to do so would result in not being able to operate under the new regulatory and payment systems. Similarly, in the late 1990s and 2000s, companies were forced to realize that nearly everything might potentially become electronic. This change especially impacted brick-and-mortar retailers. Although these are extreme cases, the point is that outside forces can force change. Don't be guilty of being too committed to your plan. Instead, your plans need to be flexible enough to allow for market changes. That is not to say that you should change your plans frequently. If you have a good plan, and there have not been significant changes in the business environment, stick to that plan. Don't waste time replacing an effective strategy.

Executing the Strategy

Strategic plans need to be simple enough for the average employee to understand his part in their implementation. This is a simpler task in a small company than in a large one. Strategies of small companies often are more tangible due to the nature of the business, whereas large companies develop more grandiose strategies that seem to have no real bearing on their daily operation. Note that it should not be this way. All plans—for small and large companies—should be implementable. Effective implementation of Hoshin Kanri is necessary for successful strategy execution. Hoshin Kanri helps management translate strategies into implementable goals and actions. Upper management sets the corporate strategy and drives the strategy through tangible goals and projects at each level of the organization. Figure 2-6 shows a simplified representation of this concept. Each level of the organization can use PDCA (Plan, Do, Check, Act), developed by Dr. Deming, in order to drive performance improvements.

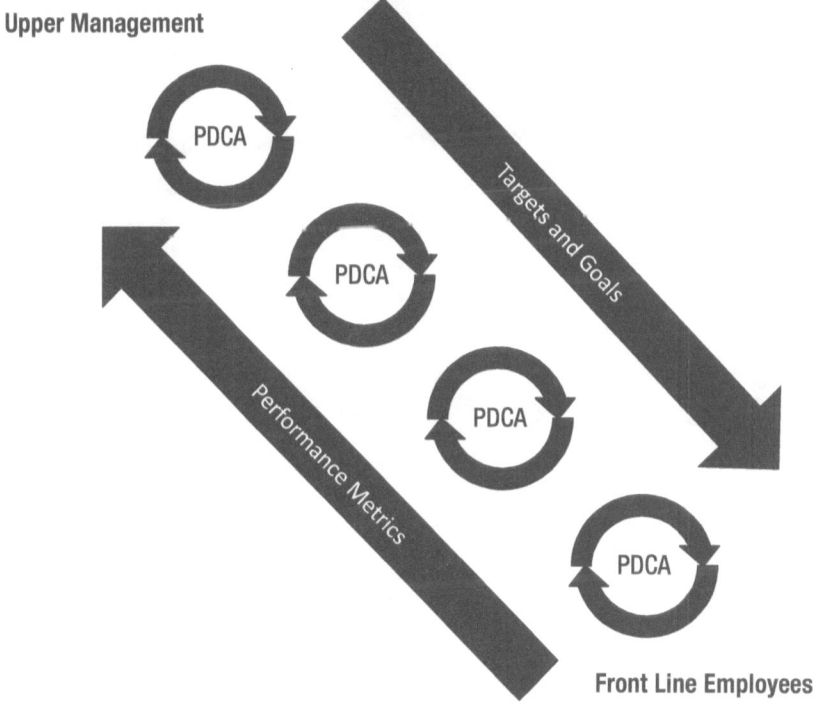

Figure 2-6. Hoshin Kanri Simplified

At each level of the organization, initiatives are designed to support the strategies of the levels above it. This concept makes the sometimes vague strategic plans tangible for every employee, although there are challenges to implementing them. These challenges include being able to dissect the strategies into smaller and easily understood pieces. Large corporate strategies are often difficult to simplify. Of course, if we expect them to be executed, we must be able to get the company to understand them. It is therefore a good idea to simplify them.

Another challenge is effectively prioritizing the tactics supporting the strategic plan. Most organizations do not make this prioritization process an effective part of leadership. For those without a formal process, an impact/effort matrix, as shown in Figure 2-7, is a simple way to prioritize work. When using this tool, a team assigns an impact and effort for each project. Easy projects with high impact are the first priority. Difficult projects with a low impact rarely get accomplished. The final challenge is using meaningful metrics to show progress on each level of the strategy deployment.

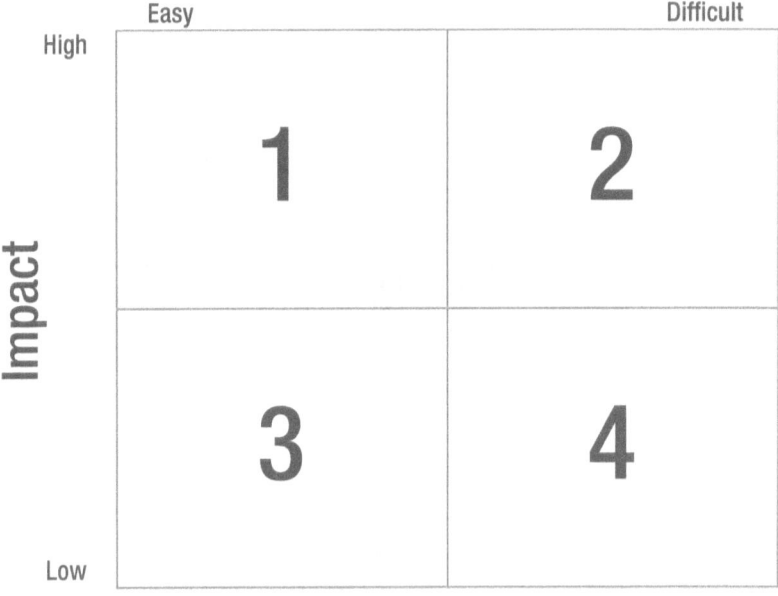

Figure 2-7. Impact/Effort Matrix

These tools, if utilized together and correctly, should help you implement a consistent strategy to run your business. They can help reduce the waste during the planning process.

Waste from Strategy and Management Based on "Fluffy" Outcomes

Until the mid-1950s, growth was about marketing, and marketing equaled sales. The job of the marketing department was to persuade a customer to buy a product. It didn't matter what the customer needed; what mattered was the product that the company made. Then, persuasion became the name of the game. In the 1960s and 1970s, companies started to see how this mindset wasn't working. They started to tailor their products to actual customer needs. Unfortunately, this was all lost in the 1980s, 1990s, and still today. Strategy itself seemed to become the most fundamental concept. This was a top-down mindset—CEOs ruled.

Both the practitioner realm and the academic circles exploded with books and research on strategy: how to create a strategic plan, how to create a mission statement, and how to perform a SWOT analysis. All of this study was very "fluffy," meaning it had remarkably few tangible specifics. It was not based on solid customer needs or research, but instead, just what the CEOs dictated. This trend, coupled with the stock market booms and crashes, seemed to shift the attention of the businesses to the indicators already described, such as growth and stock price.

In his popular book, *Making the Numbers Count*, Brian Maskell outlined the case to accountants and chief financial officers to change the way that they measured business functions.[4] These overarching indicators, such as profitability and debt-to-equity ratio, do not provide enough information to get a clear picture of a firm. At least not clear enough to formulate an effective strategy. Maskell discussed new costing methods, process management, concurrent engineering, and life cycle analysis. Dr. Deming started this movement with his criticism of the systems of absorption that are often used in accounting that lead to destructive business decisions.[5] Metrics must be relevant to the operations at hand rather than easy to get or commonly used accounting values. Lean Six Sigma methods value this approach because you cannot change the output of your processes by focusing on the output. Rather, you affect the output by understanding the inputs that drive performance.

We learned this in high school algebra through the formula $Y=f(X)$, but have somehow forgotten to consider this when operating businesses. We chase sales through price cutting or by making deals in order to meet a quota, rather than doing what truly drives sales, which is making customers happy. If you analyze the factors that drive customer satisfaction, you'll have a formula that

---

[4]Brian Maskell, *Making the Numbers Count, 2nd Edition* (London, England: Productivity Press, 2009). p. 1-243.
[5]W. Edwards Deming, *Out of the Crisis* (Boston, MA: MIT Press, 1986). p. 1-507.

you can use to drive sales through service and value, rather than less healthy strategies. It is not the output that matters, but rather the inputs. You should measure the Xs, not the Ys.

> **Note** Use Y=f(X) in all situations. Don't drive your business by focusing on the results. Focus on the things that drive results.

Accounting measures happen in monthly, quarterly, or annual cycles. This is far too infrequent to adequately affect operations. Rather, if you focus on measures that predict the monthly financials, you can drive those inputs, view them on a regular basis, and improve overall performance. Many of you have heard of SMART (Specific, Measurable, Attainable, Relevant, and Time-Bound) goals, but still try to run your businesses without them. Business success is not typically the effect of making one or two great strategic decisions; it's the direct result of making intelligent decisions every day. In order to make effective decisions, you need real-time data that influences management. You also need the experience and industry knowledge to react to that data and to improve performance.

Strategy must include the overall vision of the organization as taught in MBA schools. But it must also go way beyond what is taught in these classes. It must also include steps that are necessary to achieve this vision. We see mission and vision statements that talk about being "world class" or "best in class." We also see statements such as "meet or exceed our customer requirements." These are cliché strategic phrases that have no real meaning. How do you measure "meet or exceed our customer requirements?" You don't. However, you can measure things like dock-to-dock time or development cycle time, both of which could predict the ability to meet customer requirements (assuming that your processes are capable of meeting their requirements). If you take the time to develop strategies, you must take the time to understand the variables that reflect the success of your strategy and the inputs that drive those variables. Effective leaders will work on finding key metrics to tie to strategy and then delegate the implementation of the strategy to trusted employees. They do this by communicating the vision and showing what success looks like.

An example of this type of strategy can be found in a company like Aneonline. (We understand this is a relatively unknown company, but unfortunately, it is hard to find companies with great strategies.) This company is a small, online marketplace owned by an Australian company. Aneonline's strategy is, "We intend to provide our customers with the best online shopping experience from beginning to end, with a smart, searchable website, easy-to-follow instructions, clear and secure payment methods, and fast, quality delivery."[6] Every single one of these desires is specific, measurable, attainable, relevant, and time-bound. Searchability of a web page can be measured. Payment methods can be assessed. Delivery can be measured for quality and speed. Crafting a strategic plan through goals like "growth," on the other hand, is meaningless. Strategy must begin and end with measurable goals.

Having measurable strategies is somewhat difficult, due in part to the traditional organizational structure. This structure includes departments including sales, marketing (sometimes included in sales or vice versa), accounting, and operations. Each department is incentivized to be at odds with the others, rather than focus on the overall health of the organization. The performance metrics focus on individual performance and are used in order to incentivize people to improve individual performance rather than the health of the organization.

Note Strategy must begin and end with measurable goals.

We have essentially taken the fundamentals of what Toyoda taught us and perverted them to fit Western culture, therefore making them less effective. Maybe it is time to consider getting rid of the traditional organizational structure and instead have cross-functional teams that focus on each of the business areas. The concept of sales, inventory, and operations planning used in many organizations is a step in this direction, but does not address the root issue, which is the need for departments to consider the health of the whole company rather than how good each department looks. For instance, we should include operations and sales in investment decisions. The lack of knowledge about the overall operation of the business leads each individual to drive the metrics that he feels are important. In some cases, these may be the right metrics, but in many others, they are not. It is impossible to develop a strategy at the upper level of a company, when the individual department's needs are not known, considered, or integrated. (We discuss silos later in the chapter.)

Not having a measurable strategy creates waste everywhere in your company. Everyone is running in every direction doing things with no purpose. The first step to a waste-free company is a good strategy based on the ideals outlined in this chapter. Measure the Xs, not the Ys.

---

[6]DashCamTalk, "ANEONLINE Became the Exclusive Distributor of Dabonda HD dash cam in Australia - Best Brand Awarded," http://forum.dashcamtalk.com/index.php?threads/aneonline-became-the-exclusive-distributor-of-dabonda-hd-dash-cam-in-australia-best-brand-awarded.1839/, 2013.

Waste from the Strategic Planning Process

The strategic planning process is normally extremely wasteful. Strategic plans may be hashed out in a retreat format, which deserves some discussion here, although we discuss retreats more in Chapter 5. Why is a retreat wasteful? Taking leaders out of the daily activities and focusing on a topic or issue is not necessarily a wasteful activity, but unfortunately too many retreats include special amenities like hotel stays and country club conferences. They may also include offsite team building or brainstorming sessions. These activities are all wasteful.

If you need a retreat in order to focus, then grab a space at the company and tell everyone to leave you alone. This way, company resources are not wasted on an offsite location. Skip the team-building exercises. These are neither true rest-and-relaxation events nor something more meaningful than discussing how the leaders can work better as a team. These conversations are too often guarded and a complete waste of time. We have all been part of these wasteful events far too many times.

> **Note** The cost of developing strategy is inherently wasteful. Don't add retreats, spas, catering, and more to the mix. Respect your workforce. Plan strategies in an efficient manner. Keep in mind that having a strategy that is not executed or understood is even more wasteful.

Instead of the aforementioned wasteful strategic retreats, consider this strategy session from our experience that was beneficial. The company in question brought managers from multiple manufacturing locations together to standardize operations and reduce waste. It had never been done before and had a specific purpose. They didn't rent conference space; instead, they set up folding chairs in an empty space in the warehouse. Of the various strategic planning sessions that we have been part of during our careers, this was the best one that we can remember. They didn't spend time on SWOT or multigeneration plans, because they already knew where their opportunities for improvement were. Everyone was aware of the session beforehand and came prepared with applicable information in hand. We exited the one-day meeting with a clear path to standardize operations and share best practices. How was this different from other strategic plans? It included the following:

- **Focus:** Too many organizations haven't identified the reason for their strategic plan. They put together the plan because that is what they are supposed to do. After all, their MBA professors told them they should and they have seen other companies do it, right? If the business is doing well, then why bother? If there is a gap, focus on that gap. Develop a plan to sustain current successes and bridge the gap to get where the company wants to be.

- **No soft stuff:** Trust falls don't build teams. Golf and obstacle courses don't build teams either. Teams are built though mutual respect and accountability, and by working together on work that needs to be done. The "soft" stuff you do at retreats and strategy sessions won't build your team. It is an excuse to have recreation on the company's dime. In the age of downsizing and infrequent pay raises, this is not only wasteful, but is belittling and cruel to the employees.

- **A path forward:** The outcome of the strategy must include a plan for execution. Nobody should walk out of the planning session without knowing what they or their department is doing to drive the strategy very specifically.

- **Respect:** Again, it deserves mention, leaders need to respect their stakeholders and avoid elaborate expenses for these sessions. What is the definition of elaborate? Anything outside of meals and beverages should be questioned. If the company possesses an internal resource, then why would they waste money on renting the same resource?

Business has changed over the last 20 to 30 years. It used to make sense to build business units around the world to serve regions and have sales offices in those areas as well. It used to make sense to come together and have "leadership retreats" or even frequent "strategizing sessions." Obviously, the infusion of technology has made the world a smaller place.

These logistics improvements have also given small and medium-sized businesses the ability to be global without needing locations around the world. There are times when it makes sense to build facilities around the world, such as when a customer builds a large manufacturing location and you want to serve the customer well. This happened when Bosch Siemens Hausgeräte (BSH) built facilities in the United States and China. Some German suppliers built factories near the new factories in order to provide good service to the new factory. Although local businesses got some of the new work that BSH offered, the companies who followed BSH took a large portion of the work. Why did this happen? It was the result of a good customer relationship. We mention this example because these suppliers built manufacturing locations for logistics purposes.

There are many times when logistics become less important. Technology enables companies to hold meetings through the use of Skype or Webex, saving unnecessary travel expense. In fact, with the exception of some types of sales calls or services where physical presence is necessary, the need to travel for business is nearly extinct. We know of a company in Ohio that outsources all of its IT work to a company in California. So why do so many managers and employees travel? There is a lot more about this topic in later chapters, but we will briefly discuss some of the reasons here.

The chief reason is probably why we do many other wasteful things in business. It's the "we have always done it this way" philosophy. We travel to meetings with other divisions of the organization or to visit customers because we think we have to do it that way. We can't craft a strategic plan without sitting together in a room to "brainstorm."

In reality, we can hold most meetings and even technical discussions via the Internet. The downside to limiting business travel is that many employees use this as an opportunity to vacation. Think of the news stories around meetings and conferences held by the Internal Revenue Service or large banking firms. Do we think that these are the only people who do this? It is obvious throughout a company when executives waste money.

We spend so much time in constant communication with employees and customers that strategic planning workshops are frequently a waste of time. Get the data to make informed decisions, make your plan, and move on. Stop the bleeding of excess money in the name of planning.

> **Note** If your strategic planning process has not changed in ten years, change it now!

Waste from Too Much Leadership

Any discussion about strategy must contain a discussion of leadership. We discuss particular aspects of management in terms of human resources and how to calculate leadership/management excess in Chapter 5, and here we discuss the broader idea of leadership.

Management guru Peter Drucker was interviewed by *Forbes* magazine shortly before his death. In it, Drucker noted that one of business's worst problems was too much leadership, both in sheer numbers and the whole concept of charisma. He felt that there were way too many leaders walking around and very few actual managers who accomplished things. Additionally, Drucker felt that charisma was one of the most overrated concepts of all time. Charisma accomplishes nothing. In Drucker's words, "What they really need are competent managers who can do the hard work of decision making, planning, and coaching."[7]

---

[7]Geoffrey James, "6 Most Overrated Management Concepts," http://www.inc.com/geoffrey-james/6-most-overrated-management-concepts.html, 2012.

As an example, I can think back long ago to my days in college when I paid my college tuition and other bills by waitressing and bartending. Typically, the managers had worked their way up through the company. Every now and then, the big corporation way down in Florida would bring in a new manager who had never waited tables, never bartended, never washed dishes, never cooked, and was never a hostess. These people never lasted more than about 1-2 years. They burned out quickly when they realized how hard the job was, and moreover, when they realized they had no respect from their workforce. They try to replicate this experience in the CBS show "Undercover Boss," in which CEOs go undercover as workers in the frontline jobs. Typically, the CEOs seem like buffoons trying to do these jobs. Even in this forced and fictitious situation, it is easy to see that some CEOs have absolutely no idea what is required in their companies or how hard it is. You cannot be a restaurant manager without doing every single gross and hard task throughout the day.

This example is extreme, because restaurant jobs can be arguably some of the hardest. But, the lesson is no different in corporations. How can someone set strategy, set up plans to implement strategy, and set up metrics to measure success if they cannot or are not willing to do the work? This statement cannot be translated exactly in all situations. A CEO of a hospital might not know how to perform brain surgery. They might not even be a doctor—that's okay. What's not okay is when they do not understand each employee's job—what they need to know and possess to do the job and how to be successful in that job. They can't implement and measure strategy without this understanding.

Therefore, Drucker criticizes charisma because charisma in itself does not drive leadership. It is a combination of leadership and management that gets the work done. Not everyone can be a leader. Not everyone can be a manager either. But no leader can be truly effective without solid management skills. Drucker's criticism of leaders is based on the fact that so many leaders are incapable of management. (With more than 13,000 books written on leadership, there is an obvious problem.) By focusing on good management skills, true leadership can be developed. In reality, leadership roles are often filled through years of service or as a progression through ranks of management, such as in the restaurant example. Leadership, however, should be developed through aptitude and ability.

Note Leaders manage *and* inspire. One without the other is not leadership.

Chapter 2 | Strategy of Waste

> **A TRUE TEST OF LEADERSHIP**
>
> Traditional leaders are often type A personalities who may not possess the humility necessary to handle true leadership. Leaders start by leaning on the expertise of those whom they lead. They ask questions about what must be done and how it should be accomplished. The best leaders surround themselves with exceptional people. This is absolutely true. Andrew Carnegie wanted to put on his gravestone, "Here lies a man who knew how to put into his service more able men than he was himself."[8] Effective leaders leverage the abilities of others to maximize their potential and drive organizational success.

Waste from Commitment-Stuck Leaders

Robert Cialdini wrote about the weapons of influence and their effect on the decisions that people make.[9] One of these weapons is the commitment and consistency principle. Cialdini warns us that we can become victim to making decisions and then sticking with them, even when they are clearly bad, due to this psychological principle. Have you ever been in a fight with a loved one, and then realized after some time that you were wrong, but still continued to fight? This is the commitment and consistency principle. Leaders are often guilty of this.

I once had a conversation with a coworker about an initiative that we had been working on for a while. Our company had spent hundreds of thousands of dollars to implement this initiative. I commented that it had become ineffective and we should shift our focus elsewhere. My coworker said, "And throw away hundreds of thousands of dollars that we have already spent? We can't do that; we've invested too much." This is exactly the point. Even if millions are spent on a project, business leaders cannot afford to continue to invest more money just because they are afraid to be wrong and are more concerned with saving face than making good decisions.

Another example of this principle was with a project whereby, in order to make operating improvements, a leader made the decision to spend over $1.1 million on upgrades. Shortly thereafter, an engineer showed that 80 percent of the projected improvement could be reached for about $20,000. So, faced with the decision to spend $1.1 million and have a return on investment (ROI) that would take years, versus spending $20,000 with a ROI that would take months, what did this leader do? Obviously, we are telling this story as an example of commitment and consistency, so he started

---

[8]Karlgaard, Rick, "Peter Drucker on Leadership," *Forbes*, `http://www.forbes.com/2004/11/19/cz_rk_1119drucker.html`, November 19, 2004.
[9]Robert Cialdini, *Influence: The Psychology of Persuasion, Revised Edition* (New York, NY: Harper Business, 2006).

spending the $1.1 million. Initially, it seemed like arrogance or ignorance. But, after reflecting on the situation, it is clear that this leader had committed in his mind. Even when confronted with data about the inefficiencies of the larger project backed up with a good measurement system analysis, he could not change his mind.

These are just two real examples of situations where valuable resources are wasted due to the inability to see an ineffective project when you have one, and then be able to move on to better projects. This supports the previous advice to have metrics built around initiatives and goals. Then you should use these metrics to make future decisions. If you put the structure in place as you make decisions, then you empower employees to combat the automated response of commitment and consistency that Cialdini identified.

Note Don't be trapped by your poor decisions; learn from them and move on. Commitment to a poor strategy will cause continuing poor performance.

Waste from Benchmarking

One of the most frequently misunderstood principles in strategy is benchmarking. Almost everyone does it, yet very few understand when and how benchmarking should be used. Does Apple benchmark against other companies? Of course, any company in a competitive market keeps an eye on the competition, but benchmarking is often not used this way. We seriously doubt Apple spends much time pondering the moves of Microsoft and Motorola, or at least they didn't when Steve Jobs was around. We've seen some recent moves to show they are spending time benchmarking too much, and all for the wrong reasons.

Benchmarking is effective when it is used to cross industry boundaries, such as the way healthcare organizations look at aerospace or nuclear power to develop their own culture of reliability. It can help by identifying some best practices to implement, by finding ways to generate potential savings, or by identifying methods used to increase customer satisfactions ratings. It can also be used as a temperature check. You can use temperature checks to determine if you are a leader or a follower. In other words, benchmarking can help you know how competitive you are as an organization. In one of my former careers as an engineer designing appliance components, I would go to Best Buy and look at the appliances. This way, I could see what our customers, like Whirlpool, Electrolux, or Frigidaire, were offering in their appliances and then see what the prices were and also what the competitors were offering and at what prices. This told me whether we needed to look for ways to improve our designs. It would in no way tell me how to completely redesign a products or a strategy.

Unfortunately, there are more weaknesses than strengths in regard to benchmarks. One downside is the potential cost. Some suppliers of benchmarking information charge tens of thousands or hundreds of thousands of dollars to provide the data. If, after you have reviewed the data, you find that you are better than 90 percent of the market, then it is time to rest, right? Wrong! You should also perform an ROI analysis of the benchmark. If, after buying the benchmark (or doing it yourself), and calculating the labor and resource costs associated with analyzing the benchmark and implementing the changes, you do not show a profit, it would never be a worthwhile endeavor.

Companies should look at their own performance to identify targets and improvements. The ROI is much higher this way because you have taken the time to identify the root causes of waste and eliminate them. Plus, how likely is it that you are looking at companies directly comparable to your own? The risk is high that you are not. Even the exact same type of company, in the exact same industry, will not have the same employees, resources, or anything similar enough to be directly comparable. You may make decisions on the benchmark data that cause the company harm, because you're not comparing like companies.

If you use benchmarking, you should only benchmark the best. Average is not acceptable. Second best is not acceptable. Only the best applies. However, you have to realize that your company is not directly comparable to the ones benchmarked. Specifically, in a mature industry such as healthcare, where lots of data is available, benchmarking is over-utilized. It is measuring poor performance against other poor performance versus continually working toward perfection. There are always some companies that do some things well and some things poorly.

> **Note** No benchmark will tell you what factors are creating great success and which aren't, let alone how all the various factors interact.

In many areas of manufacturing (but not all), the concept of zero defects is the leading force in quality circles. Statistics are done on samples to show Six Sigma quality of 3.4 defects per million opportunities, which essentially equates to zero defects. Other companies still rely on acceptable quality standards driven by standards, such as MIL 105-E. With this standard, the company accepts a low level of defects instead of zero, feeling that for the price of the product (generally a very low priced product), they cannot expect zero defects. It is no wonder that we have injuries and recalls in the manufacturing world. The sad thing is that the manufacturing environment is about as good as it gets.

Many financial institutions are so accepting of defects that they do not keep a single profile on the consumers they serve. This leads to potential fraud because all of the divisions do not have the same view of the customers.

Healthcare is no different. Donald Berwick has spoken and written multiple times on the inefficiencies and lack of quality in the healthcare field.[10] In healthcare, a certain level of defects is considered acceptable as long as it is in line with the poor quality of such facilities. This is not because the customers want defects (who wants a healthcare defect!?), but rather because the companies expect defects since the benchmarks show that all companies have defects.

Benchmarking should never be used in this manner. In cases where you look outside your industry, like healthcare looking at manufacturing to see how they handle zero defects, it might not make sense. Benchmarking in the same industry almost always yields mediocrity, which will never generate an ROI, which will always lead to waste.

■ **Note** Benchmarking can be an effective tool for determining how you stand in the market or even for getting ideas for process innovations, but when it's used to copy others or to set targets, it *will* lead to mediocrity and underutilization of the company's potential.

Waste from Growth

Michael Porter talked about the growth trap over 15 years ago in his paper on strategy in 1996, yet we still see and hear about growth being a strategy. Porter said growth has a "perverse effect on strategy".[11] It incentivizes companies to go after the big customers for a quick win rather than building long-term and mutually beneficial customer relationships. In order to obtain the large customers, lower prices are offered, which limits profitability. The alternative is to grow by selling in low volume to customers willing to pay a higher margin for quality. Notice that there is still growth with this strategy, but there is a clear difference between growth as a strategy and growth resulting from customer service and excellent value. The former is a recipe for declining profits or a desperate move to reach some financial target, whereas the latter is a recipe for long-term profitability and appropriate growth, which the company can most likely handle without major investments.

We have witnessed management making changes to strategy that include adding features that customers don't really want, trying to steal ideas from other companies, and acquiring companies that have no real value to boost the overall revenue or to enter into new sales channels. The desire to grow confuses the company because—rather than having an internal strategy to make

---

[10]Robert Pear, "Health Official Takes Parting Shot at Waste," *New York Times*, December 3, 2011.
[11]Porter, Michael, "What Is Strategy?" *Harvard Business Review*, November-December 1996, pp. 61–78.

good products or provide services, which provides direction—the strategy is handed to the company by the highest bidder with the most volume to offer. The company identity dies in the wake of a growth strategy. Without this identity, it is increasingly difficult for managers to make decisions without a mistake, so all decisions must go through leadership.

We talked briefly on using growth as a strategic decision, but what is growth? Is growth an outcome that you are looking for? Why do you want growth? Will it make your company more profitable? Believe it or not, there is not a linear relationship between growth and any outcome that a business is striving to achieve. Growth has been studied since the 1950s and nobody has ever been able to come up with a formula that will drive it. McKelvie and Wiklund studied growth and found, "Despite hundreds of studies into explaining firm-level growth differences from 1950 until now, researchers have been unable to isolate variables that have a consistent effect on growth across studies."[12] It's not great leadership, it's not great employees, and it's not great customer service. Growth is created by a set of circumstances unique to each company in which it happens. There is no one thing that leads to growth. (Which again explains why benchmarking in ineffective).

A study was done that looked at the growth hypothesis.[13] In it, the authors found that leaders who sought growth without profitability first, failed. This is like the company seeking growth through investment capital. The only way to have successful growth is to have profitability first. This is clearly shown. Thinking that growth brings profitability cannot work. That is, as the phrase says, "putting the cart before the horse." Leaders who focus on the inputs that drive growth, rather than focusing on growth itself, will be significantly more successful. The inputs must be the focus, not the growth.

Too often, businesses try to become something they are not for the sake of growth. Every business has something that it does well and no business is good at everything. General Electric (GE) realized that it was trying to be good at everything. Even with 140 years of innovations from General Electric, they decided to sell the GE Plastics division to Sabic. Why would they do this? Because, with the exception of their appliance division, GE is not good at being a low-cost producer. They pride themselves on innovation and quality, which directly competes with low cost. (For this reason, it is surprising that the appliance division has not been sold as well.)

---

[12] Alexander McKelvie and Johan Wiklund, "Advancing Firm Growth Research: A Focus on Growth Mode Instead of Growth Rate," *Entrepreneurship Theory and Practice*, 34, no. 2, March 2010, pp. 261–288.

[13] Per Davidsson, Paul Steffens, and Jason Fitzsimmons, "Growing Profitable or Growing from Profits: Putting the Horse in Front of the Cart?" *Journal of Business Venturing*, 24, 2009, pp. 388–406.

When GE was successful in the plastics world, it was because they developed innovative plastics and could charge a premium for them. Customers think of Lexan® or Plexiglas® when polycarbonate is needed even though there are dozens of polycarbonate options. When GE lost this advantage and customers demanded competitive prices and service, GE found that the plastics business was not as profitable as the other divisions. Therefore, they sold the plastics division to a company that could increase the margins or be happy with lower ones. Most businesses are not this insightful and would have tried to hang on to the plastics business.

Growth can mean growth in sales profitability, customers served, or number of employees. The goal of any business is to make money. Even not-for-profit businesses must make money to pay employees and have reserves to handle fluctuations in business. Does growth equal higher profits? Chapter 3 talks more about marketing and sales wastes, but the pursuit of growth while reducing profitability is a main waste of sales and leadership.

So companies think that growth will increase profits. Maybe growth will give them more purchasing authority or give them more negotiating power with their customers. Erie Plastics from Corry, PA thought growth would make it profitable. That was until it became bankrupt when its biggest customer, Proctor & Gamble, chose to stop working with it. Similarly, Core Systems, LLC, of Painesville, OH grew to nearly $50 million from around $20 million over 15 years. Although it had a modest, but solid average increase in sales of about seven percent per year in revenue, it didn't save the over 400 employees who were laid off when Whirlpool Corporation stopped buying from Core Systems In both of these situations, they had a well-run business with qualified leadership and dedicated employees. Growth was the Holy Grail to achieve stability and long-term profitability. Growth led them both into making deals with massive companies, who would never value the relationship. Growth did not work out in either case.

This is a common formula that we see when we read business publications. It is so common that books have been written challenging the whole notion of growth. In the consumer market, growth creates more liability due to a potential increase in litigation. If you have taken a business law class, you have probably learned about the company with deep pockets. You don't sue poor people, you sue filthy rich people. Generally, once a company becomes large, that's when you start seeing discrimination lawsuits or product negligence lawsuits. Likewise, once a company becomes public, you begin to see the drive to pay investors, which frequently causes the leaders to cheapen products. This eventually pushes customers away due to low-quality issues. Yet, business schools teach that businesses must grow. Business leaders feel that growth is a measure of success.

If we assume that growth is the answer, how do we grow? Is it a fault of leadership or lack of resources or capacity? When faced with growth opportunities, businesses often look for loans or investors to fund the resources necessary for growth. This puts stress on the company. In order to meet the covenants on loans, the leaders make decisions to drive short-term targets at the potential expense of the company. We are not saying that companies should not attempt to grow or even take out loans to fund growth. We are saying that growth should be stable and achievable, based on real market factors. Resources should not be extended to the point of potential failure to achieve growth. It is better to grow slowly through happy customers with a real demand, who are willing to pay a decent margin, than by methods that commit you to success or failure based upon "false" growth. Rapid growth is greedy. And we all know how bad greed is. We have outlined some of these growth myths here:

- **You can outgrow an organizational or leadership problem.** Bad decisions happen regardless of the size of the company. Growth will not solve the problem, but magnify it. This mindset is similar to a married couple having a baby to "save" their marriage. The baby just brings more problems and more stress. The same thing happens in a company. The company must have a good foundation before growing.

- **Growth equals profitability.** As a young engineer, I frequently heard this justification for lower prices: "we will make it up in volume." This is like the idea of making something more efficient without improving its quality. You will only make additional bad products quicker if you make a bad process more efficient. The same holds true for growth. Growth will magnify the loss that you will have if you lower your prices and therefore lower margins.

- **Profitability improves when you control the market.** When you control the market and it is profitable, other organizations will enter the market and become competitors, either through a similar product or a substitution. This is a fundamental idea that Michael Porter discusses in his books. You will have increased profits only when you have something special: good customer satisfaction and brand loyalty. It is not a function of growth.

- **If you grow, customers will benefit.** How exactly will customers benefit? If you realize savings through growth, perhaps by economies of scale, however rare that normally is, you would doubtfully pass those savings on to the customers. Also, you will be distracted from servicing your existing customers as your customer base grows. You may need to hire additional people to service your customers, which may lower the quality of the service. And if we believe that fast-growing and highly leveraged organizations are less able to adapt to change, how do the customers benefit from that?

Note Grow only when it makes sense for your market or you will end up eroding your margins and losing your competitive advantage. And please remember, growth itself is not a strategy. That only creates waste.

Waste from Mergers and Acquisitions

How many of you have been part of a merger gone bad? We have seen at least six mergers or acquisitions (M&As) in our careers at different companies where the goal was to create synergy or growth through new customer bases. In five of those cases, the profit that was promised was not achieved. Customers at the acquired companies were either not profitable or chose to leave shortly after the merger. The only time it worked was when the founding manager continued to manage the acquired company and was incentivized as part of the acquisition to meet certain financial metrics. On the whole, M&As simply don't add much value.

M&As happen for a variety of reasons. See Figure 2-8, which summarizes different types of mergers and acquisitions, including when they can be beneficial. When M&As are made for simple, financial, investment reasons, shares of the acquiring firms decline by an average of 4 percent at the time of the acquisition.[14] This number is significantly understated, because it doesn't account for the average 30 percent premium over the actual book value of the acquired firm, which is typically paid.[15] Then, over the next five years, shareholders see a 20 percent decline in the value of their stock, on average.[16] Based on these averages, you have to be going against all odds and being extremely lucky to benefit financially from an M&A.

---

[14]Bruce Greenfield and Judd Kahn, *Competition Demystified* (New York, NY: The Penguin Group, 2005), p. 345.
[15]Ibid. p. 343.
[16]Ibid. p. 345.

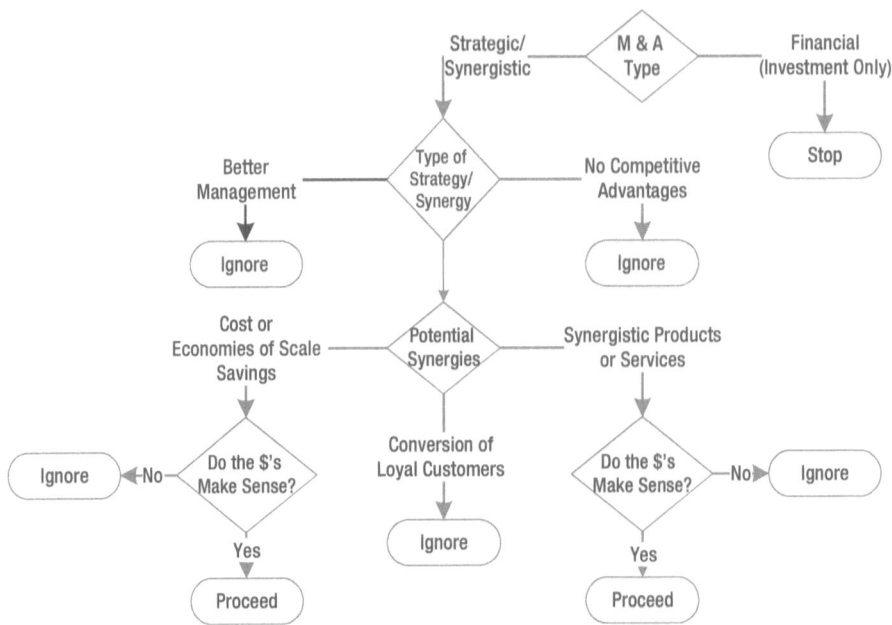

Figure 2-8. Mergers and Acquisitions

Strategic mergers and acquisitions can sometimes provide a profit. If there is no competitive advantage or synergy, obviously, they don't work or add value. Even when there are synergies, there might not be a good reason to go ahead with a merger. Michael Porter examined 33 large companies that had performed mergers from 1950–1986 and found that these companies had divested far more companies than they had retained.[17] Subsequent studies show that on average, M&As performed for synergist reasons do have an increase in operating margins, but these margins run in the range of 0.2 to 0.4 percent. Given the premium price normally paid to acquire a company, these M&As rarely make sense.

Let's look at some of the reasons why managers think synergies will be created. Sometimes, managers think that companies can, in a sense, "transfer" brand loyalty. This is completely impossible. For example, in the Pepsi/Frito Lay merger, it may make sense for logistics and economies of scale, but just because someone is loyal to Pepsi does not mean they will be loyal to Fritos. But, you can save money if the Pepsi and Fritos both go through the exact same logistics channels and therefore save on logistics expenditures.

---

[17]Michael Porter, *On Competition* (Boston, MA: Harvard Business School Press, 1998).

Many times, businesses buy other companies because they think that the good management will transfer. Normally, in this situation, the buyers feel that there is an operational or management deficiency and that the M&A will somehow overcome this deficiency. This concept assumes that the buyer has accurately assessed the company and that the buyer has the right skills to turn around the company for a profit. This is largely like the idea of flipping houses without the predictability of the local market to give an investor some idea of the return on investment. This philosophy just doesn't work. Just because a group of managers together makes good decisions and has a certain degree of luck in one business doesn't mean that the luck and experience will transfer to the new company.

An acquisition can work, however, if the two companies are truly synergistic. For example, when JM Smucker bought Jif peanut butter from P&G, they created Uncrustables, the ready-made peanut butter and jelly sandwiches. However, this brief example does not consider the fact that Smucker's may have just been able to buy peanut butter from a supplier at a good price. So, even in this example, which seems to make complete sense, there is no way to know which move for JM Smucker would have ultimately been more profitable without the acquisition.

Christine Moorman showed in a 2011 marketing survey that of those companies that plan to grow (realize that excludes everyone who does not plan to grow), about 10 percent planned to grow through an acquisition and 14 percent through a partnership. Nearly 70 percent of the companies planned on organic growth.[18] The reason for this is simple. M&As don't work as often as we would like them to. The odds of a merger or acquisition working are high enough that companies will continue to try to make them work, but they are low enough that it is likely not the best growth strategy if the goal is long-term profitability. Generally, M&As are used as someone's efforts to falsely boost a company's earnings. This just doesn't work. Beyond the fact that there is rarely added value, M&As frequently dilute a firm across more efforts and each individual product or service gets less attention.

ORGANIC GROWTH

The least wasteful growth strategy, if you desire to have growth, is *organic* growth. It leverages the capabilities of the company, serves current customers, and builds lasting relationships with new customers.

---

[18]Christine Moorman, The CMO Survey.Org, "Predicting the Future of Markets, Tracking Marketing Excellence, Improving the Value of Marketing Trends," http://www.cmosurvey.org. 2011.

So, the solution to this common business waste is not to do it. If there is a company that seems like it makes sense to acquire, look to see if there is a true competitive advantage that company has in its industry that will increase the value of your current operations. Unless you can definitively show the ability to fix any operational problems in the company that you want to acquire, don't pretend you or any consultant that you hire will be successful in getting the return on investment that you are assuming you will get from the deal.

> **Note** M&As rarely make financial sense. Do them only when there is a very obvious and exploitable synergy, like JM Smucker and Jif or Disney and Pixar.

Waste from R&D

If you are developing your own products, you need to have effective research and development (R&D) to make good products that people want to purchase. If you make products for other companies developed by those companies, you need effective R&D to create efficient and effective processes. If you provide services to others, you need effective R&D to create processes that meet or exceed customer expectations. These points are rather obvious. With 70 percent of companies with a growth strategy of organic growth, as mentioned in Christine Moorman's study, the R&D processes should be defined, if not done so already, and refined if in place. Unfortunately, there are many mistakes that can be made when doing R&D. In Chapter 3, we discuss more about market research in particular and statistics and analytics that go into understanding customer needs. Here, we focus on the overall process and some of the biggest areas of waste in R&D.

Process Mapping

One of the biggest areas of waste in R&D is having no process at all. You should create a value stream process map for the R&D and innovative functions of your firm. With this, you can design and analyze the flow of information (mostly customer data), materials, and resources required to create new products, processes, or services. This allows you to gain a full picture of the total resources involved. Often, these are overlooked, like the total amount of each employee's time in the project. By linking the process map to a Gantt chart, you can more easily recognize these connections. Likewise, by having a value-stream map of your R&D process, you can understand where the bottlenecks are and where the process is breaking down.

Eliminating Waste in Business | 53

Process maps do not need to be complicated, but they need to be done. We provide an example of one in Figure 2-9. (This example is obviously a very simplified version of the development process. A real development process would have many, many more steps and resources associated with it.) Studies have shown that once process maps are put in place, one can expect to find 60–90 percent time waste in processes during new product development.[19] The same study analyzed where typical waste occurs. The results are shown in Figure 2-10.

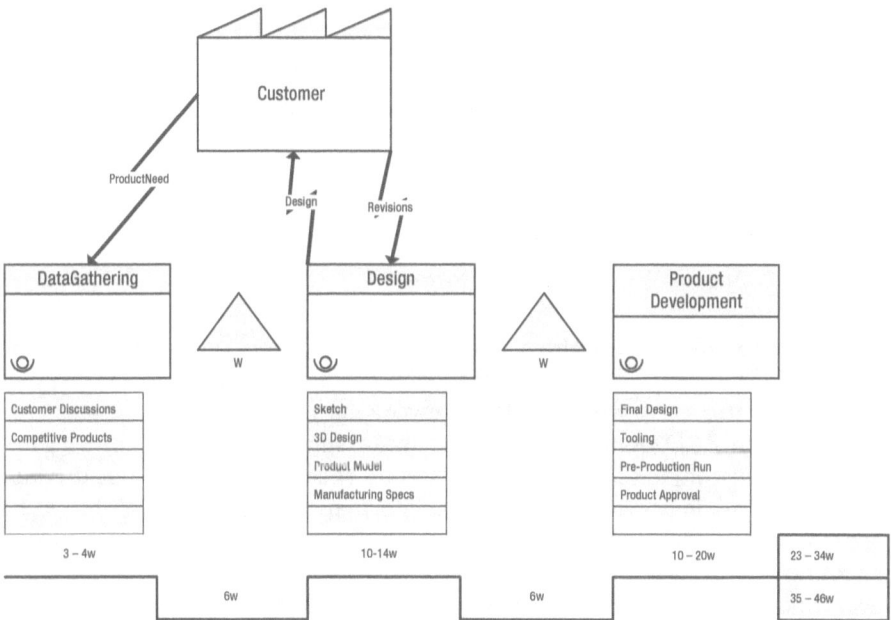

Figure 2-9. Sample Process Map

---

[19] McManus, Hugh, *Product Development Value Stream Mapping (PDVSM) Manual*, LAI, Lean Aerospace Initiative, http://lean.mit.edu/downloads/cat_view/94-products/575-product-development-value-stream-mapping-manual. September 2005.

Chapter 2 | Strategy of Waste

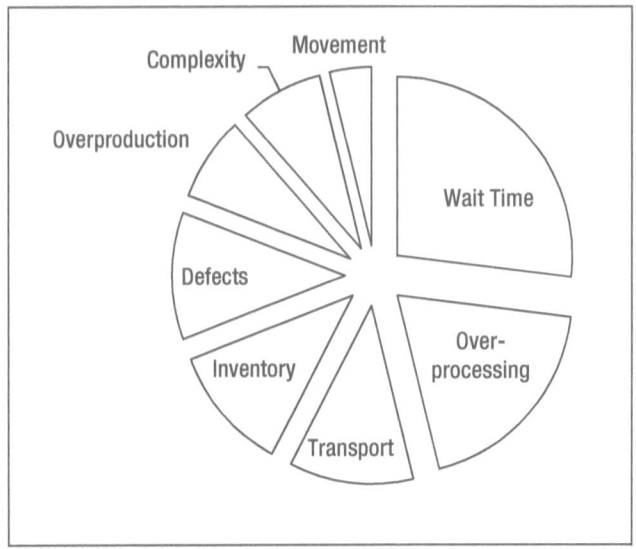

Figure 2-10. Areas of Waste in the R&D Process

This study found that the largest area of waste in product development came from waiting. This is defined as late delivery of information or delivery of information too early, which leads to rework. In order to overcome this area of waste, the R&D department should make sure that information is gathered from customer sources on time and be recent enough so that it is not obsolete. Most importantly, as soon as information is gathered, it should be processed and analyzed and entered into a database so that it can be readily found and accessed when needed. These databases should be available to everyone involved in the project, without layers of approval or delay.

Over-processing was identified as the next biggest area of waste in R&D. Excessive processing of information is defined as information processing beyond requirements. Waste in this area happens for many reasons, typically involving excessive formatting of reports because each person does not have a standard system. There is also a significant amount of over-processing due to lack of concurrent design processes and excessive approvals within the process. Turf wars often erupted when one department or person had a great idea or dataset, and did not want to share.

Transportation waste is defined as unnecessary movement of information between people, organizations, or systems. This area of waste is caused by the excess handling, reformatting, and re-entry of information. The more standardized systems are, the less the waste occurs. (We will spend time talking about these issues in Chapter 6, including how technology and IT systems can be developed to limit waste.)

Inventory waste occurs when information is unused. Think of this area almost as information overload. This waste occurs for many reasons. Sometimes people have a poor understanding of the project and its needs so they collect too much of the wrong information or there is a lack of disciplined systems for updating new information and purging old information. Defects create waste in the system typically because of human entry error or lack of validity and reliability checks of data. Overproduction occurs when information is over disseminated, typically when people send all information to everyone. Complexity occurs when the processes are overcomplicated. And finally, movement of information creates waste typically when people physically move information instead of using electronic means. This could happen because people print reports instead of using email or simply because of a bad physical distribution of people and resources.

Typically, when companies think about R&D and innovation, all they think about is how they can be more innovative. Yet, before this question is even asked, you should sit down and create a value stream map. This could save you 60–90 percent of your R&D staff's time. Imagine how much more innovative you could be if you more than double your R&D resources!

Note Stop worrying about how to be more innovative. Start worrying about how to make your R&D department more efficient, and then possibly double or triple your resources!

In addition to process-mapping the R&D department, there are a few more areas where businesses create waste. (Some of these are covered more in Chapter 3, along with some more detail on process-mapping your product-development process.)

Spaghetti on the Wall

We're sure you've heard this expression. This is a common product-development strategy where the designers create dozens of concepts and pitch all the concepts internally or to existing customers until something is chosen. This is a horrible waste of resources! If you follow a sound process based upon good data gathered from customer sources, this won't happen.

Product or Service Cannibalization

So you have a successful product or service that has gone through the natural lifecycle that all products go through. This product is near the end of its maturity and you want to get more sales. The natural inclination is to copy your successful products and "refresh" them, perhaps in a new color or a new version. After you create this new product and start selling it to your customers, you find that you have grown very little if at all. Why? You are cannibalizing your own products and driving your margins down. You are reducing efficiencies that you have built into your operation and are potentially building inventory that may be damaged or become obsolete.

This scenario can happen when you offer services as well. Maybe you introduce a new service or a new location and find minimal overall growth with increased costs. This is the result of the market being saturated by the fact that every company wants to grow.

Out of the thousands upon thousands of new products introduced every year, less than six percent featured any innovation in packaging, formulation, positioning, technology, market creation, or merchandising.[20] That means that over 94 percent of new products and services were not actually new! That means there's a 94 percent chance you are cannibalizing yourself! It is no wonder that over half of senior executives admit to being dissatisfied with the return of their new product innovations.[21]

To avoid waste, there should be extremely accurate, detailed forecasts of new and *old* product sales. (New product forecasting is outside the realm of this book, although we cover forecasting a bit in Chapter 7.) We highly recommend having a statistician with a marketing background on your staff or the help of consulting firm. This task should never be taken lightly. It should be done before launch as a forecast, and at many time intervals, post launch. The metric you are looking for here is incremental profit increase. To find that, you take new product sales, minus a loss from the cannibalized products, minus R&D expenses.

> *Incremental Profit*
>   = new product sales
>   − the loss from the cannibalized products
>   − R&D *expenses*

In most of these decisions, if you analyze your forecasts, losses, and expenses with sound statistics and analytics, you will find that more of the same is not an effective strategy. Instead, you need to find an unmet need or create a need through an innovative concept.

Don't forget to consider the best way to eliminate bad products. The typical decision process to do this is shown in Figure 2-11. The rationale is fairly straightforward. If a product is no longer meeting a specified level of profitability, the company should eliminate it. This is very short-sided. It does not consider the customer's needs and buying behavior.

---

[20]Fillman, M. W., "Breaking Tradition," *Market Research*, Vol 31(6), pp. 18-29. 1999.
[21]Landis, Steve, "Beware the Cannibal in Your Product Line," HBR Blog Network, *Harvard Business Review*, http://blogs.hbr.org/2013/06/beware-the-cannibal-in-your-pr/. June 4, 2013.

Eliminating Waste in Business 57

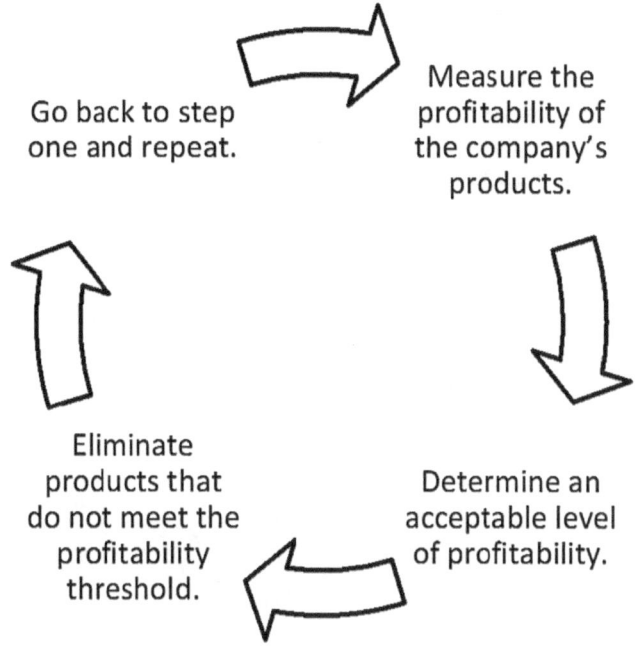

Figure 2-11. What Not to Do When Eliminating Old Products

An example of how this process can go wrong is presented in the book *Driving Customer Equity*, by Rust and colleagues.[22] They call this process the *profitable product death spiral*. Pretend that a grocery store ran an analysis and found out that high-end gourmet cheeses are extremely unprofitable. They carry price tags in the $10 to $30 range. They sit in the cooler, sometimes until they go bad. So, the grocery store manager decides to get rid of these cheeses. The next day, Sally is doing her grocery shopping. In addition to her normal shopping for the week, she is also shopping for her weekly Saturday night wine tasting party. As Sally fills up her cart with food, she goes to the wine department to select the wines for her party. Next, she makes a trip to the party section and picks out some lovely plates, paper napkins, and decorations for her party. She finally swings by the cheese section to get some cheeses to serve as appetizers with the wine. Imagine her frustration when her only options are mozzarella and cheddar. So, she checks out, leaves the store, and travels down the street to get her cheeses somewhere else.

---

[22]Roland Rust, Valerie Zeithaml, and Katherine Lemon, *Driving Customer Equity* (New York, NY: The Free Press, 2000). p. 1-304.

Chapter 2 | Strategy of Waste

What is likely to happen next week on Sally's shopping trip? Sally is busy. She doesn't have time to run to two stores. So, the next week, she does all of her shopping at the store down the street. If she is consistently able to buy all of the products she needs at a good price, she will likely become loyal to the other store. Other customers will have the same buying pattern. An illustration is provided in Figure 2-12.

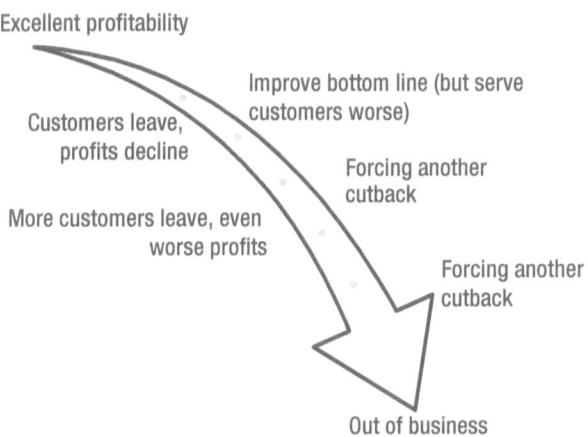

Figure 2-12. Profitable Product Death Spiral

What causes both cannibalization and the profitable product death spiral? You have to understand the buying behavior of customers at the individual level. You cannot rely on averages. Profitability comes from customers, not from products. The customers are paying your bills. You must set up information systems to track individual purchase decisions and behaviors. You need to understand complementary or competing products within your own company. (We give key metrics to understand this better in Chapter 3.) If you don't understand this, your product decisions will likely be a waste.

Don't Let Customers Design Your Products

That all being said, please realize a caveat. If you do supply a large retail company or industry giant, it is likely that you have experienced the request to design a product or service specifically for that retailer or giant, including changes to the packaging. If you believe that success is a result of differentiation and innovation, then what do you get when you take the brand and use it to become a custom manufacturer for the innovation of your customers? This is a classic issue that companies who sell to retailers face. In the name of growth, they create an environment where their products become commodities and where they are told what margin they will get for their products, how many they will create, and if they don't sell, that they will be responsible for taking them back. It doesn't take a business expert to know that the odds of long-term success in this business model are pretty slim. But, growth drives them to make these decisions. By the time they realize that they have made a mistake, the brand has been devalued. The customers who used to be willing to pay a higher price due to brand equity and quality are no longer willing to do so.

Use customer information to understand the market. Then, make decisions based upon your resources and abilities. You will never be all things to all people. You cannot forget your company's strategic goals. If customer needs are forcing you to stray from your mission, you likely need to take another look at your goals and at the targeted customer niche.

Waste from Silos

The issue of organizational silos is discussed in several chapters in this book. They are one of the single most common roadblocks to efficiency. Many companies use resources to transfer funds between departments. Each department acts as its own business and must justify its budget and expenses. In order to make their departments look good, managers will create strategies around their own department's profit and growth. Many times, departments will charge other departments for services. Process-improvement decisions are made based on the limited view of the manager's span of control. Although this might be the most efficient way to run the department, in the end it costs the company money.

The customer experiences the whole company, not the individual departments, as explained in the previous wine and cheese example. In addition, if one department saves money, but causes an equivalent or greater cost in another area through that decision, it costs the organization money. This concept is also discussed in Chapter 7, but is worth mentioning here because at some point in any company's history, this strategy was implemented. Most likely, this strategy is used to hold people accountable to meet the budget or ask only for interdepartmental services that have a real return on investment. This strategy is misguided because it makes employees care less about the overall health of the company and more about the health of their department. It sets up barriers to cross-functional work, which further degrades operational efficiencies.

Chapter 2 | Strategy of Waste

If we were to do a root cause analysis, we would find the issue of organizational structure a key problem to tackle. There are a few common options when looking at organizational structure:

- The **functional design**, the most common of the structures, has departments separated by what they do, such as human resources, finance, manufacturing, maintenance, engineering, nursing, marketing, and sales.

- The **product design** is when each product or product line has a group of the functions that you see in a functional design. This helps the employees focus on working together toward a common good rather than for their own department. However, you still end up with competition between product groups and you have duplication of resources.

- The **geographic design** features a group of entities structured around a geographic region that serves a specific customer base or product type. This typically is used in very large, spread out companies, or when geographic regions have very different needs.

- The **customer design** has groups that are focused on a single or small list of customers, where all of the functions have the same focus.

- The **matrix design** (Figure 2-13) is when there are more reporting relationships than single ones, and the structure may focus on the product, customer, or geographic type.

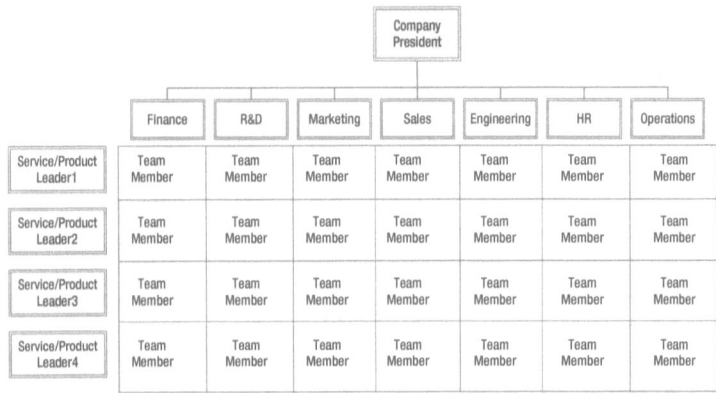

Figure 2-13. Matrix Organization

- The final structure is the **hybrid design**, which is some combination of the other designs.

The reason why the functional design is the most popular is because it allows for specialization and management that has a deep understanding of the work that the workers do. It also is easier to hold people accountable by having a single point of accountability and authority. The major downside to this structure is the silo culture and the waste that it causes. Figure 2-14 shows the pros and cons of each structure. Although each structure has its own strengths, the matrix design is the most desirable.

	Pros	Cons
Functional	Easier to manage Built-in accountability Efficiencies from specialization	Silo culture Departmental incentives Unhealthy competition No big picture view of product or customer Power hoarding
Product	Focused on the value-added function Team-based approach Product's profitability drives resources available Full understanding of each product	Little specialization Still need some corporate leadership for functions Less breadth of product knowledge and less innovation Potentially fewer resources
Geographic	Works for big companies Capacity sharing Resource sharing (warehouse, sales, and human resources) Cultural differences	Not necessarily close to customers Still has some functional design Specialization may lead to unionization and higher costs Duplication of resources
Customer	Customer-focused Team-based approach Customer group profitability drives resources available	Competition between customer segments Single customers make the group more risky Duplication of resources
Matrix	Organizationally focused Specialization of departments without the silos	Less focus Less efficient Too many masters
Hybrid	Pick and choose what works from other structures Works for big companies	Few real, proven models to mimic

Figure 2-14. Organizational Structures

The reason the matrix design is desirable is that it allows for specialized skills without the silo culture, which is a root cause of many issues in corporate America. This is a common structure in manufacturing organizations, since they require specialization. In reality, the operations must be customer- and product-focused for long-term survival. The potential inefficiencies of a matrix organization can be neutralized by effective organization, wide oversight, and prioritization. For the matrix organization to be most effective, you need to incorporate many of the solutions to waste mentioned in the other chapters of this book in order to remove barriers to success.

Implementing Strategy Metrics

Amber and Styles said, "Every metric, whether it is used explicitly to influence behavior, to evaluate future strategies ... will affect actions and decisions".[23] Companies create strategies and goals that are not meaningful. If you decide that a strategy is worth pursuing, it is worthwhile to create a metric that will show whether the performance is in line with the expectation.

Peter Drucker has said before, "If you can't measure it, you can't manage it." So why do we pretend that we can use strategies without measureable goals that are bound to a timeline? Unfortunately, becoming a manager doesn't take a special license or a show of competency. Too often, workers are promoted into management with little or no meaningful training, so even when solid metrics are in place, they don't know what to do with them. The concept of Hoshin Kanri discussed earlier in this chapter brings the overarching strategy down to a manageable and understandable number of tasks with associated measures. Of course, the company strategy still needs to have metrics associated with it, but these are the outcome metrics. The work of developing input strategies brings focus to the actions that will drive overall company success.

As discussed earlier in this chapter, you should measure the Xs, not the Ys. At the strategic level, your job is integrating the metrics from all the Xs, looking at overall numbers like profitability, and determining whether the strategy is still working. Therefore, we did not include "strategy metrics" per se in this chapter. The executive manager should make sure she is collecting the metrics outlined throughout the rest of this book and bring them together in a balanced fashion.

The balanced scorecard strategy,[24] introduced by Kaplan and Norton, helps you create a balance between financial metrics and other important, non-financial indicators such as service and quality, efficiency and effectiveness, and learning

---

[23]Hauser, John, and Gerald Katz. "Metrics: You are What You Measure," *European Management Journal,* Volume 16, No. 5, p. 517, October 1998.
[24]Kaplan, Robert S., and David Norton. "The Balanced Scorecard: Measures that Drive Performance." *Harvard Business Review,* 7t0, no. 1, January–February 1992, pp. 71–79.

and growth with your metrics in order to keep from focusing on one or two outcome metrics. The focus of most companies is often financial, which is why this method is essential. This method takes the focus away from profitability and looks at things that influence profitability, like customer satisfaction. Figure 2-15 shows the positive and negative aspects of the balanced scorecards.

Pros	Cons
Balanced	Not Actionable
Top Level Information	Data is Not Finite Enough
Linked to Strategy	
Accountability	

Figure 2-15. Balanced Scorecard Aspects

Because you have learned that top-level outcome metrics are not enough to drive performance, you need a series of actionable metrics. Balanced scorecards often show snapshots of information, which make them difficult to examine for trends and opportunities. You need to develop performance metrics that are balanced by showing the areas of the balanced scorecard. These metrics must also be tied to activities, which makes them actionable. The actual metrics to be used will vary, depending on the strategies that are unique to each organization. For instance, if, after carefully examining the market, you determine that growth is the necessary strategy, you may look at your ability to take on this growth. What will your actual strategy be to create said growth? New products? If so, what metrics will you need from your R&D and marketing departments? These metrics from your R&D and marketing departments become the driving strategic metrics.

In the manufacturing environment, capacity may be defined as the machine capacity, the labor pool available, or even the engineering capacity. Metrics such as machine utilization, time to market, order fill rates, or employee turnover rates show the barriers to growth that need to be improved in order to execute the strategy. In service industries, there are similar metrics, such as availability of service providers, time to provide service, and customer satisfaction. In both cases, these are just examples of potential metrics that you may choose.

The message here is that there is no formula to determine which measures you should be monitoring to drive your individual strategy. Nearly all of the imaginable metrics discussed in the following chapters could be appropriate. The important thing is that you understand the relationship between the outcomes you desire and the work that must be done to drive those outcomes.

> **Note** Measure the Xs, not the Ys. The job of the strategic manager is to integrate all the metrics from the Xs and reassess the strategy, not to sit back and look at profitability and debt-to-equity ratios.

Conclusion

There has been an evolution in strategy over the last 50 years. As the business environment has changed and technology advancements have happened, we need to adjust our thought process. We live in a time where the fluffy stuff won't cut it anymore. All strategies must be made with very clear goals in mind. These must be thoroughly rooted in customer needs. You should not spend precious resources in the strategy-planning process itself. You do not need retreats, boardrooms, or even catering. You need solid data, analyzed correctly, and disseminated to the right people.

Effective strategy is long term and does not require frequent manipulation (unless there are significant market changes that necessitate a new strategy). Once the strategic plan is made, stick with it. If you are counting on a "secret strategy" or "surprise maneuvers," you do not understand the true concept of strategy. Waste happens when a company jumps around from strategy to strategy with no clear direction or path. The tactics for executing the strategy may change as the business continues to learn about what works and what doesn't. Another common misconception about strategy is that companies must grow to be successful. In reality, growth can kill a company easier than improve it. Tactics around the strategy must be deliberate and invented within the company.

Companies must not count on doing what its competitors do. This approach will not create profitability. Innovation and success must be grown internally, using the skills that each unique company contains. Any strategy tactics must be measured at macro and micro levels. The macro level will show the overall progress toward the strategy, while the micro level will measure the tactics that drive the top-level metrics.

Waste Checklists

Strategic Checklist
*All "No" answers identify a potential opportunity for improvement.

Company Functions

Do you avoid silos in your operations?	Yes ☐ No ☐
Do your customers see the same company in every department or do you behave differently?	Yes ☐ No ☐
Do all your employees understand your strategic metrics?	Yes ☐ No ☐

Strategy Checklist
*All "no" answers identify opportunities for improvement.

Strategic Planning

Is your strategic plan a long-term plan with few changes year over year?	Yes ☐ No ☐
Do you have tactics that you use to support your strategy?	Yes ☐ No ☐
Do your tactics change as your business environment changes?	Yes ☐ No ☐
Is your strategic plan based on analyses of data and of your competitive market?	Yes ☐ No ☐
Have you identified what you are good at?	Yes ☐ No ☐
Have you identified your customers' needs?	Yes ☐ No ☐
Do you have goals that are specific, measureable, attainable, relevant, and time-bound to measure your strategies?	Yes ☐ No ☐
Do you have regularly scheduled reviews of your progress toward your goals?	Yes ☐ No ☐
Have you limited your costs for strategic planning by eliminating frivolous expenses?	Yes ☐ No ☐
Do your planning sessions include Focus, No Soft Stuff, A Path Forward, and Respect?	Yes ☐ No ☐

(continued)

Strategic Checklist
*All "no" answers identify opportunities for improvement.

Execution

Do you utilize Hoshin Kanri to drive the strategy throughout the organization?	Yes ☐ No ☐
Do you prioritize your work so that you have the greatest impact with the least amount of effort?	Yes ☐ No ☐
Do you understand the inputs that drive the outcomes you desire?	Yes ☐ No ☐
Is your improvement work aimed at the inputs that have the highest priority?	Yes ☐ No ☐
Do you have enough working managers and leaders to get the job done versus charismatic leaders?	Yes ☐ No ☐
Do you utilize technology to respect the time of your employees and customers?	Yes ☐ No ☐
Do you consider benchmarking as a temperature check instead of as a target-setting mechanism?	Yes ☐ No ☐
Is your benchmarking used to identify activities used in other business segments that could be used in yours?	Yes ☐ No ☐
Are your targets based upon improving your own performance levels instead of meeting some industry standard?	Yes ☐ No ☐

(continued)

Strategic Checklist
*All "No" answers identify a potential opportunity for improvement.

Growth

If you have growth plans, are they based upon customer needs?	Yes ☐ No ☐
Do you avoid growth for the sake of growth?	Yes ☐ No ☐
Can you be profitable and sustainable without growth?	Yes ☐ No ☐
If you have growth plans, are you growing using your own core competencies?	Yes ☐ No ☐
Do you understand and avoid the growth myths?	Yes ☐ No ☐
Do any mergers or acquisitions that you are considering meet make sense from a financial synergistic improvement?	Yes ☐ No ☐
Are your growth plans based upon organic growth?	Yes ☐ No ☐

Research and Development

Have you optimized your R&D processes?	Yes ☐ No ☐
Could you easily explain your R&D process to others?	Yes ☐ No ☐
Have you identified the areas of waste in your R&D processes?	Yes ☐ No ☐
Is you R&D based upon a market need?	Yes ☐ No ☐
Do you avoid creating excessive concepts to see what sticks?	Yes ☐ No ☐
Do you avoid cannibalizing your other products or services with new products or services?	Yes ☐ No ☐
Can you demonstrate a ROI on your R&D activities?	Yes ☐ No ☐
Do you avoid letting your customers design your products?	Yes ☐ No ☐

CHAPTER 3

Marketing
The Enormous Black Hole

> *I know half the money I spend on advertising is wasted; the problem is, I don't know what half.*
>
> —John Wanamaker

We'll cut right to the chase in this chapter, and you are not going to like the news. As a college marketing professor, I have dealt with the marketing waste category my entire career. How do you get the best ROI from your sales and marketing efforts? How do you figure out who your customer is? How do you target/reach your customer? The list continues. Companies often pick the product *they* want to sell (not necessarily what the customer wants) and think that if they market/advertise the heck out of it, their organization will magically grow. So many companies, from small to large, think that the more they pour into advertising, the higher their sales will be. Or perhaps, the prettier they make the package, the better it will sell. Or if they chase the latest fads, sales will magically appear.

The unfortunate news is this: there are no magic formulas, no one-size-fits-all approaches, and no quick fixes. And unfortunately, marketing efforts provide very little positive impact most of the time. Advertising tends to be quite ineffective. The moral of this chapter is that it always comes down to slow and patient maneuvers, great customer service, and word-of-mouth. If you have a great product or a service that fulfills unmet needs, and you don't get greedy or impatient and take care of every customer, word-of-mouth will travel and you will grow. The unfortunate reality is that nobody seems to want to wait for that or believe that. The good news is that in today's interconnected world, word-of-mouth travels more quickly.

> **Note** No matter what, all marketers should be primarily focused on customer service and satisfaction, brand loyalty, and subsequent word-of-mouth. These should come before any other marketing decision.

There is other good news as well. There are some ways to use traditional media and newer media outlets synergistically to create sales. In addition to word-of-mouth, these newer Internet outlets—such as blogs, podcasts, and online videos—as well as social networking applications like LinkedIn, Facebook, and Twitter—allow companies to create their own content. (We discuss these in Chapter 6.) They are no longer controlled by advertising departments, media buying restrictions, and certain space or time limitations. These options are cheaper and in many ways more effective. However, these actions must all be done with strategy and analytics in mind, and with an approach that's integrated with the more traditional channels. Additionally, as we discuss later, you *must* consider your customers. What channels do they listen to? Where are they?

The biggest challenge in marketing and advertising isn't understanding how to use these new forms of advertising; it involves two things. First, the measurement and accountability of marketing programs via analytics and business intelligence (BI) is a necessity. The company absolutely has to give the customers what they want and know exactly how to communicate with customers. "The balance of power has moved, inexorably and forever, from the company to the customer".[1]

The second important marketing priority of the day is knowing when to stop using outdated forms of advertising (please, oh please stop using billboards and television advertising). That's what this chapter is about. On the one hand, it's learning how to stop the hemorrhaging of money that leaves companies all in the name of marketing, advertising, or sales, yet never amounts to any benefit. On the other hand, it's learning how to rearrange and set the marketing department, its functions, and its duties so that everything is tracked and everyone is accountable. This ensures that the marketing department doesn't operate just because people think they need marketing, but instead, forces the marketing department to be a profit-making center in its own right.

---

[1] Baer, Jason, "Operationalizing in 2010," in *Marketing in 2010: Social Media Becomes Operational,* http://conversationagent.typepad.com/Marketingin2010.pdf, 2010.

Prime Areas of Waste

AMC's *Mad Men*, a show about advertising executives in the 1960s, makes great TV, but bad marketing strategy. If you've seen the award-winning show, you likely know what we mean. The show illuminates excess in the areas of entertaining and advertising waste. In the series, companies that hired the advertising firm allowed them great leeway to make creative advertising campaigns. In order to bring these accounts in to the advertising firm, the firm spends massive amounts of time and money on everything from dinners, to liquor, to prostitutes. Aside from the unethical nature of these behaviors, they are horribly inefficient. When they are as exaggerated as they are in *Mad Men*, most of us can see how wasteful these actions are. However, in the real world, it is harder to see the waste.

We have laid out some of these common areas of marketing waste in Figure 3-1. These are organized based on the commonly used schema of the "4 Ps" (Product, Place, Price, and Promotion). These 4 Ps become marketer's tools to satisfy customers. When the marketer picks a product that meets the customer's needs, promotes it in a way that the customer will see or hear, prices the product correctly for the customer, and gets it to the customer, better sales should theoretically result.

Figure 3-1. Areas of Waste in Marketing

We cannot really say where companies waste the most marketing money in comparison with the other areas. First, companies are so different. Some companies rightly spend lots of money on warehousing (such as Amazon.com), whereas other companies don't have or need warehouses (such as a barber shop, or most any service company). The chart in Figure 3-2 shows the average percentage of the overall firm budget that companies allot to marketing.

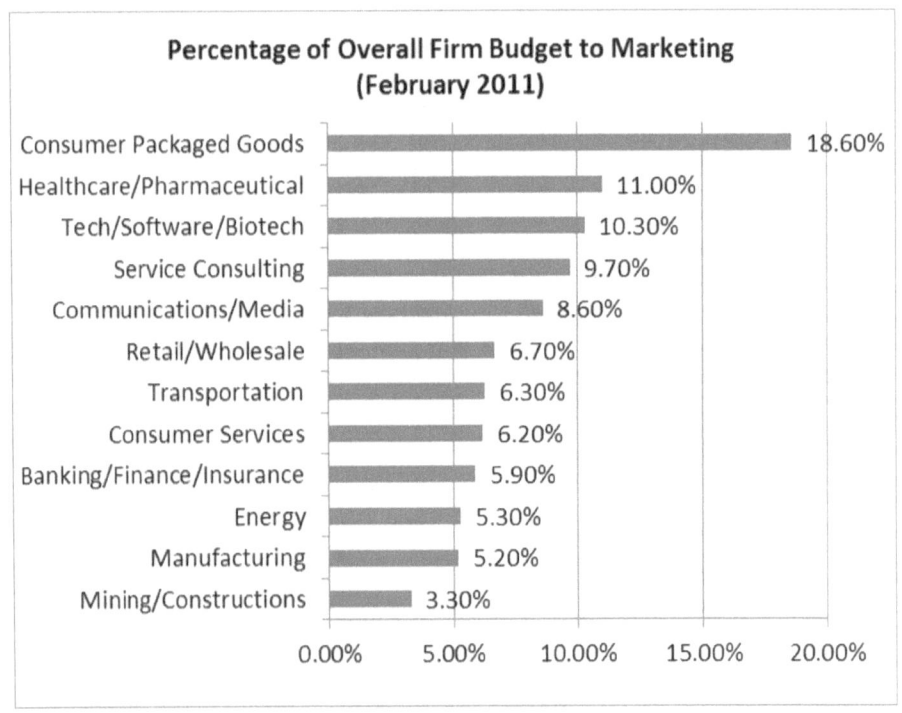

Figure 3-2. Percentage of Overall Firm Budget to Marketing. *Source:* Christine Moorman, "Predicting the Future of Markets, Tracking Marketing Excellence, Improving the Value of Marketing Trends," 2011, http://www.cmosurvey.org

Whereas our example makes sense (Amazon.com has more warehousing expenditures), it does not make sense that consumer packaged goods require more than three times the marketing budget of an industry like banking. True, consumer packaged goods require more R&D, but that certainly doesn't explain why they spend nearly twice as much as pharmaceutical companies. By looking at the chart, and turning on any TV or opening any magazine, you can quickly see that the 18.6 percent figure is evidence of a ridiculous level of overspending. This is even more disturbing when you consider the pharmaceutical example. For every dollar pharmaceutical companies spend on "basic research," $19 goes toward promotion and marketing.[2]

Another reason why it is so hard to pinpoint waste is that the expenses don't necessarily end up in the same budget line item. New product planning could be expensed in the engineering department in one company and in R&D or marketing in another. Or logistics could be included with marketing or supply chain management. Referring back to Figure 3-2, companies spend an average of 8.09 percent of their firm's overall budget on marketing. When adjusting for items that frequently rest in other categories (R&D and supply chain), it is likely that over 20 percent of firm's budgets goes to "marketing."

BIG BUSINESS OVERSPENDING

> Note that the total marketing spending of 8–20 percent is a significantly higher figure than the one presented in Chapter 1 in Figure 1-1. Chapter 1 discussed small business expenses. Large companies typically inflate their averages because they spend much more on marketing. This information brings up two very important thought-provoking issues. First, 20 percent of any company's budget is *way* too much. Imagine how much of this money a company could use to treat its employees right, lower prices, or simply make more money. Second, if the small businesses can make due with less money, why do big businesses need to spend so much more? Are sales truly a function of the amount spent on marketing? We address these issues later in the chapter.

Because of budget discrepancies, we simply present the areas of likely waste in this section. Then, we spend most of the space in this chapter dealing with how to measure and improve upon each category.

Customer Needs and Market Research

There are two interconnected, broad categories of waste surrounding the customer. One deals with not understanding the customer's needs, wants, desires, and value systems, and the other deals with bad market research aimed at attempting to understand these customer needs. It all goes back to research, and many times, it is extremely inefficient. U.S. companies, in fact, spend an estimated $6.7 billion annually in marketing research out of the estimated $18.9 billion spent globally.[3]

---

[2]Eichler, Alexander, "Pharmaceutical Companies Spent 19 Times More On Self-Promotion than Basic Research," *Huffington Post*, May 8, 2013, http://www.huffingtonpost.com/2012/08/09/pharmaceutical-companies-marketing_n_1760380.html.
[3]CASRO, U.S. and Global Survey Research Industry, 2013, http://www.casro.org/media/Media%20Facts--US%20(and%20Global)%20Survey%20Research%20Industry.pdf.

The American Marketing Association (AMA) defines marketing research as:

> "Marketing research is the function that links the consumer, customer, and public to the marketer through information—information used to identify and define marketing opportunities and problems; generate, refine, and evaluate marketing actions; monitor marketing performance; and improve understanding of marketing as a process. Marketing research specifies the information required to address these issues, designs the method for collecting information, manages and implements the data collection process, analyzes the results, and communicates the findings and their implications."[4]

According to that definition, the key premise of marketing research is collecting *accurate* information about the customer to allow decision makers to satisfy the customers. This research (as with everything in a company) must translate into real dollars. These dollars come from real, valid, and reliable information and business intelligence that helps a firm make important business decisions, such as introducing a new product that will increase profits.

As much as it pains me—a marketing professor who has spent almost two decades conducting marketing research—to say this, the problem with this assumption lies in the very word "accurate." We believe market research is a massive area for waste because it seems for most companies that it is simply impossible to collect this information with any kind of accuracy. Later in this chapter, we are going to tell you that you cannot proceed with your other marketing expenditures until you understand your customer, but the research must be done correctly. Let's now focus on just a few reasons why research tends to be so wasteful.

Wrong Market Research Techniques

There are numerous ways executives can gain information about their customers. We have listed a few of these in Figure 3-3. Most executives are familiar with or have at least heard of these. The question of market research methods rarely comes down to a marketing manager not knowing what research is or what the methods are, but instead, not knowing how and when to use them.

---

[4] American Marketing Association, Definition of Marketing, http://www.marketingpower.com/AboutAMA/Pages/DefinitionofMarketing.aspx (definition approved 2004, last accessed August 2013).

Eliminating Waste in Business

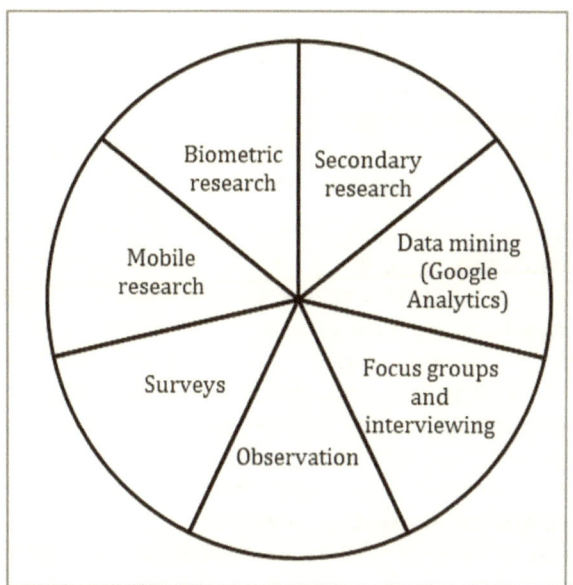

Figure 3-3. Various Types of Market Research

For example, in our careers we have witnessed the repeated and repeated and repeated use of focus groups (the redundancy is purposeful here). It seems to be very common in the world of business to bring in a group of consumers before a new product launch, sit them around a table, and ask them questions about the new product. Then, the word of the focus group is typically used as gospel when determining how and when to launch the product.

Focus groups are probably one of the worst forms of research, yet nearly all businesses use them. Focus groups, made up of about 8-12 people, can never be representative of a larger population. They generally tend to be bored housewives and older Americans—anyone who can afford to take 2–4 hours out of a day to answer questions. Then, participants almost always talk about the product in ways in which they would never behave in the marketplace. Focus groups are also subject to groupthink. The data is basically worthless.

Surveys have similar issues, and yet are also used by just about every company. You can ask and ask all the questions you want, but you have to think about who is taking the time to respond to your surveys and how well your survey questions are written. If you send the survey to customers, you will likely get very dissatisfied people or very satisfied people, or people who have nothing better to do with their time.

Even worse is data garnered from customer panels. We have seen data from customer panels where it is very obvious that more than half the responses are scammers. People are happy to get $10 a survey to take 100 surveys falsely. Additionally, surveys frequently have one or two questions and rarely get to any detailed level. For example, a question might be, "Were you satisfied with your service?" Maybe yes, maybe no, but what does that mean? It's often useless data. So, any research gathered in this manner is a waste. Don't take this wrong. Surveys can beneficial, but only when they are done properly, with good questions and a representative sample.

Today, so much data is available. You should make use of that data before taking the time and resources to collect your own. One example of this is Google Analytics. According to their website, Google Analytics can help you learn which marketing efforts are most effective, understand accurate website traffic patterns/trends, and determine which customer and customer segments are most valuable. It can also help you understand where visitors come from and what do they do on the site, how you can convert more visitors into customers, which keywords resonate with prospects and lead to conversions, and which online ad or creative is the most effective.[5] There is a multitude of this type of data available to marketers today, including Amazon Redshift. It should be about how to mine and analyze the available data first; don't waste money collecting new data until you're sure it doesn't already exist.

■ **Note** Combine newer techniques such as "big data" and biometric data with more traditional methods to create a reliable and valid picture of your customer's needs.

When data is gathered firsthand, we strongly recommend using experienced market researchers with a PhD. We also strongly encourage you to consider new techniques such as biometric data. Such data allows researchers to track eye movements over a web page or test brain waves as an ad is viewed. However, one note of caution (and probably the most important note here): no one technique should ever be used in isolation. Multiple techniques should always be employed and data should be amalgamated. Every technique has its disadvantages. By employing multiple techniques and looking at the data together, you get a better, more accurate picture. This sounds like we are arguing for more money to be spent in marketing research, which could create more waste. We are calling for more initial research, but this doesn't mean you should have some massive market research gathering project underway every day. You should consistently keep a pulse on the market and competitors, and create a schedule for other, more major research projects. Additionally, getting an accurate picture to begin with is a lot cheaper than launching a campaign with inaccurate data.

---

[5]Google, "Introduction to Google Analytics," https://support.google.com/analytics/answer/1008065?hl=en (Last accessed September 2013).

Weak Statistical and Analytical Capabilities

Once you have data from research, you need to know how to analyze it. According to a recent survey of more than 250 executives, 40 percent said they base their major decisions on judgment instead of on business analytics, many times because good data isn't available.[6] (We suspect that at least some of these executives don't want to take the time to understand the data.) This same survey found that 36 percent of managers felt that they simply did not have enough analytical talent.[7] A Harvard Business Review (HBR) study found that managers said they depend on data for just 11 percent of customer-related decisions.[8] Furthermore, the HBR study tested marketers' statistical aptitude and found that almost half (44 percent) got four or more questions wrong out of five intermediate-to-basic statistics questions, and a mere six percent got all five right.[9] Only five percent of the marketers admitted to owning a statistics textbook.[10] Another survey by CMO Insights found that only 3.4 percent of executives strongly agree that they have the right talent to analyze market research data. Refer to Figure 3-4 for the study data.

Figure 3-4. Analytical Resources Available to Companies. *Source:* Christine Moorman, "Big Data's Puzzle," 2013, http://cmosurvey.org/blog/big-datas-big-puzzle/

---

[6]Williams, Steve, "5 Barriers to BI Success and How to Overcome Them," *Strategic Finance*, July 2011, 27–33.
[7]Ibid.
[8]Spenner, Patrick and Anna Bird, "Marketers Flunk the Big Data Test," *Harvard Business Review*, HBR Blog Network, August 16, 2012, http://blogs.hbr.org/2012/08/marketers-flunk-the-big-data-test/.
[9]Ibid.
[10]Ibid.

Chapter 3 | Marketing

These statistics might be why, in spite of more data being available, fewer companies are choosing to use it. Figure 3-5 shows that a dismal 29 percent of projects in a 2013 CMO study actually used available data, down from 37 percent in 2012. Certainly, one of the first activities in any project should be assessing any available data.

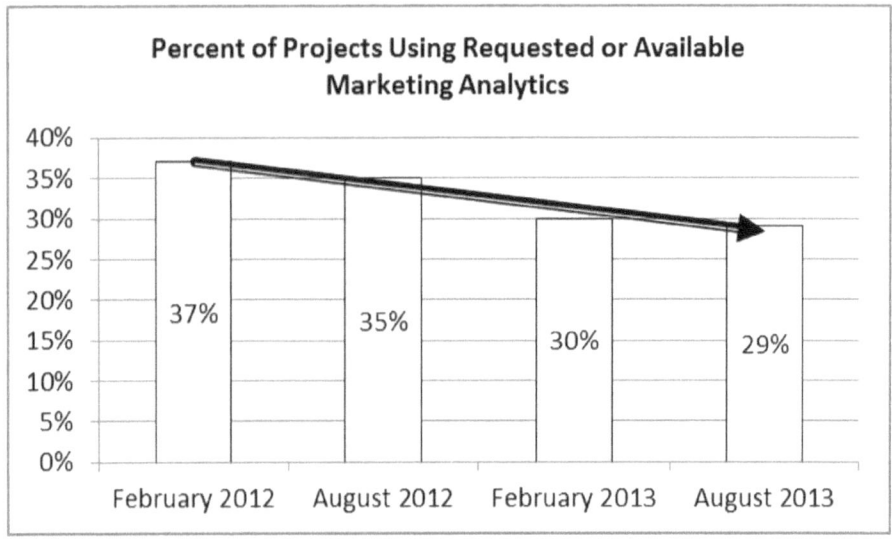

Figure 3-5. Projects Using Available Data. *Source:* Christine Moorman, "Big Data's Puzzle," 2013, http://cmosurvey.org/blog/big-datas-big-puzzle/

We do not have a lot to say on this topic. Not because it is not important. In fact, this is probably the single most important topic in this chapter. We don't spend much time on the subject for this reason: it's pretty black and white. If you do not possess the analytical and statistical tools to conduct appropriate, valid, and reliable marketing and sales analytics, find someone who can. If your company is too small, use an outside market research company (but heed our warnings later in this chapter about external research firms).

By appropriate analytics, we mean appropriate given the tools and technologies available to the market researcher in 2014. The Williams (2011) study, cited previously, lists some the terminology a business intelligence (BI) person should know (see Figure 3-6). If you or your staff finds these terms challenging, this is a sign to find someone more capable. It is simply not acceptable to "wing it" in this day and age. Any efforts designed toward collecting data are a complete waste if you do not know how to analyze the data and make sense out of it.

Styles of BI	New Age BI	Tools	Some Statistical Methods
•Reporting •Ad-hoc query •Parameterized queries •OLAP •Advanced analytics •Predictive analytics	•Agile BI •SaaS BI •Pervasive BI •Pervasive analytics •Self-service analytics •Social analytics •Real-time analytics •Mobile BI and analytics	•Scorecarding and dashboarding •Query and reporting •Statistics and data mining •OLAP cubes •ETL •EAI •Master data management	•ANOVA (and all of its forms) •Regression (and all of its forms) •Discriminant analysis •Factor analysis •Hierarchical modeling •Structural equations modeling •Cluster analysis •Conjoint analysis

Figure 3-6. Trends and Terminology in Buisness Intelligence. *Source:* Steve Williams, "5 Barriers to BI Success and How to Overcome Them," *Strategic Finance*, July 2011, 27–33

Figure 3-6 shows just a few of the many terms and tools used in business intelligence. Someone looking at supply chain analytics may care less about social analytics. For the marketing executive, BI success means having complete information about:

> "Individual customers to enable such things as better customer segmentation, more precise campaign targeting, improved customer service and customer retention, more timely campaign return on investment (ROI), improved ability to determine customer lifetime value, a better understanding of the price elasticity of demand, and improved tools for category and performance management."[11]

We cover these areas in the final section of this chapter.

Note You won't survive in the marketplace today without advanced statistical and analytical market intelligence skills. Any attempt to do research without these capabilities is a waste.

---

[11] Ibid.

Cognitive Biases and Other Irrational Consumer Behaviors

Even with the best research, you need to consider that consumers seldom know what they want. There is virtually no data to support the notion that customers understand their own decision-making processes. In fact, in the words of Robert Cialdini, customers "buy emotionally and defend rationally."[12] This logic has been shown to be true time and time again. If you ask customers after the fact why they bought something, they will very logically and rationally tell you why. If you bring someone into a focus group or ask someone on a survey about buying decisions, they will think about their decisions very rationally and give very logical answers. These answers will never explain why someone buys a worthless throw pillow, knick-knacks, overpriced coffee, pet rocks, or jelly bracelets.

There is, however, an exorbitant amount of data to show that customers are very irrational. There are literally hundreds upon hundreds of cognitive biases (tendencies to think or do things in certain ways, which are a departure from rationality). For example, the *framing effect* comes into play when Williams-Sonoma cannot sell a stand mixer for $289. However, when it's placed beside another stand mixer priced at $469, sales explode. The $289 stand mixer seems like a good deal when it's next to the more expensive item. Another famous cognitive bias is called the *gambler's fallacy*. In this fallacy, people think that if a coin flips to heads five times, the chances of getting tails next time is much higher. In actuality, every flip has a 51–49 percent chance (refer to a physics text on why it's not 50/50), regardless of the number of times it is flipped.

Marketing research, or the general study of how consumers behave in the marketplace, helps us know these little odd facts about human behavior. It provides insight into all the psychological principles and aspects of consumer behavior, from the effects of lighting and music to proper store placement. This type of research is normally conducted by psychology and marketing professors. Although not all of this research is accurate and even relevant, it is available to marketers.

The greatest challenge with this type of research is that the typical marketer does not read the sources of this information (*Personality and Social Psychology Review, Psychology and Marketing,* and *Journal of Consumer Research* are just a few examples). It would be quite a monumental task to sift through all of the academic journals across many disciplines to find a few relevant facts. There is

---

[12] Cialdini, Robert, *Influence: The Psychology of Persuasion Revised Edition* (New York: NY, Harper Business, 2006).

the even greater challenge of determining which of these irrational behaviors are coming into play and when.

On the other hand, *market research*, which is performed by a company in regard to a specific product or consumer, will likely never consider all of these cognitive biases and other issues that will destroy any well built market study. More importantly, the irrational sides of consumer behavior cannot be predicted, so it would be nearly impossible to incorporate these successfully into a marketing strategy. You cannot rationalize the irrational. Additionally, market research studies are typically focused on one particular problem, which makes it impossible to consider all the other intervening variables that affect study findings.

Note The most well designed market research cannot account for all the cognitive biases and other irrational behaviors that exist in consumers' minds. If you use enough data from enough sources, analyzed in enough ways, you will eventually filter out the noise.

We're not going to tell you how to deal with these biases, because you can't. Many astute marketers will use these biases to their advantage, almost as a form of manipulation. The Williams-Sonoma example does this. Using an advertising slogan such as "the fastest selling product" does the same thing by hitting on a social proof nerve—everyone wants to do what everyone else is doing. We like these as long as they are not manipulating the consumers, but there is a very fine line. We suggest you use the data you have to make good decisions. If you use enough data analyzed enough ways, you will eventually filter out the noise. We don't think the problem is necessarily filtering out the bad data, but instead, collecting so little data that the irrational becomes the only picture you have. We cannot say this enough times. Any business decision you make without accurate data is a waste of time and money.

Note Any business decision made without accurate data is a waste of time and money.

Marketing Silos

Another very real problem with business intelligence that comes from market research is that it does not utilize information garnered from other departments and disciplines. As discussed in Chapter 2, a large problem in many companies is the use of functional silos. A recent study showed that most marketers believe silos—both internal and external to marketing—prevent them from effectively executing campaigns.[13] Some of the most important information about customers is housed outside of marketing.

For example, imagine the company that has all of its shipping and return data housed in the warehouse. The only person who ever looks at it is the shipping manager. All she cares about is ensuring that her employees are shipping the correct product in an efficient manner. She doesn't especially notice that one product, the F-400, is being returned at a rate of 15 percent. Meanwhile, the marketing manager begins to wonder why sales are down. So, he takes the time and money to send a survey to his customers to find out what their level of customer satisfaction is. He gets a two percent response rate and it shows that his customers are happy and satisfied. Nobody seems to communicate with one another to figure it out. When looking at this very small amount of data, it is pretty easy to make an educated guess about what is occurring. There is a quality issue with the F-400. Customers are so frustrated that they had to take their time and energy to return the product; they are not going to take more time and energy to fill out a customer satisfaction survey.

Note Market research in isolation is wasteful. You must consider data from all relevant departments.

This example is, of course, overly simplistic. In the real world, businesses have data from just about every outlet available. Everyone takes their data and stores it in their own way. John puts his information in an Excel spreadsheet, Sally has SPSS files, Jim stores print-outs in hard copy on his desk. Very few companies are forward-thinking enough to integrate data from every department and from all external sites, such as industry reports, panel data, data provided from a company's CRM software, and many other sources. Very few companies integrate this information so that it can help the business make better decisions. If this is how things work at your company, market research is probably a waste. If you are running your own independent department, stop collecting data and work to integrate it before you do anything else.

Outsourcing Market Research

When market research is outsourced, this is commonly referred to as Knowledge Process Outsourcing (KPO). For the purposes of this chapter, we would like to say this. While outsourcing your market research can provide

---

[13]Teradata, "Data-Driven Marketing Delivers Enterprise-Wide Value," Global Teradata, August 5, 2013, http://www.teradata.com/News-Releases/2013/Data-Driven-Marketing-Delivers-Enterprise-Wide-Value-Global-Teradata-Survey-Says/.

advantages, it can also be a huge hole for market department waste. The largest problem with outsourced research tends to be plugging the problem into a one-size-fits-all approach.

We use an example from our personal lives to illustrate the point. Many doctors have started automatically sending out surveys after every visit. Our children's pediatrician does this with a wonderful third-party provider. The survey is very long and detailed, and it covers 90 percent of what I would consider are necessary characteristics for a good medical provider. This survey is very different from what I have seen from some other doctors. Some doctors send very short, standardized surveys that mean nothing. These are very common because outsourced providers don't know the unique needs of your business. Figure 3-7 shows a brief example of a typical customer-service evaluation.

Staff	Poor Staff	○ ○ ○ ○ ○	Great Staff
Punctual	Not On time	○ ○ ○ ○ ○	On time
Helpful	Very Unhelpful	○ ○ ○ ○ ○	Very Helpful
Knowledgeable	Very Un-knowledgeable	○ ○ ○ ○ ●	Very knowledgeable

Figure 3-7. Typical Doctor Satisfaction Survey

The biggest complaints about doctors tend to be that they are arrogant, they don't communicate well, they do not use a holistic approach, they don't seem to care, and they don't take the proper amount of time with each patient. These factors sometimes lead to customers changing doctors. Sometimes patients can't change doctors due to insurance reasons and high switching costs. But none of the information gathered from the survey in Figure 3-7 even begins to the address these issues. Typically, when you outsource your market research, you get this type of data. They just don't understand your unique product or market.

Market Research Done Right

In summary, in the words of Philip Graves:

> "Investment in market research goes beyond a simple waste of money: it corrupts an organization's ability to learn and, if that wasn't damaging enough, can lead to untold waste in the pursuit of strategies and initiatives that would never have been developed with an alternative—and psychologically informed—approach to understanding consumer behavior."[14]

If you don't conduct your market research properly, you'll not only waste money now, but you'll also waste hoards of money in the future because you enter into a series of subsequent bad decisions, each building on the last, each wasting more and more money.

Before you begin any research project, follow these simple rules:

- Define and establish the goals for your information needs.
- Conduct an information audit so you know what you have and don't have. Make sure this audit is conducted across every department.
- Thoroughly know and understand what data sources are available by big data providers.
- Gauge which methods, tools, and analytical procedures are most applicable.

Once these questions are answered, you can move to developing the structure of your market research project.

IBM conducted a study about how companies conduct market research (Figure 3-8). They found some striking differences between the top-performing companies and all others. There were drastic differences in how data was used and integrated. The line in Figure 3-8 shows how the difference between the top-performing companies and all others impacts the bottom line. Consider that companies that utilize up-to-the-minute information technology across all channels perform 5.6 times better than those that don't. Companies that adjust product and promotional offerings based on market research findings perform 5.6 times better than companies that don't. Also, companies that apply advanced analytics to determine how much to spend on media and those that detect transactions, struggle in real time, and take rapid action perform 2.2 times better than those that don't. What does this mean? Market

---

[14]Graves, Philip, "Debate: Is Market Research a Waste of Money?" *Director*, September 2010, http://www.director.co.uk/magazine/2010/8_September/debate-market-research-waste-of-money_64_01.html.

research is a quintessential part of any company's strategies and actions. But it has to be done right. You must understand market research; don't try to wing it or rely on outdated techniques. Doing so is a catastrophic waste.

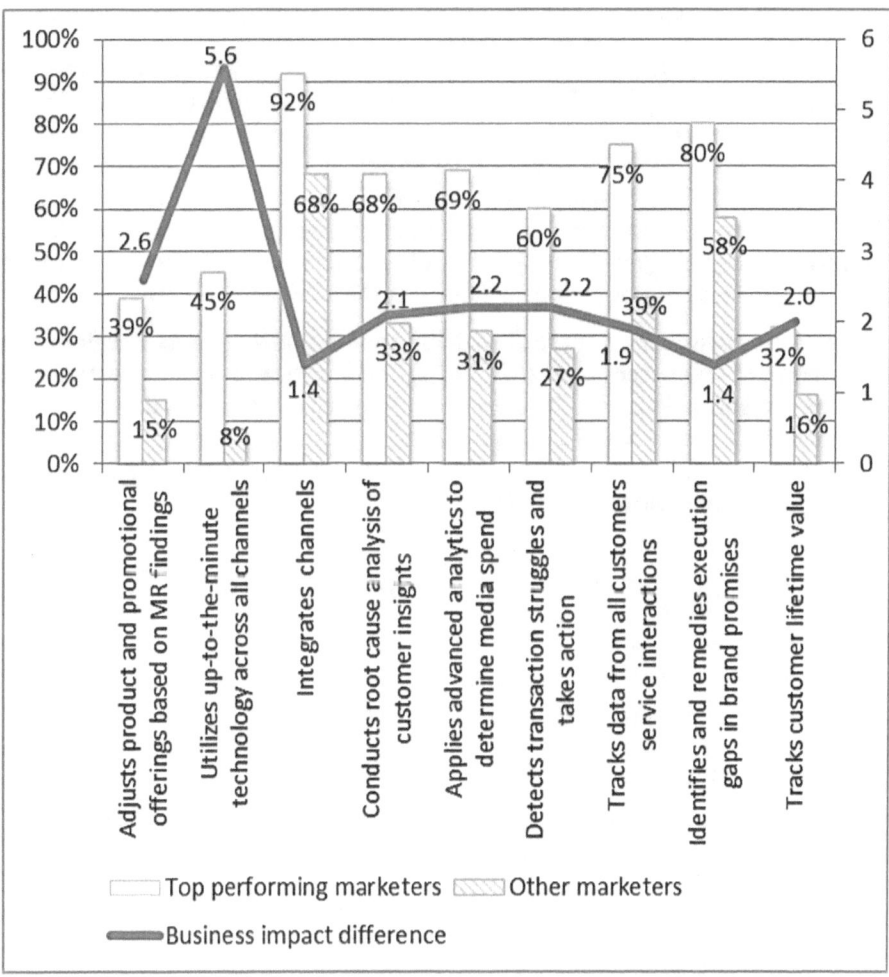

Figure 3-8. Market Research Techniques Used in Top-Performning Companies.
Source: Kimberly Whitler, "What Are The Biggest Challenges Facing Marketers According to New IBM Study?" Forbes, May 21, 2013, http://www.forbes.com/sites/kimberlywhitler/2013/05/21/what-are-the-biggest-challenges-facing-marketers-according-to-new-ibm-study/

Waste from Product Decisions

As we have and will say throughout this chapter and book, perhaps the best way to avoid waste in marketing activities is to understand that branding, customer service, and word-of-mouth are the most influential concepts! In this section, we discuss these important concepts, along with new product development.

We talked about the common misconception that a company must grow at all costs in Chapter 2. But there are areas where growth actually makes sense, such as when you're growing a current product or creating a new one. Sometimes, for the sake of growth only, leaders develop products that nobody wants or needs. The development, marketing, and sales of those products all lead to waste, because there wasn't a need in the first place. Companies do this frequently with "new" models. The old model is selling very well, but in an effort to grow sales, the company launches the new-and-improved model.

Companies spend a large part of their budgets on new product development, but may have low success rates, leading to mediocre returns on investment or worse. If sustainable growth and good profit margins are a function of innovative products and processes, then new product development is a critical part of the business. Of course, like all areas of business, there are egregious wastes in the product development cycle.

Brand Loyalty, Customer Service, and Word-of-Mouth

It doesn't matter how cool your product is, how much money you dump into advertising, or how many discounts and sales you have. If customers don't love your product, they won't buy it repeatedly. They won't tell their friends, and they will often leave in search of a product they do love. Let's look at some statistics:

- Most Fortune 500 companies lose 50 percent of their customers in five years.
- The average company communicates only four times per year with customers and six times per year with prospective customers.
- It costs 7 to 10 times more to acquire a new customer than it does to retain an existing one.
- A 5 percent increase in customer retention can increase profits 25–125 percent!

- Seventy percent of the time, customers leave companies because of bad service, 15 percent of the time due to product dissatisfaction, and 15 percent of the time due to price.
- The average company has a 60–70 percent probability of a sale to active customers; a 20–40 percent probability of a sale to lost customers; and a 5–20 percent probability of a sale to prospective customers.

Notice the cost of losing customers, as well as the cost of replacing them with new customers. If you do nothing else, keep your employees and your customers happy. Happy employees definitely make for happy customers. Happy customers make for more happy customers. More customers reduce costs. This all means higher profits. This is how to grow a business. The incremental profits you earn by keeping customers happy are presented in Figure 3-9. The incremental losses you incur by not serving customers well are presented in Figure 3-10.

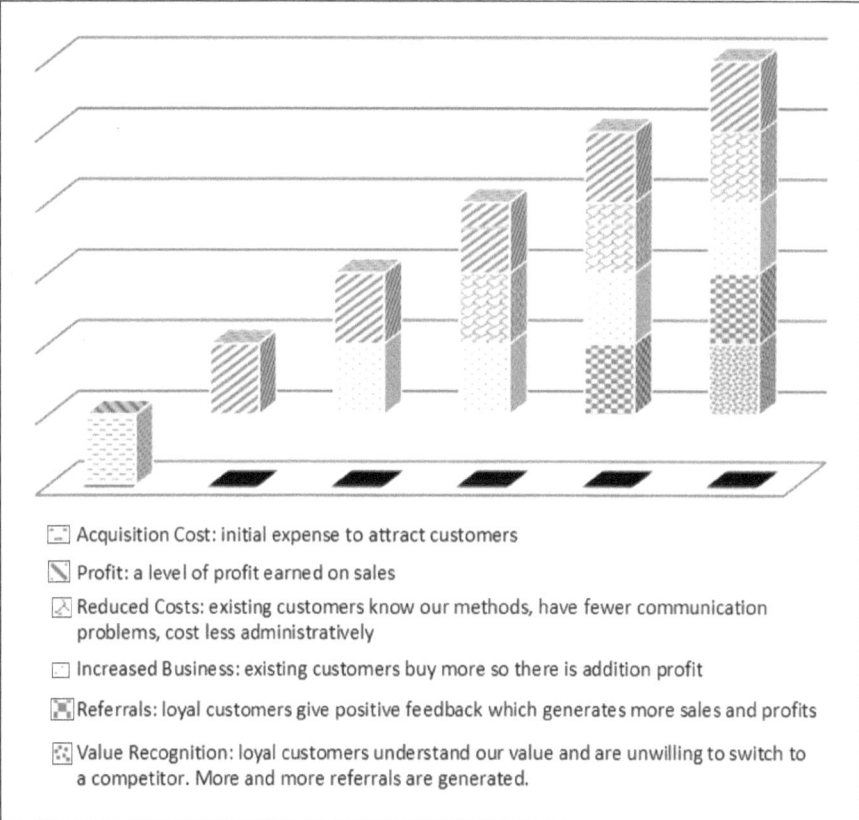

- Acquisition Cost: initial expense to attract customers
- Profit: a level of profit earned on sales
- Reduced Costs: existing customers know our methods, have fewer communication problems, cost less administratively
- Increased Business: existing customers buy more so there is addition profit
- Referrals: loyal customers give positive feedback which generates more sales and profits
- Value Recognition: loyal customers understand our value and are unwilling to switch to a competitor. More and more referrals are generated.

Figure 3-9. Customer Loyalty Leads to Incremental Profit Increases

Chapter 3 | Marketing

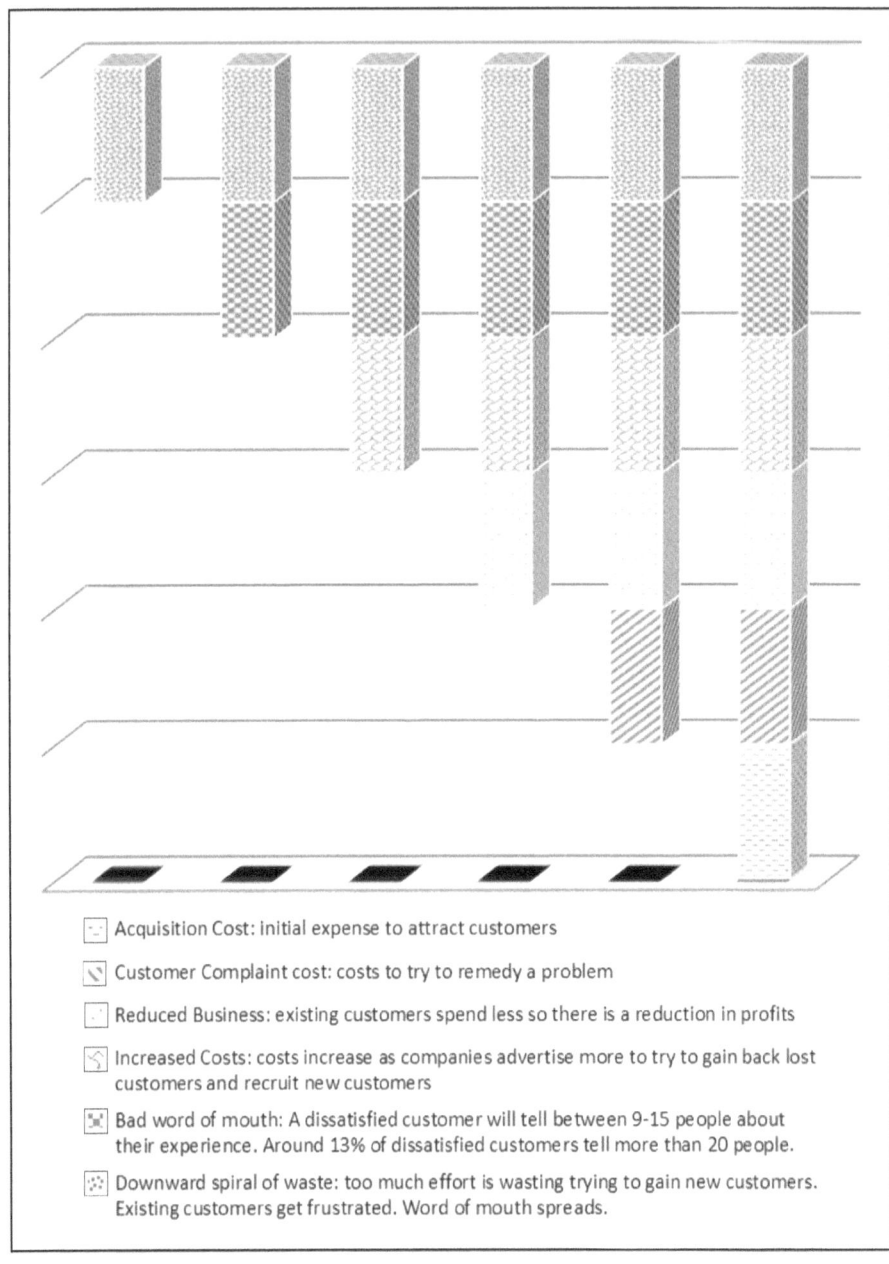

Figure 3-10. Customer Dissatisfaction Leads to Incremental Profit Loses

> **Note** If you do nothing else in terms of marketing efforts, keep your employees and customers satisfied.

Every company must know what their customers are worth and do everything they can to make them happy and to keep them coming back. (We go through the specifics of calculating customer lifetime value in Chapter 4.) Companies must communicate with customers often, but not in an annoying way. They must give the customers what they want and need to know. Companies must always provide exceptional services and product quality.

These lessons sound so painfully simple, but are many times forgotten. We once knew of a company that sold premium executive furniture. After buying a $50,000 granite board room table, one customer requested a free set of protective placemats to protect their investment, which were priced at $800. The company said no to this request, thinking that they didn't want to lose $800. That $800 easily cost them over a half a million dollars in future sales. Think not only about the future purchases that did not happen, but also all the bad word-of-mouth that was likely spread. Not investing in customer service and brand loyalty creates countless waste. You need to consider the following steps to build loyalty among customers.

Create and Maintain a Brand Personality

First, make sure you understand why your customers chose you. There is a whole line of really fluffy, cheesy consumer behavior research on "brand personalities." But, as cheesy as it sounds, it is helpful. Customers think of brands, products, and services the same way they think about personalities. Further, customers choose brands the same way they choose friends. These attributes must be in sync with how the customer views himself and his aspirations.

For example, we feel a stronger loyalty and connection with our small, locally owned, organic grocery store. You get the feeling from the store when you enter. You smell the organic-store smells (coffee, herbals, and international spices). There are almost always free samples. They give kids free bananas and apples. The same clerks work the registers. The entire place just feels healthy and hippie-ish. As you read through this, you can probably picture the traits of this store: healthy, wholesome, family friendly, customer oriented, and environmentally friendly. These characteristics suit us, and make us want to come back. Some reading this might think this sounds like a terrible place. That's okay. No product is going to suit everyone.

You have to give the customer an overall experience, or they won't have a connection to your product. This connection has to be very powerful. It makes no logical sense, but when I shop at a different grocery store I actually feel guilty, almost as if I were cheating. This feeling comes from the overall experience they've created. This store has never advertised and has only a minimal website. That's not where the connection is created. It comes from how customers are treated during every transaction. This is one of the biggest places where countless marketing dollars are wasted. The single most important thing any marketer should do is create a brand personality and overall brand experience and connect it deeply to the target market.

Meet and Exceed Expectations

Part of market research entails knowing what your customer wants in terms of an experience and expectations. This goes beyond not only understanding what they want in a product, but also includes what will make them happy. This is all based upon expectations. Some people are quite loyal to McDonald's and go back time and time again. If you ask these people why they go, we seriously doubt it is for the highest quality beef. People go to McDonald's for consistency, low price, and quick service. When someone goes there and gets that, they are satisfied. But, obviously, if you went to a five-star restaurant and got McDonald's-quality beef, you would be disappointed.

People expect different things from different providers and it is the marketer's job to understand those expectations. As long as the expectations are met or exceeded, the customer will be satisfied and quite possibly become loyal (and then begin to tell others about their positive experiences).

Here's another example. As parents of four children, we have dealt with many daycare providers. We are constantly amazed by how many daycare providers know very little about what parents want from a daycare. Just from our personal experiences, we have found enormous differences in what we value as parents and what providers try to provide (see Figure 3-11).

> **What Parents Want**
> - Consistency in care (same teacher throughout the year)
> - Flexible/affordable
> - An "experience" that is loving and comfortable

> **What Daycare Providers Think They Should Provide**
> - Four-year degrees and certifications from the teachers
> - Rigid pricing structures
> - Saftey and clealiness

Figure 3-11. Sample Perception Gap Between Customer and Provider

Now you might look at this simple diagram and think, of course, every parent wants all of the things in Figure 3-11. First, we have made this example very simplistic, so we are sure there are many things we are missing. But second, you must understand the subtle differences between the various levels that customers consider when they perceive products and services. Refer to Figure 3-12. At the most basic level, there is the generic product. In a daycare, obviously, everyone expects that their children will we taken care of, fed, cleaned, and so on. Parents expect that children will be safe and happy. If these items are not provided, parents will be upset, but these things alone will not "satisfy" a customer. These are basic expectations that have to be met.

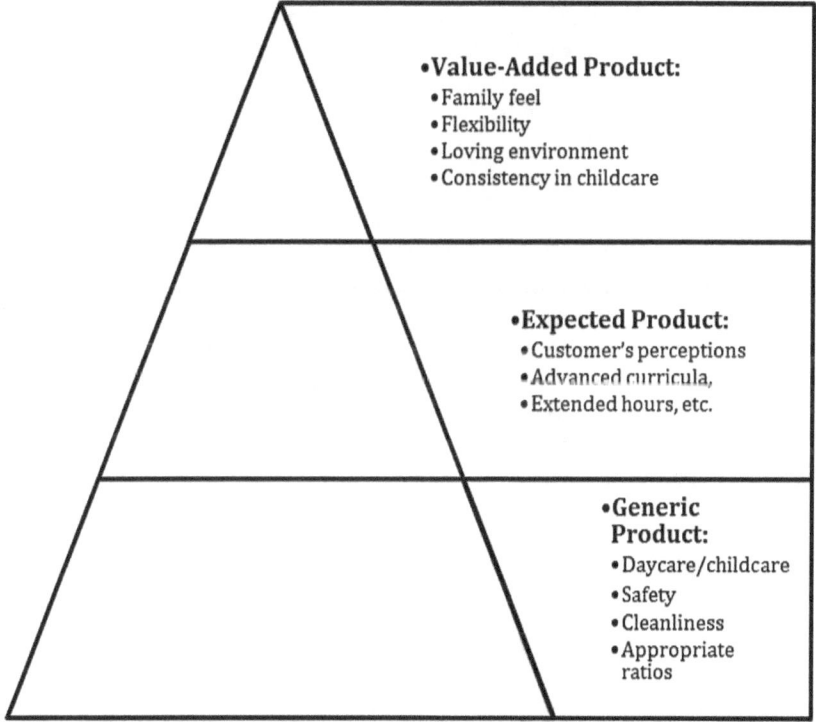

Figure 3-12. Levels of Expectations in Products and Services

Beyond that, there are expected products. In a hotel, a customer expects economy at a Motel 6 and luxury at the Ritz Carlton. In the daycare situation, based on the individual customer's desires, items like advanced curricula, extended hours, and other factors that differentiate between providers might come into play. These attributes still don't provide "satisfaction." They merely differentiate between providers. One parent is going to need a 24-hour daycare; the next parent will want a certain teaching style or curricula.

Finally, customers want the value-added components of a product or service. These are the items that provide the satisfaction, the brand loyalty, and the eventual word-of-mouth. When looking at the value-added components of a daycare (family feel, flexibility, loving environment), how often do you see daycare care providers concerning themselves with these goals? They typically get hung up on the generic and expected product. These do not create an overall brand experience and they don't really satisfy a customer to the point of being brand loyal.

As you read this book, think to yourself, do you know which value-added product/service attributes your customers care about? If not, any marketing efforts are wasteful because they are likely targeted in the wrong direction. This is the message that has to be communicated through your marketing expenditures. The only way to understand the customer's desires is through good market research. Most research does not get to the deep level of understanding that we refer to here.

Be Consistent

The final component to building brand loyalty is consistency. If you create a brand experience, understand your customer's value-added needs, but provide the brand experience haphazardly, you will not see improvements. Brand experiences must be consistent. As previously described, McDonald's is a great example of consistency. Customers aren't in search of high-quality beef; they are in search of consistency and affordability at McDonald's. Most customers are fairly forgiving and will accept a mistake or two. But over the life of the relationship, you have to provide consistency.

Encourage Word-of-Mouth Referrals

So, now that you understand better what it takes to create loyal customers, how do you get customers to spread the word? You don't. Referral programs and Facebook likes are frequently seen as desperate attempts to get customers when you haven't figured out what you should be doing right. Our current daycare does an excellent job at providing the generic product and the expected product, but has virtually no value-added products. They are very clean and safe and do everything by the book. The teachers all have four-year degrees and they have a very advanced curriculum. However, we feel like we are going into a "business" there. There's no homey feel. Our children have rotated through multiple teachers so the extra connection with each teacher is missing. And they are not flexible with special needs.

We get weekly e-mails about their referral program. If we refer someone to their program, we will get $100 off the next month's tuition. There are also random opportunities for $5 Starbucks gift cards if we "like" them on

Facebook or leave a positive comment about them on an external site. I have in the past referred people to daycares. I have taken the time to leave both bad and good comments about daycares, doctors, and establishments on websites. I never did any of these things for money. There is only one way to build word-of-mouth. You must build value and satisfy your customers!

■ **Note** Identify customer's brand personality desires and value-added product desires through good market research. Then provide these. Doing so builds value, customer satisfaction, and brand loyalty. Brand loyalty encourages word-of-mouth referrals. No referral program can override the natural chain of events.

Overpaying for Branding

Branding is key to getting return customers and word-of-mouth business. While a nice memorable brand or logo won't create loyalty, it helps give the customers something tangible to identify with. In fact, companies have been known to acquire other companies just to take over the brand and use it to increase business. However, there is no reason to spend time and money on "branding." We feel that is a waste. There is no correlation between how much you spend on your brand and your overall brand identity. Figure 3-13 shows the disparity between some very well-known brands where there was zero investment and others where the investment is extreme. The average company spends between $2,500 and $10,000 to develop a logo, whereas some of the most famous brands, like Coca-Cola, Google, and Twitter, spent very little or nothing to develop their logos.

Brand	Amount Spent on Logo
Coco-Cola	$0
Google	$0
Twitter	$15
Nike	$35
Enron	$33,000
NeXT	$100,000
London 2012 Olympics	$625,000
Pepsi	$1,000,000
BBC	$1,800,000
BP	$211,000,000

Figure 3-13. Logo Expenditures. *Source:* Stampler, Laura, "Here's How Much Money the World's Biggest Brands Spent Designing Their Logos," *Business Insider,* August 14, 2012, http://www.businessinsider.com/heres-how-much-money-the-worlds-biggest-brands-spent-designing-their-logos-2012-8?op=1#ixzz2tdDDvK5Z

Does a fancy logo build your brand? How about advertising? We explore the advertising wastes in the promotion part of this chapter, but it deserves mention here.

Automotive makers are big on using commercials to build brand awareness and brand loyalty, but in reality it is a combination of a few factors that influence buyers. These factors include the look of the car, performance specifications, buyer history, budget, features, and the items we just talked about in the brand loyalty section. Certain vehicles like the Ford Mustang and the Dodge Charger have a strong base of loyalty due to their history as classic cars and their design, but even the popularity of these cars does not make one loyal to an entire company.

As we just discussed, companies need to deliver consistent quality at a fair price to make others talk about the products or services. Take Sears, for example. Sears built its reputation for standing behind its products through the Craftsman tool line. Many people in the 1980s and 1990s would pay extra and go to Sears to buy all of their tools, including power tools, because of the quality that they would get for the money spent. Sears also had a great reputation for its appliance sales and service. It built the Kenmore brand to stand for a reliable appliance with features only offered at Sears. While working in the appliance industry, I learned that all of the major appliance manufacturers build Kenmore products. Kenmore still was a high-quality brand because of the changes that even the low-quality and low-price suppliers had to make to meet the Sears standards.

> **Note** A creative logo will not build brand loyalty. Don't waste the money.

That's the thing about brand loyalty. It takes years, if not decades, to build solid brand loyalty, and you do it by having good, consistent performance. No beautiful logo can create loyalty. The loyalty can disappear with a few simple mistakes. Remember the formula introduced in Chapter 2: $Y=f(X)$. Brand loyalty is the Y in this formula and there are many Xs that drive that Y. Buying a logo and spending money on advertising are wasteful activities when your goal is to build a brand. In order to avoid this waste, instead build a good product or service at a fair price, learn what your customers desire, and be consistent. Let your customers build your brand awareness for you and be brand loyal. Look at Google. Their logo changes daily.

New Product Planning

Waste from a new product development process usually comes from not knowing when to kill projects that are obviously doomed to failure, as well as having an inefficient process. Both can cost the business money, potential market share, and customers who will never be replaced.

Killing Bad Products/Projects

Robert Cooper and Scott Edgett invented the stage-gate product innovation process to help companies identify bad products or bad projects prior to completion so they can kill them. This process was designed to fix the first major source of waste, which is not killing projects or products that should be killed until it is too late. The process is similar to milestones in a project-management method, with the exception that at each milestone there is a decision to keep or kill. There is also a group of cross-functional leadership who makes the decisions. Leaders often introduce new waste to eliminate other waste. The stage-gate process is another example of this. There is preparation for each gate, which requires resources. Also, there are resources used to work on the projects between stages that may not proceed past the stage-gate. Both of these wastes are acceptable because they are better than the waste associated with fully developing a failing product.

In contrast to the stage-gate process, Figure 3-14 shows the reality of most product development processes, whereby the company develops its own products or processes rather than being a contract manufacturer or developer for someone else's ideas. The company starts with many ideas. Some of these ideas are immediately killed during the first review. A cross-functional team of leaders might decide for some reason that the concept will not be successful. This is the first project tollgate and the first time projects are killed. The remaining list of projects is then vetted against the market, investment costs, and projected margin. This leads to the second tollgate. At this stage, ideas are killed because they don't meet minimum requirements, are cleared for progress to the next stage, are postponed for a future product development cycle, or are flagged for some changes to be cleared for progress to the next stage.

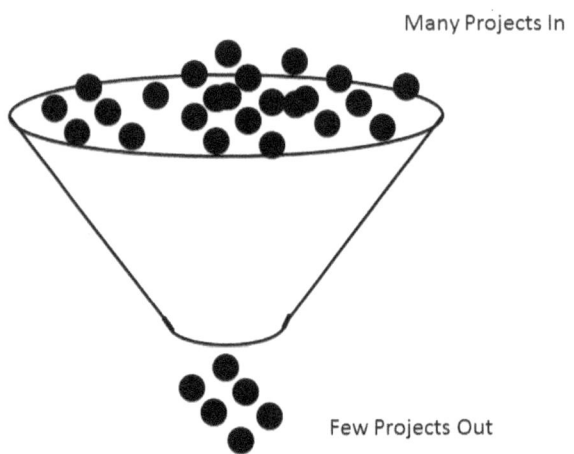

Figure 3-14. Project Funnel

At this point some creative people, who probably make between $60,000 and $120,000 per year, have come up with ideas. The majority of these ideas will go nowhere, but that is actually the least wasteful part of the process. Instead of finding out what the customers want, this is the "spaghetti-on-the-wall" strategy. These ideas are vetted using gut instinct. Gut instinct is analogous to wasting hundreds of thousands of dollars.

The other stages beyond these initial stages will vary depending upon the product or service being developed, but the idea is that the project teams will work on the deliverables for each tollgate in order to have their project progress to the next stage and eventually to market. Along with the waste from work directed toward meeting the deliverables, there is also potential "wishful thinking," which involves presenting invalid data at these tollgates. The teams are motivated to make their projects look attractive regardless of reality, so there is additional waste that must be introduced to validate the numbers. In order to avoid these wastes, the project teams shouldn't perform their own analysis. Independent parties should test any assumptions, validate the data, and prepare those portions of the tollgate that need objective opinions. This helps not only by ensuring honest information, but also by allowing the creative and motivated team members the freedom to develop the best product.

Eliminating Waste in Business

Note While setting up new product development processes creates waste, it is much less wasteful than pushing bad products through the cycle. Have cross-functional teams analytically evaluate products at each tollgate.

Inefficient Product/Project Development

By ensuring that each deliverable from each stage is in place to help with the go-forward decision is also part of making a good product or service, you can minimize wasteful activities. For instance, ensuring that the product or service is priced correctly can help lead to success, so controlling costs and reporting on them frequently are not wasteful activities. It is important that any tollgate process ensure that project deliverables or minimum performance thresholds are met to have a purpose beyond an approval process.

As with any process, no product development process is perfect. Figure 3-15 shows some data on a study conducted with 1,000 companies. The study shows that just having a development process in place with certain characteristics can be correlated to the outcomes of the project. So we can conclude that not having a process in place is a mistake and waste. Additionally, you must have a well-documented and well-utilized process. If not, they are just wastes that keep the company from realizing its full potential.

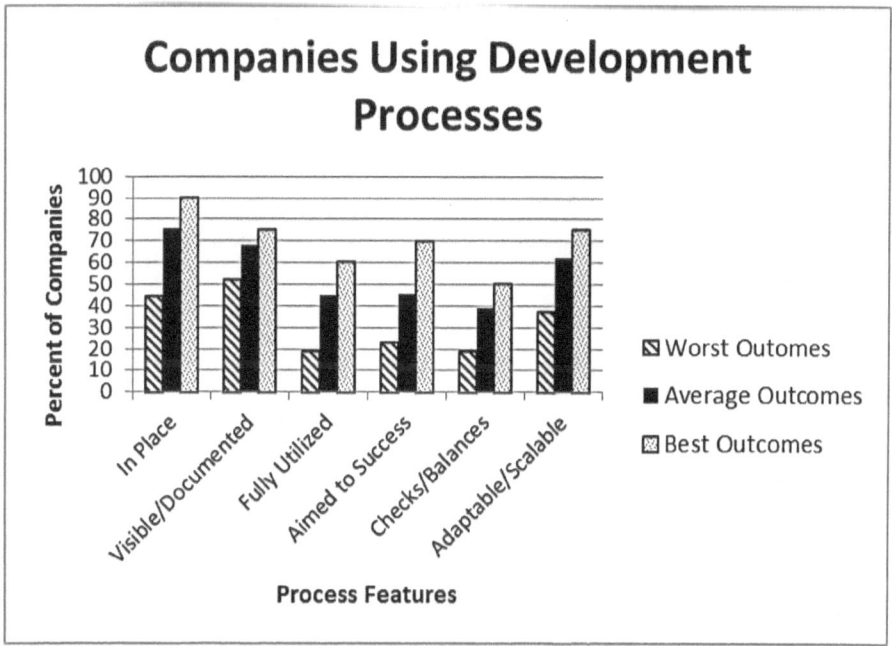

Figure 3-15. Outcomes from Using Development Processes. *Source:* Cooper, Robert and Scott Edgett, "Best Practices in the Idea-to-Launch," Reference Paper #45, Stage-Gate International, 2010

> **Note** New product development processes must be visible and well documented, fully utilized, and flexible. There must be multiple checks and balances along the way.

In order to develop a good process, you start by mapping out the next few development projects. The reason that you don't go back to recent projects is because you will have to try to remember the details of the previous projects. By mapping out the projects as they happen, you will have a more accurate process map. Along with mapping out the process, you will want to note how much time each step takes, including any wait time between steps. Assuming that there are sufficient differences between the next few projects, this will give you a good basis to develop a standardized development process that you can build upon with continuous improvement.

You can now start developing the standard process. Identify the common elements from each project. This is the skeleton of your standard process. A development process usually kicks off with some kind of information gathering, whether it is gathering customer requirements or market data. This is an opportunity to create a standard form, which you can then use on all projects.

Once you have a starting point for the information gathering, along with a process skeleton, you can start looking at all of the process steps that were not common on the projects that you mapped. You may want to ask some questions like:

- Why did we do this step?
- Did the customer require this step?
- Was this step a regulatory requirement?
- What was unique about this process that made this step necessary?
- Did we get what we expected from this step?
- Why would we use this step in the future?

The process of answering these questions will lead you to a decision point in your standard process. This will identify under what circumstances you will deviate from your process skeleton to perform this special step. Repeat this analysis on all of your process steps. Figure 3-16 shows a simple version of a process. The normal process is only three steps, but if you have a special requirement, it turns into a five-step process. Obviously, your product development process will have many more steps.

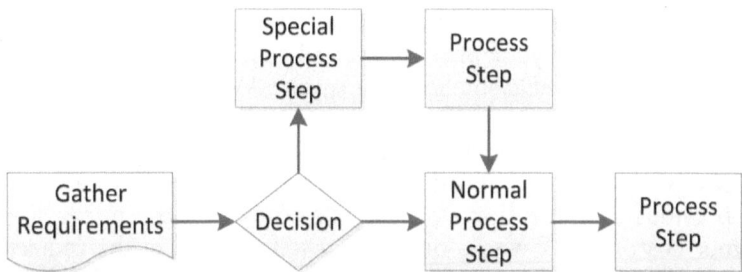

Figure 3-16. Initial Process

Once you have the process mapped with all of the potential decision points to understand how complex your process is, you can label the times for each step on the process map. With this information, you can see how quickly you can complete a simple project versus the time it would take to complete a more complex project. Figure 3-17 shows how long it takes for each step. In this example, the gray areas are the simplest processes. This simple process is eight weeks long, according to the process map. But, if our decisions take us to a more complex process, the process could take between 12 and 17 weeks. Once all of the paths are identified, it is time to ask some questions about whether our standard process is the right one.

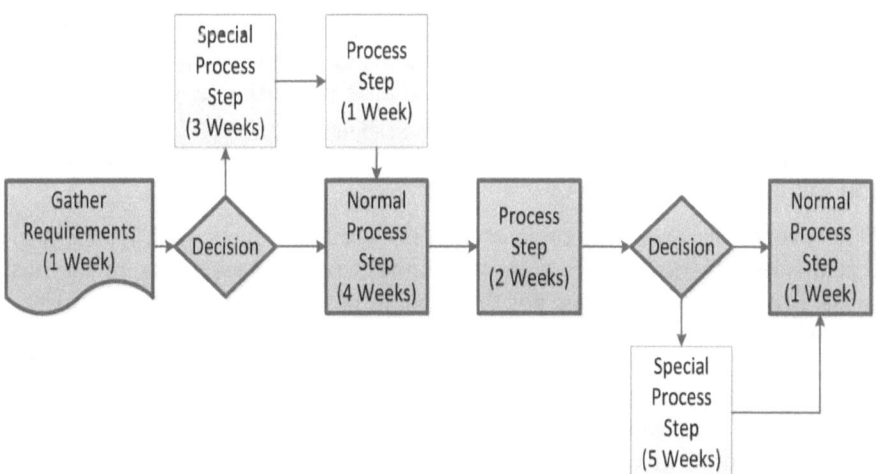

Figure 3-17. Process with Data

First, you validate that the process meets your requirements or the requirements of all of your customers. If it does, you move on to looking for waste in your process to make it more efficient. If the process does not meet your needs, then you find out what you must add to meet those requirements and add it. When you have your process with all requirements met in place, it is time to make it more efficient. So, you may ask, 'Why we would improve efficiency of our processes when we meet our customer expectations on timeliness?" You do this to improve your competitive advantage. If your customer needs you to develop your products or services within 17 weeks, as shown in the previous example, then you are able to meet those needs. If you can offer your customer 12 weeks or less and still meet all of the requirements, then you will likely get more sales due to happy customers and a differentiating skill.

You can make the process more efficient by eliminating steps through automation, by eliminating activities that don't add value, or making the steps take less time. You can also automate approval processes. You may want to consider removing some of the stage-gate criteria to reduce analysis time. Even if you choose not to offer the time savings to your customer, you can use the time as a buffer to help with critical chain project management. This is where you take the just-in-case time built into each project step and remove it. You save the time in a buffer, added to the end of the project. You may also put smaller buffers prior to major milestones. By removing the extra time in each process step, you are more likely to finish on time and not need the buffer.

Once you have your process map and have eliminated the wastes discussed in Chapter 2, you need to put together your structure for your project to help ensure success. The first step to getting any project off the ground, whether it is a product development project or a process improvement project, is to have a good sponsor. The sponsor should have the authority to help push the project forward through the stage-gate process. The project documentation should identify the sponsor as well as the cross-functional team that will work on the development project.

The overall development cycle should be documented as well. Typically, this cycle is determined by the customer's needs or the seasonality of the business. This timeline brings up another source of waste in organizations. This is the waste caused by starting the development process too late to follow the process that you have designed. This late start may be the result of multiple delays including customer commitment delays or senior management review delays. This waste causes you to spend extra resources trying to hit deadlines with less time. This delay may also cause you to miss your deadlines, leading to unhappy customers. In order to avoid this waste, the process needs to have drop-dead dates where a project does not move forward unless it is kicked off prior to the deadline.

Although you should have an idea of what the customer needs are at the project kickoff, once the team is put together, you should conduct a needs analysis. The tool that you use will depend upon the experience of the team and what type of project you are working on. Data from customer complaints, customer requests, or warranty issues can be used to help support this analysis.

Cost Management

Changes during product development cause a great deal of waste. In order to avoid this waste, you can identify the process for handling changes prior to project kickoff. This process includes how time will be negotiated or how you can get additional resources to execute the changes. This is especially important because in a matrix-style organization, it is likely you will not be working on only one project. Your time constraints mean that changes affect not only the current project but also those concurrent projects that share human resources with the changing project. Designing the process using the project buffers mentioned earlier will help you manage change. (We discuss more about how to manage your projects and avoid wastes in Chapter 8.)

Note Product development follows a process. Take the time to develop efficient and effective processes in order to make product development your strategic advantage.

Waste from Packaging

Consumer product companies often spend a lot of time and money designing and building attractive packages to catch the consumer's attention. This is not wasteful activity. Studies have shown that up to 75 percent of purchasing decisions in Europe are made in the store. In Brazil, the percentage is 88. In the United States, it is 70 percent.[15]

There are four types of waste that can be created from packaging: waste in packaging because the package is poorly designed to utilize the point-of-purchase (POP) decision processes; waste from the use of expensive or unneeded materials; waste from damage to the product; and waste because the packaging creates excess logistics expenses. Businesses must balance these wastes to ensure that sales are achieved with a solid profit margin and without product damage. In order to avoid the first two wastes, you need to have a good product development process with POP needs-identification and package durability studies.

---

[15]Liljenwall, Robert, "The Power of Point-of-Purchase Advertising: Marketing at Retail," Point-of-Purchase Advertising International, Washington, DC, 2004.

The packaging design has a definite ROI when properly done. Sales volume can increase when a package is attention grabbing. There are a few rules when designing packaging:

- Grab attention with colors and create curiosity.
- Know your competitors' packaging. You will be sitting right beside them.
- Use eye-catching market research, not just on your product, but with your product mixed in with your competition's.
- The unique selling points of the product should appear very clearly on the front on the package. Think billboard mentality. Do not include a lot of small detail on the front.
- If your product will be sold online (and on Amazon.com), make sure the product description includes the unique selling points. Customers are more willing to read online than in the store. Give more detail about the product's ingredients, instructions, and so on.
- Be kind to the consumers. Don't make it difficult for the consumer to store or use the product.

On the other hand, some companies have realized some benefit to designing packaging at a minimum cost. Those who ship via UPS and FedEx have designed packaging to meet the requirements of the sorting equipment used by these logistics giants. Others like Walmart use packaging design and reusable packaging materials to minimize costs while maintaining the POP display benefits. IKEA designed its packaging for shipping and warehousing and used the space savings to build elaborate showrooms to drive the purchase decisions.

Promotional Expenses and Advertising Effectiveness

As explained earlier, brand loyalty is more important than just about everything else. Getting a good product or service out there, one that fulfills market needs and that subsequently creates brand loyalty and word-of-mouth, is the best path to marketing success. Because this theory is seldom followed, an enormous source of waste in business is from promotional expenditures, which typically includes everything from sales to advertising. As mentioned, there tends to be the notion of increasing advertising expenditures in hopes that it will increase sales.

It's not that promotion necessarily is the largest source of waste; it's that people think it tends to be the largest enigma in companies. You might think you need to advertise because it's what you're supposed to do. Many companies have no idea whether their advertising dollars are generating sales. In reality most types of advertising is ineffective and executives often fail to understand how to incorporate the newer forms of advertising and promotions.

Many companies are starting to understand the idea that traditional media (such as TV, magazines, and newspapers) is no longer the best outlet to reach customers. In fact, Procter & Gamble (P&G) recently laid off 1,600 staffers, mostly marketers, "because Facebook and Google can be *more efficient* than the traditional media that usually eats the lion's share of P&G's ad budget."[16] But a question remains; what is efficiency? How do you measure it? How do you determine your best strategy? How do you determine where you should spend your money?

Even though some firms like P&G have mass advertising departments to determine their promotional strategies, they still seem to struggle and get the messages wrong. When those types of companies can't figure it out, how can the small business owner prevent do it?

We see two large areas of waste in promotion. The first is not knowing which media to use and the second is spending way too much money in the promotional budget. We conducted our own completely unscientific survey. In our study (and yes we are using the word study loosely), we asked over 100 people to think about products they had purchased in the past year and tell us why they brought those products (we ended up recording a total of 129 shopping experiences). We know that customers will work to be very logical in defending their purchases. So, we are not capturing all of the emotions that go into purchasing. We know our sample is not representative of much. We also know that we are not capturing some of the underlying effects that might be happening, such as the "sleeper effect." In this, a person sees an ad, but doesn't even remember seeing it. They are drawn toward the product at a later time.

In our survey, we got a fairly broad range of business-to-consumer products. Clothes were by far the largest category (see Figure 3-18).

---

[16] Andzulis, James "Mick," Nikolaos Pangopoulos, and Adam Rapp, "A Review of Social Media Implications for the Sales Process," *Journal of Personal Selling and Sales Management,* Volume 32, Number 3, Summer 2012, pp. 305–316.

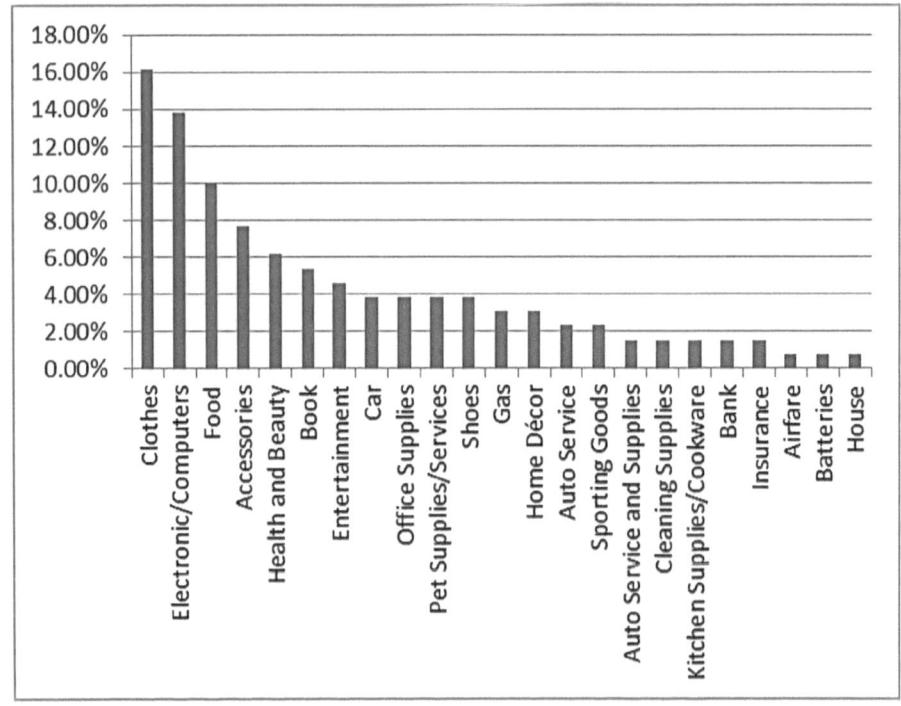

Figure 3-18. Percentage of Purchases by Category in Our "Study"

Figure 3-19 shows the main reasons why people chose the product they did. An overwhelming 28 percent of the purchases were made because of brand loyalty. Word-of-mouth encompassed seven percent. Taken together, these two factors accounted for over a third of the purchase decisions. These reasons stretched across all categories of products. We suspect that this number would be much higher if the products required more investment, such as houses and cars, instead of clothing and iPods. Although there are a couple high-investment products in Figure 3-19, the majority are not.

Eliminating Waste in Business

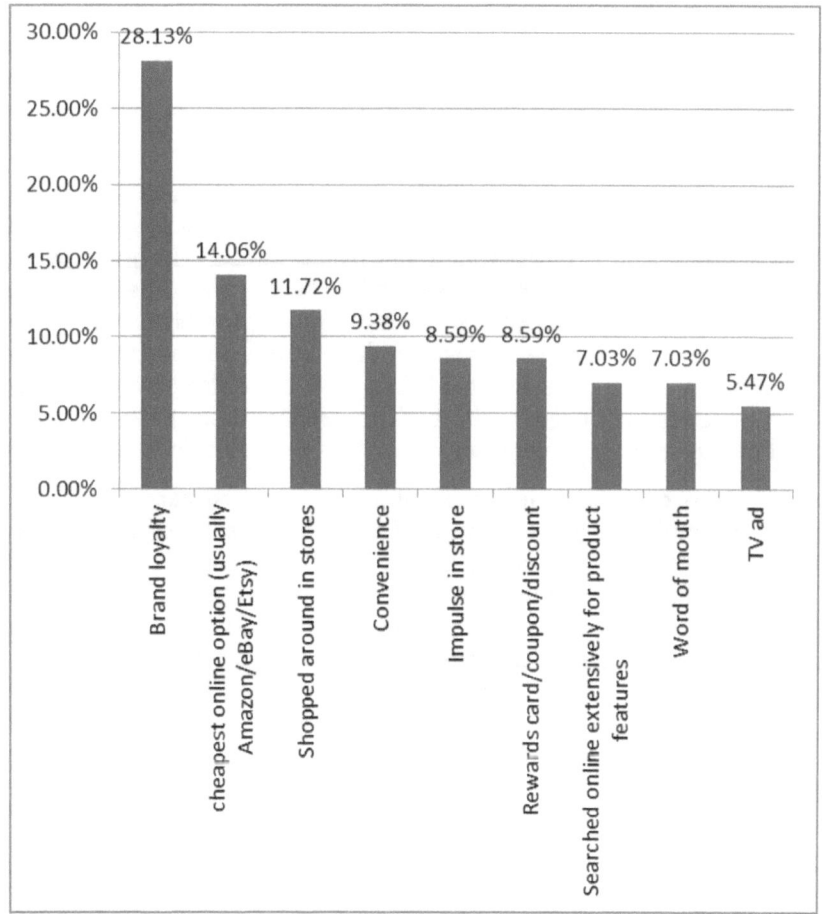

Figure 3-19. Reasons for Purchases in Our "Study"

Establishing brand loyalty and spreading it via word-of-mouth is the single most important thing any marketer should and can do. Measuring the impact and success of brand loyalty and word-of-mouth efforts should always come first.

The second biggest way that buying decisions were made in our survey was online searching for the cheapest price (14 percent). This typically was not truly "searching for the cheapest price," but instead, "I went to Amazon and searched for the cheapest price," or "I went to Etsy and searched for the cheapest price." Therefore, in almost every case, this wasn't really a function of price, but instead a function of being "brand loyal" to an online retailer. Once again, loyalty matters. Or in the product world, getting your product displayed in the right place on the most user-loyal sites matters. Then, make sure you are cost effective among your competitors. Between this and the "convenience" factor, which accounts for more than 9 percent of purchase decisions, you could almost go back to the old, location, location, location, mentality. We might not be talking about the right street corner anymore, but location clearly still matters.

Shopping around in stores and purchasing impulsively account for almost 12 percent and almost 9 percent, respectively. In order to capture these spending dollars, you need to have effective packaging. More than seven percent of the purchases were made after significant online research. We believe this to be the determining factor for the large majority of any high-involvement, high-dollar purchase, whether it is B2C or B2B. In order to win these buyers, you need updated product information on your website that is easy to find and also have those product features match buyer's needs (refer back to product design). We also feel that content marketing is very important here, which we discuss in Chapter 6.

The only two categories left are coupon or reward card usage at 8.59 percent and purchase made from a TV ad at 5.47 percent. That means, out of all the purchases in our survey, a small number of purchases (five percent) were made because of some form of advertising. Rewards cards or coupons are doubtfully bringing new customers into a retail outlet or to a new product. Many times these are sent to already loyal customers. These are either not necessary and wasteful, because the customer was going to buy again anyway, or they are effective. These can create more loyalty because the customer feels the provider is taking care of them or the coupon gets the customer to act quicker or at a certain time. It is up to you to do the research and determine the motivation and outcome of coupon usage.

This brings us to the puny five percent of purchases that were made because of advertising. Keep in mind that these purchases were all made with fairly inexpensive products in the B2C realm. If this "survey" were taken on a more extensive scale, such as with larger purchases in the B2B realm, this figure would disappear to almost nothing. It is uncommon for promotional effort to generate sales on large items.

In terms of thorough analyses of real advertising dollars, probably the best study of advertising efficiency ever conducted was done by Cheong and Colleagues (2013). It studied the top 100 advertisers (which make up 49 percent of advertising) over a 22-year period (1987–2007).[17] In a very fancy regression equation, the authors found that advertising inefficiency has increased over time. You would think that with more tools, bigger databases, and better analytical techniques, advertising efficiency would get better. However, this study found that approximately 59 percent of top advertisers are inefficiently using their ad dollars.

---

[17] Cheong, Yunjae, Federico de Gregorio, and Kihan Kim, "Advertising Spending Efficiency among Top US Advertisers from 1985 to 2007: Overspending or Smart Managing?" working paper.

Six forms of advertising were examined: magazines, newspapers, TV, radio, outdoor, and the Internet. The total spending in each category is shown in Figure 3-20.

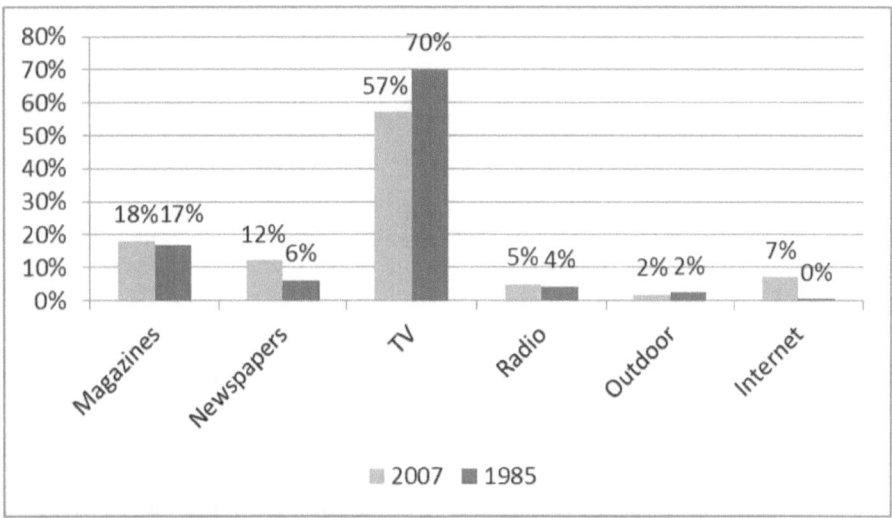

Figure 3-20. Total Advertising Spending by Media Category. *Source:* Cheong, Yunjae, Federico de Gregorio, and Kihan Kim, "Advertising Spending Efficiency Among Top US Advertisers from 1985 to 2007: Overspending or Smart Managing?" working paper

The most inefficient forms of advertising are magazine and outdoor spending. Although no forms of advertising were actually found to be efficient, the "best" form of advertising was the Internet. It was found to be neither efficient nor inefficient. This inefficiency is basically over-advertising. When companies over-advertise, the additional money spent on advertising creates no additional sales. Many times, the added money actually decreases sales, because consumers become turned off by the barrage of advertising.

Note Magazine and outdoor advertising are the most inefficient.

As far as individual advertisers, 59 percent should actually reduce their spending on advertising in order to produce the same amount of sales, all because of their high degree of inefficiency. In fact, 30 percent of the top advertisers demonstrated low advertising efficiency (below 20 percent). The proportion of inefficient firms overall has increased from 1985 (52.46 percent) to 2007 (64.84 percent). Likewise, the level of efficiency has declined since 1985.

In fact, the mean efficiency score of all leading advertisers for the 23 years was .69. In order to become efficient, advertisers need to produce sales using approximately 31 percent fewer inputs than they did over the 23 years. In fact, the inefficient advertisers among the top 100 must cut $4.28 million per year in magazine ads, $4.21 million per year in newspaper ads, $12.24 million per year in TV spots, $1.35 million per year in radio ads, and $.88 million per year in outdoor ads, and obtain the same sales to be considered efficient during the period 1985–2007. The percentages of advertising that are inefficient and efficient are shown in Figure 3-21.

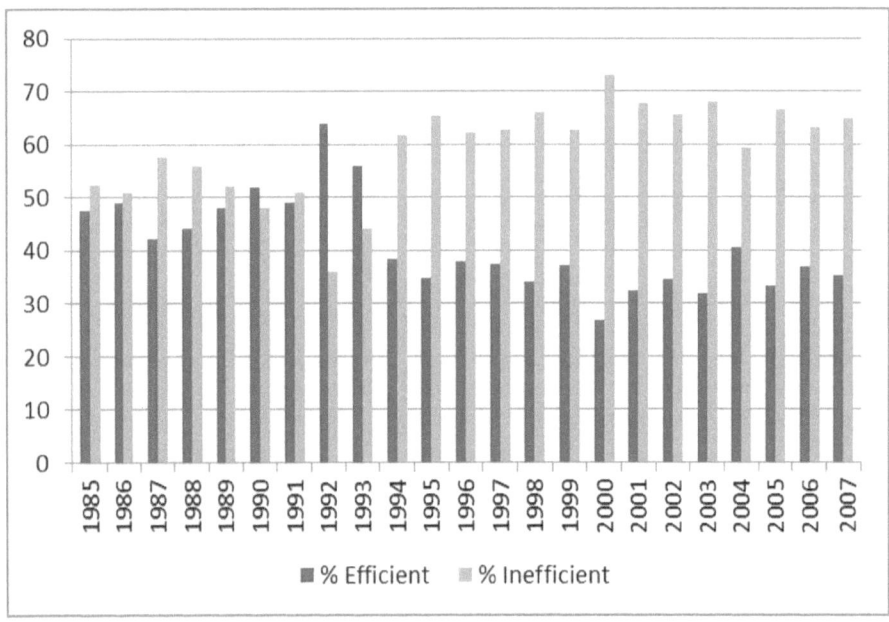

Figure 3-21. Total Percentage of Inefficient and Efficient Advertising. *Source:* Cheong, Yunjae, Federico de Gregorio, and Kihan Kim, "Advertising Spending Efficiency Among Top US Advertisers from 1985 to 2007: Overspending or Smart Managing?" working paper.

When looking at slack analysis, you can also see that much of the advertising across all six media classes could have been reduced while maintaining the same sales levels for the last 23 years. *Slack* is another measure of advertising inefficiency. The higher the slack, the more inefficient the medium is. Outdoor advertising has the lowest overall slack and TV has the highest overall slack across 1985–2007.

Eliminating Waste in Business

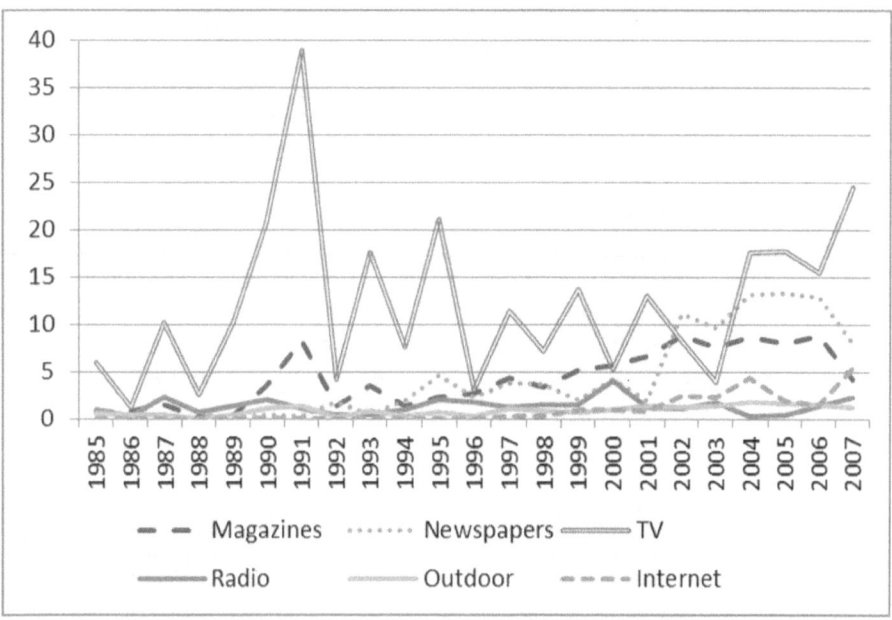

Figure 3-22. Ad Slack: Where Advertisers Need to Cut from Their Budget. *Source:* Cheong, Yunjae, Federico de Gregorio, and Kihan Kim, "Advertising Spending Efficiency among Top US Advertisers from 1985 to 2007: Overspending or Smart Managing?" working paper

▪ **Note** Get out of the "we advertise because it's what we've always done," mindset! Companies are significantly over-advertising! Use small, targeted, personal promotions.

Much of the overspending in advertising is due to the reward structure set up between advertising agencies and businesses. Until relatively recently, compensation has largely used a mark-up or commission system in which agencies charge clients approximately 15 percent of all media billings.[18] This system encourages advertisers to buy the most expensive media, not the most efficient one. Likewise, the account managers who buy the time get internal promotions and recognition based on their media buys.

There's also the whole notion that advertising brings in sales. It is seen as a sort of insurance policy against potential declining sales. Also, advertising is easily understood and somewhat comfortable. In the complicated, fragmented media market, it just may be the easiest thing to run to.

---

[18]Belch, George, and Michael Belch, *Advertising and Promotion, 9th Edition* (Columbus, OH: McGraw-Hill, Irwin, 2009).

We discuss how to measure advertising effectiveness in the metrics section at the end of this chapter, but we have an important moral here: You have to look societal changes each year. How has your customer changed? Are their searching and buying habits different? What is happening with the economy, the world, in politics, socially? You do not want to be chasing fads and trends. You want to adjust promotional expenditures yearly, but only with a proper data and analysis. Also, do not fragment yourself just to reach one or two tiny niches. Find your best few niches and understand their buying behavior. Have the best product you can, that is key. Always have a great quality product or service and do what you can to help the word-of-mouth spread. It won't happen quickly, but it's a waste of money to try any other way. Do not feel you have to advertise because that's what everyone else does. It is clearly not working for anyone, even the Fortune 500 companies.

Waste from Price

The act of pricing incorrectly is a huge source of waste. Pricing too low results in lost profits, whereas pricing too high results in lost sales (and therefore profits). Price wars lead to company failure, not growth. When a company attempts to grow by offering lower-priced products than its competitor, everyone loses. The company loses its reputation for quality, service, and brand. One of the single most studied concepts in marketing is the price-quality relationship. We know, hands down, that when consumers see a low price, they equate it with low quality. This is why Toyota can sell a car at a certain cost under the Toyota brand and sell the same car with minor changes under the Lexus brand for much more money. Higher cost gives the customer a feeling of greater value.

Additionally, as we have explained, the most important thing to consider is brand loyalty. You are never going to capture brand loyalty by selling at a discount. Best case scenario, with a sale or discount, you might bring in a new customer. But it does nothing to create long-term loyalty. It sounds very cliché, but it's true; you need a differentiating competitive advantage, and price is not it.

Low Cost

Because low-cost strategies typically drive down profit margins, the company needs to lower the actual product quality through the use of fewer materials, cheaper materials, or reduced service levels. This can be seen in every product-driven industry. As the product matures, the quality goes down due to pricing pressures and the need to maintain a certain margin. In service industries, companies try to outsource call centers and service repair functions to save money.

The best companies, however, continue to innovate and build brand loyalty so that they can charge a premium for new features. When companies focus only on low-cost strategies, they might have to lower the research and development budget in order to afford a lower profit margin. This starts a downward spiral where the lack of innovation within the organization makes the technology of that organization obsolete. Ultimately, this forces the company into extinction or into a situation where they have to reinvest in innovation to escape the low price strategy spiral.

Figure 3-23 shows how consumer decision drivers changed between 2010 and 2011. This shows an increase in trust, innovation, and branding. The biggest change was a decrease in the effect of price on the purchase decision. This information is in the wake of the recent recession, when you would think more people would be concerned about price. Even in this economic situation in the United States, not only did price reduce as an influencer by over 15 percent, but it is the fourth out of the six factors measured in regards to driving purchase decisions. Consumers value quality, trust, and service more than price. Branding is inclusive of service, quality, trust, innovation, and brand (logo/name). If you consider this fact, it further diminishes the minimal effect that price has on decision making.

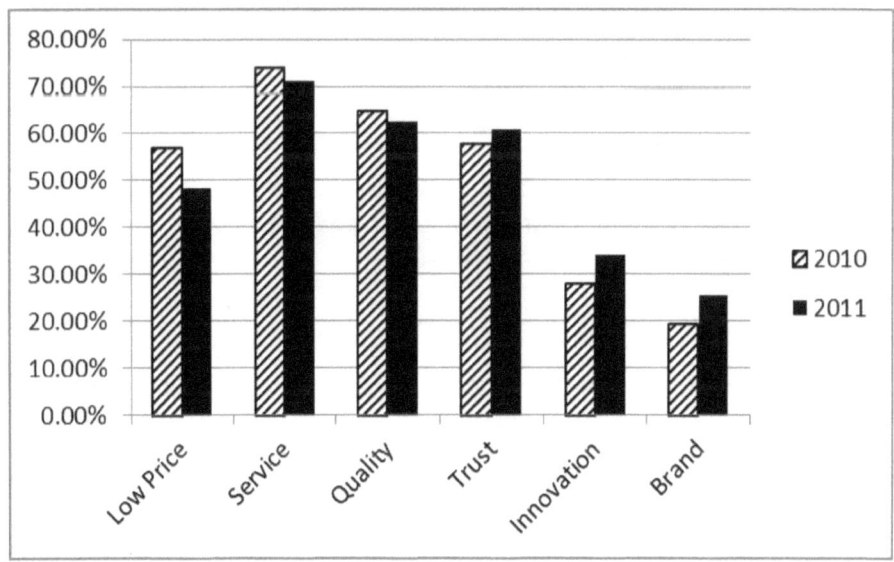

Figure 3-23. Change in Consumer Decision Drivers. *Source:* Moorman, Christine, CMO Survey, *Highlights and Insights*, February 2011, TheCMOSurvey.Org

Further, when customers leave one company and go to another, it is rarely due to price. In reality, customers leave a company only 15 percent of the time due to price. The biggest reason customers go to other companies is due to poor service (70 percent of the time), followed by product dissatisfaction (15 percent), which is likely a quality or feature issue.[19]

So why do business leaders think that price drives sales? Because of one of the biggest business wastes: "That is the way we have always done it." Furniture stores, for example, think they need to have a sale every week to draw customers into the store.

Businesses often realize when their prices are high due to lack of sales, but more often than not, businesses price their items too low or offer unnecessary discounts. Parker Hannifin realized this mistake when a new CEO took control and challenged the cost-plus margin pricing strategy that Parker Hannifin had been using for nearly 90 years.[20] As engineers and production personnel found less expensive ways to make their products, the prices were cut as well. This rationale was not based upon any insight into what the customers were willing and able to pay. His team of pricing experts and consultants found that prices could be raised up to 25 percent in some cases. After an across-the-board price increase, some customers chose to go to another supplier, but most were retained at Parker Hannifin due to the value that their components brought at even at higher prices. After the success that this new strategy brought to Parker Hannifin, they employ pricing experts for each business line to maximize profitability.

Note   Pricing should always be based on what the customers are willing to pay (provided there is a profit). Don't ever use a cost-plus system and never engage in price wars!

Discounts

Pricing discounts are like low-price strategies. The discounts aren't the primary driver of the purchase decision. Discounts should be given only when there is a good financial reason for them. Such discounts may be given to incentivize the customer to pay invoices quicker. This may be a good strategy for a business that does not have profitability issues, but is challenged with limited cash flow. Payment terms are a type of discount. Automotive and

---

[19]Manning, Gerald, L. Michael L. Ahearne and Barry L. Reece, *Selling Today: Partnering to Create Value 12th Edition* (Upper Saddle River, NJ: Prentice Hall, 2012). p. 1–544.
[20]Aeppel, Timothy, "Seeking Perfect Prices, CEO Tears Up the Rules," March 27, 2007, http://online.wsj.com/article/SB117496231213149938.html.

aerospace customers push 45- or 60-day payment terms. These terms turn the supply chain into a bank for the final manufacturer. This strategy makes sense only when there is no other choice or there is a large pool of cash that allows you to give these terms without having to borrow money. If your company is leveraged and offers payment terms that delay payment of invoices, you are paying the interest for your customers and further eroding your margins. You might as well offer them a pricing discount. Avoid this waste by thoroughly understanding the normal discounts and terms offered in your industry. This knowledge, along with the knowledge of pricing strategies, gives you the weapons you need to negotiate the best deal possible with your customers while maintaining your margins.

In the B2C world, there are certain times when it may make sense to offer a one-time price reduction to bring customers to your product. This might work if you have a new product and are encouraging customers to try it. Just remember, customers are always happy to take future price reductions, but not as happy to take future price increases. For example, when new electronics hit the market, they are always priced high. There is a whole separate stream of research based on which customers will buy the new TV at $2,000 and those who will wait three years until it is $700. However, how often do you hear about the company who brings a product to the market at $700, and three years from now customers are waiting to pay $2,000? This pricing strategy exists only in cases like collectibles and rare items.

Note Discounting, sales, and coupons make sense only in unusual circumstances. They should not be used regularly.

General Motors had a policy where every year the suppliers were required to reduce pricing due to "operational efficiency improvements." This was really just margin erosion, which eventually made them unprofitable. One year, when a three percent reduction was requested, my company gave an over 20 percent price increase. We had a unique product and capabilities so it was a calculated risk. General Motors paid the increased price, which in the long run, made the relationship less combative. This is just one example of how smarter pricing and discount strategies can increase your bottom line and improve customer relationships. Nobody will ever say no to a discount. Make sure you offer them only when they are truly needed.

Waste from Bad Place Decisions

The last area that contains marketing waste is when the transaction occurs. This is especially true with smaller companies, where you may consider your personal relationship with suppliers. The entire supply chain, from the raw materials to consumer purchases, is a potential source of waste. This waste starts with the supplier relationships. When a company is new, it overpays for materials and services due to its lack of negotiating power. It also experiences lower levels of service from those suppliers. At this phase, the waste from poor supplier relationships is obvious. As the company grows, it will gain purchasing power and also will likely change what it needs from the suppliers. These changing needs may include delivery schedules, quality levels, and services. Some of these new needs provide value to the customers, while others are the result of the leaders of a growing company applying a formula used at other companies because they feel that is what must be done.

One example of an increasing requirement may be asking your suppliers to become ISO 9001 certified. We have always been big fans of a properly designed and implemented management system because of its capability to eliminate waste. Unfortunately, we too often see and hear business leaders implement management systems so that they can hang the flag and court customers who want to work with ISO-certified companies. This is where the supplier-customer relationship actually can drive waste. In a company where ISO 9001, TS16949, AS9100, Joint Commission Standards, ISO 14000 or other standards are implemented for a customer, without the leadership actually utilizing the benefits, certification is wasteful. This same certification can provide substantial value when it is used to develop effective business processes that focus on quality and service. This is just one example where supply chain relationships can drive waste. (We talk more about the specifics of supply chain relationships in Chapter 8.)

The distribution of goods is another source of waste. Companies go through great efforts to hide these wastes. In distribution between businesses, the suppliers of large companies will often create warehouse or manufacturing locations close to the customers to provide just-in-time inventory or to reduce shipping costs. This reduces the shipping costs to the customers while potentially increasing the supplier costs, thus driving waste through additional staff. When the analysis makes sense to locate warehouses closer to your customers, this decision is not a waste. Unfortunately, as stated earlier, many business leaders believe that they should do this because other companies do it.

In distributions between businesses and retail or consumers, there are other wastes. Retail locations not often maintain a large amount of inventory on hand for most items, which results in the wasteful activities associated with small and frequent shipments to those retail locations. Retailers also have problems estimating future sales and have too much inventory on hand. In order to feed this process, there are inventory-counting and shelf-stocking wastes. Likewise, there is waste in discounting products that haven't sold.

To reduce these wastes, you can ship directly to the customer or to the store for the customer through the use of online shopping. Figure 3-24 shows a projection in the growth of ecommerce sales through 2017. Twenty-six percent of all holiday sales in 2012 were from the Internet. In 2013, that number rose to almost 39 percent.[21] Beyond the convenience to the customer, one reason why ecommerce is so popular is that it is often less expensive than traditional retail. Even though free shipping is a myth because the shipping cost is just put into the price, the reduction in distribution costs makes the online shopping a viable option for producers and consumers. The only part of the supply chain that loses is the retailer, who then has to compete with online sales.

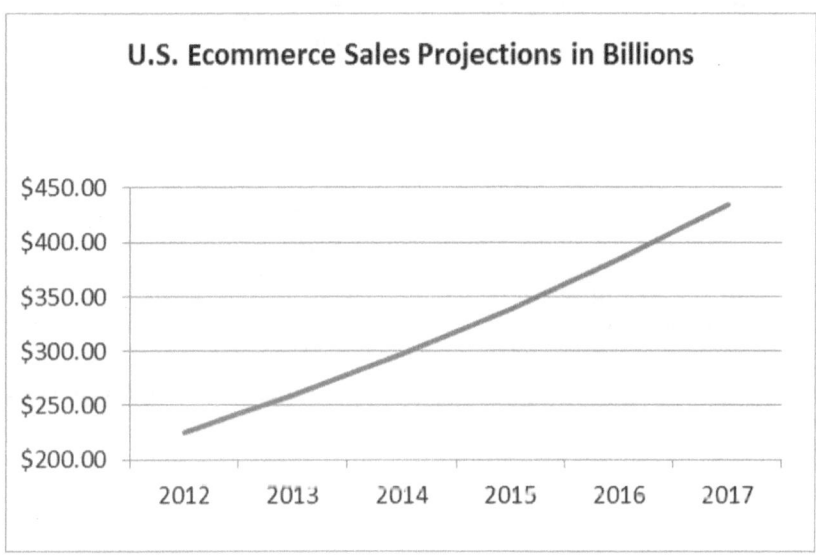

Figure 3-24. U.S. Ecommerce Sales Projections. *Source:* eMarketer, "Retail Ecommerce Set to Keep a Strong Pace Through 2017," April 24, 2013, http://www.emarketer.com/Article/Retail-Ecommerce-Set-Keep-Strong-Pace-Through-2017/1009836

Walmart has found a way to benefit from both retail and online sales by reducing shipping and warehousing costs through the site-to-store program. With this program, Walmart can offer more variety than it can afford to offer in its stores. It doesn't assume the risk or cost of carrying any inventory, because it is shipped from the producer to the store. Walmart also uses its vast distribution network to minimize the shipping costs rather than giving the shipping funds to FedEx or UPS. (In Chapter 8, we discuss how to identify operational wastes and eliminate them as Walmart has done with its site-to-store program. We also look more at other logistics issues.)

---

[21] Marvin, Ginny, "Holiday Mobile Orders Shot Up 50 Percent In 2013; Social Commerce Remains Negligible, Organic Still Dominates," *Marketing Land,* January 9, 2014, http://marketingland.com/holiday-mobile-orders-shot-up-50-percent-in-2013-organic-dominates-email-grows-social-remains-inconsequential-69958

Marketing Metrics

This quote by Roger Best is frequently mentioned, but often forgot:

> "The cockpit of the 757 Boeing jet is a maze of instruments (analytic tools) that produce flight performance data (metrics) that are critical to the safe and efficient flight of a 757. It would be impossible to fly a 757 without theses analytic instruments and performance metrics. Yet, companies invest millions or billions in marketing and sales strategies with no clear measure of their performance impact or efficiency."[22]

Top executives have voiced concerns over the lack of metrics available to support marketing activities. The quote "In God we Trust, All others bring data"[23] holds true in all areas of business. With CEOs feeling that there are no actionable metrics in the marketing field, it is no wonder that the marketing department is often easily downsized and undervalued. It is also no wonder that there is enormous waste from marketing dollars.

All of your marketing activities need to be validated by data. Too often, we have seen marketing materials inferring that certain activities have driven a return on investment. In other words, the advertising department runs an advertising campaign, sales go up, and the marketing department claims a positive ROI. Unfortunately, these claims are not often easily substantiated. Most marketing activities can be considered waste unless you can rigorously measure their effectiveness.

This rigor includes setting a baseline performance through a reliable measurement method. Then, you must maintain the measurement method after marketing activities have occurred to show the effect of those activities. It is also crucial to evaluate other potential factors that are driving sales. For instance, a consumer product company cannot claim that a marketing campaign drove Christmas sales necessarily because the holiday season itself may be the driving force.

The leading scholars will tell you that *net marketing contribution* is the very first metric you should calculate. To get it, you should take net overall company profit (after expenses) and then subtract marketing and sales expenses, and this overall total is your marketing contribution. For example, if Apple made $13.5 billion net profit (from $36.54 gross profit) and had $3.12 billion in marketing and sales expenses, the net marketing contribution is $10 billion, which represents a 34 percent marketing ROS (Return on Sales). This example

---

[22]Best, Roger D. "Getting Started Using Marketing Metrics," http://www.marketingmetricssolutions.com/pdf/MMH%20-%20WP%20Final%20RB.pdf, (last accessed August 2013).
[23]Hastie, Trevor, Robert Tibshirani and Jerome Friedman. *The Elements of Statistical Learning* (2nd ed.). New York, NY: Springer, 2011).

is actually in the field's leading text on marketing metrics. However, nothing could be more wrong. This assumes that every sale Apple ever made on every iPhone, iPad, and all of its products and services came from marketing. This is extremely short-sited and even egotistical.

With marketing being a key function in all companies, the marketing section of this book is the largest. Even small companies without named marketing departments spend a lot of their resources on marketing activities. We have divided the various areas of marketing into categories in this part of the chapter to discuss the metrics in each of those areas. These metrics are by no means exhaustive, as marketing metrics themselves could fill a book. We have tried to highlight some of the most important ones.

Customer Metrics

As we have said and as research has shown, it is much cheaper to retain customers than to get new ones. That means that measuring your customer satisfaction is critical to the long-term success of your business. Likewise, the goal of any marketing campaign should be to create brand loyalty.

Customer Satisfaction

Everyone needs an overall level of satisfaction. This can be found quite simply by asking customers on a regular basis how satisfied and/or dissatisfied they are. Most organizations measure customer complaints in some way. The motivation for this measurement is often tied to minimizing legal issues or avoiding bad public relations issues. The need to monitor and control consumer satisfaction has been heightened by the growth of social media because consumers now have a bigger voice. Unfortunately, by the time you get customer complaint data, it is too late to avoid a bad customer experience. The reaction to the complaint is the opportunity to create a stronger customer relationship or destroy one altogether. Customer compliant data can be measured in both qualitative and quantitative methods. The quantitative data helps you understand and predict future issues by monitoring trends and the scale of warranty issues. The qualitative data helps you understand how you can improve customer service and what the overall view of your company is.

Customer compliments are similar to customer complaints, but they also allow you to make process changes that turn individual positive customer experiences into the way that all customers experience your products or services. Customer compliments are normally qualitative in nature, so the customer's reactions must be understood in order to be able to improve through the feedback.

Effective management of customer complaints and compliments leads to customer retention. Most importantly, you do not want to be reactive and wait for comments to come your way. Instead, you should focus on being proactive by regularly sending out surveys. As already described, make the surveys long enough to capture the right data, but not so long that customers do not want to fill them out. For example, our pediatrician sends a survey via e-mail every time we visit the office. Sometimes I delete the e-mails (when I'm too busy). When I have five minutes, I fill them out. With four kids, I am there enough and filling out enough surveys that they likely have a good idea of what I want. In the "open comments" section (which every survey should have), I said that I love the doctors and nurses, but the office looks a little dumpy. About 3–4 months later, the office had new carpet, paint, and chairs. I imagine that I was not the only one who said that. This brings us to the most important point—don't just collect data, act on it!

> **Note** Satisfaction surveys are critical. Regularly collect data relevant to customer needs and make the necessary changes to keep customers satisfied.

A customer impression of quality, value, and service is the ultimate goal. Unfortunately, business leaders make mistakes, leading to customers leaving the organization. In a consumer market, the percentage of customers who purchase only one time should be measured and understood. For some reason, these customers have only purchased one product or service. You need to understand why that happened so you can make any changes necessary to avoid this in the future. You may want to survey those customers to try to figure this out. These metrics are typically calculated in a CLV (Customer Lifetime Value) equation, covered in Chapter 4.

In B2B relationships as opposed to B2C relationships, it is often easier to identify unsatisfied customers and determine the reason they are unsatisfied. Business customers tend to give you multiple opportunities to succeed and will cease to do business with you if you fail.

Customer Expectations

We have said now many times that satisfaction should be measured on relevant attributes. But what does that mean? We will not go into full detail here, but marketers must know exactly what it is that makes customers happy. Refer back to our daycare example. Everyone knows parents expect daycare centers to be clean and safe, but how many people realize that customers want more? Survey data can also be used to measure these gaps. In the early 1990s a group of researchers developed the SERVQUAL model (see Figure 3-25) to help marketers analyze the gaps between expectations and what the marketing provided. Data from customer satisfaction surveys and "gap" survey is perceptual, and thus, not "hard" data. However, it is still important information to have. Each gap should be measured and processes should be put in place to minimize each gap.

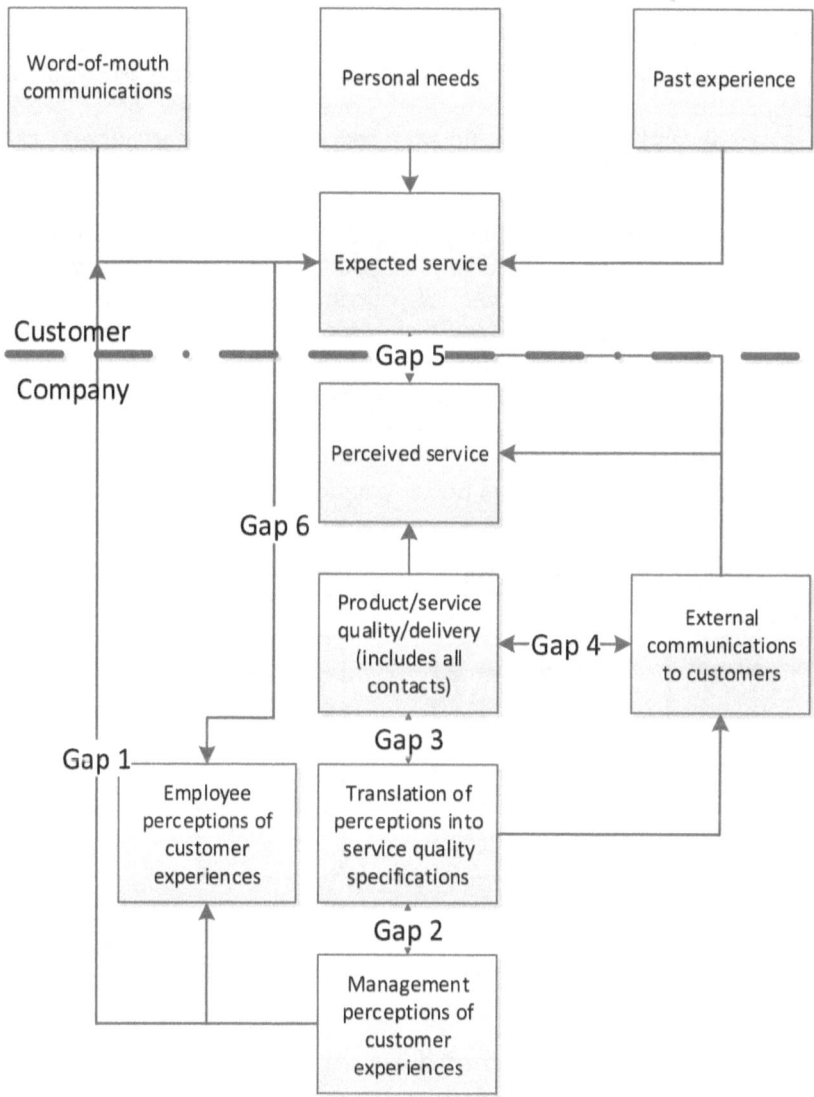

Figure 3-25. SERVQUAL Model. *Source:* Parasuramann, A., Valerie A. Zeithaml and Leaonard L. Berry, "SERVQUAL: A Multiple-Item Scale for Measuring Cosumer Perceptions of Service Quality," *Journal of Retailing*, 1999, vol. 64, No. 1, pp. 12–40

Customer Value

As mentioned, we cover customer lifetime value fully in Chapter 4. You should always know the full "worth" of every one of your customers. This data is more quantitative and therefore, many times, more helpful is predicting future customer behavior. This helps you better plan future marketing activities, leading to less waste.

Brand Preference

You must not only know exactly how much your customers like your products, but also exactly how much they "prefer" them over other products. There are several stages of brand preference development. Surveys can be used to collect this data. Figure 3-26 shows some of the items that should be measured to collect this data. Part of being a preferred brand includes a "share-of-wallet" measure. In this, you need to assess how much of your customers' wallets, as a percentage goes to your brand. If out of your annual gas spending, you spent ninety percent of your money at Circle K, seven percent at Speedway, two percent at BP, and one percent at other random gas stations, Circle K marketers could assume that they are the preferred brand and have a much greater share-of-wallet. You can also start to assess why the missing ten percent was spent at other gas stations. Was it because of a random event like a vacation, or due to location? When analyzing this type of data across many consumers, marketers can better plan future needs and actions.

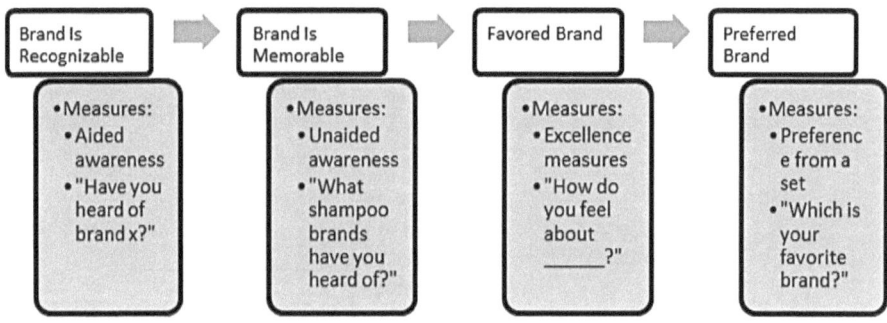

Figure 3-26. Brand Preference Development

Repurchase and Recommend Intentions

Many researchers feel that repurchase and recommend intentions are the most important metrics to use. Obviously, repurchase intent is a measure of whether the customer plans to purchase the brand again. Recommendation intent is a measure of whether they would tell their friends about a brand. Most studies do show that these two metrics are the most powerful. Therefore, surveys should include these two measures. As part of this metric, you should also capture word-of-mouth data, as described earlier in the reputation-management section. Sometimes, you don't see these measures on a survey, but when customers talk positively (or negatively) about you online, they go beyond merely recommending you to becoming a consumer advocate.

> **Note** Repurchase and recommend intentions are quite possibly the most important metric in terms of customer satisfaction and brand loyalty.

Product/Service Development

When developing new products, it is often a mistake to consider all sales from the new products as incremental improvements, when in reality there is a normal cannibalization of profits from current products. Therefore, when you consider the value of a new product, you must reduce the sales or contribution margin of the new product sales by the amount of reduced sales you have in similar legacy products. We call the product of this calculation the *net new product sales* because it is the gross new product sales minus the change in legacy product sales. The following formula shows how to calculate this metric.

$$NNPS = GNPS - (PYLPS - CYLPS)$$

GNPS = Gross New Product Sales

PYLPS = Prior Year Legacy Product Sales

CYLPS = Current Year Legacy Product Sales

NNPS = Net New Product Sales

You must also look at research and development spending as a percentage of the company's margin. You need to monitor the expense of research and development as a percent of margin to be able to know if you are increasing the proportion of your research and development expense. The appropriate value of research and development spending will depend upon your business model.

$$\%RDE = \frac{RDE}{M}$$

RDE = Research and Development Expense

M = Company Margin

%RDE = Research and Development Expense as a Percent of Margin

To start measuring individual project success, you need to take a page from the activity-based costing model (ABC), which we talk about more in Chapter 7. The basic concept of ABC in regards to product development is to look at the incremental cost of the individual product or service that you are evaluating. All research and development expenses can be split into two categories:

- **Research and development overhead expense.** The costs accumulated for development projects that are never completed.

- **Research and development activity expense.** The costs accumulated for each successful development project.

When evaluating the success of a specific project, you should not include the sunk costs associated with the projects that were failures but rather the costs associated with the specific project that you are evaluating. The other costs of R&D should be minimized through better processes for selecting projects early in the development cycle. The rejected projects should not negatively reflect upon the successful ones. Now you can measure the ROI of R&D. This is measured to see how long it takes to recuperate the expenses incurred from new product or service development.

$$RD\_ROI = \frac{(NNPS - NPE) - RDE}{RDE}$$

NNPS = Net New Product Sales

NPE = New Product Expenses

RDE = Research and Development Expense

RD_ROI = Research and Development Return on Investment

Tracking the ROI for research and development helps keep you from wasting money during new product development processes.

Price Metrics

We have found many times that the most underutilized metrics are pricing metrics. Companies look at their costs, sometimes look at what the competitor is doing, and then randomly pick a price. When sales drop, they either have a discount or run an advertising campaign without considering pricing. I once had a small class project in which the students performed marketing research for a small beauty salon. The students all found that sales were dropping at the salon because the pricing was too low. The owner continually dropped prices over the last couple of years, thinking that she was losing business because prices were too high. Instead, she had priced herself so low that customers saw her as a competitor for places like Supercuts and Great Clips, only more expensive. You must have metrics in place to examine what customers want to pay. As we already said, you need to make a profit, but you cannot use cost-plus pricing or continual discounting. Be sure to follow the steps outlined in Figure 3-27 when determining pricing.

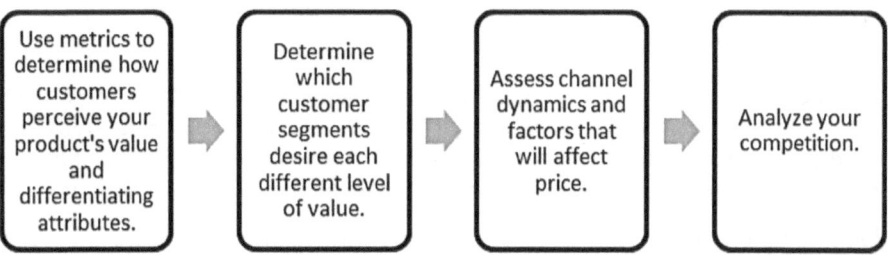

Figure 3-27. Price Metrics

Promotions Metrics

There are numerous categories of promotional expenditures and metrics. We have tried to highlight a few of the more important ones so that you can eliminate some waste in your marketing department.

Direct Marketing

There are many metrics that you can use to assess the effectiveness (and therefore the waste level) of marketing campaigns, such as response rate, conversion rate, and churn rate. We cover these in Chapter 4. However, we have a cautionary note here.

Consider the practice of sending out e-mail campaigns to a list of consumers based upon a past sale or a purchased list. Say you send out 20,000 e-mails. Only 8,000 people open the e-mail, which leads to about 1,000 people going to the company website. Of those 1,000 visitors, 250 end up purchasing your product. Now consider that each customer is worth $5,000. Is this campaign worth it? Many marketers would say that it absolutely is worth it because this generates over one million dollars in sales. But, how do the 19,750 people who were sent an e-mail and didn't buy the product feel? This is a common waste we see in multiple marketing methods. We seem to think that the time wasted by the receivers of our communications is worth the sale gained. Of course, the goal is to sell products or services, but what is the collateral damage caused by this selling technique? What if we need to get in touch with those customers for an important reason? Would those customers open our e-mails if we repeatedly send them solicitations?

It is also difficult to truly understand the value of a direct mail or e-mail campaign. Marketers tend to ignore the downstream value of a new customer when evaluating these campaigns. We know it is a lot less expensive to keep a current customer than it is to get a new one. Therefore, it's important that we understand customer lifetime value when evaluating new campaigns. You have to look at the holistic effects of campaigns on all customers, not just at the raw sales data.

Advertising

Much of the waste in advertising comes by using the wrong metrics. Advertising metrics are typically as follows: reach, frequency, cost per point, cost per thousand, gross rating points, impressions, media impressions, number of clips, target rating points, accuracy of coverage, and advertising value equivalency.

Unfortunately, these metrics do not tell you how many people paid any attention to your ad or whether the customer decides to purchase your products because of the ad. Therefore, the more important metrics are like the ones we described in the customer satisfaction and brand preference sections. Once an ad is run, it doesn't matter how many people sat mindlessly on their couch while the ad was on TV. What matters is how many people's behaviors changed. The first of these metrics is brand awareness. Technically, brand awareness is a combination of brand recall and brand recognition. This is now measured through a combination of three online metrics. The first is the impressions or how many times your content is viewed. This helps tell you how many people are interested in your advertisements. The second is customer engagement or how many brand-specific searches are made. This helps you know if consumers are looking or talking about your brand. The final metric is *reach*, or how many customers you are reaching with your content. If your campaign is online, all of these metrics can be measured using a tool like Google Analytics. If brand awareness is a critical element to your business, then you should be using these metrics to measure the effectiveness of your efforts. If you do not use online campaigns, you still need to capture data for awareness, engagement, understanding, and belief. It is just harder to come up with this data. Some tools that you can use are eye-tracking studies, newer biometrics studies, and the old fashioned starch tests.

Finally, you must assess which behaviors changed because of the promotion. Here, you are looking for metrics such as the following:

- Asked for more information
- Increased the amount of purchase
- Increased the frequency of purchase

- Purchased
- Recommended
- Subscribed

In essence, we suggest three layers of promotional metrics. First, you need to assess the typical measures such as reach and frequency. Do not stop here. It is easy to say to yourself, "Cable is so cheap, what do I have to lose?" A lot. If you come across with the wrong message to the wrong people, you can turn people away. You must make sure you understand the customer's needs and expectations. Based upon those, you can institute metrics for customer awareness and engagement. Finally, and most importantly, you have to tie promotional campaigns to actual behaviors. This can be done many ways; some are tools like surveys or split runs.

Conclusion

Perhaps the largest waste in marketing happens because marketers do not invest the proper time, money, and resources into the research. As mentioned, we are not talking about research for the sake of research. Typical approaches do not assess real consumer needs. Bringing in a random group of people for focus groups will never get to real needs. Instead, triangulate data from multiple processes to get a clear picture. Make sure some data is gathered from newer methods and media, such as big data and biometrics. Do not farm out your market research to a third party unless you are sure that they understand your unique products and customers.

Additionally, through your research, assess customer satisfaction and brand loyalty. These are the most important variables when considering a company's long-term sales. No funny advertising campaign can generate sales and make customers come back in the long run. Advertising is hugely ineffective, so stop overusing it. When considering social media, make sure that you are creating true value for your customers and not just doing what you think you need to do. Customers need to be satisfied before they will create positive word-of-mouth. You need to create satisfied customers, not a million dollar logo, to keep customers coming back.

Finally, measure, measure, and measure some more. Make sure you have metrics for all of your marketing activities. If you don't measure, you don't know what is effective and what is bringing more customers to you.

Waste Checklist

Marketing Checklist

*All "no" answers identify a potential opportunity for improvement.

Customer Needs and Market Research

Do you use newer methods of market research instead of relying on focus groups and surveys?	Yes ☐	No ☐
Do you utilize big data like Google Analytics?	Yes ☐	No ☐
Do you utilize competent market researchers with PhD-level skills to design and analyze your data?	Yes ☐	No ☐
Do you use multiple techniques when collecting customer data?	Yes ☐	No ☐
Do you employ marketing personnel capable of studying data using statistical methods to help make decisions?	Yes ☐	No ☐
Do you use data sources outside of the marketing department for market research?	Yes ☐	No ☐
Prior to beginning research, do you define and establish goals?	Yes ☐	No ☐
Prior to beginning research, do you conduct an information audit to see what data you have?	Yes ☐	No ☐
Prior to beginning research, do you know and understand what data is available through big data?	Yes ☐	No ☐
Prior to beginning research, do you gauge which methods, tools, and analytical procedures you will use?	Yes ☐	No ☐

Marketing Checklist

*All "No" answers identify a potential opportunity for improvement.

Product Decisions

Do you consider not cannibalizing your current products for the sake of growth?	Yes ☐ No ☐
Do you focus on your brand loyalty, product quality, and customer service to drive word of mouth?	Yes ☐ No ☐
Is part of your product strategy keeping employees happy to help drive good service?	Yes ☐ No ☐
Do you focus more energy on keeping current customers happy then pursuing new customers?	Yes ☐ No ☐
Does your brand have a personality that your customers feel good about?	Yes ☐ No ☐
Do you understand how your customers view your company?	Yes ☐ No ☐
Do you know what your customers care about? What value do you add?	Yes ☐ No ☐
Is your brand experience that you offer to customers consistent and reliable?	Yes ☐ No ☐
Do you encourage word of mouth through your marketing promotions?	Yes ☐ No ☐
Do you spend more money on providing a good product that building your brand?	Yes ☐ No ☐
Do you know the inputs that drive your customer loyalty?	Yes ☐ No ☐

Marketing Checklist

*All "no" answers identify a potential opportunity for improvement.

New Product Planning

Do you use a stage-gate process to help kill ideas before you waste resources on them?	Yes ☐ No ☐
Are your stage-gate decisions based upon unbiased information instead of gut instinct?	Yes ☐ No ☐
Do you have a well-defined product development process?	Yes ☐ No ☐
Are you constantly refining your product-development process based upon lessons learned?	Yes ☐ No ☐
Do you actively look for ways to shorten your product development cycle?	Yes ☐ No ☐
Do you have change-management procedures as part of your process?	Yes ☐ No ☐
Do you design your packaging to catch the attention of your customers?	Yes ☐ No ☐
Do you consider logistics needs when designing packaging?	Yes ☐ No ☐
Is your packaging designed to make it easy for the customer to use the product?	Yes ☐ No ☐

Marketing Checklist

*All "No" answers identify a potential opportunity for improvement.

Promotion, Price, and Place

Do you use promotion activities that reach your target customers rather than rely on traditional TV, print, and outdoor? Yes ☐ No ☐

Do you price your products based upon the value to the customer rather than the cost of the product? Yes ☐ No ☐

Is your pricing strategy consistent with your desired brand image? Yes ☐ No ☐

Do your discounts that you offer provide a real return on the investment? Yes ☐ No ☐

Are the locations of your company and suppliers based upon business and customer needs? Yes ☐ No ☐

Metrics

Do you have metrics to measure the effectiveness and efficiency of your marketing operations? Yes ☐ No ☐

Are your marketing metrics relevant to business performance? Yes ☐ No ☐

Do you establish baselines to measure the effectiveness of your activities? Yes ☐ No ☐

Do you measure customer satisfaction, expectations, and value? Yes ☐ No ☐

Do you measure brand preference and why consumers repurchase? Yes ☐ No ☐

CHAPTER 4

Sales

Waste by Not Treating Sales as a Science

> *Nobody counts the number of ads you run; they just remember the impression you make.*
>
> —William Bernbach

There are many misconceptions about the entire sales field and sales department being an enormous source of waste. When we think of sales, many of us think of the guy in the business suit, sitting on the plane, having a drink on the way home after making maintenance calls to several customers. Perhaps the biggest misconception is that all you need to do to be a salesperson is have great people skills—that somehow this image we just portrayed is who a salesperson should be, that guy flying around the country, wooing his customers.

For decades, salespeople have been the folks who are extremely charismatic, those who can play a game of golf, and those who can wine and dine clients. No one really assumed that you needed a college degree to sell. And as for sales managers, they were typically selected from the sales ranks, with the best sales reps being offered a promotion into management. Other than adapting to new sales force automation, there was really no need for salespeople to update their skill sets or use statistics during the sales process. All of these practices are outdated and wrong.

Perhaps the greatest cause of waste in sales is treating sales like it has always been treated. By that, we mean falling into these myths just described, by hiring those "veteran reps" who have a book of contacts and who are good "people" people. As we have said so many times before, there is a very real need for analytics in every department. Sales, especially, has been undergoing a Gestalt shift in recent years. When it's done right, it is incredibly scientific and analytical. When it's done poorly, it becomes a game of throwing as much stuff against the wall in hopes that something sticks.

Prime Areas of Waste

One of the biggest sources of waste in sales occurs from not treating sales like manufacturing. Just as in manufacturing, you have to understand and calculate sales-force productivity. This concept is so misunderstood that even in academic literature, the concepts of *sales performance* and *sales productivity* are incorrectly used interchangeably. Productivity and performance are impacted by different things and create different results. That is why we provide a description of sales productivity—to help you avoid waste associated with it. Through this analysis, you can learn whether you are overstaffed or understaffed and whether you need to hire more salespeople. There are many misconceptions about hiring in sales, proliferated by hiring agencies that want to make a lot of money doing things like personality testing. We talk about why this is typically a wasteful process and how to hire using more scientific approaches.

Another effect of not treating sales like a science is the lack of value-stream mapping in sales. Once again, just like in manufacturing, you should understand how these processes occur and how you can make them work better. In addition to this, we also cover sales expenses. Such an enormous part of a company's budget is devoted to sales expenses that it is critical to limit the expenses to avoid waste. Sometimes things like trade shows or travel are necessary, but many times they just create waste. We cover these topics later in this chapter.

Sales Productivity

Sales jobs make up almost 11 percent of all occupations in the United States.[1] When you factor out all the non-business related jobs that the U.S. Bureau of Labor Statistics tracks, such as manufacturing, mining, construction, food service, law enforcement, and others, sales accounts for well over 50 percent of business occupations. In fact, as a college professor, I tell my students the interesting statistic that 50 percent of all college graduates, no matter the major, go into some kind of sales.[2]

Why is this the case? Is sales that important? Does it take that many salespeople to sell products and services? As we show in this chapter, sales *is* that important. But it certainly doesn't need that many human resources! It ends up needing an excessive amount of resources because it's so poorly managed. Take academic research as an example. (This isn't a perfect example, because many times academics are busy researching topics that are of absolutely no

---

[1] Bureau of Labor Statistics, U.S. Department of Labor, Occupational Employment and Wages, March 27, 2012, http://www.bls.gov/news.release/archives/ocwage_03272012.pdf.
[2] Sales Education Foundation, SEF Annual Report, 2011, http://saleseducationfoundation.org/pdfs/sef_annual_2011.pdf.

interest or relevance to managers, but the point is still a good one.) There is absolutely not one single study of academic research that has ever looked at what "sales productivity" is. With all the volumes of research in the manufacturing realm related to productivity, you would think that it would be a no-brainer to say, "If 11 percent of the total U.S. workforce is in sales, does it matter how productive they are?" But, it hasn't been done. Many people, academics and practitioners alike, assume that productivity should be measured in much the same way manufacturing productivity is measured. By that, you look at the output per hour (or other time period) of a worker. The worker who makes ten widgets per hour must be more productive than the worker who makes five widgets per hour. Note that quality is a different metric.

Based upon that rationale, does that mean that the salesperson who sells $2 million in product in one year is more productive than the salesperson who sells $1 million in product the same year? Absolutely not. The sales rep who sold $2 million might have worked 80 hours a week, while the rep who sold $1 million may have worked only 30 hours. Also, this does not take into account different territories, customers, and buying or selling processes.

Unfortunately, an even worse metric that is perhaps more commonly used is the amount of time the salesperson spent with the customer. Any quick search of Google will show a multitude of articles on this subject and how to get sales reps to be in front of the customer more. Is the sales rep who spends 35 percent of her time every week with customers more productive than the sales rep who spends 25 percent of his time every week with customers?

Note As much as 87 percent of your sales budget could be complete waste, likely because you don't have an accurate measure of sales productivity.

In manufacturing, it is easy to say these two workers are on the exact same machine, making the exact same widget, and therefore productivity statistics translate rather easily. You cannot really do this in sales because there are way too many other intervening variables. For example, differences exist among customers, territories, and the products that each sales rep sells. Moreover, note the exception that was made about manufacturing. Productivity is not the same thing as quality. Obviously, in manufacturing, you want to increase productivity while at least maintaining the same quality level or even improving quality. How does this work in sales? These days, the sales rep does not have to be "in front of the customer" to make a sale. The customer could see a sales presentation and the order might be sent in days or weeks later. With good customer service and follow up, orders can continue at increasing rates with no direct effort from the salesperson. Sales today is much more about strategy and analytics than in days past. The most productive salesperson is the one who spends more time analyzing accounts, and less time courting them.

Chapter 4 | Sales

It is these types of analyses and questions that companies rarely consider when they're trying to reduce waste in sales. In this day and age of downsizing and concerns over efficiency and productivity, it is simply astounding that sales productivity is not more carefully considered.

The best measure of sales productivity is sales per hour. How can one rep sell $1 million in 40 hours, while the other rep sells only $500,000? Or, why can two reps sell $1 million, but one works 40 hours while the other needs to work 70 to accomplish the same sales? The Organisation for Economic Co-operation and Development (OECD) defines workforce productivity as "the ratio of a volume measure of output to a volume measure of input."[3] Thus, worker productivity is typically measured as:

$$\text{Worker productivity} = \text{Worker productivity} = \frac{\text{volume measure of output}}{\text{measure of labor input use}}$$

Therefore, in sales:

$$\text{Sales person productivity} = \frac{\text{sales}}{\text{hours worked}}$$

There is still a great room for potential variability in interpreting this simple equation. Sales could be in units or dollars; it could incorporate paid orders, canceled orders, and other factors. Therefore, many units must be measured. Then, hours worked must include a broad enough time measurement to be meaningful. It is easy to know how much a factory worker in front of a machine produces in one hour. However, because sales have seasonal, weekly, and even daily fluctuations, those should be taken into account. Also, productivity will likely be drastically different based upon the strength of the territory. There are many other factors, like those discussed previously. The sales rep's time must be measured while she's doing all daily activities that could lead to a sale. This way, sales per exact activity can be traced.

In the sales productivity studies that I have done, the best measure has typical been:

Sales Productivity

= ((Sales in dollars) / ((Total Territory Potential)
/ (Number of Reps in Territory)))
/ (Total Hours Worked)

---

[3]OECD, 2001, http://www.oecd.org/std/productivity-stats/2352458.pdf.

This formula typically accounts for the tremendous differences across sales territories by looking at sales as a percentage of total market potential and then separating by number of reps in the territory. Once the figure is calculated for each rep, a sales manager can have a better sense of who is the most efficient rep and then how to better hire, fire, promote, and motivate. These are all discussed in later sections.

However, it is these types of analyses and questions that we do not think are analyzed enough in sales. As mentioned, the typical approach is to hire the veterans with industry experience and throw them out there. It is no wonder that it takes 11 percent of the U.S. workforce to produce mediocre results. In a recent survey of 1,500 companies, sales managers listed their top three priorities to improve in the next year: (1) increase revenue, (2) capture new accounts, and (3) increase sales effectiveness.[4] We assert that if number three happens, numbers one and two will follow. Therefore, sales managers and company managers have to become more analytical about their sales departments. Once each sales rep's productivity is understood, the sales manager can begin to think about the subsequent decisions.

Bad Hiring and Firing

Thirteen percent of a company's sales force brings in 80 percent of the revenue.[5] Does that mean that approximately 87 percent of your sales budget and resources is waste? Not exactly, but it is very clear that many companies have an extremely high number of ineffective, unproductive salespeople. In terms of sales management, the average tenure of a VP of Sales is 24 to 32 months.[6] We typically don't see turnover like that in other areas. Why is there so much waste, ineffectiveness, and turnover in sales and sales management? First is the matter of simply not measuring and assessing sales force productivity, as discussed. Second is the issue of bad hiring and firing.

As we discuss at more length in Chapter 5, the hiring process is difficult for employees in any position within the company. But it is especially difficult in sales for a few reasons. There is an enormous shortage of the number of highly skilled professional sellers. By this, we emphasize the word "skilled." So many people are smooth talkers and are great with people. But, most of these veterans do not understand the analytical side to sales, both in terms of the analytics required to assess each account and the requirements of the

---

[4]CSO Insights, "Sales Performance Optimizations: 2012 Key Trends Analysis," 2012, http://news.citrixonline.com/wp-content/uploads/2012/02/2012-Sales-Performance-Optimization-Study-.pdf.
[5]Bosworth, M. and J. Holland, *Customer Centric Selling* (New York, NY: McGraw Hill, 2004). p. 8.
[6]Baldwin, H. "The Strange Case of the Vanishing Sales VP," *Selling Power Magazine,* 2010, p. 34–37.

sales process today. You would never hire an engineer to do brain surgery, nor would you hire an accountant to design a building. It is so unbelievably difficult to break free of the mindset that sales is a science, not an art. Since we literally have over 100 years of hiring unqualified salespeople, many of whom have succeeded, it is very difficult to recognize that there is a better way to go about sales. These outdated, inefficient, and extremely wasteful approaches must die.

Consider the cost of a bad hire in sales. The investment to hire and train a new salesperson ranges from $75,000 for a tele-salesperson to more than $300,000 for a more senior sales position.[7] Think about how much money is lost because of an ineffective or bad sales rep in the field. They are losing accounts and perhaps causing some customers to leave. Then, after they leave the job, the waste rises even more as a new salesperson needs to be trained.

Most companies will admit that they do not fully understand how to hire sales reps. Figure 4-1 demonstrates that only 5.7 percent of companies think their hiring practices exceed their expectations, while 40 percent say they meet their expectations.[8] Almost half know how poor their practices are.

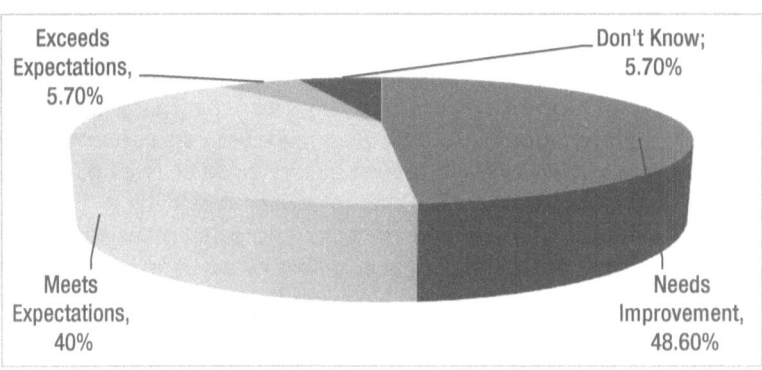

Figure 4-1. Satisfaction with Hiring Practices

Let's take a look at some of the wasteful hiring practices that occur specifically in sales.

---

[7]The HR Chally Group. "The Route to the Summit," *The Chally World Class Sales Excellence Research Report,* 2007.
[8]CSO Insights, 2010, retrieved from http://www.csoinsights.com/Topics/Hiring-and-Retention.

Wasteful Hiring Practice #1: Building a Personality Typology of the Star Salesperson

Given how most companies don't understand how to hire sales reps, of course everyone is concerned with more effective recruiting. However, more attention to the process does not necessarily correlate with more success. Most companies look for candidates who share common traits with their superstar sellers. (Many of the companies that I have done consulting for have done this very thing.) They have the top 5–10 percent of their sales force take extensive personality assessments. Then, they create a new assessment tool based upon these traits of the top performers. Finally, the company hires only candidates who possess these same traits.

This method is so wasteful. First, you have to consider the enormous amount of money given to the testing service to develop the new test and perform the testing. In fact, it was the companies who sell their personality testing services that created this bad idea in the beginning. Second, consider the errors within this method. For a number of reasons, it is very difficult to identify the unique characteristics of top salespeople. Unfortunately, the superstars are anomalies and the traits they share might not produce success in other candidates. There are so many other issues—just think about a few. Do those top candidates have the best territories? Do those candidates produce consistent, long-term success? Do those candidates mesh well with their managers and might fail with a different manager? It is for these reasons, among many others, that this hiring method is extremely wasteful.

Wasteful Hiring Practice #2: Having No Strategy

We will be brief here because this practice is highlighted in Chapter 5. Many companies hire poorly because they do not understand the strategic hiring process. Just like with other business decisions, hiring decisions are often based on "gut instincts" instead of on analytical procedures and techniques. These decisions are frequently made utilizing the outdated tools of the past, as discussed in the next section.

Wasteful Hiring Practice #3: Using Traditional Hiring Techniques

Like strategy, this problem is also covered in Chapter 5. Suffice it to say that research has shown that the methods most commonly used to screen and hire candidates are actually less predictive of success than the flip of a coin.[9] Interviews, job shadows, looking at education and experience, checking

---

[9] Hunter, J & Hunter, R. "Validity and Utility of Alternative Predictors of Job Performance," *Psychological Bulletin*, 1984, 96 (1). p. 72–98.

references, and other mainstay recruiting tasks are not valid. In fact, as can be seen in the data in Figure 4-2, every selection tool commonly used, except personality testing, is less accurate than flipping a coin, which provides a 50/50 accuracy rate. (Please note that this is not personality testing as described previously.) Hiring is one of the most wasteful processes in businesses, yet businesses keep using the same approach because, "this is the way we have always done it." How many of you have stepped back and thought about reengineering your hiring process?

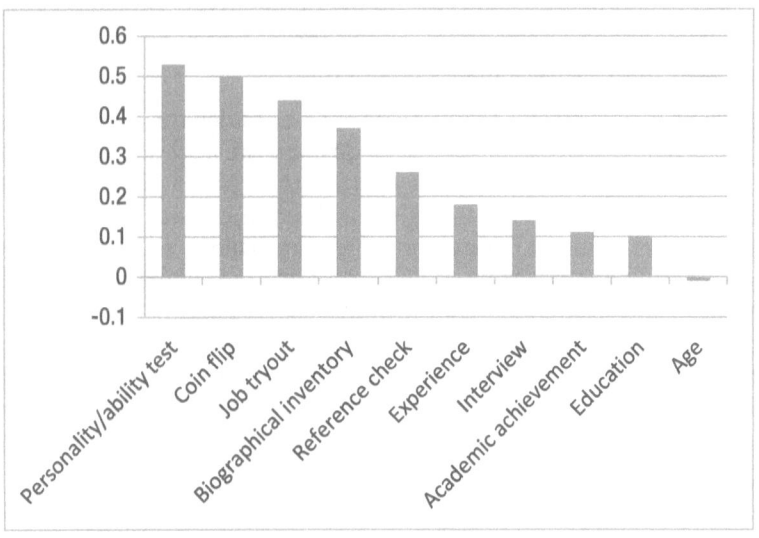

Figure 4-2. Hiring Methods and their Accuracy Rates. (*Source:* Hunter, J & Hunter, R. "Validity and Utility of Alternative Predictors of Job Performance," *Psychological Bulletin*, 1984, 96 (1). p. 72–98.)

Wasteful Hiring Practice #4: Recruiting/Promoting from Within or from the Same Industry

One common approach is to promote from within. We are not saying this is bad, but it doesn't always work in sales. Companies look at their best sales reps and try to promote them into sales manager roles. This is probably the single biggest reason that the average sales manager tenure is 24-32 months. While salespeople need to be analytical, that role does not require the analytical and statistical abilities that a sales manager needs. To be effective, a sales manager has to understand enough statistics to be able to create sales forecasts and has to be analytical enough to develop quotas, compensation plans, and sales territories. Likewise, sales managers need to be able to calculate more sophisticated equations and models, such as Customer Lifetime Value

(CLV) calculations. Typically, what happens in the hiring process is that the best salesperson gets the promotion, but does not understand these statistics. He "wings it" for a while and then quits or gets replaced when results are poor.

Another extremely common hiring tactic in sales is to search for a candidate who has "3-5 years of industry experience." Likely because this is the way things have always been done. An interesting study was performed by Gallup, in which they actually found a negative correlation between same industry experience and success.[10] In fact, in my personal consulting experiences with companies, I almost always find a negative correlation between years of experience and sales performance and productivity. Perhaps this is because having same industry experience typically makes someone "set in their ways" and less able to think in new, creative ways. Further, the longer someone has been in an industry, the less coachable they become. They are also more likely to be burned out.

Note In sales especially, having same industry experience creates waste!

No/Weak Training

After the right candidates are selected, regardless of the skills that they walk in the door with, new sales employees should be trained. Then, training should be continued throughout their career as customers, products, technologies, and sales processes change.

Many times this training is thought of as waste. Companies try to minimize it. If a sales rep is in training, not in the field, they are not making money. However, most organizations realize an average ROI for the typical training program within six months. The real waste is in not providing any sort of training at all, not doing enough training, or utilizing unqualified trainers.

But as we said, sales training is often considered a waste. And in fact, research shows that within 60 days of a typical training event, 87 percent of the skills gained have been lost by the sales force.[11] Even more concerning than the "stickiness" of sales training is the question of how applicable the training is to the needs of a particular sales force. A fundamental reason why sales training increasingly fails to deliver its expected results is that it is simply the wrong training from the start.

---

[10] Phelps, G. "Creating Paths to Success," *Gallup Management Journal*, 2010, retrieved from http://gmj.gallup.com/content/286/creating-paths-success.aspx.
[11] The HR Chally Group. "The Route to the Summit," *The Chally World Class Sales Excellence Research Report*, 2007.

Frankly, sales training programs are often viewed as generic one-size-fits-all cures to every selling malady. Not enough consideration is usually given to the specific business needs of the sales force and their specific selling challenges. Much sales training is done by sales training firms. They generally provide generic, canned programs that focus on very basic skills, like questioning and objections handling. Although these are important skills, given the changes in the sales environment, salespeople should be more focused on the roles of the market analyst and planner, selling team coordinator, customer service provider, information gatherer, sales forecaster, and market cost analyzer. These skills are rarely covered in these generic programs.

Furthermore, the single biggest difference between top performers and poor performers is listening skills. Eighty percent of the selling process should be devoted to understanding customers' needs; studies show an average 50 percent error rate in terms of salespeople understanding their customer's expected performance levels.[12] In fact, 47 percent of salespeople admit to having no clue about their customer's biggest concerns. In order to completely understand customer needs, salespeople must have analytical skills. They must be able to research customers to identify needs. They must utilize their Customer Relationship Management (CRM) software to collect this data, both pre- and post-sales. Then, they must use this information to determine the right questions to ask and listen intently while questioning the customer. This skill set is beyond what is typically taught to salespeople.

Only an average of 10 percent of sales training is devoted to questioning and listening skills, whereas 40 percent of sales training is designed to increase product knowledge. And while 81.5 percent of firms provide product knowledge, only 51.5 percent provide communication skills training. Salespeople are also not currently being trained on how to listen to the needs of today's very diverse buyers, such as production engineers, quality assurance personnel, design engineers, and other technical staff that makes up the buying center. Thus, any sales-training program must devote lots of time to listening and analytical skills.

■ **Note** Training should focus on analytical skills aimed at researching and understanding the customer.

---

[12] The HR Chally Group, "The Chally World Class Sales Excellence Research Report," 2007. HR Chally Press.

Any good sales training program is going to cost a lot of money, and many managers think of this as a waste. Continually developing and updating the skills of the sales force is one of the most critically important elements of the future revenue of a company. Even though it sounds like sales training can be a waste, and many times it is, not performing the training is a much larger source of waste. Having sales reps in the field who are unqualified wastes the company's money in terms of sales expenses and labor, and wastes tons of future money in lost revenue. The sales rep is the front line/face of the company. Above all others, those who interact with the customer must be thoroughly knowledgeable.

We discuss training in Chapter 5. The issues here are the same. Any good training program first begins with a needs and gap analysis. Then, the training should be built to fill those gaps. Many times, sales managers will say, "sales are down, I must need training." Then they will call a sales trainer and set up a program. This skips the critical step of finding out what is truly going on. Data must be gathered and analyzed. Why are sales down? What is really going on? Is it a volume issue, pricing issue, or a customer-satisfaction issue? Are salespeople making too many phone calls and not spending enough time researching? None of these questions can be answered without data. This data is necessary to find out what the training should cover, who should be included in the training, and how the training should be conducted.

Training is an inherently perishable good. As soon as salespeople leave training sessions, their new knowledge and skills begin to deteriorate. The only defense against the rapid and constant evaporation of the training investment is to further invest in reinforcing new skills. Whether the training is supplemented with follow-up sessions or reinforced through management coaching, most people need repeated exposure to new information in order to retain it.

Further, the more content packed into a training session, the more reinforcement is subsequently required. To address this fact, organizations should move away from large training sessions (like annual sales meetings or new hire orientations), where a year's worth of knowledge is dumped onto salespeople. Instead, just-in-time training should be implemented, whereby very specific skills are taught only as they are needed by the sales force. Sales managers can know when this information is needed only if they are continually gathering data on their sales force.

By providing the training in close proximity to the time the salespeople actually need the skills, an organization can improve the likelihood that the learning will stick. Additionally, you should provide training in smaller, more digestible chunks, so the salespeople can concentrate on mastering one or two skills before moving on to others. Ideally, companies should train in two-day sessions every quarter. By providing timely and more focused training, based on actual, hard data, top sales forces are achieving better training outcomes and dramatically increasing their salespeople's capabilities.

Finally, to ensure that sales training is not wasteful, the sales manager should measure the sales force on many dimensions before the training, immediately after the training, and 6 and 12 months post-training. In sales, at a minimum, we suggest gathering the following information about every sales rep at each of these time intervals:

- Total sales volume by unit
- Total sales volume by dollars
- Percentage of market potential
- Sales expenses/costs
- Number of orders
- Average size ($) of orders
- Batting average (orders/calls)
- Number of canceled orders
- Number of new accounts
- Customer conversion from lead to first-time buyer
- Customer conversion from first-time buyer to repeat buyer
- Number of lost accounts
- Percentage of time meeting quota
- Customer satisfaction

While it is impossible to calculate the waste from not training, using these data points, you can calculate ROI for sales training and ensure that the training you are doing is not wasteful.

No Sales Process/Value-Stream Mapping

We've said it many times, but one of the largest areas of waste in the sales department is failing to use science and analytics. Just as processes are set up, measured, and improved in manufacturing, sales should have processes as well. Both the sales-management function and sales force should have their own distinct processes. Formal sales processes provide the sales force direction in terms of "how to sell," provide sales management with a framework from which to manage, and enable measurement and continuous improvement of the sales force's performance.

The idea behind value-stream mapping is that you map out every step that adds value in the eyes of the customer. Two main objectives are then accomplished. First, all ancillary steps that do not add value can be identified and eliminated. Activities such as maintenance calls with no measureable goals and paperwork with no purpose can be cut. Second, processes can be analyzed in order to speed them up or find and eliminate bottlenecks.

> **Note** Failing to treat sales management and sales processes analytically creates waste.

CSO Insights routinely conducts studies of organizations, and in their recent study on sales processes, the following results were found for companies that have sales processes in place (refer to Figure 4-3). It is important to note that only 25.7 percent of the companies surveyed actually had "formal" sales processes in place, whereas 42.2 percent had informal processes in place. The data is still very telling; clearly, sales processes make an impact on a company's bottom line.

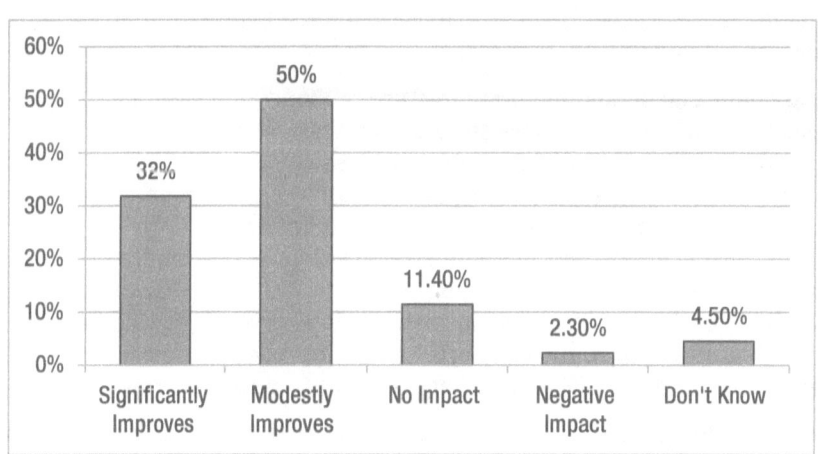

Figure 4-3. Sales Processes Impact on Sales Performance. (*Source: CSO Insights*, "Sales Processes," 2013, http://www.csoinsights.com/Publications/Shop/Sales-Performance-Optimization.)

When looking at this data, 82 percent of CSOs believe that sales processes improve performance. It is very likely that the other 18 percent either don't understand how to set up and implement sales processes correctly or do not have the resources to do so. If this is true, then why do 75 percent of businesses not even have sales processes? Again, because it is so easy to look at the way things have always been done. Sales has always been a group of "people people" who just aggressively schmooze customers. This outdated thinking is incredibly wasteful.

Steps to Create Sales Processes

There are several necessary steps a company must take to establish and implement formal sales processes. First, companies can begin by analyzing best sales practices in other companies. As we discuss throughout this book, benchmarking can produce bad results if it's done incorrectly. This is because every company's processes should be designed around the very specific ways a customer buys products. Customers in different industries rarely buy in the same way. However, seeing how other companies do things can help jump-start the decision-making process. In other words, you would never want to photocopy another company's sales process map, but it can be a source of ideas to get your processes going.

Next, the sales manager should conduct value-stream mapping, or sales "blueprinting," in order to understand how the sales process flows through the entire sales pipeline. Part of this is to define the parts of the sales processes and understand how they fit together. Likewise, when examining the processes, you should work to ensure that sales planning also includes information about a multitude of variables, such as materials, labor, equipment, logistics, and anything else that affects the process.

Some things that should be formalized are prospecting, customer analysis, and presentations. Every single task should have a metric associated with it so that you can measure the sales processes as if they were production processes. You will have waste, especially if you do not track the productivity of each step with each rep. Then, you should focus on continuous improvement principles, stressing important outcome variables such as customer satisfaction or customer retention. Remember from Chapter 2 that $Y=f(X)$, so you need to have a true understanding of what sales activities drive the outcomes that you want. With these steps, you can begin to develop sales processes that help the organization become efficient and effective, with much less waste.

Figure 4-4 demonstrates an example of a value-stream map for the request for proposal (RFP) quoting process in a fictitious company. This is an example of an extremely inefficient map. But, from this, you can begin to see where your weak areas are. By examining your map and then outlining the processes and their associated times, you can quantify the inefficiencies. As you can see, there are many bottlenecks to the process. The sales rep might be waiting as long as 1,440 minutes for a response to a quote. If this organization is one in which RFPs were standardized, much of this time could be eliminated. Figure 4-5 shows the same company with a new value-stream map, after the inefficient processes are eliminated.

Eliminating Waste in Business   145

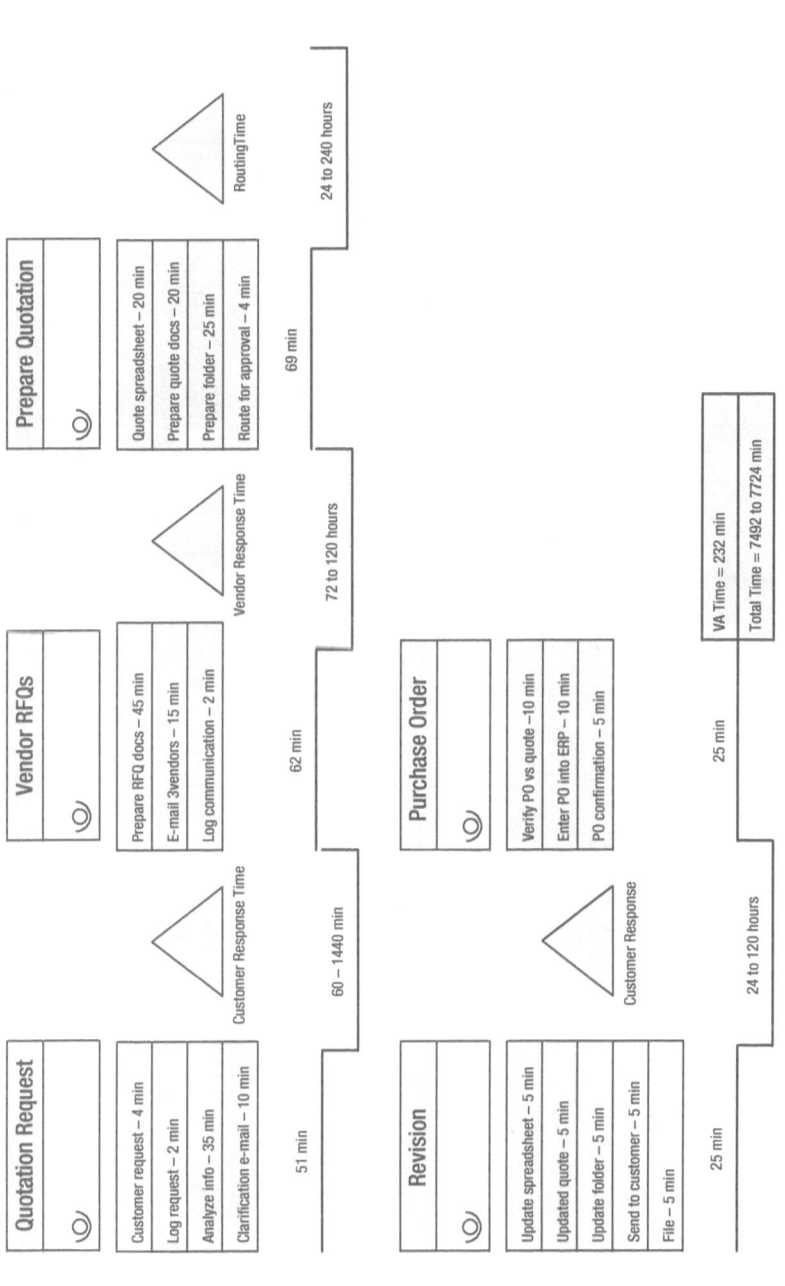

Figure 4-4. Sales Value-Stream Map with Inefficiencies

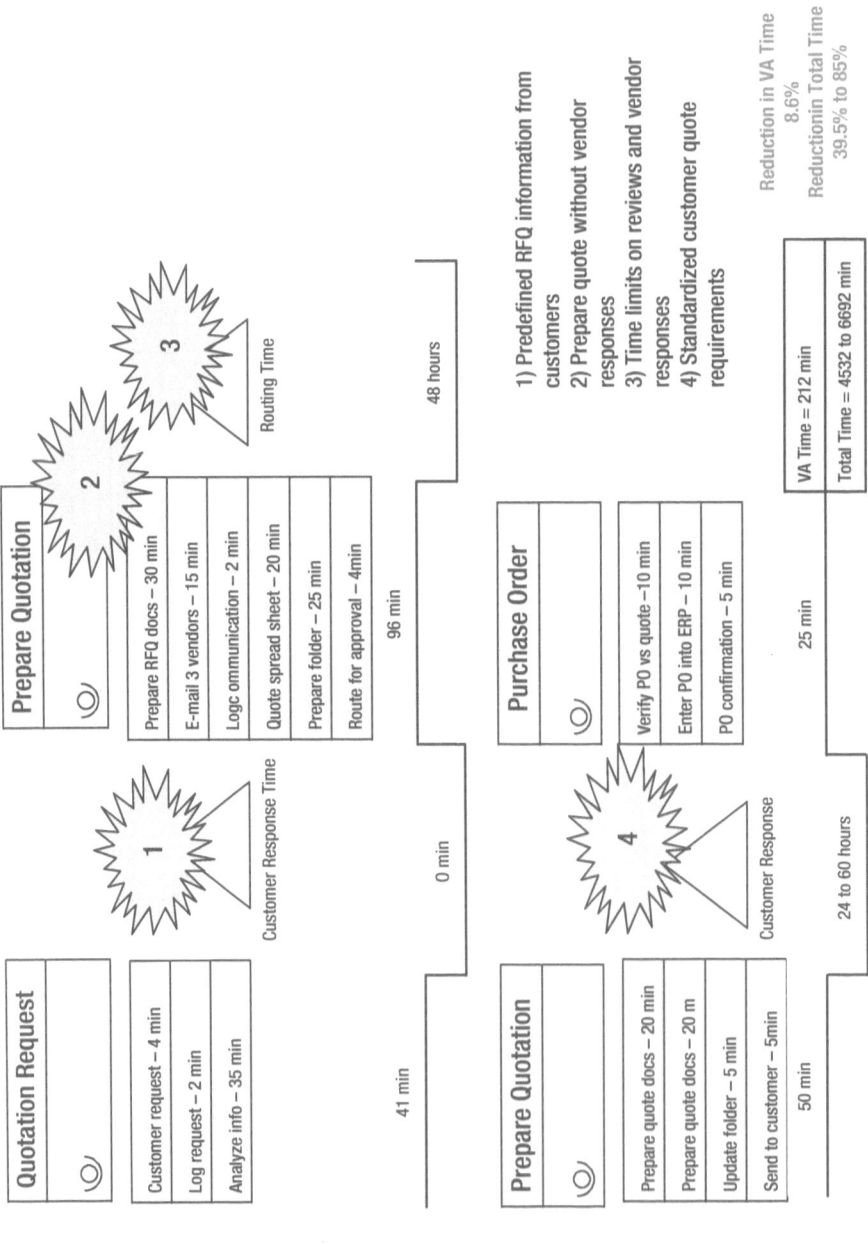

Figure 4-5. Sales Value-Stream Map with Inefficiencies Eliminated

Many times when the map is created, the manager can see processes that are a complete waste. Current research shows that sales reps try to spend more time with customers, when in fact that doesn't add value. We think everyone just assumes that the rep who spends the most time with the customer has the highest sales. In fact, if you search online, there are studies everywhere about where sales reps spend their time. Do your sales reps spend ten percent of their time in front of a customer? How about 30 percent? Does that equate to higher sales?

When you think about sales like you would manufacturing with distinct processes, think about how crazy it is to worry about time with the customer. As described, if a worker can manufacture 100 widgets an hour, we assume that he is more productive than the worker who can make 50 widgets an hour. We would never say that the worker who spends seven hours a day in front of a machine is more productive than the worker who spends five hours a day in front of a machine. So, why have sales managers and sales academics alike become so obsessed with the idea of time in front of the customer?

To some extent, it does make sense. Obviously, if you take an extremely inefficient salesperson who cannot get their paperwork done in a reasonable time and doesn't plan travel well, they will likely have limited time with the customer and low sales. But, on the other hand, think of the two categories of biggest waste that sales reps have with the customers: the maintenance call and entertaining.

We now know how wasteful entertaining in sales is. Wining-and-dining, golf, cold-calling, and other wasteful processes should go. Now it's all about strategy! The sales rep who is the most productive spends the most time researching the account. Through this, they add value. They add value by not calling on unqualified accounts. They add value by researching answers to questions ahead of time and not wasting precious time with the client asking questions that can be found on Google. As described, every process must add value. This benefits the company and the customer. The value-stream map helps achieve these benefits.

Through the map, you should be able to identify the value-add and ROI for every process. This will take a lot of time when you do it for the first time. You may even need to hire someone who is a sales efficiency expert the first time. Once the map has been created, you can begin to eliminate waste in sales, and as a consequence will likely start making your customer happier with increased service levels.

Note Map every sales process. Eliminate or reduce steps that do not add value. Continually revise your map as your processes become more efficient.

Not Treating *Every* Marketing Activity Like the Sales Process

Here the waste is not in sales, but in forgetting how important sales is. Most everyone involved in sales has referred to some form of sales process like the one shown in Figure 4-6.

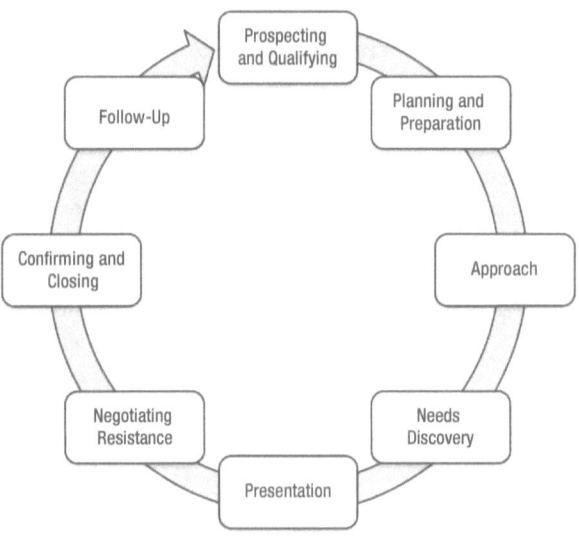

Figure 4-6. Sales Process

We encourage you to treat every single marketing activity like a sales process. Imagine running your typical advertisement. You think you want to build brand awareness. Then, you look at your budget to determine media vehicles and frequency. Hopefully, you do some thinking about what media your audience watches/reads. Then, you run the ad and probably do some rudimentary tracking. However, we suggest that much of the waste created in marketing, as discussed in the last chapter, would be avoided if every marketing process was treated like the sales process.

In order to this, you need to start your advertising campaign by prospecting and qualifying—*qualifying* being the keyword. As we have said numerous times, you do not want to use the "throw the spaghetti against the wall and see what sticks" philosophy. In sales, you should not simply buy a lead list and cold call like crazy. Cold calling doesn't work. Instead, you want to do as much research as possible. Here, just think about not allowing yourself to move forward in the process until you have qualified every account. This is where sales reps spend most of their time. Do you spend almost all your marketing time doing research? Then, do you prepare a needs identification analysis prior to running that campaign? Again, the idea is to understand why your customers buy and what benefits you should stress in the ad. Then, there should be follow-up to close the sale and follow-up to keep customers brand-loyal. These processes are all just normal parts of the process in sales. It is really scary that they are not in all marketing activities.

As I was driving to work a few weeks ago, I saw an ad for my university's basketball team on the back of a metro bus. It was as dirty as could be, barely viewable, covered in a gray sheet of road salt. Who attends my university? Do they attend because of the basketball team? Do they typically see metro bus ads? Do they equate a university education with the dirtiness of roads and cars during a Northern Ohio winter? The answers to these questions are quite obvious. Again, we went through the entire process of advertising waste in Chapter 3, but please think about the sales process in all your activities.

> **Note** You should establish sales processes not just for sales, but for all marketing activities.

Sales Expenses

Executives spend almost three times more on sales and expenses than they do on advertising expenses.[13] The average company spends 10 percent, and some industries spend as much as 40 percent of their total sales revenues on sales expenses.[14] Just as we discussed in regard to sales force productivity, it seems odd that so many resources, in terms of both people and money, are needed to support the sales function. The biggest sales expenses are labor costs, travel, and entertaining. There are other costs that can be very large, such as technology and supplies, but we address those in later chapters. Here we focus on the three big expenses: sales travel, entertaining, and trade shows.

Sales Travel and Entertaining

If you look at the raw numbers on sales travel, you will see that companies that spend more on travel have marginally higher sales. These studies are generally poorly conceived. Is the travel creating the higher sales, or do companies with higher sales tend to expand their travel budgets and therefore travel more?

---

[13]Zoltners, A. A., P. Sinha and S. E. Lorimer, "Sales Force Effectiveness: A Framework for Researchers and Practitioners," *Journal of Personal Selling and Sales Management,* 2008, 28(2), p. 115–131. (Special issue on enhancing sales force productivity.)
[14]Ibid.

Some studies show that travel went way down during the recession of 2008 and 2009, and therefore, sales went down. Was it the travel or the recession that caused sales to go down? Also, we don't know of any published studies that have looked at the ROI difference between travel and electronic contact mechanisms.

I currently have a very large study underway that looks at all the variables that impact sales productivity and performance.[15] I have yet to find any data that shows that travel increases sales. As mentioned, the most important variables for boosting productivity and performance are analytical skills and time spent researching and analyzing accounts. Obviously, you do want to spend time with your reps. You cannot ignore your customers and have high sales.

However, in order to make sure travel budgets are most effectively used, you need to make sure reps visit with customers only when there is a specific, measureable goal associated with that contact. Customers will be more satisfied and respect you more if you respect their time. They will see you and/or your reps more as the solution-providers you should be than if you are there simply to sell products and services when they need them. Additionally, most people appreciate documents being sent via e-mail and demonstrations being made through presentation software online, rather than taking their whole day to escort a visiting sales rep.

While the principle of reciprocity is real (the more time you spend with someone, the more they feel obliged to give you time or something else back), in this day and age, you will not be successful for long because of your ability to bribe clients with golf and steaks. This is especially true now, for example, given the enormous fall in people who play golf. Now, only about 8 percent of Americans play golf in any capacity. Only around 1.2 percent of Americans consider themselves active golfers.[16] The bulk of these players are in their late 40s and 50s. Workers, especially of generation X and Y, are just simply too busy to engage in recreational activities, especially during work hours. As a sales rep, you might actually offend someone by suggesting an entertainment activity. They could be thinking, "it must be nice to have such an easy job where you have so much free time." There is a small percentage of workers that still appreciates and even expects to be wined and dined. This number is very small and shrinking every day.

---

[15]Orr, Linda, "Sales Force Productivity: Definition, Measurement, and Determinants," working paper, 2014.
[16]Fitzpatrick, Michael, "Golf's Decline in America: Work/Life Balance Is the True Culprit," *The Bleacher Report,* March 29, 2011, http://bleacherreport.com/articles/648286-decline-of-golf-in-america-worklife-balance-is-the-true-culprit.

Save travel for the most important events. This is typically the initial needs discovery and presentation portions of a sale. Send only those reps and employees who play a critical role in the sale. As you'll read in Chapter 7, your reps can fly coach and stay at reasonably cheap motels. Get out of the mindset that you travel in sales because it is what you have always done. It doubtfully boosts sales.

Note Travel does not increase sales. Only travel when it's absolutely critical to the bottom line, when you have a specific measureable objective, and when other forms of technology cannot be substituted.

Trade Shows

Trade shows can be a tremendously profitable venture or a black hole of expense. (Unfortunately, from what we have seen, they are typically the latter.) The Center for Exhibition Industry Research (http://www.ceir.org/) provides valuable research data about the impact of trade shows. Some of these facts are shown here:

- The average company allocates 21-32 percent of its total marketing budget to events and exhibiting (more than any other marketing category).
- More than $24 *billion* is spent annually by U.S. exhibitors for trade shows.
- Seven out of ten trade show attendees plan to buy at least one product.
- Seventy-six percent of attendees asked for quotes and 26 percent signed purchase orders at trade shows.
- Seventy-two percent of show visitors say the show influenced their buying decision.
- Sixty-four percent of attendees tell at least six other people about the trade show.
- It costs 22 percent less to contact a potential buyer at a show than it does using traditional field sales calls.
- Yet 98 percent of the marketing people in charge of their company's trade show budget haven't received even one hour of formal exhibit education.

If trade shows take up so much of a company's budget, and can be so important to sales, why is so little effort in the way of training devoted to them? I work closely with a VP at a local trade show display and service company.

During sales calls, he asks customers why they go to trade shows. The most common answer he hears is, "so people know we are still in business." If this is your reason for investing in trade shows, you are creating massive waste!

As you can see in the statistics, trade shows can be quite beneficial. In fact, they provide a way to get face-to-face contact and time with buyers and are often cheaper than having to travel all over the country to individual customer facilities throughout the year. Trade shows can help organizations build brand awareness, get leads for new business, network with others, build partnerships, see current clients, see many buyers at the same time, write new orders, or launch or demonstrate a product.

No matter what the goal, you need to with one in mind—a *measurable* goal. Measurable means quantifiable. An example would be to obtain 300 qualified leads or close sales of $10 for every $1 spent at the trade show. Based on this goal, you should have a better sense of which shows to attend, where, and how often. This should also help you build a budget. There are free calculators available online to help calculate your trade show ROI. One is by The Center for Exhibition Industry Research (http://roitoolkit.exhibitsurveys.net/Home/Welcome.aspx). No matter what approach you use, you absolutely must have a goal, must produce measurable targets, and must then calculate the ROI (estimated before and measured afterward). There are very sophisticated computer programs available that aid with trade show lead and sales tracking. Without measurable goals in mind, trade shows will likely be very wasteful.

Note Trade shows are frequently very wasteful because there are no measurable goals, no training, outdated and boring equipment and displays, and no ROI. Make sure you do your homework first. When you do, trade shows can be very helpful.

Weak Statistical and Analytical Capabilities

Statistical and analytical skills are needed in many areas of sales, even beyond creating processes and analyzing expenses. Every sales and operating decision should filter down from the sales forecast. (In Chapter 7, we discuss forecasting.) Without an accurate sales forecast, you cannot know how to distribute sales territories. Without this knowledge, you could have too many or too few reps in a territory. This leads either to wasted reps or lost sales. All resources must be devoted based upon this forecast. Do not "wing" forecasts. Do not rely on last year's figure, plus a gain. Do not rely solely on a survey of buyer's intentions. These actions are all dangerous and wasteful. Utilize advanced statistical techniques to calculate an accurate forecast.

■ **Note** No decisions should be made until you have an accurate forecast. Use numerous statistical methods so that you can improve accuracy.

Weak Territory Management

Having better territory alignment can create a five percent boost in profitability.[17] In a study of 4,800 territories in different industries, 25 percent had too much work for the sales force to handle effectively, and 31 percent had too little work to keep the salesperson busy.[18] That very loosely translates into almost 50 percent of territories being ineffectively designed. Territories should be organized in order to obtain thorough market coverage, establish a salesperson's responsibilities, evaluate performance, improve customer relations (give the right customers the right treatment), reduce sales expenses by reducing travel, and allow better matching of salesperson to customer. This way, excess waste is not being created simply because of a lack of prior analytical skills and planning. So that territories are not wasteful, you should follow the process outlined in Figure 4-7. This process is described in more detail in the following sections.

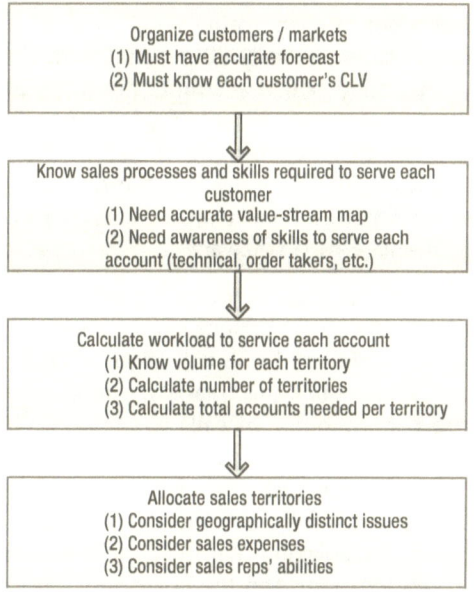

Figure 4-7. Territory Design Steps

---

[17] Baldwin, H., "The Strange Case of the Vanishing Sales VP," Selling Power Magazine, 2010, p. 34–37.
[18] Ibid.

> **Note** Almost half of territories are inefficient and wasteful due to poor design. Use a strategic and analytical process to define territories, and revise it often.

Organize Customers and Markets

The first step in territory design is to organize customers based on their "value" to the company. To begin this process, information is taken from the past purchasing information and information deemed from the sales forecast. This is a critical step because, honestly, not all customers are created equal. Some customers need more service than others, some provide the company more money, and some have different needs that can be handled only by certain types of sales reps. If sales reps do not spend their time with the right accounts, they simply cannot sell to their full potential. A sales manager has to know who their key accounts are before they can successfully place salespeople in the proper territories.

There are numerous ways you likely already divide your accounts. The simplest and most frequently used way is the "single factor method." In this, a single factor is used to divide accounts, typically into A-, B-, and C-level accounts. This is a decent method and is better than nothing. It allows you to determine where reps should spend their time, typically 80 percent with their best accounts. It also allows you to determine which accounts are small enough to be better served by a customer service rep instead of a full time, high-paid salesperson. This method, while being the most simple, is also prone to the most errors, and therefore can be wasteful. There are much more complex methods available. Many are now automatically calculated through a company's Customer Relationship Management (CRM) software.

No matter how the customer segmentation is performed, there are other factors that you must include during account segmentation. First, a simple breakeven analysis should be performed on each account to find out if an account is even worth having. To conduct this analysis, you should calculate the total cost per call and the total number of calls to close business, and determine the total net selling days, average calls per day, and other total direct expenses to arrive at a breakeven point. Other things that you need to consider are account growth, volume potential, competition's share (including the competitors and the likelihood of displacing them), financial well-being, industry leadership, willingness to experiment, and the customer's price sensitivity.

While outside the discussion of this book, in a real situation, the sales manager should go much beyond a simple account division and use some method to look further into each account. The Miller Heiman (1998) method is a common one, but there are several other methods as well. More or less, each individual account needs to be assessed in great detail to really understand what its true potential is, how it should be serviced, and which reps should handle which accounts. After some time, sales reps can begin to develop an "ideal customer profile." Using basic demographics and psychographics, they can predict a pattern of likely sales. This will enhance efficiency and decrease waste, by not calling on unqualified accounts.

Know the Sales Processes

We have already discussed the concept of creating a value-stream map. Once you've created one, you'll understand better which processes are required to service each account. Now that you just segmented your accounts, you can look at each account, especially your better ones, and determine what you need to do to service each customer appropriately.

Analyze the Workload

Once a thorough assessment has been made with regard to how to organize customers and how to prioritize accounts, salespeople need to be placed on accounts and in territories. This should be done using a workload analysis. However, before a workload analysis is preformed, there are a few additional considerations a sales manager needs to think about. First, sales force productivity, or the ratio of sales generated to selling effort used, needs to be assessed. In the early stages, the addition of salespeople increases sales considerably more than the selling costs. As salespeople continue to be added, sales increase at a decreasing rate until a point is reached when the costs to add a salesperson are more than the revenues that salesperson can generate. Then, over the course of a salesperson's career, some salespeople are simply more productive than others. CRM systems can track a sales rep's activities and run some basic calculations so that managers can calculate productivity and examine any issues of difficulty. Also, sales managers must take sales force turnover into account. It is very costly, should be anticipated, and dramatically affects productivity.

Once a manager has the information about productivity, he can begin to develop a salesperson-workload analysis, as shown in Figure 4-8. This analysis shows a manager how many total reps he needs for adequate market coverage. As a manager you might find out, for example, that you have five reps in one territory, but really need only three, whereas in another geographic region, you have three reps but should employ five. These analyses are vital for achieving high levels of sales productivity and for maximizing territory coverage in order to maximize revenue. You cannot calculate the results until you track the sales reps' productivity on an hourly basis for several weeks, either by using productivity journals or by using CRM program entries.

Step 1: How many accounts at each level?		
Class A:	100 accounts	
Class B:	200 accounts	
Class C:	300 accounts	
Step 2: Estimate length per time of sales contact and frequency (per each account)		
Class A:	30 minutes a call x 15 calls a year =	7.5 hours a year
Class B:	20 minutes a call x 10 calls a year =	3.33 hours a year
Class C:	15 minutes a call x 2 calls a year =	0.5 hours a year
Step 3: Compute total workload		
Class A:	100 accounts x 7.5 hours a year =	750 hours/year
Class B:	200 accounts x 3.33 hours a year =	666 hours/year
Class C:	300 accounts x 0.5 hours a year =	150 hours/year
	Total	1566 hours/year
Step 4: Compute total work time available per sales rep		
45 hours a week x 48 weeks =	2160 hours/year	
Step 5: Allocate percentage of total work time to selling tasks		
Selling tasks:	35%	756 hours
Nonselling/Admin:	40%	864 hours
Traveling:	25%	450 hours
Total	100%	2160
Step 6: Determine total number of salespeople		
Salespeople needed = 1,566 hours / 756 hours	2.071429	(The company should employ 2 reps)

Figure 4-8. Workload Example

Assign Territories

One of the large areas of waste is when companies fail to continually revise territories. Customers grow and leave, territories grow or shrink. You should continually monitor the efficiency of your accounts. By combining the forecast, the customer analysis, the sales value-stream map, and the workload analysis, sales managers can develop territories in a non-wasteful manner. Obviously, travel time and each sale rep's abilities need to be taken into account. When assigning sales personnel to territories, managers should rank the sales force using these criteria: relative ability, product and industry knowledge, energy level, persuasiveness, and verbal ability. There are now sophisticated territory-mapping and territorial-routing software programs that can do much of the work described here.

One final issue that sales managers must consider is whether sales activities will be performed in-house or outsourced to independent contractors. Whether you are considering a manufacturer's rep, selling agent, or telemarketing firm, you should always complete an ROI. More importantly, you should think about how your customers will be served. If there is loss of customer satisfaction possible, you should probably keep the duties in-house. Few things are more important than how customers view you and your firm. Once your image is tarnished, it's hard to get it back.

No Productivity Tracking and Weak Evaluation Processes

Do you really know who your best reps are? Or do you just know who sells the most volume? I have worked with many companies in consulting capacities and have rarely seen a company who really knows who their best sales reps are. As discussed in the productivity section, there are many ways to measure both performance and productivity. Are you going to measure gross units or dollars or are you going to measure net profits after sales expenses? Are you going to abandon performance and look at productivity? Are you not going to care about outputs at all and just look at inputs? You could track total strategizing time, calls, presentations, or something similar. Maybe you have team sales and you need to figure out a way to adequately divide sales across the team.

> **Note** Do not rely on one evaluation measure. Use many, including input measures.

No matter which method you choose, you will produce waste if you do not use multiple measures to evaluate performance and productivity. Without the right data, you will be basing your decisions on the wrong data. All the data points must be based on the processes that you established when you created your value-stream map. This ensures that the process is efficient. In short, you must measure everything that's relevant, based on your goals and objectives, and then revise your goals and objectives and plans based upon the data on an ongoing basis.

Likewise, do not count on reviewing your reps only once a year. If you wait until then, it may be too late, as problems may be insurmountable. With regular targets and tracking, it is easier to make sure reps are working to their full potential.

Automated Dialers and Telemarketing Firms

A big trend in sales now is to use automated dialers or telemarketing firms to help with prospecting, appointment setting, and low-level C accounts. Earlier, we talked about sending these C-level accounts to customer service. It can be quite wasteful to have high-paid sales reps servicing accounts that buy a very minimal amount of product every year. Although this approach is okay, we have seen outside firms produce more waste in lost customers than any savings that are produced.

First off, don't use automated dialers! Ever. Just about everyone alive today knows what's coming when you see an 800-, 877-, unknown, or something similar number. We know the pause after we say hello and we can almost see through the phone at the poor rep who just got handed the call and is struggling to read the name that just popped up on their screen. I have frequently informally surveyed my classes about this subject. We never answer our phones when we do not recognize the number. I haven't found more than one or two students who will answer the phone to an unknown number. Using these systems is impersonal and ineffective. Any savings you have in sales reps salaries will be lost due to customers leaving or not buying.

Another trend is the use of outside firms to make prospecting and appointment calls. Be extremely cautious with telemarketing firms! Do not do this! We do not even like having administrative assistants call to set appointments. I work closely with a CEO of a large Fortune 500 company who once came to me complaining about these new techniques. His words summarize everything wrong with this method. He said, "If I'm so important, why can't you take the time to call me yourself!"

> **Note** Avoid automated dialers and appointment-setting firms at all costs!!!

A very rudimentary ROI analysis will show huge savings by outsourcing these functions. Sales reps are expensive, whereas telemarketing callers are often paid minimum wage. Any ROI analysis should include more complex variables, such as customer satisfaction, short-term and long-term outcomes, lost current and potential sales, lost chance of up-selling and cross-selling, and any other damage that might be created by not servicing your customers in the correct manner. Even with the C-level accounts, no one's account segmentation is perfect. You may have a C-level account that's a local sole proprietorship. They are set to expand 1,000 percent over the next ten years. Obviously, within a few years, they will go from a C to a B, to likely an A. A third-party firm will not likely pick up on these nuances. They rarely continually document data and calculate future customer lifetime values. It is okay to let C-level accounts be handled by customer service departments, but we suggest these be in-house departments. You are better off having well-trained, in-house college interns than an outside company.

Sales Metrics

One study showed that only 25 percent of sales executives are using analytics to look at their business and processes.[19] That is so sad. All executives should use analytics. If we do nothing else in this book than help you understand the importance of analytics, then that will be a huge improvement. Just the mere act of making smart decisions will dramatically cut your waste. We outline some of the most important sales analytics in the following sections.

Customer Lifetime Value

Everyone making customer decisions should understand customer lifetime value (CLV) for each customer. In its simplest form, CLV represents the present value of benefits, less the burdens from customers. The assessment of CLV is a complicated task; however, with the rapid growth of database mining, the vast availability of data on customers, and the abundance of models available, the task of assessing CLV is easier than ever. CLV-based segmentation can aid sales reps and marketers in determining what segments they should (or should not) try to create a more profitable relationship with and how to achieve that relationship. An extremely basic CLV calculation worksheet is provided in Figure 4-9. Note that the time value of money is not included in the spreadsheet. Any projection of future earnings should factor that into account. A dollar today is worth more than a dollar in five years. Once you complete this worksheet, you can add it to the information used to classify accounts.

---

[19]*Accenture*, "Connecting the Dots on Sales Performance: Leveraging the 2012 Sales Performance Optimization Study to Inform Sales Effectiveness Initiatives," 2013, http://www.accenture.com/SiteCollectionDocuments/PDF/Accenture-Connecting-Dots-Sales-Performance.pdf.

The Lifetime Value of a Customer

Customer name:

Basic Formula

Estimate # of customer transactions in a lifetime	×	Number/ quantity of purchases per visit	×	Avg price per purchase ($)	−	Cost to acquire customer	=	CLV

Projected Formula, 5 Year Period

	Revenue (Include gross revenue generated)	−	Cost to service this customer, including marketing and costs of making and	+	Referrals (Add net value of referred accounts)	=	Profit ($)
Year 1		−		+		=	
Year 2		−		+		=	
Year 3		−		+		=	
Year 4		−		+		=	
Year 5		−		+		=	
TOTAL:							

Figure 4-9. CLV Caluculations

CLV calculations can be laborious and require advanced statistics, but are perhaps one of the most important metrics you'll use. You cannot create an accurate forecast and therefore cannot make any of the other decisions we recommend without accurate CLV numbers. Even though the chart looks simple on the surface, each of the individual variables can be difficult to estimate.

Estimating total purchases over a lifetime can be quite tricky. Using the data you have, which may be in your CRM system, you want to look at three variables: how recent the sales were, the frequency of sales, and the number of sales. Meaning, how recently did the customer purchase, how often did they purchase, and how much did they purchase. When looking at these numbers, you can start to gauge if a customer is purchasing more and more often, or if the purchases are slacking off. As part of this, you want to look at your churn rate. The churn rate is the number of customers who stopped purchasing your product or service during a given time period. The formula follows:

$$Churn = \frac{number\ of\ customers\ lost}{number\ of\ new\ customers}$$

You also need to calculate customer acquisition costs (CAC) and other expenses required to service a customer. The formula for customer acquisition follows. When calculating it, you want to be very careful to include only those costs associated with each customer. Also, don't forget to include every cost associated with a customer. Expenses like samples and visual aids are easy to forget. If your CAC increases, your sales and marketing might be becoming more inefficient.

Customer Acquisition Costs (CAC)
= All sales and marketing costs (advertising, salary, commission, bonus, overhead, etc.) per period
/ number of customers in that period

Another metric is the time to payback. This looks at how quickly you are making your money back on your CAC costs.

Time to payback CAC = CAC / Revenue

As you will notice in the CLV spreadsheet, referrals is an extremely important measure. The more referrals you get, the more valuable each customer becomes. Likewise, studies have shown that new customers who buy because of word-of-mouth or referral are twice as valuable as customers who buy because of short-term advertising campaigns.[20] For every customer, find out how they came to you (through referral, Internet search, etc.). Based on these numbers, you should be able to calculate a CLV.

Pipeline Analysis

Every sales rep and sale manager should have an idea of the pipeline conversion rates. These tell you how wasteful or productive your sales reps are. Figure 4-10 shows a simplified pipeline analysis. In this, you can see that sales

---

[20]Villanueva, Julian, Shijin Yoo and Dominique M. Hanssens, "The Impact of Marketing-Induced vs. Word-of-Mouth Customer Acquisition on Customer Equity Growth," *Journal of Marketing Research*, 2008, 45 (1), p. 48–59.

reps are being rather wasteful in their lead selection. You actually want fewer leads going in because you want to make sure your reps are qualifying the accounts. You want them to work smart, not hard. The actual appointment-to-sales rates, however, are quite good. This indicates that when the sales reps are in front of the customer, they are doing their job. In this instance, waste could likely be reduced by having the reps take some prospecting training.

Sales Rep	Leads	Appointments	Lead/Appointment Conversion Rate	Sales	Lead to Sales Conversion Rate	Appointment to Sales Conversion Rate
1	24	2	8.33%	1	4.17%	50.00%
2	22	5	22.73%	3	13.64%	60.00%
3	30	2	6.67%	1	3.33%	50.00%
4	22	2	9.09%	2	9.09%	100.00%
5	20	7	35.00%	1	5.00%	14.29%
6	28	3	10.71%	0	0.00%	0.00%
7	32	8	25.00%	1	3.13%	12.50%
8	23	5	21.74%	4	17.39%	80.00%
9	20	4	20.00%	1	5.00%	25.00%
Avg	24.56	4.22	17.70%	1.56	6.75%	43.53%

Figure 4-10. Pipeline Analysis

Trade Show Metrics

If you're attending trade shows, you need to keep good ROI measures of your success. So many people attend trade shows just because it is what they think they should do. As described, trade shows can be quite profitable and a good source of well qualified prospects. However, they can be extremely wasteful too. You must understand what goes into a trade show and what comes back out to know if you should be attending trade shows. Some of the more important measures are in the following.

> Cost per contact
> = Entire trade show cost or investment
> / gross number of contacts generated
>
> Cost per visitor reached
> = Entire trade show cost or investment
> / Prospects who visited the booth

Industry average for costs for visitors reach ranges from $116 – $195.

> Cost per qualified lead
> = Total trade show cost or investment
> / qualified leads generated

Make sure, when examining these metrics, that you incorporate all expenses. Trade show venues will charge you for every little thing they can, from space to electricity to ice and cups. And don't forget your sales rep's travel expenses and some figure for the lack of ability to service other accounts while traveling.

Conclusion

Like every area of business, the sales function has various areas of waste that you need to address. The bulk of the waste in sales is created by not treating it like the analytical process it is. Business leaders tend to think of sales as a function of charisma instead of a real skill. Sales research and practice, however, show that following structured processes can yield more consistent sales results. Because you might be used to the waste from sales as being the way that you have always done it, you need to analyze your processes. Improvements need to start with the way that you are measuring sales activities. Every activity should have an associated metrics so that you can identify and eliminate waste.

The data that you get from the sales processes should lead you to better hiring, training, and managing of your sales employees. You can then focus your limited resources on activities that provide a ROI because you understand what truly affects sales. By learning to see the sales processes as a kind of manufacturing process, you can identify and improve upon them.

Waste Checklist

*All "no" answers identify a potential opportunity for improvement.

Managing Your Sales Force

Do you measure sales force productivity based upon sales generated per hour of work?	Yes ☐ No ☐
Do you consider the sales territory potential when evaluating sales force productivity?	Yes ☐ No ☐
Do you evaluate skills that drive sales when you hire a salesperson?	Yes ☐ No ☐
Do you understand what makes your best salespeople successful?	Yes ☐ No ☐
Do you hire based upon the characteristics of your best salespeople?	Yes ☐ No ☐
Do you have an analytical approach to hiring?	Yes ☐ No ☐
Do you avoid using traditional hiring techniques as your main method of vetting candidates?	Yes ☐ No ☐
Do you hire outside of your industry?	Yes ☐ No ☐
Do you provide training based upon your skills assessments of salespeople?	Yes ☐ No ☐
Do you provide frequent training to keep the sales force skills relevant?	Yes ☐ No ☐
Does your training include analytical skills like forecasting and cost analysis?	Yes ☐ No ☐
Do you measure the effectiveness of your sales training on the outcome of increased sales or customer satisfaction?	Yes ☐ No ☐

Eliminating Waste in Business

Sales Checklist
*All "No" answers identify a potential opportunity for improvement.

Sales Processes

Do you have a sales process that is identified, understood, and followed?	Yes ☐ No ☐
Have you worked to remove waste from your sales processes?	Yes ☐ No ☐
Are marketing activities integrated into sales goals and activities?	Yes ☐ No ☐
Do you analyze the benefit of sales travel?	Yes ☐ No ☐
Do you understand how often you customers want to see your sale people?	Yes ☐ No ☐
Do you know the value you get from attending trade shows in regards to sales?	Yes ☐ No ☐
Do you optimize your trade show presence through booth design and follow up processes?	Yes ☐ No ☐
Do you require your sales people to have analytical capabilities?	Yes ☐ No ☐
Do you use analytics to design sales territories?	Yes ☐ No ☐
Do you truly understand the workload of each of your sales people?	Yes ☐ No ☐
Do you assign territories based upon the strengths and weaknesses of each sales person?	Yes ☐ No ☐
Do you evaluate your sales force outcomes and productivity?	Yes ☐ No ☐
Do you avoid automatic dialers and telemarketing firms?	Yes ☐ No ☐
Do you use sales metrics to monitor your effectiveness and improve your processes?	Yes ☐ No ☐

CHAPTER 5

Human Resources
A Source of Value or a Source of Waste?

> *99 percent of all employees want to do a good job. How they perform is simply a reflection of the one for whom they work.*
>
> —Mark S. Hoplamazian, President, Hyatt Hotels

It is not difficult to find someone who feels like the human resources (HR) department is a source of waste and frustration. Whether it is outdated forms with no meaning, a constant barrage of repeated signatures, sexual harassment seminars—or just about any of the functions HR performs, in fact—it seems that there is always a perceived waste of money associated with the HR department. How did such an important function become such a source of waste?

The HR department is responsible for many functions in an organization. In the case of human resource management, responsibilities include manpower planning, job analysis/description, wage analysis, recruitment, performance appraisal, training and development, employee motivation, benefit administration, dismissal, and labor relations.

HR: SUPPORT OR BUSINESS FUNCTION?

There is a debate as to whether the HR department is a support function or a business function. In our definition of any department, the deciding factor as to whether it is a support function or a primary business function hinges upon whether the department directly affects the production of the product or administration of the service to the customers. Based on this definition, functions like human resources, finance, information technology, and quality control are support functions. That being said, these support functions are still a necessary part of business, but this changes the level of control that these functions should have.

Unfortunately, in the administration of these HR activities, many organizations introduce waste. Much of this waste is created because HR tends to forget they are a support function and that their job should be to support others, not to control. And some of this waste is created because activities occur in which there is no added value. For instance, employee evaluations are a key function of human resources. One such example is the use of an electronic Excel file or an online system with multiple steps to create the evaluation. Once you get the right form, you have to enter goal and performance information. Then, the employee has to enter their performance information into the form. Finally, you have to review the employee's self-evaluation and add your comments. After you do all of this, then you schedule time with the employee to discuss the evaluation, which may take anywhere from 15 minutes to an hour. All told, this process can take 45 minutes to a couple of hours per employee.

If this information provides value or dictates future pay increases, this time is well spent, but in fact the employee evaluation process rarely accomplishes anything except to create a paper trail used to discipline employees.

So, in order to limit the waste in each of these areas, you need to analyze the value that each activity offers the organization. As a support or business function, if value is not added, then the process should be dropped. As we've said time and again throughout this book, any service or function that doesn't add value is inherently wasteful.

Note Much waste is created in HR because it is treated as a business function. Instead, HR should be treated as a support function. To make this switch, every process must undergo a value analysis.

For example, while we are sure it happens at some point in some organization somewhere, we personally have never seen an HR professional thoroughly engaged in productivity and manpower analysis. This is likely due to a lack of formal training in doing these types of analyses. HR professionals tend to be involved in the implementation of staffing decisions rather than the analysis of labor. This can lead to a lack of understanding the number of workers needed in each department. With such a knowledge gap, the HR department depends on the management staff to decide how much personnel is necessary. Since managers often look to add labor to resolve efficiency and effectiveness problems, this lack of knowledge of productivity needs by the HR department can lead to overstaffing. A healthy relationship between managers and HR professionals includes checks and balances where HR understands enough of the needs to challenge excess staffing requests. The manager should control and HR should support when needed. Managers and HR professionals should make sure their needs are communicated to each other to avoid these problems.

When it is necessary to hire personnel to fill a role, HR recruitment personnel can draw from the wrong candidate pool, leading to a poor hire. When HR doesn't fully understand the needs of the organization, ineffective staffing is the result. When managers don't fully understanding the job market, they are more likely to give HR a poor definition of the position's requirements. So lack of understanding by both departments drives waste in the organization. This waste can manifest itself in many ways. You could end up having an employee who is in a position that is not a good fit for his skills. Even if this is a good employee that the manager is happy to have on her staff, he still does not meet the business need that justify the role. This creates waste because the original needs are not being met. Also, an employee is doing work that might not be needed. Also, you could end up with an employee who has higher expectations of the role than what the company is actually looking for. In this case, the new employee is not challenged, and is undervalued and demotivated. This employee will likely look for a new job as soon as he realizes that the role is not a good fit.

If you combine the lack of knowledge of business needs and the lack of understanding of business roles, it is a formula that leads to poor HR decisions. We once analyzed temporary, part-time labor versus full-time labor. The prevailing HR opinion was that temporary or part-time labor was a cost savings over hiring full-time employees. This is because the company could avoid benefit expenses and could hire employees at a lower hourly rate.

Our analysis looked at the productivity level from units per hour measurement, the quality reject levels, and the product line. The goal of this analysis was to determine which products were best suited for temporary labor. I performed a multiple regression analysis based upon a large set of data to determine which factors drove high productivity and high quality. We found that in all product lines, the lower costs of labor did not offset the loss of productivity and quality gained with full-time, skilled employees. We made the decision to reduce the number of temporary employees and adjust our production methods to ensure that we maintained a stable and skilled workforce.

> **Note** Perform productivity analyses prior to filling positions.

This is just one example of the prevailing knowledge of how to manage human resources can be incorrect and can lower company profitability. Over our careers we have seen companies copy a successful strategy from one organization, but with poor results. HR departments absolutely should be aware of trends in labor management, but also cannot afford to be ignorant of their company's unique needs. This ignorance leads to bad decisions, such as relying on a steady stream of temporary labor when what you want is a stable and skilled workforce. We show throughout this chapter that, in order for HR to provide value and not add waste, they must serve in a support function. It is job of HR to support management and help fulfill needs of the various departments. This process must be performed in an analytical manner so as to not create added waste—as well as to begin to eliminate existing waste.

Wasteful Hiring Processes

One of the key roles of HR is to provide a candidate pool for hiring and ensure that a proper hiring process is used to meet not only company needs but also legal requirements. We have mentioned how not understanding the needs of a position can cause waste. Where else is there waste in hiring? The waste is in the process itself. Figure 5-1 shows a simplified version of a hiring process.

Eliminating Waste in Business

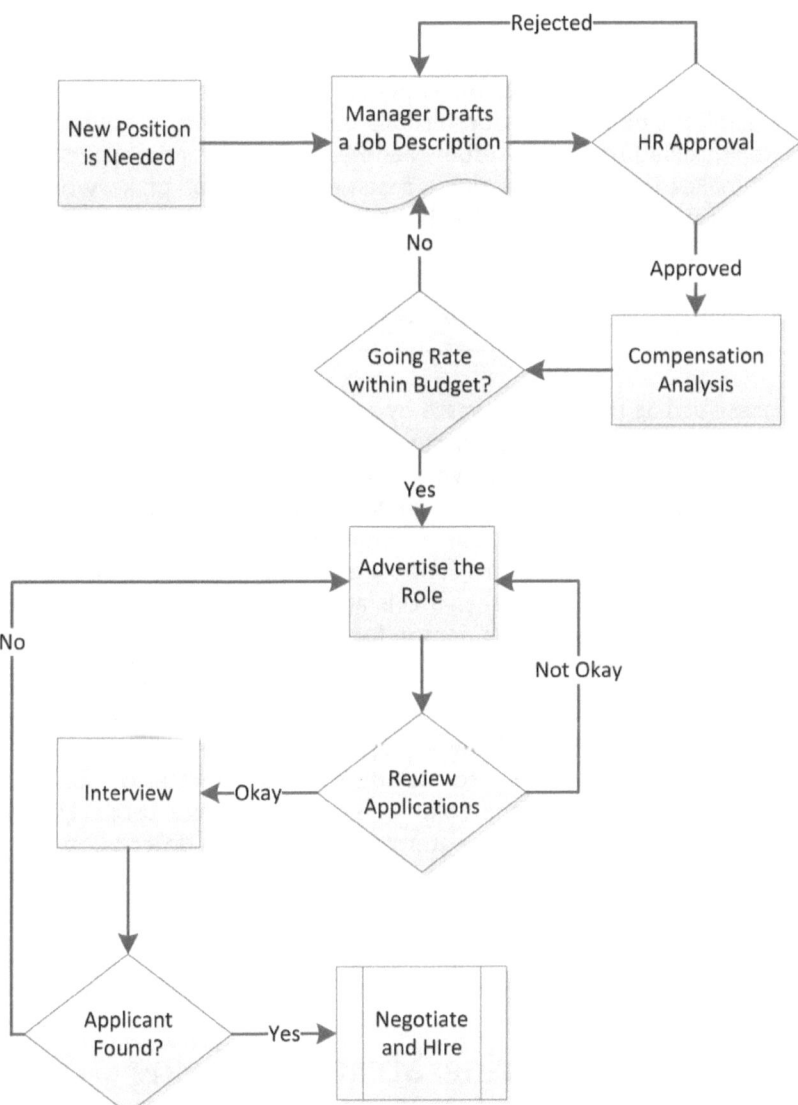

Figure 5-1. Typical Hiring Process

Although these exact steps aren't used in every company, it is typical. If you analyze this process, you will notice that the compensation analysis occurs near the beginning of the process. Thus, the compensation then affects the job description so that the hiring budget can be met. So in this process, meeting a certain employee cost is a higher priority than getting the right skills for the job. This is going to create waste. Having the wrong employee for the job at any cost (even a cheap one) is wasteful.

What we leave out of this simplified process are some of the very common HR practices used to build a pool of applicants. Many times, HR uses keyword searches to search resumes and HR personnel reviews of candidates to create an applicant pool. If HR doesn't fully understand the role, what makes a recruiter qualified to review resumes and eliminate potential applicants? This process makes the art of creating a resume with clichés or keywords more important than having the right skills or qualifications.

Note Hiring must be controlled by the person in charge of the position.

Processes such as these drive waste by potentially eliminating the best applicant for the job or wasting resources reviewing resumes without the proper knowledge. This process works very well for established or frequently filled positions, but any position that has unique qualifications must follow a different process. Unfortunately, in our attempts to simplify hiring processes, we design simple processes that are supposed to fit all situations. Not having the right process for each hiring scenario is another source of waste, because it often leads to hiring the wrong person for the job.

This issue can be solved by creating two or three hiring processes. The decision points included with these processes eliminate the need for prescreening processes where sufficient HR knowledge is not available. The compensation process will also be modified to include the market rate for similar roles and adjust the budget for the role. This ensures that a properly qualified candidate is found, rather than watering down the job description to justify a lower compensation rate. Businesses are a complicated set of coordinated processes, and the hiring processes must be designed to support these processes. In order to accommodate these needs, a strategic hiring process must be followed.

Non-Wasteful Hiring: Strategic Hiring

Good hiring practices start with a sound strategy and require some work, both prior to interviewing candidates and after hiring the best ones. Any experienced HR professional would likely know the work that is necessary, but unfortunately many lack the knowledge or resources to follow the process every time. This is a waste of the opportunity to capitalize on the talent of your people in HR and new recruits. Figure 5-2 shows the steps necessary for effective hiring. We describe each of these steps in more detail in the following sections.

Eliminating Waste in Business

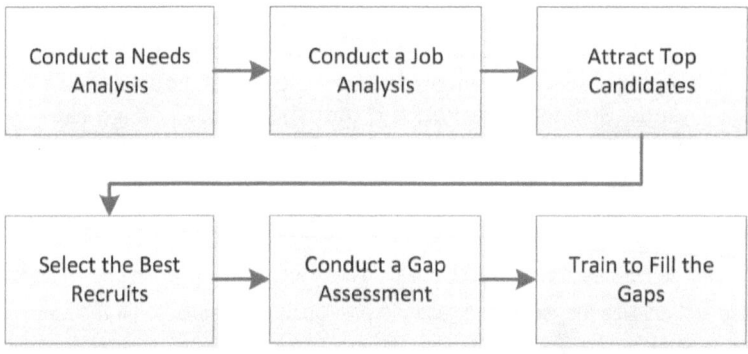

Figure 5-2. Effective Hiring Steps

The key to creating non-wasteful hiring practices is to make sure that the processes fit the exact need. We wrote this section intended for skilled positions. Obviously, there are many unskilled positions in firms that can be filled with identical processes and likely handled through HR. However, for the skilled positions, the persons who understand those skills best must take the lead in the hiring process. Any attempt to do this in a one-size-fits-all, non-strategic manner will likely create waste.

■ **Note** Attempting to cram the hiring process into a one-size-fits-all approach, so that HR can that the lead, will likely create waste. Hiring should not be taken lightly and should be handled by those who best understand the needs of the position.

Needs Assessment

Many times, organizations skip the crucial first step of needs assessment. When a company decides to fill a position, there are a few key questions that the leaders must ask every time:

- **Why is the position necessary?** As simple as this question is, we find that leaders sometimes add people to fix problems caused by poor processes or lack of sufficient resources in other areas of the organization, such as up-to-date information technology. You must perform productivity analyses of current employees. By forcing yourself to answer this question, you may avoid hiring someone who is not necessary and, therefore, avoid waste.

- **What gap does this job fill?** Sometimes we hire to replace people who have moved on to another job. This is a great time to evaluate what work is lost by their departure and whether that work is necessary. Whether this is a new position or a replacement, it is a good time to upgrade or downgrade the role to fit your specific needs. Business, market, and industry needs change rapidly and employee skills and resources should change to meet those needs.

Note Just as businesses change, so does the need for positions. When positions are vacated, you should first analyze the need to replace the position. It might need to be replaced, but with a different type of job.

- **How long will it take the new employee to be effective?** If hiring a new employee is a solution to a specific need, you should have realistic expectations about how long it will take for the new hire to add value. Without realistic expectations, you are likely to be disappointed. If the company needs are quick and short term, you should perhaps consider outsourcing.

Job Analysis

The job analysis portion of the hiring process is important because too often we start a job description with template language such as, "candidates should have a bachelor's degree and should have 3-5 years of experience in a similar industry." These criteria might not be what is actually necessary. Sometimes these are valid criteria, but what about fresh perspectives? What are the actual job duties? Do you need industry experience to do sales order entry or even engineering, or do you need the skills to do those jobs regardless of the industry experience? As a hiring manager, you need to know the answers to these questions.

If you are hiring a business analyst, for example, you may start by looking at a current job description for this title within the company. If one does not exist, maybe you do some research on what the typical duties of a business analyst are so that you can create a job description. If you know you need the position, why do you need the position? What duties do you need performed? You do not want to fall into the common mistake of finding existing job descriptions online. This is very typically what HR does. This act drives you to write a generic job description that does not meet your specific needs. You may also eliminate the best candidate through criteria that is not necessary for the role. HR should have minimal input in these steps. They do not do the job you are seeking. They do not even directly manage the job, so their knowledge is minimal.

Once you determine the correct characteristics for the job, you'll know where to look for these candidates and how to attract them. You wouldn't look for a seasoned engineer with a variety of work in her design portfolio on a college campus, for instance, so why would you assume a newspaper ad or a posting on an online job board will bring you the right candidate?

Attract Top Candidates

The method that you use to attract candidates will depend on the job analysis and requirements. There is not much specific to say here, other than you need to make sure that you understand the needs of your potential candidates. Needs can come from many places, so once you have the job description, create a profile of your ideal candidate. Needs might include flexible hours, autonomy, opportunities for professional development, or variability in tasks. The candidate's personal and professional needs play a part in identifying them. There should be transparency about the job during the entire process. If you, as a hiring manager, know the person can work flextime or at home, as long as they work 40 hours a week, be sure to communicate that. It's important for working parent to know.

In this part of the hiring process, HR's input should be to help the hiring manager and the potential employees. Many times, this process becomes more difficult because HR has certain forms that need filled out and certain places where ads need to be posted, such as to fulfill affirmative action requirements. Typically, no one in the company knows the laws better than the HR department. Thus, they can be a tremendous source of knowledge. Be sure the laws are being followed, but also make sure not to overcomplicate the process at this point.

Select the Best Recruits

Companies use many methods to select recruits. Every company uses interviews as a method to evaluate potential recruits, and they may utilize other tools such as testing, social networking reviews, or reference checks. The interview process is probably the most unscientific of all of these, with the possible exception of reference checks. There are resources available to prepare interviewees to give favorable responses to the standard interview questions like, "What is your greatest weakness?" or "Tell me about when you have overcome a difficult situation at work?" Many times there are interview forms to fill out as a record to support that the interview was fair and there were good reasons to hire or not hire. Of course, there are limits to what you can ask because of potential discrimination issues, so most personal questions are off limits. The reality is that the only value in an interview is the ability to get an idea of the person's personality and how well the person would fit into the team. The rest of the interview process creates waste. You may weed out the very poorly prepared candidates with the interview process, but any person who has taken the time to prepare and has a decent *EQ* (a measure of emotional intelligence) will do fine in the interview.

When you conduct an interview, it is more instinctual than anything. You are looking for basic aptitude to perform the work. You are also looking for attitude and personality to see how well the person will work and fit into the team. Avoid the typical interview questions where you can and try to make the interview more conversational. This allows the candidate to relax some as well as overcome any coaching or preparation that a candidate may have had.

> **Note** Interview for fit and personality. Let the other selection tools help you measure other qualifications.

Personality tests can measure decisiveness, energy, enthusiasm, results orientation, maturity, assertiveness, sensitivity, openness, tough-mindedness, emotional intensity, intuition, recognition needs, motivational needs, sensitivity, assertiveness, and even ability to trust and likelihood of deviant behaviors. IQ tests measure intelligence. Industry-specific knowledge tests can reveal how much the candidate knows about the industry. Many companies use drug or nicotine tests to avoid potential liability or ensure lower insurance costs. These are just a few of the tests available, but many of these are necessary only when you have a tight candidate pool or you have questions about specific candidates that you would like to hire. Many HR departments standardize these tests for all new hires without regard to potential weaknesses in a specific candidate. This can be a large waste of resources.

> **Note** Most personality tests are basically the same. Save money by using free tests.

Many of the tests are expensive and not that helpful, and are just moneymaking ventures for the companies that create them. The better, more psychologically sound tests can frequently be found for free in academic literature. A brief search through Google Scholar will provide many of the most accepted psychological tests. These tests can easily be placed on a site like Qualtrics or Survey Monkey at very little cost. An intern or someone in HR could then cull the data to see if it matches desired personality characteristics. If you don't feel comfortable doing this, pay an academic researcher to find the right tests for you, set up the survey, and set up an easy-to-use program to manage the incoming data. This one-time investment will be significantly cheaper than paying an outside company anywhere from $75 to even $500 per candidate!

> **Note** Pay a one-time investment to set up candidate testing. Never pay a reoccurring per-candidate fee. EQ tests (discussed next) are the most important and predictive.

Current research shows that the best test to give to new hire is an *emotional intelligence test*.[1] Emotional intelligence (EQ) accounts for about 75 percent of the variance in candidates' success rates.[2] So, if you are going to spend your money on any new-hire test, we recommend a good, sound EQ test. Then, remember that the differences among all the other tests are just based upon who patented a particular test. Figure 5-3 shows many of the typical pre-hire personality tests. No matter which one you use, they all end up creating the same four quadrants, which originated, believe it or not, from Freud and other psychologists. There is basically no difference among the tests in their ability to predict the success of new hires.

Hippocrates: Melancholic Myers-Briggs: Sensing/Perceiving/Feeling Keirsey: Artisan/ Guardian Marston: Submission DSI: Behavioral DISC: Steady Wilson: Amiable Freud: Oral	Hippocrates: Sanguine Myers-Briggs: Intuitive/Feeling Keirsey: Idealist/Advocates Marston: Inducement DSI: Conceptual DISC: Influential Wilson: Expressive Freud: Omitted
Hippocrates: Phlegmatic Myers-Briggs: Intuitive/Thinking Keirsey: Rationalists/Engineers Marston: Compliance DSI: Analytical DISC: Compliant Wilson: Analytical Freud: Anal	Hippocrates: Choleric Myers-Briggs: Sensing/Judging /Thinking Keirsey: Guardian Marston: Artisan DSI: Dominance DISC: Dominance Wilson: Driver Freud: Genital

Figure 5-3. Similarities Among Personality Tests

---

[1] Orr, Linda, "Sales Force Productivity: Definition, Measurement, and Determinants," 2014, working paper.
[2] Hunter, J. E., & Hunter, R. F., "Validity and Utility of Alternative Predictors of Job Performance," *Psychological Bulletin,* 1984, 76(1), p. 72–93.

In addition to the waste of paying for these tests and analyzing them, savvy candidates may be able to fake the results of some of these tests. There is also the question of whether positive scores on these tests actually result in higher performing employees. In many positions, with some basic intelligence as a foundation, a loyal and hardworking employee can be trained to do whatever is necessary.

Another area where HR can help managers is by reviewing candidates' social networking web pages. Frequently, some less desirable candidates forget to clean up their online presence and leave clues about their poor decision making. This says a lot about a candidate's EQ. There have even been some studies to show that the more a person engaged in social networking, the more narcissistic they are.[3] Whether or not this is true, people blindly leave tons of details about themselves online.

Another source of waste are the candidate's references. Reference checks are typically unreliable because potential employees will give you the best references that they have. Everyone can find at least three people who will say good things about them. Checking with the prior employer will get you a canned response confirming that the candidate worked at the company, but unless the HR department violates standard policy, that is likely all that you will get. We feel that for this reason, reference checks are a waste. So, if you decide to use reference checks, if the candidate will allow, ask for 10-20 references and then tell the candidate that you will call three of those references at random. Many companies have completely abandoned traditional reference checking now in favor of reviewing LinkedIn recommendations. Just like with reference checks, these are also biased, but at least there is very little time investment in obtaining them.

If you do continue to use reference checks, and if you don't have a concern about a specific candidate, it is best to keep it simple and look at the qualifications and the results of the interview. Use a tool to help you figure out the best candidate without personal bias entering into the decision. The specific tool that you use will depend upon what you like, but one example is the qualification matrix shown in Figure 5-4. Each critical qualification is weighted on its importance and then each candidate is rated using a scale, such as 0, 1, 5, and 9, or 0, 1, 3, and 9. Although the qualification matrix is not a perfect method, if you solicit feedback from others who are interviewing the candidates, you will get a good idea of the best candidate for the job.

---

[3]Panek, Elliot T., Yioryos Nardis, and Sara Konrath, "Mirror or Megaphone?: How Relationships Between Narcissism and Social Networking Site Use Differ on Facebook and Twitter," *Computers in Human Behavior*, 29(5), September 2013, p. 2004–2012.

Weights	Qualification 1	Qualification 2	Qualification 3	Qualification 4	Qualification 5	
	20%	20%	40%	10%	10%	100%
Candidate 1	9	5	9	1	0	6.5
Candidate 2	5	5	5	5	5	5
Candidate 3	9	9	1	0	1	4.1
Candidate 4	9	9	5	9	9	7.4

Figure 5-4. Qualification Matrix

■ **Note** Reference checks are usually wasteful. There are better and more analytical ways to judge a candidate.

Conduct a Gap Assessment

Once you have identified the best candidate, you should do a gap assessment prior to the start date. It is important to do this prior to the start date so that you have a plan to fill those gaps in the first few months when the new hire starts.

To perform this gap assessment, you should go back to the tool that you used to evaluate all of the candidates. It is rare to find a person who meets all of the qualifications that you want to have for the job, so there will be gaps, even with the best hire. If you use the qualification matrix example in Figure 5-4, candidate 4 met all of the qualifications except the one with the heaviest weight. Strictly looking at the numbers, you would select candidate 4, but you may have also selected candidate 1 because of the importance of qualification 3. In either case, there is a gap to be filled. You identified the gaps in the selection process so now is the time to come up with an action plan to fill those gaps. The goal is to have a fully productive employee within six months. That's where training comes in.

Train to Fill the Gaps

Not all gaps can be filled with training, but many can. Gaps that cannot be filled with training are filled by giving the employee additional experiences. For instance, in my own personal transition into the hospital environment from manufacturing, I possessed the process improvement and high reliability skills but was lacking industry knowledge. In my first few weeks, I lined up time in various clinical and support areas to gain some firsthand knowledge of the operations and the challenges that each area faces. Although this is not a substitute for experience, it was a great opportunity to see current operations from a fresh perspective and identify opportunities for improvement.

If the gaps can be filled through training, make sure that the training is designed to give the new employee a way to demonstrate the new knowledge in the work environment. It may be necessary to repeat the training periodically to ensure relevancy and the ability to maintain the information. For example, in a sales career, it is necessary to train reps regularly in the newest products or services as well as in current sales techniques.

Motivation: Why It's Wasteful and How to Do It Right

According to a recent Gallup survey, 70 percent of U.S. workers are "not engaged" or "actively disengaged" at work.[4] This equates to an estimated $450 to $550 billion loss of productivity.[5] "Organizations with an average of 9.3 engaged employees for every actively disengaged employee in 2010-2011 experienced 147 percent higher earnings per share (EPS) compared with their competition in 2011-2012."[6] In fact, the Gallup report also showed the effects of negative employee engagement. If you refer to Figure 5-5, you'll see that disengaged employees have major effects on companies. Unfortunately, there are more negative effects of disengaged employees than positive effects of engaged employees.

---

[4]Gallup, "State of the American Workplace," 2013, http://www.gallup.com/file/strategicconsulting/163007/State%20of%20the%20American%20Workplace%20Report%202013.pdf.
[5]Ibid.
[6]Ibid.

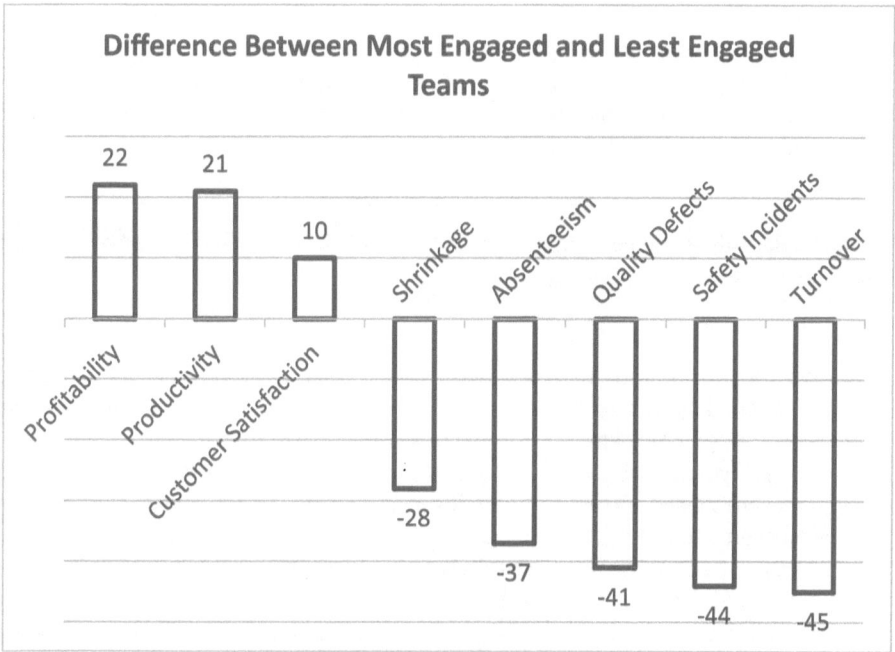

Figure 5-5. The Effects of Engagement on Company Outcomes. (*Source:* Gallup, "State of the American Workplace," 2013, http://www.gallup.com/file/strategicconsulting/163007/State%20of%20the%20American%20Workplace%20Report%202013.pdf.)

Given these facts, a crucial job of HR should be to increase engagement and motivation. Right? Not really. Again, as with hiring, much waste is created by HR trying to control the motivation and evaluation processes. The bulk of the motivation should come from the employee's direct supervisor or department. Likewise, every person is motivated differently. If you research reward systems, you will find ideas from employee engagement techniques to compensation techniques. Not all of these techniques will motivate all of your employees. Some can be quite effective though, such as building trust with your employees by setting clear expectations and then allowing them the autonomy to work on those priorities. Unfortunately, many HR professionals and managers tend to utilize one-size-fits-all techniques, which are not so effective.

Rewards

We both have boxes full of plaques and certificates marking achievements that were recognized by current and former employers. These items did not motivate either of us to do our job or to work harder, likely because we are internally motivated. In fact, there have been times that we were upset by the wasted paper, wood, or plastic that went into the award and the wasted money that was used to fund it. There can be some degree of demotivation to the award in that employees might think, "Why don't they care what would make me happy?"

■ **Note** Rewards should be hard to obtain and used only for extraordinary performances. Also, only use them for externally driven people.

Rewards can be effective if they are tied to performance that exceeds the norm. When they are expected as part of doing a normal job, rewards lose their value. Also, the person must have a personality that appreciates receiving awards. Typically, the only people who appreciate these types of rewards are those who have external need for recognition. (If you have paid money for personality testing at hire, you should have this information at your disposal.) Many people would rather have a bonus or extra time off work. If a plaque costs $250, you could likely save money by giving your employee Friday afternoon off or making Friday work-from-home day. This will then enhance productivity in the long term, thus boosting profits.

Team Building

People spend as much time at work as they do at home, so companies obviously have concluded that activities to build the relationships within their teams are helpful. Scheduled volunteer activities, baseball outings, or retreats are just a few examples of team-building opportunities. The reality that these leaders miss is that work relationships are shallow and based largely on the need to get along with people, whether or not you actually like working with them.

Teams are not built by going into the woods and tackling an obstacle course or going to the bar after conducting a strategy retreat. Typically, team-building exercises have a physical nature to them. These can actually have a negative effect on employees who feel embarrassed by the inability to perform. Additionally, if the event happens over the weekend or during typically non-working hours, employees resent the time away from their personal lives.

Most importantly, if you think you need team building, you need to look at why you have a bad team. No team-building exercise is going to overcome deep, underlying problems within organizations. Teams are built through effective work, where the team members challenge each other and work together toward a common goal. Trust and respect must be present in all situations, especially from management. The relationships built in this way last longer and are less superficial than those developed through a "trust fall."

> **Note** If you think you need team building, stop. Figure out why you have issues first. Most often the issues are a result of bad management.

Celebrations

At least twice a year we are invited to some work-related celebration. We attend these celebrations out of obligation and leave as soon as we can without making our distaste for the activity obvious. This may seem to be a pessimistic view, but if you watch the interactions between people in these banquets, you can see that the majority of attendees are there for the same reason, to look good. The concept of pizza and meetings is not new to workers in any industry. If you meet certain targets set by the organization, everyone will enjoy a cheap pizza party to celebrate the achievement. If you fail to meet the targets, you will be chastised and there will be no party. Do these activities really motivate people? Or more likely, are people motivated by their internal values to do their best?

Again, find out will motivate your team. Banquets are extraordinarily expensive for the company and the employees. Costs can quickly exceed $10,000 on space and catering alone. Employees frequently need new attire and childcare. Have you taken the time to find out if employees are really motivated by these events? Your employees with externally driven personalities may appreciate these events. Likewise, those earlier in their careers, who have not become jaded by such events, might like them. However, most people are demotivated by celebrations and see them as an intrusion of time and money.

Picnics and Holiday Dinners

Along the same lines as these celebrations are the annual parties that companies throw for employees. Company picnics are common. A picnic may occur at the company site with free food and some entertainment. Maybe a facility tour for the family is available. In the few times that I have seen company picnics cancelled due to financial distress, HR managers have been concerned about the negative effect on the employees. What I have found is that employees are more concerned about having their jobs than whether or not they will be served a hotdog and some chips while playing corn hole with co-workers.

Additionally, the infamous holiday dinners provide no real value to employees. I have seen these a few times as a way to celebrate the holidays with employees. Although the free food is nice, how is this supposed to motivate an employee? What are you trying to motivate him to do? Eat? Not to mention the horrible statistic that states that 44 percent of males said they've had an affair with a co-worker at a holiday office party at least once in their lives.[7] Whether you believe the validity of these frequently quoted stats or not, employers should certainly do everything they can to avoid potential lawsuits and chaos!

■ **Note** Don't waste your precious resources on banquets, parties, and events that employees feel obligated to attend.

Bonuses

Bonuses can be a great way to motivate employees. In fact, for sales people who earn a good portion of their compensation from bonuses or commission, it is a great motivator. When the bonus is individualized and ties directly to their work, it is very effective.

Organization-wide bonus programs don't motivate employees unless the company is small. We have seen many companies with profit-sharing bonuses where a percentage of all profits (regardless of the size) are split equally between all employees. Due to the small size, the individual employees affect the company profitability, so the bonus program motivates them to work hard to meet profitability goals. In larger organizations, the entitlement bonuses have the opposite effect. With organization-wide goals that seem out of reach and hard for the individual to affect, the employees become demotivated and just take the bonus if they are lucky to get one.

An entitlement bonus is the annual bonus that may tie to a few metrics but is normally paid out to employees as a reward. If an entitlement bonus is put in place and then taken away, you take an unmotivated employee who gets a bonus and turn him into an angry employee with no bonus.

In a large organization, bonuses should be split based upon department-specific objectives so that the individual can be motivated by the bonus program. Employees should know exactly how to accomplish the given metric and receive updates about their progress throughout the year. In fact, smaller quarterly or monthly bonuses are more motivating than one big, year-end bonus.

---

[7]Ruth Houston, "Shocking Statistics Reveal Link Between Office Christmas Parties and Infidelity," *The Examiner*, December 15, 2011, http://www.examiner.com/article/shocking-statistics-reveal-link-between-office-christmas-parties-and-infidelity.

Wage Increases

Wage increases can be an effective motivator if the increase is based upon performance. In the attempt to be fair and equitable, wage increases often take a socialist route, where the highest available increase is some small percentage, like 2-3 percent, which is based upon the achievement of some individual goals set earlier in the year. If the manager wants to provide a larger increase, she must promote the employee to a new position that pays a higher rate rather than just give a larger raise. Similarly, if the employee gets to the top of the compensation range for the current position, any raise would require a promotion.

These policies create an environment in which employees don't feel that hard work is related to a large increase, so they are motivated to look for higher-paid positions rather than focus on doing good work. In my career, I have received as large as 20 percent increases in a single year, entirely based upon performance. With this potential, any employee who is financially motivated would be motivated to work hard. This also encourages an employee to stay with the company that is appreciating their work.

Employee of the Month

Does having your picture on the wall or a special parking spot motivate you? This is one of those laughable motivation techniques that is still prevalent. It is so laughable that a movie was created to show how ridiculous the practice is. At best this strategy creates unhealthy internal competition when the goal should be to improve the overall team performance. This technique is almost always wasteful and demotivating.

Note Employee-of-the-month awards are wasteful.

Motivating Without Waste

Given that so many of these techniques are wasteful, why do so many companies use them? The answer is simple. Because it is what they have always done. They've always had banquets, they've always had a Christmas party, and they've always had an employee of the month. Very little thought typically goes into the whys behind it. Employee satisfaction and engagement in America is horrible. Satisfied employees are better employees. So, in order to achieve these outcomes you must take a fresh approach to your motivational practices.

Know Your Employees

It may sound like a no-brainer, but it is so frequently forgotten—every employee is different! Numerous studies show that employees of smaller companies are happier. This is likely because the bigger the company, the more standard the policies, and the bigger the company, the easier it is to get lost in the shuffle.

Managers must sit down with their employees on a regular basis and ask them directly what they want to make them happier in their jobs. Take the approach of the sky's the limit. You have to let employees know that you emphasize with their needs and wants. They may ask for things that are financially or otherwise impossible, but that doesn't matter yet. After you have shown them that their opinion matters, you can negotiate for something that works. Then, you must follow up to make sure their satisfaction is increasing.

Also, you must follow up as needs change. An employee's needs in their 20s are a lot different from their needs in their late 30s, with kids and family obligations. Likewise, the needs and desires of empty nesters will again be different. Different generations are motivated by different things. Different personality types are motivated by different things. Different positions in different industries are motivated by different things. Standard HR policies generally create more disengagement than engagement.

Note Every manager should know exactly what each employee wants to be happy.

Have Great Management

Numerous studies show that the number one demotivator is a bad boss. This might be a really tough realization, if it is your employees who are unproductive, but it is hard to argue with the multitude of studies. Employees must trust their managers. They must be able to trust that their manager has their best interests in mind.

Happy employees also feel that their managers are competent. It is nearly impossible to be motivated to work hard when you know your manager doesn't know what he is doing or talking about. This does not mean that you have to know everything to be a good manager. Employees will typically love it when a manager says, "I don't know how to handle this situation. That's why I hired you. You are smart and capable."

Manage Positively, Not Negatively

Through years of child development studies and workforce studies, we've learned an important thing: reward the good, ignore the bad. Instead, we tend to ignore the good and punish, or "coach" the bad. Rewards should be tied to positive accomplishments. If an employee has a weakness in an area, do not ask them to do that thing. You are never going to have the perfect employee. Instead, you should find employees that possess different skills. Then, nurture and encourage each employee to develop the skills that they are good at.

Healthy Employees Are Happier

Numerous studies have shown the impact of health on engagement. This gets worse when the employee feels that the employer does not support their needs. Do whatever is needed to help employees be healthy. Encourage sick employees to stay home. Encourage time off for doctor's appointments. Give time off to go to the gym. Companies talk out of both sides of their mouths on this topic. They say that you should stay home if you are sick, but if you are sick too often, you get fired. They say they want you healthy, but they really want you at work. Implement policies that reward healthy choices. This is another reason not to have banquets, pizza parties, and donuts in meetings!

We discuss better motivators throughout the next sections. The key is that the motivators of the past are not only ineffective, but are many times demotivating.

Increased Productivity

The process of improving productivity is an operational issue that managers should address. HR professionals may be involved in pay-for-performance or piece-work productivity compensation. We discuss productivity in more detail in Chapter 8. Here, we look at HR tools that can be used to encourage productivity.

Education and Training

Education and training opportunities are undervalued in business today. This is considered an extraneous expense that is often cut as businesses look for ways to meet their budgetary needs. I once worked with a leader who had the opposite opinion. He preferred to hire people who wanted to get their education as direct labor workers. The theory that he had was that those employees may be more motivated to succeed due to longer-term career goals, they may be easier to train, and they may be promotable. Even though there is an expense related to subsidizing the education of these workers, they would be more promotable or exportable. Promotable employees build the internal talent of the company, and at a lower cost than finding experienced workers externally. Exportable employees are also good, because the next group of workers come in at entry level wages, which helps keep direct labor costs lower.

There is a famous story of a CFO asking a CEO whether the company could afford to train employees, only to have those trained employees leave the organization. The CEO asked the CFO if the company could afford *not* to train them. Companies that choose not to offer competitive educational opportunities to their employees fail to motivate good employees to stay. The reality is that there are always employees who choose to leave after being educated. Some companies minimize this by requiring employees to pass a probationary period prior to being eligible for educational assistance and then requiring employees to repay any expenses incurred if they do not stay at the company for some period of time after the education is completed. For a person who is intelligent and motivated without the resources to go to school full time, this is a good option. For companies, not only do you get an intelligent and motivated employee, you probably will have that employee for four-eight years, depending upon the amount of education that they get. Who loses in this deal?

Some employees have reduced what they will pay for employee education rather than eliminating it. Although this is a better option than eliminating the benefit, it is still short-sighted. In a competitive environment, the benefits package can have a great deal of influence over the decision to work for your company.

> **Note** Invest in your people!

On-the-job training is less contested than educational assistance programs. Typically, specific training is targeted more at the work being done in that company rather than toward a degree. Even in these situations, you may hesitate to provide training due to the fear of losing employees. Don't. You must have a competent workforce to succeed.

Employee Evaluations

As mentioned, employee evaluations can waste time and energy without having productive outcomes. Over the years, I have talked with other managers and leaders who struggle with developing measurable goals for all of their employees, performing the measurements, and then using the measurements for the employee evaluations. There is no point in creating measurements so that you can check the box for HR. If the employees perform measurable activities that are important to you, measure those activities for the evaluation. If they don't, don't force a measurement onto your employees.

Companies have forgotten that the evaluation process is for the benefit of the employee rather than for the benefit of the company. The sad reality is that many employees get feedback only once a year when these evaluations are performed. Competent managers talk with employees frequently and give feedback in the moment so that positive behavior is repeated and negative behavior is avoided. In such an environment, the employee knows what to expect during their evaluation because they've been hearing it all year.

Now keep in mind that we believe in structured processes with measurable outcomes. This is different from evaluating people. We should not force our methods to evaluate employees to be like those that we use for equipment or processes. The evaluation form should be very simple. First, there should be a section to discuss whether all of the employee's skills are relevant. This is so that the employee can benefit from feedback on where she can improve. Next, there should be a section about interaction with others. This is not an opportunity to be punitive; there are other processes for this. This is the opportunity to discuss areas for improvement and develop strategies to make those improvements. There should also be a section about the efficiency and effectiveness of the work performed. All employees need to be competent. This is the employee's opportunity to understand where they need to improve. You may choose to talk about initiative taken or some other areas important to your business. The total number of sections on the evaluation form should be fewer than six. There should be a rating system on some kind of Likert scale and room for comments.

The outcome of the evaluation is a document that the employee can take with her, and that contains her goals and strategies for development over the next year. This document should not be used to create the compensation for the employee. The frequent use of evaluations to design compensation make the evaluation ineffective. Management is either overcritical or not critical enough because of this fact. The overcritical may not want to give high raises so they may be critical to avoid this. The under-critical may not want the employee compensation to be affected so they may sugar-coat the evaluation. The employee may feel more defensive because of the implication that the evaluation affects compensation. All of this leads to evaluations that do not benefit the employee; instead, it's just a process that you must go through every year.

■ **Note** Employee evaluations are for the benefit of the employees, not the business.

Employee Surveys and Suggestions

Large companies tend to survey their employees as a way to better understand what drives employee behaviors. The idea to survey employees and have employee suggestion programs is a good one. One fundamental of a culture of continuous improvement is the need to engage the process experts in improving their own processes. The process experts are the employees. In a smaller company, the surveys may be less formal. Managers build good working relationships with their workers so that opinions and ideals can be shared freely. This should also happen in larger organizations, but unfortunately a culture of fear built by a structured employee evaluation program designed by HR professionals often prohibits employees from speaking freely.

As bad as it is not to solicit employee feedback at all, it is even worse not to act on it when you do solicit it. Not listening to employee feedback is a great demotivator. This does not mean that all employee ideas are good ones or that they should all be implemented. All employee ideas should be taken seriously and addressed, either by using them or by explaining why you are not using them.

Administration Positions

In the days before computers, managers needed secretaries to perform tasks that they were not able to do in a workday, such as type a document multiple times until it was perfect. Now there is less of a reason for administrative roles. These roles include assistants to answer phones, file documents, manage schedules, and create documents. Don't get us wrong. Most of those people that we know who do this work are very efficient and effective. The issue is not the quality of or need for the work that administrative assistants do.

The waste in this area stems from the fact that office processes are so inefficient that this work is necessary. In order to be effective, a person can focus on only a few projects at a time while managing their daily tasks. With this limited scope, an assistant is not necessary. We have worked in multiple companies where the need for administrative assistants was phased out. In one very large company, the CEO and CFO manage their own schedules, file their own documents, answer their own phones, and create their own work schedules. Truly great administrative assistants can be retrained to do other jobs. This way, they begin to add value and they are typically happier because they are building their resume with new skills.

Paid Time Off

One area where companies can save money as well as motivate employees is in the paid time off. Some industries have "use it or lose it" paid time off policies, where each year, the employee time off is reset. Typically, companies try to minimize the paid time off for employees and do a good job having policies to control this. The waste comes from the administration of the time off.

The most effective paid time off policy that I have seen was based upon managerial control. Managers were responsible for monitoring and administering time off for each employee. There was no fancy system to track each person's time off. Sometimes, in the name of efficiency, we add work that makes us more inefficient. By centralizing control of paid time off, you take the power and decision-making away from management. You also take away management accountability, which produces weaker managers. Employee management is the job of managers. HR is there to help with issues.

Flextime and Working from Home

Many companies are embracing flexible work options. In fact, according to Gallup, employees with more flextime report a 44 percent higher well-being.[8] Flextime allows workers to set their own schedules. Many companies encourage workers to work from home. Work-from-home workers work longer (46 versus 42 hours) and are slightly more engaged (32 percent) than employees who work on-site (28 percent).[9]

I worked with a consulting group whose employees spent part of their time working at home with a video link to the company. I could see that they were working, yet they avoided travel costs and the waste that happens from employee interpersonal interaction. My office phone rings to my computer and cell phone. I can take a work phone call anywhere I can get an Internet connection. I can make a presentation and even give control of my computer to someone around the world through the use of collaboration software. I have a faster Internet connection and better computer hardware at home than I have in my office. Most work-at-home people have a similar situation.

Unfortunately, there is a lack of trust in many organizations that prohibits people from working at home. Likewise, there is such an ingrained culture of thinking people need to be at the office, that it is hard to see the work world in other ways. Also, as noted in Chapter 2, it is hard for people to realize that they don't need all the meetings they have.

Both of us get more work done at home than we do at work from a sheer productivity standpoint. The benefit of the office is the interaction with co-workers on team projects. Each company has its own individual needs. Obviously, a manufacturing line worker or a mechanic cannot work remotely. Companies should evaluate the work of each person and leverage technology to utilize the ability to work at home. As long as there are productivity expectations and measurement methods in place, this can allow companies to lower facility, utility, and maintenance costs, while increasing productivity and satisfaction.

---

[8]Gallup, "State of the American Workplace," 2013, http://www.gallup.com/file/strategicconsulting/163007/State%20of%20the%20American%20Workplace%20Report%202013.pdf.
[9]Ibid.

Contingent Workforce

There are many times your company does not need a full-time employee, but needs a consultant or part-time employee who is available two to three days a week. This schedule works well for many talented workers who simply cannot work nine-to-five jobs for various reasons. It also minimizes your company's fixed labor expense.

Many accountants would argue that labor is a variable expense, but those of us who have managed a workforce understand that it is difficult to hire good people, so people are not a variable expense. When evaluating the use of a contingent workforce or temporary workers, you need to understand the role you are trying to fill. Companies are guilty of trying to maintain a large number of workers who work on a part-time basis in order to avoid employee benefit expenses. As a leader, you need to be careful not to do this. Forcing workers who want or need full-time employment to fill part-time roles only hurts you by giving the workers a reason to leave. Temporary workforces also require more supervision, training, and handoffs. The analysis that I did a few years ago that looked at employee productivity and quality based upon employment status showed with a high degree of confidence that temporary workers produced a lower-quality result with less efficiency than full-time employees.

A contingent workforce needs to benefit the employee and the employer. I have seen this work where a talented person with great experience worked 30 hours a week as a contingent worker because she was dedicated to being a mom. Her work was some of the best marketing work that I have seen and she maintained her family needs. The company benefited from her experience. She benefited from the flexibility.

Employee Benefits

When I worked at Core Systems, LLC at the turn of the 21st Century, there were a lot of families who worked there. Core Systems did not pay hourly workers a high wage. As a matter of fact, a person could make more money working at McDonald's than at Core Systems. What I found out was that many of the workers worked there for the benefits. The health benefits were cheap in comparison to other companies and the network was flexible. This experience taught me something about people's motivations. Managers assume that employee decisions are based upon salary, when in reality each person has his own needs. The topic of employee benefits includes much of what we have discussed in this chapter. In addition to these benefits, employee benefits also include investment and ownership options, health plans, and many other creative benefits offered by companies that understand that benefit plans can be a competitive advantage.

These are competitive advantages that differentiate your company from others and attract top talent. Benefit programs can be a disadvantage when they are cut and are not competitive. Good talent can be lost because the right benefits are not available. This is an important concept to consider, given the current state of the healthcare system and the implementation of the affordable care act. With medical costs increasing at a greater rate than inflation, companies struggle to minimize costs. Before you do this, make sure that you understand your employees' motivations. You might just lose good employees that make you more money than their medical expenses because you are revising your benefit options. Also, realize that good healthcare enables you to have healthier employees, which again increases satisfaction and productivity.

HR Metrics

HR metrics are many of the same metrics used by managers. Motivation methods need to be analyzed for a return on investment. As discussed earlier, bonus programs and wage increases should not be entitlement programs or ways to trick employees into thinking they are earning more money when, in fact, their wealth is dwindling.

There should be metrics that determine where your company stands in relationship to competition for the same labor. You need to consider the roles within your company and who competes for your skilled labor. In jobs such as information technology, sales, marketing, quality control, supply chain management, or others, the industry skills are less important than the technical skills. You are competing with the whole region in multiple industries for these workers. The analysis of compensation and benefits programs needs to extend beyond your own industry.

Productivity

Productivity is the amount of something produced using labor resources. The product or service will vary depending on the industry, but the productivity concept does not vary. It is measured as paid hours per unit or as worked hours per unit. The unit may be a service or product, but is something that can be measured and understood.

Managers and accountants often argue about productivity. Managers want to meet 100 percent productivity, and accountants want to count only value-added activity. The percent productivity doesn't really matter. What matters is that there is a consistent measurement method in place, goals for improvement, and progress toward those goals. The actual productivity measure matters only when there is a benchmarked comparison that you must make.

> **Note** You must track, measure, and improve the productivity of all employees. If someone is not adding value, why are they doing their job?

Benefits and Compensation

Part of HR's goals is to minimize cost and maximize talent. This is done in various ways. One method is to get comparative data on job descriptions and measure where you are in the range. You create a normal distribution curve and try to hire people below the median value for that job description and maintain overall wages around the media. Figure 5-6 shows how this curve may look.

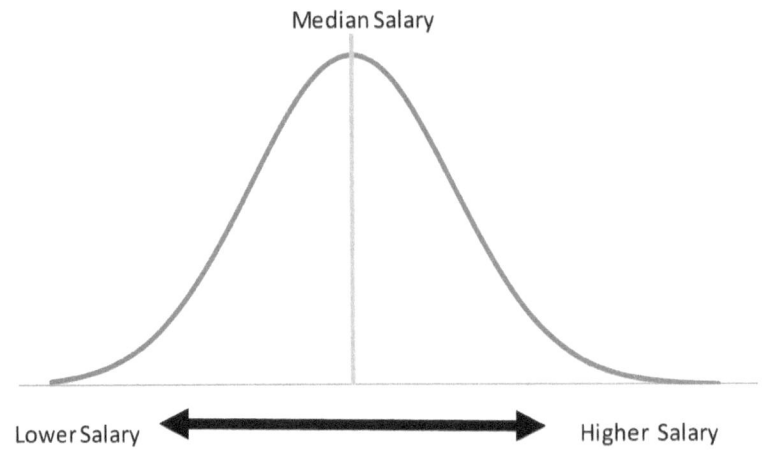

Figure 5-6. Normal Salary Distribution for a Job Description

Another metric used to measure compensation is benefit cost per employee. The point behind this metric is to minimize this expense while maintaining a benefits package that will make your company attractive to potential employees. This metric helps you identify escalating benefits costs and should trigger some action to look for ways to reduce these costs.

$$\text{Benefit Cost per Employee} = \frac{\text{Total Cost of Employee Benefits}}{\text{Number of Employees}}$$

As we stated, we are not fans of these metrics. Never try to normalize your employees' salaries or benefits so that you fit a standard average. If you are paying significantly above average but have even better performance, who cares? You have found a formula that works for you!

Employee Satisfaction

As discussed earlier in this chapter, employee satisfaction is hard to improve. It is also hard to measure. Companies may use a survey tool like the Likert scale to measure employee satisfaction, but these measures are only as good as the trust the employees have in the confidentiality of the survey. If employees are truly unsatisfied then they will likely not trust the validity of the survey results, even when the survey is conducted by a third party. However, we strongly encourage you to track employee satisfaction on a regular basis. There are better measures of employee satisfaction.

Employee turnover is a good measure of employee satisfaction, because the ultimate measure is whether or not the employees stay. What is the right employee turnover percentage? This depends upon what you want for your company. Some amount of turnover is healthy. In a low wage job where training costs are relatively low and sufficient controls are in place to ensure quality, a turnover percentage of 25 to 30 percent may be okay, as long as the money saved by the low wages from new employees exceeds the cost to train the new employees and there is a sufficient workforce pool in the area. In a skilled labor job where training and risk of quality defects are an issue, a much lower turnover percentage would be acceptable. Here's one formula for calculating employee turnover:

$$\text{Employee Turnover} = \frac{\text{Employees Leaving over 12 Months}}{\text{Average Number of Employees}}$$

TURNOVER BENCHMARKS

We caution you not to rely too heavily on turnover benchmarks. The job pool in your area is not likely to be the same as the benchmarking groups you are looking at. It is also a reasonable assumption that if you aim for average turnover along with average wages, you will have average performance.

Turnover can be quantified in monetary terms as well as a percentage of the workforce:

$$\text{Turnover Costs} = \text{Cost of Separation} + \text{Vacancy} + \text{Replacement} + \text{Training}$$

The final measure of employee satisfaction that every company should measure is the absence rate. Although a reasonable absence rate is to be expected due to health and family issues, an overall absence rate for the company or a department indicates how satisfied the employees are. Happy employees come to work.

$$\text{Absence Rate} = \frac{\text{Number of Days Absent from Work}}{\text{\# of Employees} \times \text{\# of Work Days}}$$

If you monitor all of these metrics for employee satisfaction, you can identify if you have opportunities to improve.

Workers' Compensation

Workers' compensation is not just a cost of business that you try to minimize. It is a measure of both employee satisfaction and how well your internal safety programs are designed. If you have high or increasing workers' compensation costs, you need to evaluate your training and safety programs for effectiveness. If you find that your processes are well designed then you may have an employee engagement issue.

$$\text{Workers' Comp per Employee} = \frac{\text{Total Workers' Comp Costs}}{\text{Average Number of Employees}}$$

Benchmarking can be an effective way to identify poor performance and workers' comp issues. Your goal should be a workers' comp per-employee cost of $0.

Recruiting

Recruitment is a key function of all HR departments. It is a vital role because the quality of your workers will often define the quality of your company. Because having the right people in key roles is essential to success, you have to be good at filling the right positions with the right people in a short time. The first way to analyze the effectiveness of your recruitment activities is to look at the number of good applicants you get from them. If the applicants you get don't get hired, your recruitment source is ineffective. To have an efficient and effective hiring process, you need to have a high yield percentage.

$$\text{Yield Percentage} = \frac{\text{Number of Applicants Hired}}{\text{Applicants from the Source}}$$

A long recruitment process is frustrating to managers and to high-performing applicants alike. The time it takes to fill the positions is a key metric for monitoring how well your recruiting process works.

$$\text{Time to Fill} = \frac{\text{Total Time to Fill All Positions}}{\text{Number of Positions Hired}}$$

Notice that the recruiting metrics don't highlight expenses related to the new hire. Recruiting personnel often get hung up on reducing the cost to hire employees and minimizing the total compensation. It is much more important to ensure that you are getting the positions filled with the right skills in a timely manner than it is to minimize the costs associated with hiring.

Conclusion

Human resource management can be a source of value or waste within any organization. In order to maximize the value while eliminating the waste, make sure that all efforts are in conjunction with management priorities and not due to bureaucracy. Efforts of human resource management need to be focused on strategies that provide the organization and employees value. Hiring should be based on the company's needs. Employees should be motivated through techniques that truly motivate performance instead of cliché methods such as picnics and holiday dinners. Human resources employees must be fully engaged in business operations as a valued advisor to management and an advocate for employees. If HR works on improving these areas, there will be no need for a chapter about HR wastes.

Waste Checklists

Human Resources Checklist
*All "no" answers identify a potential opportunity for improvement.

Hiring

Is your primary goal of hiring to find the best candidate for the job?	Yes ☐ No ☐
Is the hiring process controlled by management?	Yes ☐ No ☐
Have you looked at having different hiring processes for different job types?	Yes ☐ No ☐
Prior to hiring, do you conduct a needs analysis to ensure that you are hiring the right role?	Yes ☐ No ☐
Prior to hiring, do you conduct a job analysis to define what skills you need?	Yes ☐ No ☐
Do you target potential candidates based upon what your typical candidate may use to browse for jobs?	Yes ☐ No ☐
Do you avoid using traditional hiring techniques as your main method of vetting candidates?	Yes ☐ No ☐
Do you hire outside of your industry?	Yes ☐ No ☐
Do you only interview for fit and to ask specific questions?	Yes ☐ No ☐
Do you use appropriate tests to evaluate skills and fit?	Yes ☐ No ☐
Do you have an economic way of testing instead of relying on a third-party that may be overcharging you?	Yes ☐ No ☐
Do you review the online presence of the potential candidates?	Yes ☐ No ☐
Do you use a quantitative method to review each candidate to take some of the emotion out of the decision?	Yes ☐ No ☐

HR Checklist
*All "no" answers identify a potential opportunity for improvement.

Working with Employees

When you bring on a new employee, do you do a gap assessment to define developmental needs?	Yes ☐ No ☐
Do you proactively provide regular training to boost employee skills?	Yes ☐ No ☐
Are your rewards methods based on things your employees actually want?	Yes ☐ No ☐
Do you build teams through positive work experiences instead of activities outside of work?	Yes ☐ No ☐
Are any celebration dinners or events at the request of employees?	Yes ☐ No ☐
Are your bonuses based on individual or team performance measures?	Yes ☐ No ☐
Are your wage increases based on performance rather than inflation adjustment or entitlement?	Yes ☐ No ☐
Do you avoid employee-of-the-month type activities?	Yes ☐ No ☐
Do you know what motivates your employees?	Yes ☐ No ☐
Do your employees like their management?	Yes ☐ No ☐
Do you reward the good rather than just punish the bad?	Yes ☐ No ☐
Do you actively work to keep your employees healthy?	Yes ☐ No ☐

HR Checklist

*All "no" answers identify a potential opportunity for improvement.

Productivity

Do you encourage employees to get education and training?	Yes ☐ No ☐
Do you financially support employees to get education and training?	Yes ☐ No ☐
Are your employee evaluations for the benefit of the employee rather than a document that HR requires?	Yes ☐ No ☐
Do you take action based upon the results of employee surveys and suggestions?	Yes ☐ No ☐
Do you evaluate the positions that may not be necessary, such as administrative positions?	Yes ☐ No ☐
Is your paid time managed by the manager rather than by a complex time-keeping system?	Yes ☐ No ☐
Do you offer flextime and the option to work from home?	Yes ☐ No ☐
Do you utilize contingent workforces where you need a part-time skilled employee?	Yes ☐ No ☐
Do you hire full-time employees when you need full-time employees?	Yes ☐ No ☐
Are your employee benefits a competitive advantage to getting good workers?	Yes ☐ No ☐
Is human resources involved in improving employee productivity?	Yes ☐ No ☐

Human Resources - General

Is your human resources a support function instead of a function that dictates policy?	Yes ☐ No ☐
Do you human resource processes depend upon managerial input?	Yes ☐ No ☐

CHAPTER 6

Technology
Waste by Using Software as a Solution

> *The first rule of any technology used in a business is that automation applied to an efficient operation will magnify the efficiency. The second is that automation applied to an inefficient operation will magnify the inefficiency.*
>
> —Bill Gates

This quote from Bill Gates explains partly why technology can be a source of waste. Too often companies rely on technology to solve operational problems. Not only will technology magnify inefficiency, but it will also magnify ineffectiveness and the ability to meet customer needs. How many times have you heard justification for a large technological improvement being a gap in a current process that is causing the company issues? Technology is never a moneymaker; it's never a profit center. Don't use technology just because it is fashionable to do so. Technology is a tool to aid other processes. The other processes must be efficient, the right technology must be implemented, and employees must have proper training. With those key pieces of the puzzle, technology can help improve efficiency.

Is There Anything Good About Technology and Marketing

You have to be careful when looking at technology in any area of your businesses, including the marketing areas. Banner ads don't work. Popups don't work. Spam e-mail doesn't work. Unsolicited text advertising doesn't work either. The trick to using new technology to advertise your products or services is to make the content relevant. This is why we suggested having an effective blog or content marketing source that drives consumer traffic to your website. If you're using popups, e-mails, or text messages, ensure that the content of these communications provides value to the consumer beyond hearing about your company. Don't create apps or blogs just because you think you should.

Instead, evaluate your customers and determine what they are doing in these areas. If your current customers or the customers you want are spending a lot of time working in apps, spend some time finding out what they value and consider creating an app. If you can create an app that your customers will use, you will likely get some benefit from it. The key to benefiting from any strategy of utilizing online tools, social media, apps, or e-mail is to ensure that you are offering benefit to your customers. If you keep this in mind, you will have a greater chance of success in your strategy.

When to Jump on the Social Media Bandwagon in Marketing and When to Run

Social media has changed the way many people communicate. While there still is no consistent definition, most researchers agree that social media is a platform for individuals to interact with others with common interests and associations. The interaction between consumers and companies has changed the way that companies create products and services.

Some predict that using social media for marketing in the United States will reach over 30 billion dollars by 2014. This is a five-year increase of over 4,000 percent.[1] We thought, given the huge push in our society to be digital, social media should be included in the technology chapter. Like any other technology or marketing media, social media marketing sometimes makes sense and sometimes it doesn't.

Consider for example an apple farm in our area that we absolutely love visiting. They have a year-round farmer's market where you can always get the cheapest and freshest produce, in addition to their homegrown apples. They also have events that fluctuate with the season: pick your own strawberries in May/June, homegrown blueberries in July, and peaches and tomatoes by the boxfull in August. They used to have one simple website, with a page for contact information and directions, a page for the history of the farm, and a page for current events and which crops are in season. This all changed a few months

---

[1] Ang, Lawrence. (2011). Community relationship management and social media. *Journal of Database Marketing & Customer Strategy Management*, 18(1), 31–38.

ago. Now when you go to the home page, it has no information or events page. Instead it states, "See us on Facebook for current events." Then, you go to the Facebook page and it says that the latest happenings are on Twitter. Then you go to Twitter and you get the one line about what is happening, with very little detail (of course, it's Twitter).

Many users who have to go through this maze of clicks will be long gone. In fact, the average consumer spends about 10-20 seconds on a webpage.[2] If they get frustrated or the page loads slowly, they will spend even less time on the site. If we were not already loyal customers who have an interest in knowing what is going on at the apple farm, we also would not bother going through the extra clicks. (Likewise, we seriously doubt apple farm visitors fit the high social media using profile.) Why would this farm change their online methods? We believe that the apple farm either was likely guided by a well-intentioned, but not analytical marketing consultant and/or they just thought they had to do it because it's what everyone else is doing.

Social media has changed the way many of us communicate. The interaction between consumers and companies has changed the way that companies create products and services. Seventy-five percent of Internet-using adults in the United States use online social media regularly.[3] This shows that there is a definite opportunity for companies to advertise, but only the right products or services can benefit from this kind of advertisement. Likewise, it must be done in the right way.

Before embarking on a social media campaign, companies need to identify the goals of the campaign. Just like with any advertisement strategy, marketers need to understand who the customer is and how this ad strategy is going to reach that customer. Since social media is a two-way communication method the social media strategy has to include a value to the customer in addition to promotion for the company.[4] The company must determine how a social media presence can benefit the customers, such as by providing a better understanding of the product or service. Likewise, social media can be used as a tool for the marketer to get information back from the customer.

---

[2]Nielsen, Jakob, "How Long Do Users Stay on Web Pages?," Nielsen Norman Group, September 12, 2011, http://www.nngroup.com/articles/how-long-do-users-stay-on-web-pages/.
[3]Bemoff, Josh, Cynthia N. Pflaum, and Emily Bowen, "The Growth of Social Technology Adoption," *Forrester Research Report,* 2008, Cambridge, MA.
[4]Andzulis, James "Mick," Nikolaos Pangopoulos, and Adam Rapp, "A Review of Social Media Implications for the Sales Process," *Journal of Personal Selling and Sales Management,* 32(3), Summer 2012, p. 305–316.

By providing tools such as content marketing, trust can be built between the consumer and the company, leading to future sales. Regardless of what value the consumer finds through social media, the company needs to use social media in a strategic way, rather than the typical "spaghetti-on-the-wall" used by many companies.

■ **Note** Regardless of what value the consumer finds through social media, the company needs to make the use of social media in a strategic way, rather than the typical "spaghetti-on-the-wall" method used by many companies.

Social Media Growth

The marketing departments in many consumer industries started using social media to promote their brands or improve the reputation of their products. As these marketers have improved their capabilities, they have developed loyalty programs or transactional marketing efforts. The most sophisticated have also developed big data and analytics. The focus is now on how to capture consumer profiles and data so that, along with gaining new consumers, marketers can take action to retain current customers.[5]

The profile of the social media market is changing, as shown in Figure 6-1. Although Facebook has the largest share of the population, others like LinkedIn have created a niche in the market. The frequent users of LinkedIn may have different needs to meet than those who stick to Facebook, so your social media strategy should be different for each group. You have to consider what type of product you have and what market you are reaching. Back to the apple farm example. As mentioned, we doubt that the apple farm visitors are regular users of any of the typical social media sites. However, for Procter & Gamble, it likely makes sense for a product such as Cover Girl makeup. Users of this product are teenagers and young adults, many of whom are regular Facebook visitors.

---

[5]Greengard, Sam, "13 Major Marketing Trends for 2013," CMO.com, Last Accessed August 2013, http://www.cmo.com/slide-shows/_13_major_marketing_.html.

Eliminating Waste in Business

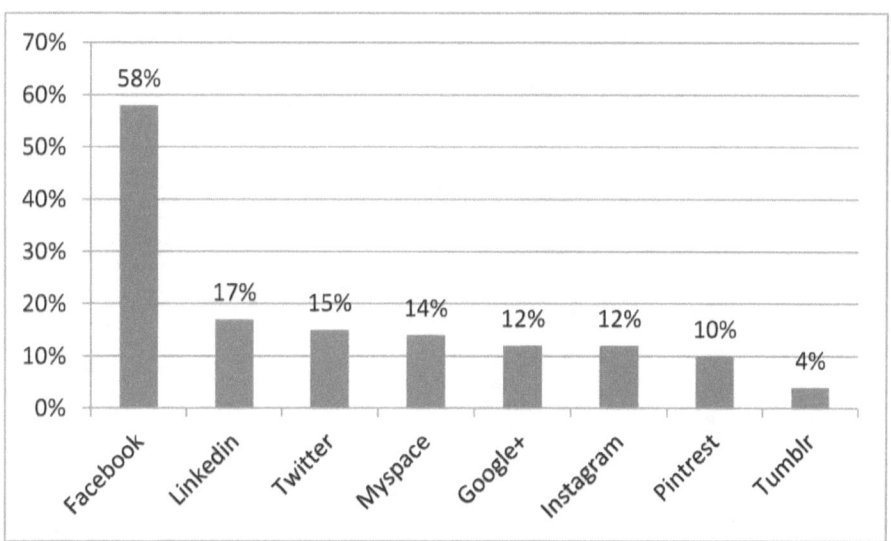

Figure 6-1. Percent of People Using Social Networks. (*Source:* Pedsicker, Patricia, "Six Marketing Trends to Watch in 2013: New Research," SocialMediaExaminer.com, Last accessed August 2013, http://www.socialmediaexaminer.com/marketing-trends-2013/.)

Marketers also need to consider how long each social media outlet will be around. It was easy to predict in 1960 that the TV will be a major part of people's lives for a long time to come. However, think of how rapidly we cycle through social media outlets. In the last 10 years, we have gone from Myspace, to Facebook, to Snapchat, Instagram, and Tumblr. Facebook has even recently admitted to having a huge problem losing the teenage audience. Because no teen wants to hang out the same place their parents do, teens will always be finding new sites as their parents slowly adopt the newer technologies. As the parents adopt, they will kick their kids forward to the next, "cooler" site.

Figure 6-2 shows the breakdown of where companies put their social media efforts. The most noticeable point when comparing this chart to the previous chart is that, although only 17 percent of the population is using LinkedIn, a full 81 percent of companies are utilizing LinkedIn for business purposes. There is extreme disparity between where consumers are and where companies are.

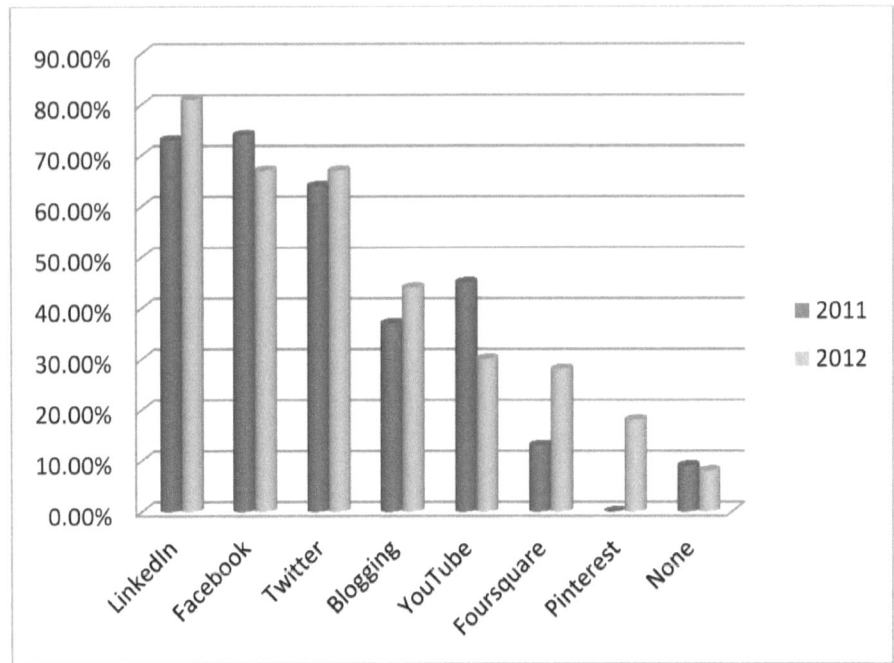

Figure 6-2. Company Use of Social Networks. (*Source:* Barnes, Nora Gamin and Ava M. Lescault, "2012 Inc 500 Social Media Settles In," 2012, UMass Dartmouth, http://www.umassd.edu/cmr/socialmedia/2012inc500/.)

Why are so many companies using LinkedIn? This is an example of how companies have identified that they can successfully market to a smaller population that has interests in their products and services. This trend is fueled by the content marketing used on LinkedIn. Banner advertisements like those used on Facebook are horribly ineffective, while content marketing engages the consumer. The trend toward more focused use of social media is an encouraging one. However, the not-so-encouraging point is that 58 percent of companies admitted that there was no ROI mechanism in place to measure the effectiveness of the time and resources they put into social media.[6]

Content Marketing

This brings us to one of our favorite forms of social media: content marketing. The top three types of content marketing are social posts and updates, e-mail newsletters, and news or feature articles: 83 percent of marketers utilize social

---

[6]Barnes, Nora Gamin and Ava M. Lescault, "2012 Inc 500 Social Media Settles In," 2012, UMass Dartmouth, http://www.umassd.edu/cmr/socialmedia/2012inc500/.

posts and updates, 78 percent send e-mail newsletters, and 67 percent use news or feature articles. Content marketing is more effective than Internet advertising because companies can track the interaction of the consumers with the content in order to determine what is important to the consumer. The company can then use these insights to target consumer needs.[7]

On the other hand, consumers are much more likely to come to your site for what is considered more credible information. Let's pretend you are a consumer looking for new, all-natural beauty products. You might start searching on the Internet for various product ingredients and how bad they are for you. After you type "skin care ingredients that are bad for you" in Google, you stumble across one particular site that is the second hit on Google. When you click on this link, a lengthy article comes up that goes through all of the toxic chemicals:

> **Harmful Ingredients in Skincare Products:** We want to protect your health.
>
> The FDA requires that all skincare companies list their ingredients in order of highest concentration first. Learn to read your lotion labels. Do your own research as well. Made from Earth skin care products never use these ingredients. Does your skin care contain these harmful ingredients?
>
> Paraben
>
> This is also known as Methylparaben, Propylparaben, Ilsoparaben, Butylparaben. Parabens are a group of chemicals widely used as preservatives in the cosmetic and pharmaceutical industries. ..."[8]

As the consumer reads through this site, they not only gain insight into the relevant topics, but they also see pretty pictures of flowers and the company's all natural products. The company gains several advantages this way: 1) The customer found the website and came to it. 2) The customer views the website in a positive, credible way. 3) The company has a chance to showcase its products while the customer is fully aware and focused.

■ **Note** Content marketing is one of the most credible, informative, and customer-oriented ways to interact with your customers on social media.

---

[7]Pedsicker, Patricia, "Six Marketing Trends to Watch in 2013: New Research," SocialMediaExaminer.com, Last accessed August 2013, http://www.socialmediaexaminer.com/marketing-trends-2013/.
[8]Made from Earth, Harmful Ingredients in Skincare Products, Last Accessed November 2013, http://www.madefromearth.com/content/harmful-ingredients-skincare-products.html.

Hospitals do very similar forms of content marketing. The Mayo Clinic has an informative page for just about every disease and condition. If you are searching for just about anything, WebMD and the Mayo Clinic are typically your first one or two hits on Google. On the same page where a patient can get information, there are links to click on to make an appointment. Content marketing is one of the most important aspects of a social media strategy.

Waste in Social Media

Social media is obviously here to stay, but it creates a lot of waste. The first waste in social media is having no plan for using the tool. Social media can be a useful tool if the efforts are targeted, but the outcome of the targeted efforts must be measurable. So the second waste in social media comes from lack of measurement. Without effective measurement and the ability to show the ROI tied to that measurement, efforts in social media are ineffective and wasteful. Tools like Google Analytics, Radiant 6, and HubSpot can measure how consumers behave with social media. However, the data provided by these companies does not show the critical link between the activity on the sites and the effect on the sales of the company.[9]

Past business reactions to technology have taught us about what to expect from the social media wave. Facebook, for example, has seen the loss of the teenaged crowd to "cooler" sites like Tumblr, as the teenagers run away from the parental presence on Facebook. This is much like the past adoption of the Internet, where every company felt that they must have a website whether it was actually needed or not. Take our veterinarian as an example. She has a very healthy practice with a loyal customer base and she does not have a website, a Facebook page, or a Twitter feed. Her business model doesn't require these things. Companies need to have a real need to have a social media presence. Companies that follow the social media wave without a good purpose are wasting their resources and maybe even frustrating their customers, like the apple farm with the Twitter account. Define your objectives before engaging in any social media strategy; otherwise, you will probably create waste. You must decide if social media can truly help you meet your objectives. Don't create a Facebook page just because it is what everyone else is doing.

Note Objectives must drive your social media decisions.

---

[9]Barnes, Nora Gamin and Ava M. Lescault, "2012 Inc 500 Social Media Settles In," 2012, UMass Dartmouth, http://www.umassd.edu/cmr/socialmedia/2012inc500/.

Social Media in Sales

To avoid waste in social media in sales, you must know why you are choosing to engage in social media and how your customer behaves and uses social media. You must track, measure, and improve your efforts. You should first perform a "social audit" to determine what your customers want from your company's social marketing strategies. Some reasons that a customer might want to view social media about your products and services are:

- Are customers simply looking for a forum to better understand a product or service?
- Do they want to interact with experienced customers to read word-of-mouth and product reviews?
- Are they perhaps looking for loyalty rewards for choosing to do business with one company over another?

These are just a few questions that you want to ask yourself to determine the needs of your customers. Some firms may need a simple blog, whereas others may need a Facebook or Twitter presence. Still others may find the most value in educational videos posted on YouTube or similar file-sharing forums such as Flickr. The customer drives this decision. Establishing a social media presence that does not attract customers or deliver additional value is a potential waste of resources and a lost opportunity to connect and collaborate. Once the message is out, make sure that there is collaboration between the sales people and the marketing department. You do not want "vigilante" sales people posting things online that are different from other messages and images the company wants to portray.

From the side of the sales rep, social media can be very beneficial. I am in the middle of a large study investigating how sales reps use social media. Finding respondents has been difficult, because many reps still do not use social media—some because of the technology learning curve, some because they feel it is unprofessional, and some due to legal reasons, like customer privacy.[10] Other studies show that fewer than nine percent of sales people use social media as a sales tool.[11] For those who have adopted social media, LinkedIn is definitely the tool of choice. In fact, in my study **88** percent of the sales reps (who use social media) have used LinkedIn, **32** percent have used Facebook, and **20** percent have used Twitter for sales processes. There does seem to be

---

[10]Dugan, Riley, Joshua Clarkson, and Linda Orr, "'I'd Like to Add You to My Professional Network...': Toward a Better Understanding of the Effect of Social Media Usage on Sales Performance," 2014, Unpublished Dissertation, University of Cincinnati.
[11]Agnihotri, et. al, 2012.

performance and productivity benefit in sales, namely in prospecting, research, and follow up. The percentage of sales people using each of these tools for each of the sales processes is shown in Figure 6-3.

Sales Process Stage	Percentage of Respondents Using LinkedIn
Prospecting for Customers	64%
Planning for the Sales Call	24%
Presentation	0%
Handling Objections	4%
Negotiating Terms of the Deal	4%
Post Sales Follow Up	36%

Figure 6-3. Sales Reps and the Use of Social Media

During the pre- and post-sales stages, LinkedIn does seem to help sales reps, primarily as a research aid. During the post-sales stages, social media can be used to update customers of new products or services. It must have a message that is integrated with the rest of the company's communications. Additionally, there needs to be very specific work-related goals. Obviously, you don't want your reps socializing on Facebook all day.

Note Social media can be a beneficial tool for sales reps, especially in the research and follow-up stages of sales. It can be used as a huge time saver, speeding along the sales process.

Technology in Marketing

Social media is just one example of putting technology to use in marketing. Fifty-seven percent of businesses surveyed by HubSpot were able to attribute a new customer to a company blog.[12] There is more technology available in the marketing realm than just social media. Opportunity exists with online presences, mobile applications, big data, and software. Seventy-eight percent of consumers research products online prior to purchasing them.[13] This means

---

[12]HubSpot.com, "The 2011 State of Inbound Marketing", February 2011, http://cdn2.hubspot.net/hub/53/file-13222127-pdf/docs/ebooks/the_state_of_inbound_marketing_final_v3-2.pdf.
[13]Jansen, Jim, "Online Product Research", September 29, 2010, http://www.pewinternet.org/Reports/2010/Online-Product-Research.aspx.

that whether you are in a business-to-business or business-to-consumer selling relationship, information about your products or services must be available online.

Reputation Management

One of the greatest things about the Internet is being able to use it to quickly spread positive word-of-mouth. You should absolutely have a devoted person responsible for tracking positive and negative word-of-mouth on social media. Tools like Google Alerts have been utilized for years by companies that understand the value of the data available to track posts and consumer sentiment. Now the available tools for reputation management have become more sophisticated. This is necessary because, with the increased popularity of social media, companies must know what is being said about their brands. Skweal allows companies to block negative comments and resolve them privately by sending the complaints to the right person. Other tools are being sold to track negative reviews in order to provide data for strategic responses to repeat issues.[14] Table 6-1 shows some popular tools used for reputation management.

Table 6-1. Reputation Management Tools (Source: DiSilvestro, Amanda, "Top 10 SEO Reputation Management Tools Online," February 9, 2013, http://socialmediatoday.com/amanda-disilvestro/1227146/top-10-seo-reputation-management-tools-online.)

Tool	Description
Trackur	Shows what comes up in a Google search or on social networks.
Naymz	Gives you a RepScore based on how people find your brand and your social influence.
BrandsEye	Basics of reputation management and competive analysis tools.
Brandwatch	Monitors keywords on social media sites.
Technorati	Tracks blog posts.
Rankur	Shows online reviews and monitors competitors.
Alterian	Looks at how you are viewed in multiple countries and with multiple demographics.
SocialMention	Monitors keywords, sends alerts, and ranks importance of mentions.
Whos Talking	Similar to SocialMention.
Google Alerts	Sends you e-mail when keywords are mentioned.

---

[14]Greengard, Sam, "13 Major Marketing Trends for 2013," CMO.com, Last Accessed August 2013, http://www.cmo.com/slide-shows/_13_major_marketing_.html.

Although many reputation-management tools are low-cost or even free, companies that choose to invest in social media due to a customer need for this interaction must also invest in the right tools to measure the effectiveness of their online presence. Table 6-1 shows only some of the available tools. These may not be the right tools for your company, so be sure to find the right measurement method for your strategy. (We talk more about social media metrics at the end of this chapter.)

Text Messaging

E-mail is for old people. It's true. Any online research about communication trends will show you that teenagers are more likely to use instant messaging, text, and social networks to communicate than e-mail. Companies are even endorsing the use of these tools for business use by installing services such as Microsoft's Lync, which provides an instant message service along with other tools.

The concern with this trend is that many companies still send e-mail as a marketing technique. This is the Internet version of those shiny direct mail cards that come in the mail, only they are much easier to ignore through spam filters and the Delete key. If the younger consumers are ignoring e-mails now, they are likely to continue this trend as they get older. Therefore, businesses must adapt. Even dental and medical offices have adopted the use of text reminders and confirmations as a way to communicate with its clients.

Mobile Apps

Traditional mobile users outnumber smartphone users 5.6 billion to 835 million,[15] so smartphone market is still relatively untapped. This may be largely due to the expense, but as mobile companies like Apple or Samsung continue to look for ways to offer less expensive options or consumers get smart about purchasing smartphones secondhand, the percentage of smartphone users will continue to grow. Even with this trend, this is an underutilized area in marketing. Applications like Pandora or many app games include popup ads similar to what would be used on a website, but as we all know, we pay about as much attention to those ads as we do the car ads on television. They are just noise in the background to be ignored. Marketers are continuing to miss the boat on where money should be spent on advertising. Figure 6-4 shows the result of a study of where companies spend their advertising budgets versus where consumers spend their time.

---

[15]Ting, Richard, "Why Mobile Will Dominate the Future of Media and Advertising," *The Atlantic*, June 6, 2012, http://www.theatlantic.com/business/archive/2012/06/why-mobile-will-dominate-the-future-of-media-and-advertising/258069/.

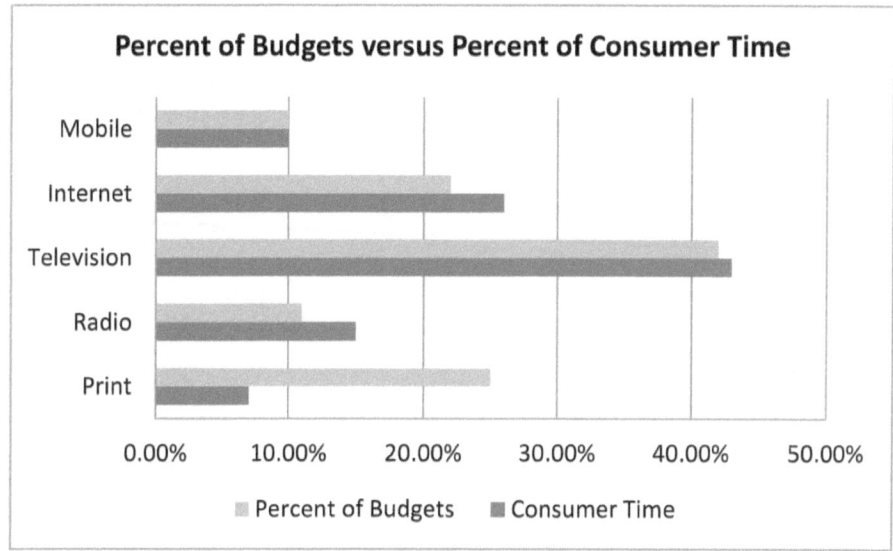

Figure 6-4. Company Spending versus Consumer Behavior. (*Source:* Ting, Richard, "Why Mobile Will Dominate the Future of Media and Advertising," *The Atlantic*, June 6, 2012, http://www.theatlantic.com/business/archive/2012/06/why-mobile-will-dominate-the-future-of-media-and-advertising/258069/.)

■ **Note** Make sure your app has the functionality that your consumers want.

The mobile app advertising market is underutilized by most companies. In fact, advertisers prefer to advertise in a dying media, such as newspapers and magazines, than explore effective ways to advertise through mobile apps. Although most consumers zone out television and radio commercials and even more ignore banner and popup ads when surfing the Internet, spending in these areas is at least appropriate to the volume of use. The waste created by using ineffective technologies is an opportunity for companies to leverage the growth of the mobile apps and secure customers. With mobile users spending over 1.5 hours using mobile applications while Internet usage has declined slightly, it is obvious that this medium deserves attention.[16]

According to a survey by the Boston Consulting Group that included 550 businesses with fewer than 100 employees, only three percent of advertising expenses were used online. Large companies use over 15 percent of their

---

[16]http://blog.flurry.com/bid/80241/Mobile-App-Usage-Further-Dominates-Web-Spurred-by-Facebook.

advertising budgets online.[17] It seems that these small businesses focus on the less expensive print advertising or the potentially more expensive direct mail. Figure 6-5 shows that while mobile web surfing activity remained stable between March 2011 and August 2012, mobile app usage more than doubled.

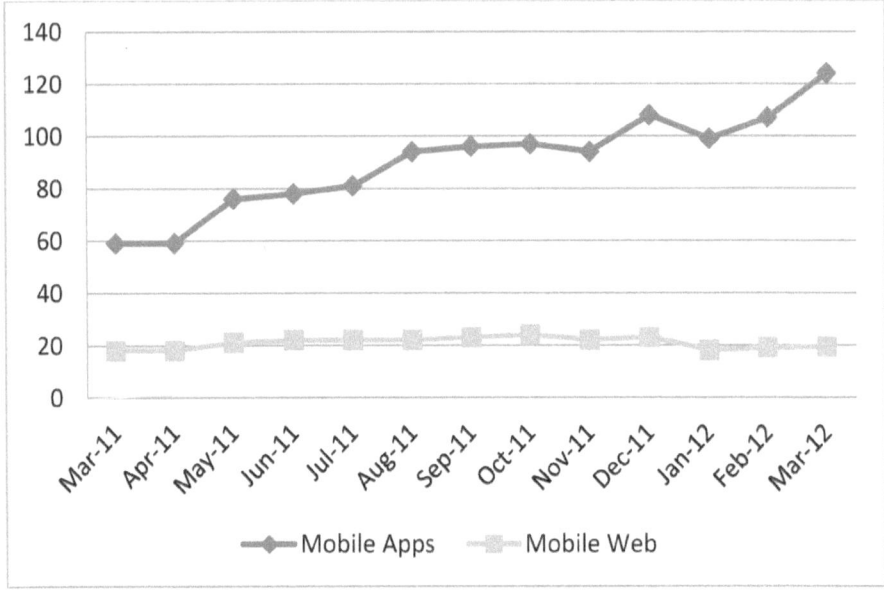

Figure 6-5. Mobile App Usage Growth vs Web Usage Decline (*Source*: Nielsen, March 2011 – March 2012, Nielsen Smartphone Analytics.)

Note Any consumer-driven company with more than 100 employees should have an app presence.

A custom app will likely cost thousands of dollars or even hundreds of thousands of dollars to create. So, although there are millions of apps available for various smartphone platforms, it is not surprising that not all small businesses have created their own apps. The cost of a mobile app will depend on the hours needed to create the app, which is a function of how complex the app is. Pursuing an app without first identifying a need is wasteful, although not

---

[17]DiGrande, Sebastian, David Knox, Kate Manfred, and John Rose, "Unlocking the Digital-Marketing Potential of Small Businesses," Boston Consulting Group, March 19, 2013, bcgperspectives, https://www.bcgperspectives.com/content/articles/digital_economy_marketing_sales_unlocking_digital_marketing_small_businesses/.

looking to see if there is a need in such a growing media outlet is probably more wasteful. Any consumer-driven company with more than 100 employees should have an app presence.

Technology in Sales

Technology has made the sales process much more efficient, and has also created whole new areas of waste. Customer relationship management (CRM) systems still seem to be a mystery to many companies and many times get purchased without being used. CRM systems can be helpful when they're implemented correctly, which we talk about in the following section. Likewise, technology has also enabled better use of analytics in sales due to the data storage capacities. However, few marketers understand how to fully utilize these technologies and do not benefit from them. Instead, many companies opt for the more wasteful traditional forms of marketing and sales (like television advertising), as discussed in Chapters 3 and 4.

CRM

It has been nearly 30 years since the first CRM program, ACT!, was introduced. Yet, only about 45 percent of sales reps use CRM systems.[18] Many sales reps and managers see them as wasteful. Many times they are.

Sales reps have hated (and we do mean hated) their CRM systems for many reasons. Most often, they feel as if CRM systems are ways for their sales managers to spy on them. The independent-minded rep normally hates this thought. Many CRMs are poor designed or at least not designed for their specific company's needs. They, therefore, become a complete waste. There is waste created by purchasing the software and because the reps are in constant struggle with difficult-to-use software. One of the reps I know, who worked with a very well known, great CRM system once told me:

> *I hate it! It is so over-engineered for what we need. We have such high-level analytical proposals for each customer so we store those in Excel. All we really need is a place to track customer info. This has made our jobs so much more difficult. They CRM's sales reps said the dashboards were completely customizable. But the company has been no help.*

---

[18]Accenture, "Connecting the Dots on Sales Performance: Leveraging the 2012 Sales Performance Optimization Study to Inform Sales Effectiveness Initiatives," 2013, http://www.accenture.com/SiteCollectionDocuments/PDF/Accenture-Connecting-Dots-Sales-Performance.pdf.

I've also heard another rep say about an even more well-known CRM:

> This is such a stupid program. I can get my contacts in Outlook, and that's all it really does. It gives lead lists, but the lead lists are like those you buy online—untargeted, outdated, and basically worthless.

When this is what you are hearing from your reps, chances are your CRM system is wasteful because it was not purchased with a clear objective and user needs in mind. On the other hand, I have worked with a company that uses the CRM vilified in the second example, and they love it. Their biggest savings came from tracking the sales reps and the sales process and using that information to boost productivity.

Figure 6-6 shows the most touted advantages of CRM systems. The data was gathered from a large study from the consulting group Accenture. Keep in mind that this data may have some bias, as Accenture gains by highlighting a company's problems, given that they are a consulting firm. However, this data is similar to what we have seen in other companies. The percentages represent how many executives in the survey noticed improvements in each of the areas.

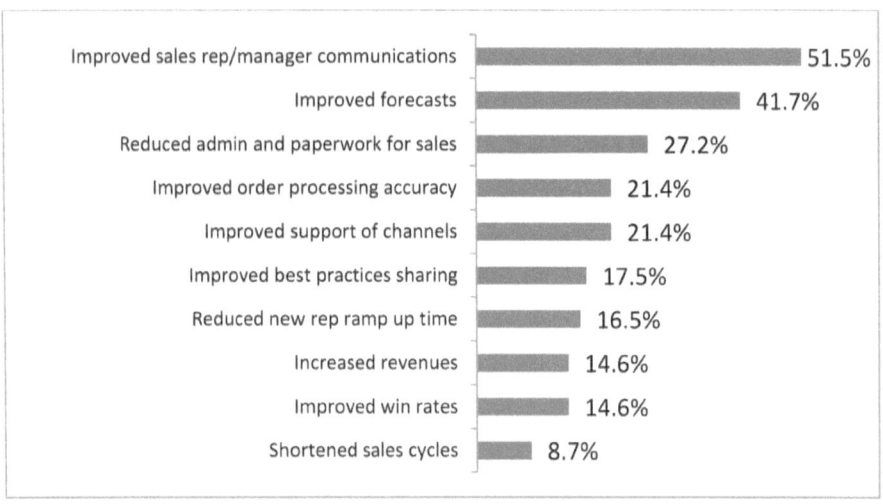

Figure 6-6. Benefits of CRM. (*Source:* Accenture 2013, "Connecting the Dots on Sales Performance: Leveraging the 2012 Sales Performance Optimization Study to Inform Sales Effectiveness Initiatives," http://www.accenture.com/SiteCollectionDocuments/PDF/Accenture-Connecting-Dots-Sales-Performance.pdf.)

If the CRM systems are implemented appropriately, you should see all of these advantages. CRM systems are great tools to record and analyze data, although any high-level analytics will still require a separate program like SPSS. In order to see real advantages of CRMs, you should follow some of the guidelines about technology implementation that we discuss later in this chapter. First, determine what you need the software to do. What do you hope that it can do? What do you need it to do? Ask the people who will use the software the most—the sales reps. Listen to their needs. When purchasing or designing the program, do not over engineer it. Then, provide proper training. Make sure the sales reps actually use the software. The only way to overcome the thought of managerial spying is to build a culture of trust. If your reps are concerned about spying, that means they don't trust management! Find out why. Be honest and open with yourself about why your reps do not trust management.

Note CRM systems can be wasteful if they're not implemented correctly. Perform a needs analysis first, then train. Don't blame spying fears on the CRM software.

Real-Time Buying and Big Data

In Chapter 3, we explained the wasteful, traditional forms of advertising and marketing. It seems that companies are in some ways stuck to those methods and in other ways they jump all over new technology without any purpose for doing so. Take, for example, technology failures such as the QR codes. It is amazing that companies still seem to be placing these little two-dimensional bar codes everywhere, from ads to posters to packaging. Yet, more than 20 years after the invention of the QR code, 93.8 percent of those with a smartphone have never scanned a QR code.[19] This figure does not even account for the percent of the population without smartphones. The failure seems very obvious. It is hard enough to get a consumer to passively sit on a couch and view an ad. What makes anyone think we can show a consumer a boring, black-and-white square, and then have the customer download a QR reader, just to get an unknown bit of information? Failures like these will continue to happen as companies try to figure out the best way to use new digital and mobile technologies. We think that real-time buying and big data hold the most promise in the new technologies available.

Over 6.8 billion cell phones are in use around the world, which has led to a change in the way consumers buy their products.[20] The smartest companies are using real-time data to offer coupons or product information based on the customer's location. For example, an interesting partnership between Visa

---

[19]"QR Codes: Why They Are Failing and What the Future Holds," *Invoke The Blog*, March 17, 2012, http://www.invokemedia.com/qr-codes-why-they-are-failing-and-what-the-future-holds/#sthash.IrJlutSF.dpuf.
[20]Hunt, Teddy, "Mobile Marketing Trends," Last Accessed August, 2013, http://dvm8run94lq3.cloudfront.net/wp-content/uploads/2013/08/Mobile-Marketing-Trends_Final.jpg.

and Gap was formed to take advantage of real-time data. When a Visa card is used in close proximity to a Gap retailer, a message is sent to the mobile phones of opt-in customers. Gap can customize the offer based on time of day, customer history, or other personalization methods. Hopefully, interested consumers will pop over to the Gap during their outing and use their special offer to buy Gap clothing.

The data available today is enormous, but must be considered carefully. For example, the average amount spent during shopping expeditions on tablets and smartphones is higher than during desktop shopping experiences. Likewise, people spend much more online than they do in the store. The latter half of this statistic makes some sense. It is easier to purchase products online; there are fewer distractions and you don't half to worry about your physical cart being too full or about long check-out lines. However, there is some dishonesty in this metric. The reality is that those with a higher disposable income are purchasing with the smartphones and tablets.

Many consumers will go to a store like Best Buy to research a product in the store and then will buy the product online at a lower price. With this trend, organizations have to be smart about the use of their marketing resources and data. Data silos and inadequate business intelligence infrastructures make it difficult for marketers to effectively leverage app development that targets consumer behavior.

Companies that have identified the need for a custom app or for a series of apps to support customer service and growth must develop internal resources to do this. Part of this resource pool needs to be targeted at using the data collected from customers and apps to improve marketing practices. Data doesn't belong in a big data center to report high-level metrics with drill down capabilities. Rather, the data must be used to drive marketing decisions that allow your company to react quicker than the competition in a way that builds value for the customer.

Waste from Technology and the IT Department

Technology is purchased for a host of reasons, some of them good and some of them bad. Many times, companies severely overspend on software or spend the right amount, but do not involve the user in the purchase so the software is still wasteful. We know of a company that spent $85,000 on a technology improvement four years ago. The technology was about four times more expensive than the other options available on the market. The reason for the high cost was that special equipment needed to be included so that the technology could be used by someone who refused to change and learn new technology. This equipment was basically obsolete as soon as it was purchased. Therefore, maintenance and repair was not an option.

So then, not even four years later, new technology and equipment needed to be purchased. This time, someone else was responsible for the purchase. They did not use the equipment, nor did they ask the users of the technology how the system was used. This person was very naïve and bought a system based on a flashy sales presentation. Another system was purchased, surprisingly again, for $85,000, still more than two times as much as many other systems on the market.

At the time of writing this book, after $170,000, the new system is not working. The users and IT department were not consulted and certain things were left out, thus making the system nonfunctional. Many of us have heard of disastrous failures such as this. There are a few basic concepts that must be remembered to ensure that technology purchases and implementations are done in a non-wasteful manner.

Software as a Solution

One common area in business is the inventory-management portion. Most of service businesses and all manufacturing businesses have some sort of inventory to manage. I have heard many times that installing a new software package will solve a company's inventory issues. None of these installations fixed all of the inventory accuracy problems. We know of two companies that, in our experience, are the best at inventory management. They had great accuracy versus the inventory on the books as verified by an audit and they had a relative lack of stock-outs (where you think you have inventory, but don't when you need it). Neither of these companies have fancy MRP (Material Requirements Planning) or ERP (Enterprise Resource Planning) systems, or a WMS (Warehouse Management System). Instead both companies have sound inventory management practices that utilize manual processes. We are using this example because inventory management is the most common reason we have seen for large information technology installations. But, the theme is the same in any installation. Good technology will not overcome inefficient processes.

EMR (Electronic Medical Records) implementations are the current wave of technology improvements in hospitals, physician practices, and testing facilities. EMR systems promise to have more accurate and retrievable information that can be shared across healthcare providers in order to improve care. The reality is that most EMR systems don't communicate well with each other. So, it is difficult to identify the same patient in multiple systems. Within the same facility, there are issues with standardized documentation practices or the correct information in the EMR, such as dosage on certain medications. Because of these inconsistencies, popup alerts and signoff processes occur so much that alarm fatigue is created. By this, we mean that the caregiver is bombarded by alarms and begins to ignore them. So, many alarms are overlooked. The benefits are then unrealized. This is another example of information technology implementation where the promised value is difficult to achieve because the former manual process was not adequate and its issues were passed along to the electronic process.

Customer Relationship Management (CRM) software in sales is the same. Sales reps who are great at recording all their information about their customers will do great whether or not they have a fancy system. CRMs are great, if used correctly. The manager should first set up processes to ensure that all sales reps record all customer information. Then, they have to be encouraged to use that information to make decisions, such as how much time to spend with each account and what to do next with each account. Only those reps and managers who have the appropriate strategic mindset and training will benefit from the system

The key here is that software is rarely the solution but is actually a way to automate a process or maintain good records of a process. Any other expectations of a software implementation are likely wishful thinking.

Note Software is a tool, not a solution.

Not the Right Software

Most companies have standard software packages such as Microsoft Office that provide e-mail, word processing, spreadsheets, and presentations features, but other tools beyond these basic ones are not always provided. The tools that are available may not be the right ones. The decision makers who make software purchases might not know which software is best for the job.

Software might include something as simple as the accounting system used by the company. Most accounting systems perform basic functions such as invoicing customer, paying vendors, inventory, and payroll. Many of these systems don't perform simple functions that are necessary for business. Specifically in the manufacturing sector, only a couple of accounting systems handle revisions to products in the bills of materials (or the recipe for the product being made) while allowing for manufacturing and design changes to be traced. There is also normally not much flexibility in the way that inventory is handled. This is true of both the small software companies and the large ones that market their "solutions" to companies. I have seen and used manual processes and tools such as spreadsheets and Microsoft Access databases to fill in for the shortcomings of these software packages. Every person using the software needs to list their "must haves" prior to the purchase of new software.

Another common problem is with software implementations that cost millions of dollars, but don't perform the necessary tasks without a third-party application. These tasks may include creation of financial statements, sales forecasting, report writing and distribution, and employee hiring/management. A well-intended software upgrade can lead to additional expenses and uncoordinated work due to shortcomings not identified in the selection process.

On a smaller scale of waste, although it happens more frequently, is when companies don't supply individuals with the software they need to do their job. Tools such as Microsoft Visio or Microsoft Project are not standard-issue programs even for those job functions that benefit from their use. If employees are not given the right tools to do the job, they end up creating more work by modifying the tools that are available to them. From personal experience, we have seen gross amounts of productivity loss due to inadequate technology resources.

■ **Note** Lowest price and popularity are not the best ways to pick software. Do a current and future needs assessment.

Not Utilizing Software Potential

We know of a company that bought a software package to track movements of items through its processes. This software shows where each item is at any point in time and how long it has been at that stage of the process. This information can be seen in real time from any workstation in the company. The only reports that are available were provided by the software vendor. This company spent hundreds of thousands of dollars implementing this system, including software, hardware, and employee training, but did not spend the additional ten thousand dollars to have the custom report writing capability or the ability to create interfaces with other systems without the software vendor support. Why would anyone do this? This decision has led to many users downloading detailed data (hundreds of thousands of records) into spreadsheets and spending hours sorting the data to look for KPIs (key performance indicators) to monitor the business operations, when the software is fully capable of producing a report to do this.

I can't even count how many times I have asked whether a company-wide software package has a function that should be used and heard the answer of "yes, I think it does, but we never use it" or "we didn't buy that module, but I hear it works well." Prior to making decisions not to use standard software functionality, a cross-functional team should evaluate what is not being used and what the company loses by not utilizing the software potential. Even when the company will not immediately need to use a function of a software package but foresees a future use, a plan to revisit the decision on whether or not to use the feature should be put in place. Once the software is purchased, make sure all employees have proper training. Many times, software is not used to its true potential because people do not understand the tools they have at their disposal.

■ **Note** Don't limit the benefits of new software by not fully implementing it.

Report, Reports, and More Reports

While teaching Lean Six Sigma, one example that is frequently used to highlight extreme inefficiency is the overproduction of reports by organizations. I often tell the story of report usage that I used in Chapter 1 of this book, in which the manager took every report off the system to see if anyone would actually notice if they were gone.

Another story I tell is how I get reports pushed to me by one of our large vendors. This vendor does quality analytics, operations analytics, contract negotiation, and consulting for us. As part of their services, I get bombarded with e-mails every two weeks. I got so many reports via e-mail that I set up a rule in Microsoft Outlook to automatically delete anything that came from that vendor. This worked well until I started working with some consultants from the same vendor; I realized I was not getting e-mails that I needed.

In my current role I am often asked to push reports to people rather than providing easy access to the same information that the users of the data can get whenever they want. I always resist these requests because of the story that I just told. The average business user gets over 100 e-mails per day.[21] This means that many of these e-mails will likely get ignored. The last thing that any business user needs is to receive too many e-mails with reports that they don't use. Instead, employees need to be able to access the few reports that they use in an easy and customizable way.

---

[21] Radicati, Sara, Quoc Hoang, "Email Statistics Report, 2011–2015," May, 2011, The Radicati Group, Inc.

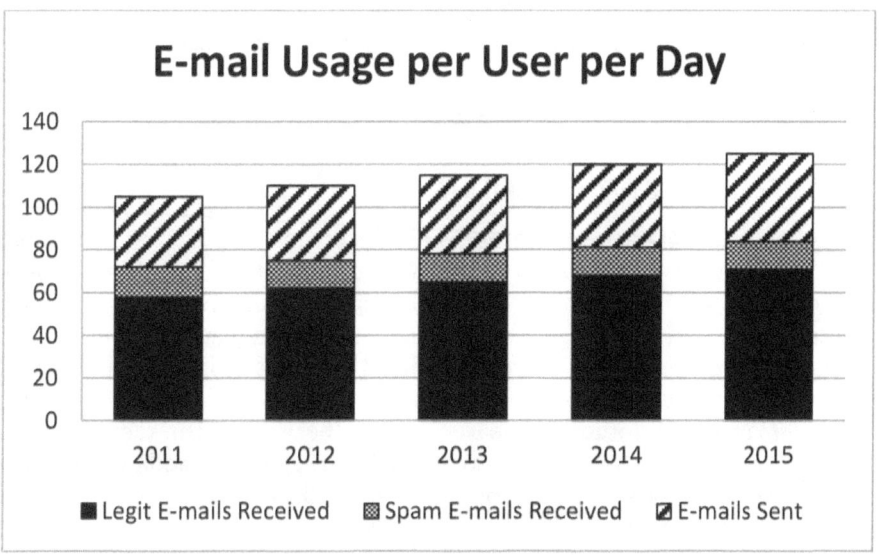

Figure 6-7. E-mails per User Per Day (*Source*: Radicati, Sara, Quoc Hoang, "Email Statistics Report," 2011–2015, May 2011, The Radicati Group, Inc.).

For any organization that has multiple computer systems, report management becomes even a bigger deal. Your financial statements may come from one system, cost data comes from a second system, productivity from a third system, and quality from a fourth. And so on and so forth. Even the best-intending IT teams that create a central repository of reports where users can access PDF or RPT versions of reports from multiple systems end up removing the functionality that the reports may have in them.

The most mature organizations set up IT infrastructure where work lists are created in the main IT system rather than a report to be analyzed. Alerts are used to identify performance of a process that is not representative of regular performance. Analyses are completed using business intelligence (BI) tools with self-service data cubes and filters with the ability to drill down to detail information if needed. This is part of the dream of the use of big data and BI tools that many organizations pursue. The process toward this dream starts with looking at the reports that you push to workers and evaluating how you organize your data to make it easy to navigate and produce reports.

For small and midsized organizations, it is often sufficient to have one or two IT systems to do key functions. When selecting these systems, it is best for small and midsized organizations to consider embedded reporting features to see if the self-service data access is available. Larger organizations need to start by having each key system with self-service data access capability in conjunction with a larger BI strategy that is tied to business needs.

> **Note** Reports should add value to key business processes. Users who need reports should have easy access to them.

Data Access and Distribution

Whether your data access strategy is via documents, reports, or data cubes, you must have a data security and distribution strategy. For manufacturing and many service organizations, these strategies are determined through the company role and some regulatory requirements. Data that is secured is often cost, margin, or personnel information. Small and midsized organizations have an easier time determining data access and security requirements because of the smaller workforce and clearer roles. In healthcare, the same information is secure as the information mentioned earlier. But, in addition to those requirements, private health information must be protected in accordance with regulatory requirements.

All of this is obvious, so why have a section on waste regarding data access and distribution? The issue is that the IT personnel with master data access may not understand the data or how it could be used to drive improved performance. Users of the data may manually re-create information that is already stored in a more reliable manner in a current software, due to a lack of knowledge of the availability of the data elsewhere. This is wasteful not only because of the work put into collecting and storing the data, but it is also dangerous. Software managed by IT departments is often built with security to ensure that nobody unintentionally accesses information not meant to be seen by them. In areas like healthcare, this is important due to privacy needs of patients, but in any organization, critical data should be protected.

The answer to the data access and distribution issue is not an easy one. IT departments try to manage this access concern through role-based access, domain groups, and approval processes. The challenges are in making sure that the roles and domain groups are appropriate. In addition, the approval process should be simple enough that potential users are more likely to get appropriate access than to create their own data repository. As the amount of data increases, it becomes more important to make data experts available to users. Making data readily available prevents users from trying to re-create it for their own needs.

This may surprise data security professionals, but security can become so high-level that it puts the data security at risk. The processes may actually drive more potential for leaks. For instance, in my work with consultants, it is sometimes necessary to share data. This is pretty easy for small quantities of data where the byte size limit does not exceed what is allowed by IT, but when the data sizes exceed those limits, other options need to be available. I have seen high-priced encrypted flash drives. This is okay if both parties have security profiles that allow the installation of the encryption software and there is an interpersonal connection. Otherwise, some type of file transfer method is needed.

For example, I worked with a consultant who was trying to get a file to me. We tried e-mail. It didn't work. We tried my file transfer system and he could not access it through his security. We tried his file transfer system and I could not access it through my security. So, he created a Gmail account for the purpose of transferring the file to me. He e-mailed it from the new Gmail account to the new Gmail account. Then he gave me the login information to get the file from the Gmail account inbox. This was the method that he chose because again, due to security, neither one of us could use a popular method such as Dropbox or Google Drive to transfer the file. None of our internal tools worked.

In this example, we weren't dealing with private information that would have violated either company's security policy. It was actually a file to help do complex calculations and create a dashboard. The point is that a company's attempts to secure data can make it less secure. Companies can disable the ability to access external e-mail accounts and add other more extreme barriers, but I guarantee that a determined person will find a way to do their job regardless of these barriers.

■ **Note** Make your data more secure by allowing appropriate access to data and tools.

IT Training and Skills Gaps

We've all been there and seen it. Something goes wrong and an employee calls IT. IT's first question is usually, "Is the computer powered on?" This is an extreme example, but PC support technicians will tell you that power issues or a simple restart of the computer fix many of the computer issues that cause the average user to need help. Unfortunately, many workers are expected to use technology, and they never receive the proper training. If you do not train your workers to use the technology you buy, you're likely creating waste.

At one of my former employers, we decided to bring in a college professor in IT to teach many of our employees how to use Microsoft Excel. After days of training, the employees still could not perform the duties that we needed them to perform. There is no one-size-fits-all approach to training. With the level of IT implementations that companies put effort into and the wide spread use of Outlook, Word, Excel, and PowerPoint, IT training is a key to many organizations. Why are we so bad at it? We put money into computer labs. We pay employees to learn in these labs. We spend hours developing materials for training. So why is it still so bad? We don't actively do two steps that are main keys to success.

The first step is determining what the user needs to know. We want to train the user how to do everything. For example, there is very little reason to teach the average Excel user how to do conditional formatting, use a solver, link to external data sources, or edit macros. Most users of Excel probably need to how to use about ten formulas and format cells. Yet, when we train users in Excel, we try to teach them everything. More specialized software is the same. We need to determine what people need to know in order to actually train them well. I have sat through days of software training when probably 80 percent of the material was background information or about functions that I will never use.

The second step is determining what the user already knows. We assume a basic competency level when we train employees and we are not consistent in our assumption. This is not only the case in IT training but pretty much all training makes assumptions like this. When I went through my Lean Six Sigma Black Belt training, at least half of the material was review. I was bored. The teacher was excellent and the material was interesting, but I already knew it. Over-training is a large source of waste in IT. Under-training is also a waste. I have trained people in the use of multiple hardware and software systems. In nearly every class there are people who probably could have learned in 15 minutes what I taught in a few hours. All of that time was waste. There also is normally someone who, after hours of instruction, still cannot do the basic functions. All of that time was waste. Without first knowing the capabilities of those being taught, you run the risk of wasting their time by over- or under-training.

> **Note** Do competency analyses and determine learning requirements prior to training people.

Heads in the Cloud

While more technical definitions exist, at its most basic level, cloud computing involves storing and accessing data and programs over the Internet instead of from your computer's hard drive. There are many opinions on why businesses should embrace cloud computing. Cost reductions due to paperwork reduction, lower hardware costs, and lower personnel costs to maintain the hardware are one reason. By using the cloud, your IT staff is focused on maintaining your network and handling routine PC support functions. This frees your staff to perform value-added functions like maintaining databases and supporting the technology needs of the workforce. Figures 6-8 shows the average savings per company from a group of companies surveyed in various areas of business. Figure 6-9 shows the total savings ranges for the responding companies.

Eliminating Waste in Business | 227

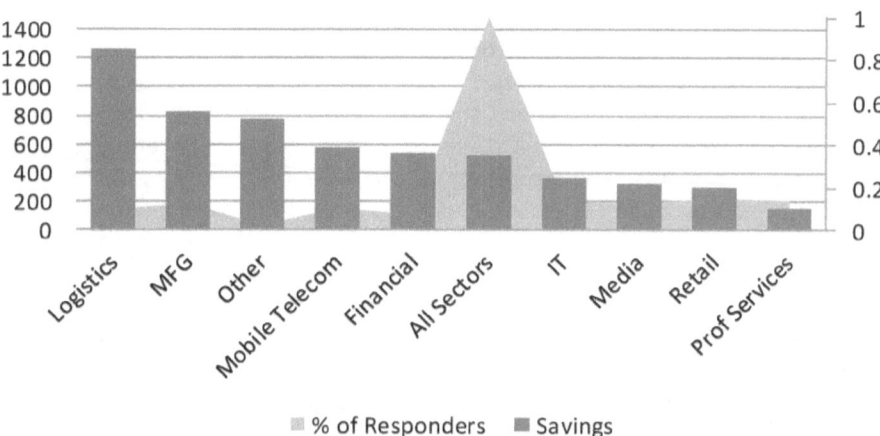

Figure 6-8. Average Savings in Thousands from Cloud Computing. (*Source:* Columbus, Louis, "Making Cloud Computing Pay," *Forbes*, April 10, 2013, http://www.forbes.com/sites/louiscolumbus/2013/04/10/making-cloud-computing-pay-2/.)

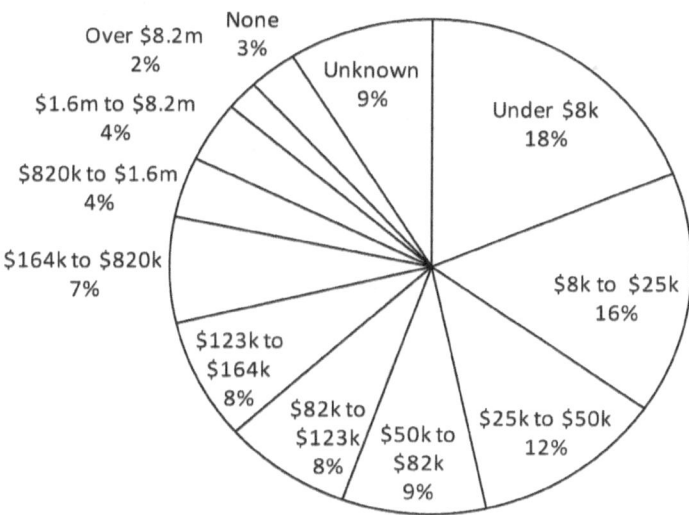

Figure 6-9. Percent of Responders with Ranges of Savings. (*Source:* Columbus, Louis, "Making Cloud Computing Pay," *Forbes*, April 10, 2013, http://www.forbes.com/sites/louiscolumbus/2013/04/10/making-cloud-computing-pay-2/.)

The amount of resources you use on the cloud can change easily, much like your utility usage. Currently, IT resources are more like fixed assets. By making IT a variable cost, it helps companies control expenses. Due to this scalability, smaller companies can access better technology on an a-la-carte basis, which would not be possible without the cloud. Companies can collaborate more easily with cloud services. There are many companies using Google Drive, Dropbox, or other similar applications to manage projects around the world and share documents. The availability of the resources via any Internet connection allows users to access information via any PC or mobile device. This is particularly useful for workers with a mobile office. If you remember from Chapter 5, work-from-home employees are more productive and the cloud can allow this to happen. In teaching, I have been able to make my classes 100 percent paper-free. To do this, I have eliminated all paper expenses and countless hours of my own time sorting through papers that needed to be graded. Students get instant access to feedback and they can complete assignments even on snow days.

There are also some disadvantages to the cloud. The first one is that you must be connected to the Internet to use it. Some applications allow you to work offline, but most do not, so it is difficult to work while traveling or in areas without good data service. The reliability of your connections is also an issue. The cloud computing service providers typically can provide very high levels of reliability, but they cannot provide for a highly reliable connection. The potential savings gained through going from localized software to the cloud could easily be eliminated by lost productivity due to downtime. A strategy that includes cloud computing must also include redundancies in the network connectivity to avoid any downtime.

A responsible collaboration with IT and legal will result in a good contract with your cloud service provider, giving you reliable security and an assurance of getting your data once you decide to discontinue services, but it is more difficult to ensure that you have a way to use your data once it is transferred to you. Since the database structure of your data can be in various forms, you need to have a plan to ensure that you can use your data once you get it. Although you may have good legal contracts ensuring that your data is destroyed on the service provider side, you must have a way to verify this destruction. Both usability of data history and data destruction protocols should be included in your contract with the cloud computing service.

Figure 6-10 shows the top cloud computing benefits from the same survey referenced in the *Forbes* article. As you can see, the benefits of cloud computing are mostly in the IT area but also improve the ability to grow and invest in the business. This is not surprising given that if you are given more resources, you will use them to improve your business. Over half of those surveyed noted that they were able to compete with larger businesses once on the cloud. This is perhaps the greatest benefit to the cloud. Prior to the cloud, small companies had to rely on manual processes or their own creativity with the basic database and spreadsheet applications available to them. Those more fortunate companies could buy second class software applications and servers to run them and be at a disadvantage to their competitors. Now many of the top-quality software companies offer a cloud application that is scalable and is a good alternative to the onsite application. The number one waste with cloud computing is being a small-to-midsized company and not taking advantage of the cloud.

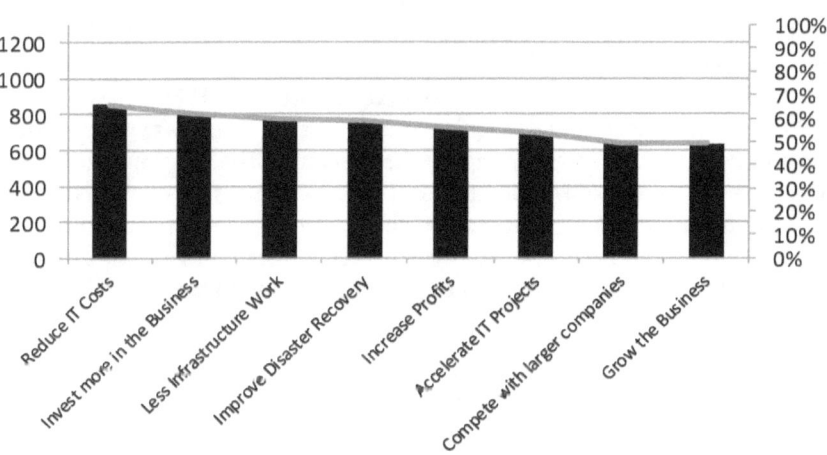

Figure 6-10. Cloud Computing Benefits. (*Source*: Columbus, Louis, "Making Cloud Computing Pay," *Forbes*, April 10, 2013, http://www.forbes.com/sites/louiscolumbus/2013/04/10/making-cloud-computing-pay-2/.)

Note All companies can benefit from the cloud, but small and midsized companies cannot afford to ignore it.

Outdated Technology

We have worked with a variety of companies in our careers. We have seen totally paper processes in manufacturing facilities with vegetation growing out of cracks in the floor and water leaks in the ceiling. Conversely, we have also seen space shuttle components being assembled with robots and workers tracking quality checks on laptop computers in real time while the assembly is happening. Various levels of technology are in use across all industries. Commonly, companies who leverage technology are able to produce higher-quality products or services with greater customer satisfaction. So why don't companies invest in technology? It is likely a combination of limited financial resources and lack of knowledge of what is possible.

One company we know of used 20-year-old computer technology and produced shipping paperwork on carbon paper. Forecasts were printed on a dot matrix printer that crashed frequently. The result of this was lost or late orders that would never be found because the carbon copy of the order was lost in transit. Invoices sometimes weren't sent to customers who received products due to lack of traceability. Although this is an extreme story, it is not uncommon for companies to get stuck with outdated technology.

Healthcare workers still use pagers and fax machines for many of their business processes. I was asked to page someone one day and had to be taught how to do this because I hadn't seen a pager since the 1980s. I also think the only time I have used a fax machine in the last 15 years was when I bought a house. But healthcare has deep pockets. That is the predominant belief in government anyway. Why not upgrade? The answer is the same. Resources are wasted on inefficient processes rather than invested in technology. Many healthcare providers did not seriously invest in technology until the government decided to help pay for it with meaningful use dollars.

In order to respond quickly to changes, whether it is variability in a manufacturing process or information related to a patient, companies need to have technology that reports information on close to a real-time basis. I have spent hours in meetings where leaders discuss the results of data that is six to nine months old, all the while pretending that the information is relevant to today's operations. In a chapter on technology and waste, it is important to note that perhaps the single biggest waste is not using technology to improve processes and to access actionable data. Don't get us wrong, technology can drive wasteful activity in any organization, but you can almost guarantee that you will not be able to effectively compete over the long term without taking advantage of the benefits of good technology.

Note The greatest technology waste is not using technology.

Centralized or Decentralized IT

Much like the human resource management function, the information technology (IT) function has lost its way in some companies. IT is a support function that helps to maximize the efficiency of the core business operations. But in some organizations, IT sets policies that end up becoming barriers to organizational efficiency. In an effort to reduce expenses, for example, large companies with large IT groups have centralized purchasing of software and hardware. This is a great thing for regular business users such as accountants, sales, nursing, or manufacturing personnel, but it can cause problems for users who need more computing power than the regular user.

Also, IT's general lack of knowledge of a department's software needs can lead to decisions not to purchase software that has a good operational return on investment. Who better knows what kind of CRM system they need than the sales manager and sales force? The IT department might understand how a program works and what installation issues will be present, but they won't understand why the software is being purchased and what functions it needs. If IT is purchasing items on its budget, then why would it care if the department that is using these tools gains operational efficiencies? It is impossible to calculate an accurate ROI if you do not understand the potential gains, which requires a functional understanding. The goal of IT leadership at this point is to reduce IT costs, not to make sales more efficient.

Having the opposite approach can also be detrimental. A certain amount of standardization is necessary in IT. Companies that do not have some oversight of software purchases may end up with dozens or even hundreds of applications that do not communicate with each other or duplicate work. This approach costs money because the software is likely not at the best price because it is purchased in small volume. There is also the support needed to ensure that the hardware and software work properly. Also, there is support needed in the setup and the training for all of this varied hardware and software. Unfortunately, most employees don't have enough IT knowledge to take care of their own workstations.

What makes the most sense, although it is not common, is a hybrid of the centralized and decentralized approach. Figure 6-11 shows which IT functions should and should not be centralized. The reasoning behind this hybrid model is that there needs to be an appropriate amount of standardization and centralized control of IT policies, but without becoming a hindrance to operations. By allowing operations to make decisions on new software and hardware purchases within reasonable guidelines established by IT, the best of both models is achieved. IT can also ensure that if software is used in one area of the company and a request for similar software is made, that if possible, a single software is used to meet all of the needs for both departments. Of course, like anything, there are situations where this does not make sense, such as when a special set of skills is necessary to use the software and there is little need to collaborate between users.

Centralized Functions	Decentralized Functions
- Software Vendor Management	- New Equipment Budgeting
- Hardware Vendor Management	- New Software Budgeting
- Technology Support (PCs, Printers, Projectors, etc)	- Maintenance Costs on Department-Specific Software
- Network Maintenance	- Technology Usage Policies
- Maintenance of Master Software Lists	- Evaluation of New Software Capabilities
- Equipment Maintenance Costs	- Justification for New Expenses
- Database Administration	
- Custom Software Creation	
- Business Process Analysis	

Figure 6-11. Information Technology Centralization

Another place where centralization fails is when companies decide to save money on software costs by purchasing versions where you need to be connected to the company via a VPN or remote login on a server in order to use the software. This causes a barrier to anyone who may need to work outside of the office and cannot secure a good Internet connection. This of course is easier for IT but not for those users who are affected. If worker productivity is affected, the software savings is likely negated. Again, a proper ROI analysis must include all potential gains and losses.

■ **Note** IT is a support function. Core business operations should always take priority over IT efficiencies.

Technology Metrics

IT departments have lots of metrics about the performance of the systems at their disposal, assuming the systems are designed correctly. These metrics include ways to measure system performance to ensure that the hardware is working properly and metrics about the software performance to identify bugs that need to be fixed. Many other metrics in IT are focused on productivity of personnel or basic project management. There are a few key metrics, discussed next, that all IT groups must keep in focus in order to be successful, but note that not all IT groups monitor these metrics.

Social Media Metrics

Social media is new enough that metrics are still being developed to show the success of its campaigns. Early in their development, the metrics were largely financial. Now, we are starting to see more metrics that capture other data from social media. This goes beyond mere financial measures, but does, of course, ultimately correlate with financial returns. Figure 6-12 shows some common social media metrics that can be used to measure success. As noted earlier, you should pursue social media only if your customers get value from the interaction. If you decide to pursue social media, you must have an effective measurement system in place and have goals associated with your activity.

Metric	Definition	Percent of Companies Using This Metric
Hits/visits/page views	Number of unique views of the web page	40.90%
Repeat visits	Number of repeat visits by a single customer	24.90%
Conversion rate (visitor becomes a buyer)	Percent of visitors who buy something	21.10%
Followers	Number of people following you on Facebook	30.50%
Sales levels	Sales from the site	8.70%
Revenue per customer	Sales per customer	9.20%
Web mentions	Times your company is mentioned on the web	16.20%
Customer acquisition costs	Cost to acquire new customers	10.20%
Profit per customer	Dollars left after all expenses	4.50%
Online product/service ratings	Online ratings (number of stars)	6.00%
Customer retention costs	Amount of money needed to retain a current customer	3.00%
Net promotor score	How likely your customers will recommend you	9.80%
Other text analysis ratings	Various defintions	8.50%
Abandoned shopping carts	Number of times someone starts a purchase but does not complete it	2.80%

Figure 6-12. Social Media Metrics. (*Source*: Moorman, Christine, "Measuring Social Media ROI: Companies Emphasize Voice Metrics," May 23rd, 2013, http://cmosurvey.org/blog/measuring-social-media-roi-companies-emphasize-voice-metrics/.)

The main challenge with social media metrics is to ensure that you are looking at valuable metrics to drive the performance you need. This is true in all business areas where metrics are used, but in other areas, there is more history on commonly used metrics. As new metrics are created in the social media realm, marketers may be tempted to use metrics that don't translate to bottom-line success.

Performance Metrics

To help avoid waste in IT, you should have metrics to determine where bottlenecks lie in your IT infrastructure. You also want to assess the degree of under- or over-utilization of your systems.

Response Time

Response time is the amount of time it takes the system to respond to users during the highest utilization of the hardware. High response times may indicate that you have inadequate hardware or need to change the times of the day when your process jobs use your current infrastructure.

Infrastructure Utilization Percent

This is the percent of the infrastructure capacity utilized throughout the day. You should look at the peak utilization as well as the variation of the utilization. High utilization should trigger discussions about how to improve the performance of your current hardware or upgrade to new hardware.

Unplanned Downtime

All IT departments have downtime on applications due to the need to apply patches and fixes to the software or to upgrade to the latest features. There are also downtimes to perform hardware upgrades or basic maintenance. Although users don't like any downtime, unplanned downtime is the worst because there are no plans to handle it. Tracking unplanned downtime will help you identify repeat issues. When you track this downtime, you should include a process to identify the root cause and the action taken so you can look for patterns in your data.

Customer Satisfaction

As a support function, IT must be customer focused and measure how satisfied the users of the IT systems are. This satisfaction should include the quality of the hardware used, the quality of the network, the quality of the applications, and the quality of service from support personnel. Companies often try to minimize IT expense and in the process of doing this, sacrifice performance, which leads to greater organizational costs. A broad measurement of customer service will lead you to understanding where you should be spending money, whether on upgrades or process improvement.

Project Management

IT personnel are often big supporters of project-management techniques. Most of the PMP (Project Management Professional) certified people I have known have worked in IT. Project leaders are rewarded for delivery implementations and upgrades that are on time and on budget, so basic project-management metrics need to be in place to ensure that these goals are met.

In addition to these, you cannot forget to measure the scope and quality of your work. What good is a project that's delivered on time and on budget when the end users are unsatisfied with the result? I have also seen cases when the scope was reduced to the point where the new software did not deliver the improvements that were promised and the users were very unsatisfied, but the project was on time and on budget. For these reasons, all IT projects should have key metrics around all four areas, with a higher focus on quality and scope than on time and budget.

Return on Investment

We include a basic ROI calculation in the Chapter 7. IT capital expenses normally come from needing a new system, either because the old one is inoperable and no longer supported by the developer or to gain some return on investment through new features and more efficient processes. There needs to be ongoing measures of the actual ROI on IT projects to show the credibility of future project ROI calculations. When beginning new projects, part of the ROI discussion needs to include exactly where the ROI will come from and how it will be measured. Ideally, any consultant or software company will agree to these estimates and put some of their fees at risk for meeting these performance objectives.

Conclusion

Technology is still an ever-changing area in business and there is no reason to believe that it will become less important in the future. Your challenge is to make sure that you use technology to improve your businesses at a quicker rate than your competitors. Technology can help you overcome many obstacles, but it is not the solution to fixing poor business processes. Since almost all areas of business can benefit from technology, it is easy to get too many people involved in purchasing and maintaining IT systems. In order to avoid having dozens or even hundreds of disparate systems in use, you must have a good IT governance process that is flexible but effective. Your IT processes need to ensure that you efficiently and effectively select the right software applications and utilize them to their fullest capability to drive performance. Data access must be managed efficiently to avoid data duplication created from frustrating IT processes. The right mix of reports and self-service data cubes need to be available to ensure that all employees have access to the data they need. And of course, there should be a single source for accessing information.

Since lack of skill can curtail any efficiency that comes from technology, you must accurately assess user skill and provide adequate training to get all users to a proficient skill level. Companies need to avoid relying on outdated technology and look for ways to leverage the right level of technology to support business operations. When cloud computing is a better option, you should put the right tools in place to get maximum value from the cloud, with minimal risk of data loss or security breaches.

The greatest waste of technology is not using it. The second greatest waste is not using it correctly. The third greatest waste is letting technology use you. Technology is a set of tools that your company chooses to use. The goal is to make employees more efficient and effective. If at any point you spend more time taking care of your technology than running your business, you should evaluate your technology strategy.

Waste Checklists

Technology Checklist
*All "no" answers identify a potential opportunity for improvement.

Social Media

Did your customers ask you to create social media outlets?	Yes ☐ No ☐
Does your social media use benefit your customers more than your company?	Yes ☐ No ☐
Does your social media use provide desired information to your customers?	Yes ☐ No ☐
Are you doing social media because everyone else is doing it?	Yes ☐ No ☐
Is your social media offering used frequently by repeat customers?	Yes ☐ No ☐
Is the social media that you chose targeted at your customer demographics?	Yes ☐ No ☐
Is content marketing part of your social media strategy?	Yes ☐ No ☐
Do you measure the effects of your social media use?	Yes ☐ No ☐
Is your social media controlled by a centralized function to control the message?	Yes ☐ No ☐
Are the authors of social media content experts?	Yes ☐ No ☐

Technology Checklist

*All "no" answers identify a potential opportunity for improvement.

Technology in Marketing

- Are you using technology for reputation management? Yes ☐ No ☐
- Are you utilizing text messages as an option to communicate with customers? Yes ☐ No ☐
- Are you supplying your customers with mobile apps that provide value to them? Yes ☐ No ☐
- Are you evaluating whether traditional marketing outlets (TV, print, radio, billboards, etc) provide a real return on investment? Yes ☐ No ☐

Salesforce Automation

- Were your sales people involved in the selection of your CRM? Yes ☐ No ☐
- Does your CRM provide value to the sales manager and to the sales staff? Yes ☐ No ☐
- Do you use existing big data where it exists to answer customer questions? Yes ☐ No ☐
- Do you actively collect customer data to improve the customer experience? Yes ☐ No ☐
- Do your sales people collect data to influence their sales activities? Yes ☐ No ☐
- Do you utilize technology to respect the time of your employees and customers? Yes ☐ No ☐
- Do you use benchmarking as a temperature check instead of a target-setting mechanism? Yes ☐ No ☐
- Is your benchmarking used to identify activities used in other business segments that could be used in yours? Yes ☐ No ☐

Technology Checklist

*All "no" answers identify a potential opportunity for improvement.

General Information Technology

Are your software purchases strategic and coordinated to meet business goals?	Yes ☐ No ☐
Is your software built to follow your operational processes rather than your processes designed to meet the software?	Yes ☐ No ☐
Are IT decisions made by business leaders instead of by IT leaders?	Yes ☐ No ☐
Are workers involved in IT purchasing decisions?	Yes ☐ No ☐
Is the IT function decentralized with some central oversight?	Yes ☐ No ☐
Do job functions determine software needs for employees?	Yes ☐ No ☐
Do you utilize all key functions of owned software applications?	Yes ☐ No ☐
Do you have a way to manage your reports and make reporting easy for employees to access without e-mailing reports to them?	Yes ☐ No ☐
Do you routinely analyze reports to understand their purpose?	Yes ☐ No ☐
Does your data access policy allow employees appropriate access, thus eliminating the need for re-creating data that is not accessible?	Yes ☐ No ☐
Is your data access based upon job function?	Yes ☐ No ☐
Is your data security designed to make it easy to do the job without a workaround?	Yes ☐ No ☐

Technology Checklist

*All "no" answers identify a potential opportunity for improvement.

General Information Technology

Do you evaluate employee skill levels and offer appropriate technology training based on those skill levels?	Yes ☐	No ☐
Have you evaluated using cloud technology for some or all of your software needs?	Yes ☐	No ☐
Do you have Internet connectivity redundancies in place if you use cloud computing or if rely on the Internet for key company functions?	Yes ☐	No ☐
Do you regularly evaluate technology that you use to determine if it is ineffective or outdated?	Yes ☐	No ☐
Do you have performance metrics in use for your technology?	Yes ☐	No ☐
Do your performance metrics drive changes in your operations?	Yes ☐	No ☐

CHAPTER 7

Finance

Accounting for Your Waste

A bad system will beat a good person every time.

—W. Edwards Deming

Finance and accounting operations are by their definition effective because the people who perform these functions, and the functions themselves, are very detail focused. The issue in this area of business is the efficiency of operations. Now before all the business leaders with finance backgrounds throw this book away, we are not saying that finance people don't work hard. Some of the hardest working people we know have worked in accounting or finance. The question is whether all of the activities that we do in these areas of the business are value-added activities. Friends of ours who are financial leaders in their companies have admitted that not all of the work that they do provides value. We are not just talking about some of the hoops that they jump through for regulatory compliance. Some of the analyses and internal controls that they put in place cause waste and provide little improvement for the organization. Some examples of these controls are the auditing of the financial records or segregation of duties. Although these are necessary activities, they provide no value to the organization. This chapter is about the waste in those processes and how you can limit that waste to create a leaner organization.

Tiered Approval Processes

We all have approval processes in our companies. But, when you have extra processing due to redundant approval processes, your processes are extremely wasteful. Moreover, consider that when more than one person is responsible for any given activity, then nobody is responsible.

I once did a lot of quoting for products to sell to customers. We had a pretty good process to turn around quotes. We had a pool of suppliers that was committed to giving us good prices and delivery times. We also had a nice spreadsheet that we could use to calculate the internal cost and margin we could expect from our products. For our larger customers, we had contract rates we used that made the formula rather mistake proof. The spreadsheet was password protected so the formulas could be changed only by the two people who knew the password. By limiting the people who could use the spreadsheet, there was less chance for error.

We also had a format for our request for quotes from our suppliers, which made it difficult to get inaccurate supplier quotes. And we *always* got at least three competitive quotes. Our suppliers would provide a quote in two or three days, which worked well because our customers rarely gave us more than a week to provide a complete quote. By the fifth day, we had the completed quote ready for the customer.

But then our accounting department wanted to ensure that all quotes were properly evaluated prior to being sent to customers. The process included a review and sign off by eight executives for every quotation. Due to a variety of factors, including travel schedules, the average turnaround time for a review became ten days. So this internal process to ensure that all quotations were properly analyzed ensured that our company was unable to submit any quotations on time. Therefore, we were disqualified from every negotiation process and could not get any sales! Although the process was well intended, it caused more problems than it solved. Ultimately, our Vice President of Engineering told all people who were creating quotations to submit to the customer as soon as he had evaluated the quotation and to "get the signatures after you sent it."

This is just one example of a tiered approval process causing waste. Similar things happen in processes designed to control expenses. For example, consider the manager who has a spending limit of $1,500. In such a situation, in order to avoid the tiered approval process, spending isn't discouraged but rather creative spending is encouraged. I have caught people splitting expenses between multiple purchases in order to avoid expense caps and still get the full expenditure paid for. Although this is not an ethical practice, I have seen it used multiple times with no negative recourse. So along with the waste of time in coming up with a creative way to get around accounting policies, now the expenses associated with each payment to a vendor are double or triple because of multiple invoices and multiple sign-offs and approvals.

To get rid of this waste, you need to make each manager in control of her budget. Structure each department so that it runs like its own business. A manager who is empowered to think like a business owner is more likely to control expenses. Nobody in an accounting or purchasing department knows more than you about what your business unit needs. If the manager is not capable of doing this, she probably is not going to be a good manager overall and either should be coached into developing these skills or replaced.

> **Note** If more than one person is responsible for an activity or process, then no one is. Eliminate your tiered approval processes in favor of accountability.

Travel and Business Expense Policies

Travel policies must be structured to avoid abuses. Almost ten years ago, I spent some time in sales. The sales manager had quit in order to pursue another job, and I took over at the request of our division president. I used to love traveling with the prior sales manager. We stayed almost exclusively at Hilton hotels. We flew business or first class whenever we could. And we ate great. We went to fancy steak houses and famous restaurants. The company had no policy on travel. No limits on any expenses whatsoever. Such extravagance is an obvious source of waste. But when I took over the sales role, the company's travel expenses were cut by more than half. And I traveled more often than the previous guy.

Another example comes from the academic world. Professors spend thousands going to academic conferences every year. Professors write conference proceedings, which are frequently research in progress with little impact to the discipline. These proceedings do not affect research, teaching, or tenure. The conferences are typically at very nice hotels in very nice locales, such as Marriott on the beach in Tampa, Florida. There are even many conferences in fancy Mediterranean locales. There are a lot of fancy meals and alcohol at these events, all on shrinking budgets.

Travel, whether business or academic, should not occur unless it is a bona fide value-added activity. Certainly travel policies must be structured to allow reasonable expenses when customer interaction is needed, but they also must be limited to lower expenses when employees are traveling and not meeting with customers. In sales, as described in Chapter 4, the need to see customers in person is becoming less necessary every year. Even when there is a need for the salesperson and customer to get together, there is no need for expensive entertaining. Specifying maximum amounts to be spent on food, lodging, and airfare with a policy to pre-approve amounts that are expected to be greater is a good approach to controlling travel expenses.

Conferences and trade shows, as noted in Chapter 4, can be beneficial when there is a specific outcome planned. If you sell or purchase products where trade shows are a main avenue to get sales leads, there is a true business purpose. If there is some knowledge that can be gained only by attending a conference and that knowledge will lead to a change in the operations of your organization, then there is a true business purpose. Otherwise, you should question whether the expense is necessary. Conferences and trade shows are often an excuse to get out of the office or see past colleagues.

These types of activities should be justified with a specified purpose and measureable outcome, much like what you would expect for a project. What is your baseline measure of performance? What is your goal? How will you know if you achieved your goal?

Similarly, business lunches can be a tremendous source of waste. The waste comes in many forms. The obvious one is the actual expense of the meal, which we put conservatively at $10 to $15 per person. Just compare how much a person could save by packing a lunch. With an average cost of $5 to $10 per lunch and working 250 days per year, you spend between $1,250 and $2,500 per year. This is 2.5 to 5 percent of the median household annual income.[1] The average number of workers per household is 1.22.[2] For families with more than one worker, the annual lunch expense could be 5 to 10 percent of their income. Now imagine how much the business lunches could cost.

Lunches are also wasteful due to the fact that all the workers are not working and being productive while they are at lunch. There are conflicting studies about this. Some studies show that workers are more productive if they take a break for lunch. Others show that it is better to work straight through lunch and get done early. While stopping to eat lunch is all wasted "down-time," people are more creative while their brains are doing low mental energy tasks. Many people get their best ideas in the shower or while vacuuming their home. These low mental energy tasks allow the brain to be creative. However, many times, lunches are very long—upwards of an hour—and are not really low mental energy tasks. If you are eating with co-workers, you might still be at a high stress level because of focusing on managing your reputation and talking about office politics.

We are not saying that you should not give your workers breaks. Some workers may feel rejuvenated by them. Many people need to run errands and will feel and be more productive after they have cleared their personal to-do lists. However, trying to conduct business over lunch is typically very wasteful. Using lunch breaks to encourage team building in similarly wasteful.

Note Travel and meal expenses don't lead to happier employees or happier customers. Create robust policies with checks and balances to avoid these wasteful expenses.

---

[1] U.S. Census Bureau, Current Population Survey, 2009 to 2011 Annual Social and Economic Supplements, "Three-Year-Average Median Household Income by State: 2009–2011 and Two-Year-Average Median Household Income by State: 2010 to 2011," http://www.census.gov/hhes/www/income/data/statemedian/index.html.
[2] U.S. Department of Transportation, "Census Transportation and Planning Products," April 28, 2011, http://www.fhwa.dot.gov/planning/census_issues/ctpp/data_products/journey_to_work/jtw1.cfm.

Budgeting

A few weeks ago, I was discussing the budgeting process with a colleague. He shared with me his experience as a leader in the United States military. He managed a budget and at the end of the year, he would purchase surplus supplies. My colleague did this because if he did not spend the money, his unit would not get as much money the next budget cycle. Sadly, many businesses use this same process.

Companies or departments with revenue and expenses are relatively simple to operate. Figure 7-1 shows a simplified budget process for a sales dependent business or department. The strength of your budget is largely dependent upon your ability to predict revenue and costs. A basic concept of business is that if your revenues are greater than your costs, you make money. In a small company, this concept is not forgotten. A financially sound small company makes money because each expense is controlled and spent only if it is necessary. There is no such thing as spending as much as you can at the end of the year so that you can get the same budget the following year.

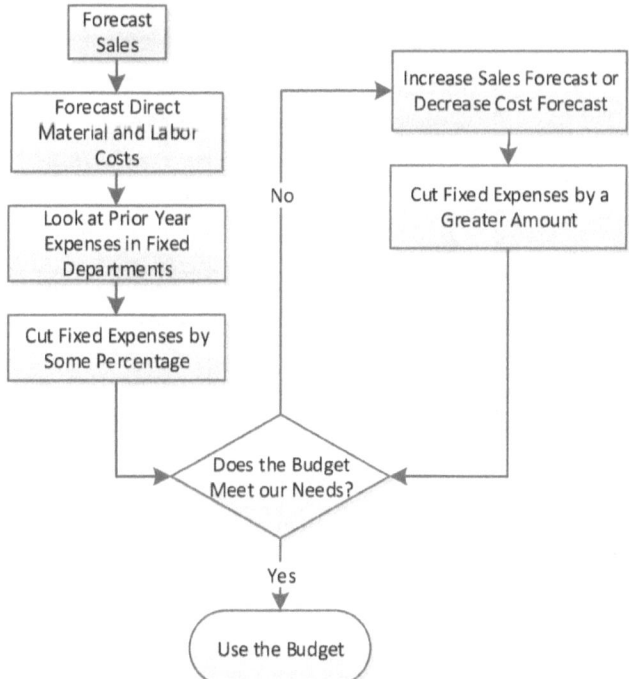

Figure 7-1. Simple Budget Process

Large companies, however, allocate their large pools of money to all of the departments. Due to the scope of the operation, this allocation is not based upon need or expense minimization but rather on entitlement. If you needed $200,000 last year then you must need $200,000 this year, right? This is a disease in budget management. We talk more about productivity in Chapter 8, but each department's expenses must be based upon the work to be done and not on past performance.

Forecasting

Part of creating a good budget is accurately forecasting revenue and expenses. We have both seen very questionable forecasting methods used by companies. Yet, all decisions filter down from the forecast. For example, managers need to know how much inventory to have on hand, how much workforce to employ, and how much cash flow will be on hand. As Figure 7-2 shows, the impact of erroneous forecasts can be very dangerous.

	Forecast ↑	Forecast ↓
Customer Relations	• Money Wasted	• Unhappy Customers Can't Get Their Products
Distribution	• Not Enough Capacity to Meet Demand	• Too Much Capacity. Too Much Expense
Finance	• Cash Is not Earning Interest	• Not Enough Cash
Inventory	• Too Much Inventory	• Too Low Inventory
Pricing	• Price Cutting to Force Sales	• Price Increases Due to Capacity Constraints
Production	• Too Much Production, Unsold Items	• Not Enough Capacity for Customers
Profits	• Low Profit Due to High Expenses	• Low Profit Due to Lack of Sales
Promotion	• Not Enough ROI for Promotion	• Not Enough Promotion to Drive Sales

Figure 7-2. The Impact of Bad Forecasts

Accurate forecasts are rare in business for many reasons. This is usually because the company has chosen not to change the way it forecasts. Again, companies do things the way they have always done them, even despite new computer software and hardware programs that can handle much more sophisticated models.

Asking your customer to tell you what your forecast should be is normally a poor choice, but many companies and even whole business sectors use this method. One reason this method is a poor choice is that buyers typically overstate their future purchases. Also, this method is not suitable in estimating sales for the long term, especially in unstable industries in which there is irregular demand. More or less, if there are large fluctuations in the industry, buyers are not going to know how to predict them any better than anyone else in the industry. If the company using the forecast is a B2C company, they could not use this method to any great reliability. Household consumers are too numerous, making this method rather impracticable and costly. Also, a basic limitation of this method is that it is passive and does not expose and measure the variables under management's control. Buyers do not know what is going on inside a company.

There are a few companies who have created great software to forecast using multiple quantitative methods. Unfortunately, many companies don't collect enough of the right data or employ the right analysts to effectively use this software. With the basis for most budgets being the sales forecast, you simply cannot afford to use the guess-and-pray method that many companies use.

Instead you should use several methods to identify the lowest and highest forecast alternatives and realize that your actual forecast is somewhere in between. If you cannot break even at your lower forecast, then you need to tighten your budget. Once you have done this, you should create contingency plans to achieve the high forecast if it happens. This plan should be triggered by some leading indicators of your forecast accuracy. You must understand your industry to know which methods to use and to use them accurately. Figure 7-3 shows some common forecasting techniques, along with their strengths and weaknesses.

	Strengths	Weaknesses
Naïve	• Easy • You don't need to be analytical	• Inaccurate if there are any changes
Jury of Executive Opinion	• Gets input from all key business areas • Executives have a broad view of the business • It is quick	• Lots of executive time • Disconnected Executives may not understand the current sales landscape • Not good when you have lots of products • One or two influential people may dominate the process
Delphi Method	• No need for group meetings • No group thinking pitfalls • Get positive and negative opinions • May be done via email or survey	• Only willing participants. May not have good knowledge. • Time consuming • Might have a high dropout rate
Sales Force Composite	• Gets input from those close to the sales • Gives details by product/ customer/ territory • May improve sales force morale	• Sales people may underestimate • Can take a lot of sales force time • Sales people may not understand the economic situation
Survey of Buyer Intentions	• Based on customers plans • It is an excuse for good customer service • Inexpensive	• Customer may overestimate • Not all customers are willing to disclose their plans
Moving Averages	• Simple • Good for lots of products • Good for products with stable sales • Smooths out random changes	• Needs a lot of sales history data • Slow adjustments to changes • Equally weights all sales periods even though current periods may be a better gage for future sales • No way to test the results with statistics
Exponential Smoothing	• Simple • Give more weight to recent information • No expensive software • Accurate for short term forecasts	• Much searching may be needed to find appropriate weight • Poor for medium- and long- term forecasts • Erroneous forecasts can result due to large random fluctuations in recent data
Decomposition Method	• Simple • In most forecasting software • Looks for major factors like trends and seasonal data • Breaks down sales	• Needs lots of historic data • Not good for long term forecasts • No way to test the results with statistics

Figure 7-3. Some of the Available Forecasting Methods

Qualitative methods of forecasting are nice because they are cheap and work well when you have limited data, but they are not the most accurate. Stable industries with minimal fluctuations may use the naïve forecast and assume that the next period will be the same as the prior period. Executive forecasts ask the opinions of the company executives. The Delphi method is a structured form of the jury of executive opinion, with multiple rounds that take the executive opinions and whittle them down to the best answer. The sales force composite is a similar forecasting method, but only includes the sales force's opinions. The buyer intentions method is simply asking your customers what they will buy. All of these methods have bias and significant room for error, but are very cheap and easy. If you use any of these methods, you should absolutely combine it with a quantitative method.

Quantitative forecasting is great if you have enough good data and the skills to analyze it. With time-series forecasting, you look at known future events to predict sales based upon similar past events. When conducting a time-series analysis, you look for trends, periodic movements, cyclical movements, and erratic movements. Trends are movements in a time-series where a linear or curvilinear performance can be seen. Periodic movements include patterns like seasonal sales. Cyclical movements include long-term fluctuations like business recessions. Erratic movements include special events like wars, strikes, snowstorms, hurricanes, fires, and floods.

Moving averages are forecasts developed using a rolling mean to predict future sales. For example, if I were to use a five-year moving average, I might forecast sales for 2017 by averaging 2011–2016. Then, to forecast 2018, I would get the average of 2012–2017. This continues as the years go along. This method is especially helpful if you have growth, as the rolling nature of the average will account for the continued growth. Exponential smoothing is a type of moving average with weights that give more credibility to recent data. A weighted average allows you to pick which periods will have the greatest weight in the analysis. This is helpful if, for example, you wanted to lessen the impact of years that vary because of recessions.

There are also many other more complex forecasting methods. Every business should either employ a statistician who can perform forecasting or hire a statistician as a consultant at least once a year. You absolutely should not just wing your forecasting. You have to know how much your sales will be or all other business decisions could be drastically affected.

Forecasting is probably one of the most important things a business can do. The waste here is in not creating an accurate forecast. As was shown in Figure 7-2, not forecasting appropriately can be disastrous and wasteful. Take the time and resources to forecast accurately. If not, you will pay by not really budgeting well and dealing with the downstream effects of a bad budget, such as the ones outlined in Figure 7-2.

Zero-Based Budgeting

In a zero-based budgeting company, each department or function gets a full cost-and-needs analysis. The budget is based upon the current and future needs of the department, not prior performance. Not only does this encourage a real analysis of the ROI, but it also helps foster some budget responsibility.[3]

In order to build a functional zero-based budget, you first need to understand your costs. This is where having knowledge of activity based-costing is essential. Simply defined, activity-based costing is a method in which you define the incremental cost of each activity performed. Traditional cost accounting takes all costs that are not directly attributed to each product or service and spreads them across all products or services based upon some metric such as machine hours. In activity-based costing, only items that can be attributed to a product or service are assigned to the costs. All other costs are extra expenses in addition to the product or service. This is helpful because if you have an activity that costs you $100 and you charge $150, you understand that each time you do that activity, you earn $50 to pay for overhead and profit. If another activity costs you $75 but you are able to charge $150, then you are able to get $75 each time you do that activity. Obviously, you should try to do the second option more than the first.

Once you understand the cost versus revenue for activities that provide revenue for your company, you can analyze the other expenses for a return on investment. For instance, if you need to have marketing activities, a data-based ROI calculation can justify those expenses, although you may not be able to attribute that expense to a single product or service.

With all of this data in hand, you are ready to start your zero-based budget. You start with analyzing the products or services where your costs are higher than your revenue or where your contribution to the company beyond direct costs is small. Are there opportunities to reduce expenses? Be honest with this question. Think about all the areas of waste we have identified in this book. Can you get a higher price? Is there an interaction between this product or service and a higher priced item? Maybe in a healthcare organization, screening or testing activities yield a low or negative margin, but if a serious health issue is found through these activities, then a higher margin results. You may decide to keep or even increase the volume of the low margin work because your data shows that the number of high margin procedures will pay for those activities. In this case, you may make the argument to add the costs of these low-margin jobs as a part of the activity-based cost for the high-margin jobs.

---

[3] Bain and Company, "Zero-Based Budgeting," May 8, 2013, http://www.bain.com/publications/articles/management-tools-zero-based-budgeting.aspx.

The following is an example in which you may choose to discontinue a product. Once the true costs are understood, this part of the analysis is easy.

$$Cost = \$200$$
$$Revenue = \$250$$
$$Contribution\_Goal = 35\%$$

$$\frac{Revenue - Cost}{Revenue} = Contribution$$

$$\frac{\$250 - \$200}{\$250} = 20\%$$

The harder part of the analysis is deciding if there is an interaction between the sales of this product and the sales of another product. I once worked to eliminate the third largest customer for my company because when we did this analysis for the whole body of work, we found that it cost us more to sell the products than if we didn't sell them at all.

Once you have identified the fate of each of your products or services, you need to look at your fixed overhead. What basic functions do you need? How many resources do you need to support them? For instance, if you know that you get a certain amount of invoices to pay per month and you know how long it takes you to pay each invoice, you can easily figure out how many people you need in accounts payable. You need to do this for all remaining departments in the company.

Once you have done this, you look at what is left from your sales forecast and the risk associated with the forecast. What additional strategic initiatives do you have? What are their priorities? What margin must you maintain? This helps you figure out what you can do next. Your budget should cover the basics of operations. The sales forecast with your highest risk level minus the costs that you have identified as essential should provide you with your margin. The remaining margin is what you have left to support strategic initiatives.

Of course, this is a simple representation of the overall concept of zero-based budgeting, but there are books based upon the topic that explain this in more depth. The point of this section is to make you realize that one solution to the entitlement budget disease is the zero-based budgeting method. It can help you identify large sources of waste in your organization and determine how to eliminate them. Even if you apply some of the concepts associated with zero-based budgeting, you will see a positive effect on your bottom line.

> **Note** Look at activity-based costing and zero-based budgeting as ways to improve your financial performance and better understand your business.

Fake Numbers

The world of accounting does not just exist to count real money. Accounting does sometimes use statistics that have no real value. They use factors, such as an efficiency factor, to make the numbers work. Although these are generally accepted accounting principles, you need to operate your businesses on more than a cash basis. What did you provide that will bring you revenue? What was the unit cost for that product or service? How much do you owe your creditors? When you receive money from your customers and pay your bills, how much is left? The point is that whether you are looking at operations management or accounting, the facts and figures that you should look at must have real and tangible meaning.

For instance, there is no point in having good absorption costing statistics if you are producing inventory that you will not sell. You need to do absorption costing for GAAP, but you should make your decisions based upon a combination of variable costing and the actual sales forecasts, along with other real numbers. I once watched a factory manager build inventory to absorb the fixed overhead without the supporting sales to get rid of the inventory. This act caused significant strain on the organization since now all of its cash was in inventory.

> **Note** Make sure that the metrics that you use actually make you money.

Getting and Keeping Money

Many U.S. businesses operate on the same premise that U.S. consumers use. If they don't have the cash, they will get a loan or credit to pay their bills. This works fine if you have the income that exceeds your commitments. In fact, many financial professionals will tell you that you should have a certain amount of debt and equity. There are pros and cons to both debt and equity financing. Figure 7-4 shows some of these issues to consider when looking for external funds.

Equity		Debt	
Pros	**Cons**	**Pros**	**Cons**
Less risk	Investors have a voice	Bank has no say in your business	Money must be paid back in a certain amount of time
Credibility by association with investors	Investors want a higher return	Relationship ends when the loan is paid	If you have cash issues, you may default on the loan
Longer-term view	Some investor ownership	Interest is tax deductible	Too much debt may keep equity investors away
Profits can go into the business	You may need to cash in your share and walk away	Loan can be long- or short-term	You are more vulnerable in slow periods
More cash on hand	Hard to find the right investor	You can plan on the regular expenses	The repayment costs may be high
No requirement to pay if the business fails			Business assets or personal assets may be collatoral

Figure 7-4. Debt versus Equity (*Source*: National Federation of Independent Business, "Debt vs. Equity Financing: Which Is the Best Way for Your Business to Access Capital?", October 17, 2009.)

There is risk in both financing options so the best option is cash. For example, my parents bought the house I grew up in with cash. They never worried about paying a mortgage because there wasn't one to pay. I have known a few people in my life who have done this and have yet to know one who regretted this. A business that is wholly owned and supported with cash reserves is better prepared to handle business fluctuations. There are no loan payments or even lease payments that must be covered to stay in business. If there is a downturn in the economy, a solid business with no debt and cash reserves just reduces its variable costs. Companies who have debt or equity commitments don't have this luxury. Referring back to Chapter 2, many companies need to borrow because they think they need cash to grow. As the studies in Chapter 2 showed, growth does not create money. Money must come before growth. Perhaps if you look at the real reason why you want to grow and think about whether you are trying to grow too quickly, you may realize you do not need to borrow.

There are many other reasons that businesses get in a position where they need cash. Small businesses can get squeezed between large customers and large suppliers. The suppliers demand high prices and favorable payment terms while the customers demand low prices and favorable payment terms. What happens when a company is in this position? The company either uses its own cash or the loans that it holds in order to act as a bank for its customers.

Chapter 7 | Finance

This tactic can get out of hand very quickly. Pretend Company ABC buys raw materials with net 30 payment terms. This means that ABC needs to pay the supplier within 30 days. The company takes 45 days to produce its products once it receives its materials. The customer requires ABC to hold 30 days of inventory on hand. When the customer orders the products, it demands a single monthly invoice with net 75 payment terms. Figure 7-5 illustrates this example.

Supply Cost	$100		
Annual Interest Rate	10%		
Monthly Interest Rate	0.83%		

	Day Number	Inventory Money in Use	Money Financed Due to Payment Terms
Receive Material	0		
Pay	30		
Produce	45	15	
Ship	30	45	
Receive Payment (Min)	75	120	$3.38
Receive Payment (Max)	105	150	$4.24

Figure 7-5. Payment Term Example

Although the dollars seem small in this example, it could present a problem on a larger scale. Consider if this is a company with $3,000,000 in sales and a 30 percent material cost. That means that this company is borrowing between $30,000 and $40,000 just to provide good payment terms for customers and suppliers. The better option is to have the cash on hand without borrowing to cover these terms.

Each company has individual needs and the reality is that sometimes you need to get extra cash through equity or debt. The point is that you should not leverage your company too much because of the risks of doing so. Too many companies fail because they don't plan for bad times and take on too much debt or other ownership for the sake of growth. Don't get caught in this trap. Any good finance person will tell you that you should make sure that you have months of cash on hand to pay for your bills. If your regular use of cash for business depletes those resources too much, you should consider your options for debt and equity. You just need to make sure that you understand the downside to that decision. More importantly, you should think about your business needs and whether they have gotten out of hand.

■ **Note** Cash is king. Make sure that you don't over-leverage your company or lose control by taking on too much equity financing.

Managing Business Taxes

The key waste in business tax management is the ignorance of the tax codes. We have all heard stories of wealthy executives or politicians who pay very low tax rates. Is this because these people are unethical? Are they smarter than the average American? The answer is that they employ people who are experts in the tax codes whose job it is to limit tax liability. The effect of taxes could influence many of your business decisions in a positive way.

Tax incentives or loopholes may make one location for your business a better decision than another, for example. There are tax benefits to the ownership structure that you choose. There are benefits that will influence your supply chain. While we all probably realize the absurdity and inefficiency of the tax code, as long at the tax code remains as complicated as it is, you must work with people who understand it so that you can take advantage of the benefits.

Since the majority of companies are not large enough to employ full-time tax experts, using consultants can be a good option. Such consultants can ensure that you reap all of the tax benefits to which you are entitled.

■ **Note** The biggest waste in business taxes is not using the tax code to minimize your tax liability.

Leasing versus Buying

There are various reasons to lease assets rather than buy them. These include, but are not limited to, the growth of technology, how long you need the asset, tax benefits, and financing options. You must also look at the terms for leasing or purchasing agreements available to you. Every business has risk, so you want to make sure that you don't put your business or yourself at risk if you find you have to break the lease or purchase agreement.

Technology

In areas where technology changes rapidly, it's wasteful to purchase an item when you can keep up with technology through lease agreements. This is partially why the SAAS (software as a service) model using cloud computing has become popular, as discussed in the Chapter 6. Essentially, you are leasing software and hardware because it would cost you more to keep up these items internally than to use cloud computing.

As discussed, for small-to-midsized companies, the lease versus buy decision comes down to economics. The price per user for the software is lower than the cost to buy the software and hardware and maintain those assets with internal personnel. The point at which it makes sense to buy technology and support and upgrade it will vary depending on the company size and the software and hardware in question. You should always make sure that you evaluate both options if they are available.

Timeframe and Industry Volatility

Leasing is a perfect way to handle short-term needs when a long-term purchase would not make sense. More importantly, if you can get used items and don't need the latest technology advancements, such as the case in many industrial applications, buying makes more sense.

For instance, when working in the injection-molding industry, I have looked at the decision to lease or buy the molding machines, ancillary equipment, and other items such as powered industrial trucks. Due to the dynamics of this industry, including the frequent bankruptcies, it is often a better decision to buy these items. The challenge in doing this is ensuring that you maintain similar models of equipment so that maintenance costs are low.

The restaurant industry is very similar. So many restaurants go out of business all the time that it is almost always preferable to buy used equipment. In another industry without this level of volatility, the lease decision could be a better option because cheap, good-quality equipment may not be available. Overall, many executives get caught up in the notion of needing the latest and greatest things. If customers do not enter the area where the equipment is used, there is absolutely no reason to buy new and expensive items.

Taxes and Financing

We discussed the decisions to finance your company using debt or equity. One thing to consider when you are looking at leasing versus buying is how much debt you are currently carrying and how much cash you have on hand. Companies with high amounts of debt that are low on cash often tend to lease rather than buy just to avoid more debt. Some companies will actually sell assets to another company just to lease the assets back in order to build a cash reserve. This is very popular with companies that need the cash to improve their financial position or that want to invest to grow the company but cannot get good debt or equity financing deals.

There are also potential tax benefits to leasing that may drive the decision to lease versus buy. The benefits will vary depending upon the state and the details of the lease, but it is definitely worth exploring if you are considering a lease-versus-buy decision. You may be able to deduct the full cost of a purchase.

Note Failure to evaluate your options when you need new equipment, facilities, or software may lead to lost opportunity to boost your financials and to lower your risk. Also, do not let your ego lead you to buy overpriced items. Find used items when you can.

Finance Metrics

There are countless financial metrics that businesses monitor. Kaplan and Norton criticized businesses for not taking a balanced approach to looking at metrics outside of financial ones.[4] Dr. Deming also criticized businesses for focusing too much on the financial metrics. We highlight just a few common metrics that a business leader or even a department manager should understand.

Pre-Tax Net Profit

This metric is simply the total revenue from sales minus all expenses prior to taxes. This metric helps you understand how well you are managing your expenses versus your sales.

Pre-Tax Net Profit = Total Revenue - All Expenses (prior to taxes)

It is also important to know how your profit compares to your forecast. If there is a large difference, you need to reevaluate your forecasting methods.

Contribution Margin

Contribution margin is the contribution per unit of sale divided by the price per unit. This tells you how much each product or service you sell helps pay for your fixed costs.

---

[4]Kaplan, Robert S. and David P. Norton, "The Balanced Scorecard: Translating Strategy into Action," *Harvard Business Review*, September 1, 1996.

$$\text{Contribution Margin} = \frac{\text{Price per Unit - Variable Cost per Unit}}{\text{Price per Unit}}$$

In cost accounting, fixed costs are applied to products. This means that each product will increase in cost if the company has an overall increase in expenses or a decrease in sales. Contribution takes the noise out of the equation but shows what each item contributes to covering the expense of the fixed costs and, eventually, to the profit margin.

Net Cash Flow

For any given period of time, net cash flow is the incoming cash minus the outgoing cash:

$$\text{Net Cash Flow} = \text{Incoming Cash - Outgoing Cash}$$

You want this metric to be positive and large. It helps you understand if you are paying your suppliers too quickly or not getting paid by your customers quick enough.

Return on Investment

This is a key concept that all business professionals need to understand—I have seen it misunderstood many times. Return on investment (ROI) is the gain from investment minus the cost of investment, divided by the cost of investment.

$$\text{Return on Investment} = \frac{\text{Gain - Cost}}{\text{Cost}}$$

This indicator is misused when determining the gain from investment. For instance, the gain from a marketing campaign is not the sales revenue generated from the campaign, but rather the contribution margin generated from the campaign. That is, the funds generated by the campaign minus the variable costs from the new sales. But even this example is faulty. You must also factor out any other variables that might have increased sales during the same time period. You should know the ROI of every business decision and even every employee.

Current and Quick Ratios

Current ratio is current assets divided by current liabilities. It shows whether you have enough assets to cover your liabilities. You want to make sure that this ratio is greater than one. A larger number is even better.

$$\text{Current Ratio} = \frac{\text{Current Assets}}{\text{Current Liabilities}}$$

Quick ratio is cash plus accounts receivable divided by current liabilities. Again, a larger number is better.

$$\text{Quick Ratio} = \frac{\text{Cash + Accounts Receivable}}{\text{Current Liabilities}}$$

AP and AR Days

Accounts payable (AP) days shows you how many days it will take you to be clear of your liabilities. Accounts receivable (AR) days shows you how many days it will take you to collect all of your assets.

$$\text{AR Days} = \frac{\text{Accounts Receivable}}{\text{Annual Sales}}$$

$$\text{AP Days} = \frac{\text{Accounts Payable}}{\text{COGS}}$$

You look at these two metrics together because you want your accounts receivable days to be less than your accounts payable days. The gap in time between the two gives you time to invest or collect interest on your customer payments prior to paying your suppliers. If the accounts payable days is less than the accounts receivable days, that means that you have to use cash reserves or borrow money to pay your suppliers before your customers pay you. This is a problem of being a sustainable organization. It can also limit your growth potential because you would not have the cash to cover this gap.

Conclusion

The deciding factor when evaluating finance and accounting processes and procedures for waste is whether or not those functions are adding value to the organization. There are many areas that add value beyond the traditional accounts payable, accounts receivable, and financial reporting functions. By having effective policies and procedures that do not cause waste, like budgets based upon prior year performance or multi-tiered approval processes, finance professionals can help drive improvement that is felt through the company. By having seamless processes for core accounting functions, accounting departments can avoid late payment fees and take advantage of payment incentives because of the efficiency produced from these processes. So even though there is not as much waste in finance operations as in other areas of business, there is still opportunity for improvement. You should avoid tax issues by having experts on staff or on retainer help navigate decisions around taxes in order to minimize tax liability. Making intelligent decisions around leasing and purchasing equipment or software will ensure that money is not wasted unnecessarily. And finally, every business leader must have a key understanding of business financial metrics.

Finance professionals should ensure that leaders understand the metrics produced by the finance team. The greatest waste of talent in the finance and accounting areas of business is to assume that the role simply produces reports and handles regulatory issues. These roles are there to maximize value and eliminate waste. This approach is not taken often enough. Finance professionals have a great deal of information at their disposal. This wealth of knowledge and the logical thought processes that finance and accounting people often have gives your business a resource to eliminate waste. You need to ensure that you are getting value from your finance folks by involving them in your activities to improve your processes and eliminate your wastes.

Waste Checklists

Finance Checklist

*All "no" answers identify a potential opportunity for improvement.

Are your approval processes simple, with only one or two levels of approval?	Yes ☐ No ☐
Do you have travel policies in place to avoid excess expenses?	Yes ☐ No ☐
Do you reject requests to go to conferences or trade shows unless there is a return on the investment?	Yes ☐ No ☐
Do you utilize technology to limit the need to travel?	Yes ☐ No ☐
Do you travel only when a face-to-face interaction is needed?	Yes ☐ No ☐
Do you have policies to avoid abuse of business lunch expenses?	Yes ☐ No ☐
Are your budgets based on predictive models for revenue and expenses?	Yes ☐ No ☐
Are your budgets based on the work that needs to be done instead of past expenses?	Yes ☐ No ☐
Do you use multiple forecasting methods to develop your budget?	Yes ☐ No ☐
Do you use zero-based budgeting for your budget processes?	Yes ☐ No ☐

Finance Checklist

*All "no" answers identify a potential opportunity for improvement.

Are payment terms with customers and suppliers designed to avoid using your company as a bank?	Yes ☐ No ☐
Do you have a tax expert on retainer to determine where you can minimize your tax burden?	Yes ☐ No ☐
Do you evaluate leasing versus buying for all major purchasing decisions?	Yes ☐ No ☐
Does the company management understand all of the finance metrics?	Yes ☐ No ☐
Do you understand how much each part of your business contributes to your fixed expenses and profit?	Yes ☐ No ☐
Do you use activity-based costing to determine how much each of your operations activities costs incrementally?	Yes ☐ No ☐
Do you balance your debt and equity financing?	Yes ☐ No ☐
Do you try to use cash instead of financing where possible?	Yes ☐ No ☐

CHAPTER 8

Business Operations
Everyday Waste in Everyday Processes

> *Our business is about technology, yes. But it's also about operations and customer relationships.*
>
> —Michael Dell

All businesses have core functions, which we have discussed throughout this book. Business operations are the functional areas where the product or service that the company sells is produced for the customer. Whether it is a product or component made by a manufacturer, consulting advice, a cheeseburger, or healthcare services, all businesses have operations. All businesses also have operational waste. People accept this everyday waste because they become numb to it. It doesn't bother them when they walk by it every day. However, we have come to realize that the success of operations management comes down to managing the details. And every detail counts.

Like most people, we go to our primary care physician about twice per year. The person who manages the office has put decent processes in place so when we show up for our appointments, there is minimal wait. There is a process for when we go back to the examination room to ensure that little time is wasted getting our vital signs and finding out why we are at the doctor. (We have never waited more than five minutes in the exam room to see the doctor!) In the checkout process, efficiency in scheduling appointments and getting prescriptions is built into the process. Overall, it seems as if the operations manager has looked for ways to be efficient and effective.

However, you have to think about all the little areas of waste behind the scenes. A huge source of waste comes from the payment process. Like many people in the United States, we typically pay for things with a credit card. When the receptionist swipes our card, she prints out three 8.5 X 11 sheets of paper. Two pages go to us, which we recycle, and one goes to the office to file away. The office also eventually pays another company to hold the paper as a record for a couple of decades. You may be thinking that this is no big deal. A piece of paper is about five cents, and a black-and-white printed sheet is between 6 and 7 cents. So at best, this transaction is costing only 18 cents. Right?

Now consider that the group of doctors sees 500,000 people per year in the office across the 88 physicians. They all have the same credit card processing process. That equals $90,000 a year in paper costs. Now consider that as of October 2013, over 40,000 healthcare workers lost their jobs to save money.[1] Now consider that there are about 209,000 primary care physicians practicing in the United States, with each physician seeing about 4,000 patient visits per year. If all of these offices have the same credit card processing practices, that means $150,480,000 is spent per year just for paper to process credit cards. If the average healthcare provider salary is $50,000 per year, that means over 3,000 of those workers could have kept their jobs with better business processes. Of course, there are a lot of reasonable assumptions in this example. Perhaps the jobs that were lost were themselves wasteful. But we include this simple example to illustrate how a small detail can build up to a large expense if not properly managed. Imagine how many small issues like this exist in every business. It is your duty as a leader to find these wastes and eliminate them. The small wastes very likely create more potential loss than the big ones.

Waste from Inefficient Workflows and Layouts

One of my friends, who is a Lean Six Sigma Master Blackbelt trained to identify waste, once told me a story about his visit to a local restaurant. He watched the servers in the restaurant trip over each other multiple times as they tried to deliver food and get drinks for customers. The drink machine was located next to the door to the kitchen so everyone had to go through the same three-foot gap to do all of the service. This bottleneck not only affected the efficiency of the restaurant, but was also a safety concern because of the likelihood that workers will run into each other and potentially cause an injury.

---

[1] Davidson, Paul and Barbara Hensen, "A Job Engine Sputters as Hospitals Cut Staff," *USA Today*, October 13, 2013, http://www.usatoday.com/story/money/bus iness/2013/10/13/hospital-job-cuts/2947929/.

My friend looked at the layout of the workspace and actually drew an alternate workspace to give to his server as a recommendation for improvement. This happened about a year ago. There have been no changes. I wouldn't expect the owner to change the area to my friend's specifications, but I would have expected some change. The same scenario happens in all industries. We have seen offices that are safety hazards because of years of files and junk that's never used.

Lean Manufacturing Tools

A handful of lean manufacturing tools can help almost every company gain a great deal of operational improvement. If you take time to utilize each tool, you will see how much waste you have.

The 5S Process

The first of these concepts is 5S, which enables you to get rid of all supplies, equipment, paperwork, and other things that are not needed. It's like the TLC show *Clean Sweep,* but for business. Think about how much "stuff" you have in your office building that is never used. You might not think this is a big deal, but it is. This "stuff" takes up space, and space is always very expensive. It also gets in the way of efficient operations and can create safety hazards.

The first step in 5S is to *sort* out the items frequently used, the items not frequently used, and the items that are never used. The next step is to *set* the items in order by placing the frequently used items near the area that they are used. The infrequently used items are stored away from the work area. Other items are thrown away or donated. The third step is to *sweep or shine* the area by cleaning the work area or even painting it white to give it a clean look (this makes it easy to identify when it gets dirty). This sounds like a minimal change, but just the act of making something fresh and clean helps maintain the improvements. The fourth step includes creating and implementing a *standardized* process to maintain the new work area. The final step is to *sustain* the improvement by following up on it to ensure that it continues to meet the expectations set by the improvement. It is always easy to fall back into the same old behaviors. This is one of the reasons any improvement should have a conscious sustainment process embedded in it as well.

Note Sort, set in order, sweep, standardize, and sustain all work areas. This process goes far beyond manufacturing facilities and can create major improvements in every area of business.

Chapter 8 | Business Operations

5S is an easy process to implement and can help you make a safer, more efficient work environment with less potential damage to inventory. I have used this method in offices, manufacturing lines, storage areas for equipment or inventory, clinical workspaces, and even at a pharmacy. Overall, 5S will help you improve quality, safety, and workforce morale and can reduce changeover time, inventory costs, and process time, saving your organization both time and money.

There are numerous success stories about businesses that have implemented 5S. A metal fabrication company was able to increase inventory turnover by 67 percent, reduce inventory by 35 percent, and increase reliability of shipping time to 99 percent.[2] In another example, a window manufacturing company was able to increase productivity by 35 percent and reduce overtime by 45 percent.[3] It seems almost too simple that just the act of cleaning and organizing can reduce so much waste, but it is very real. Figure 8-1 shows the basic 5S process.

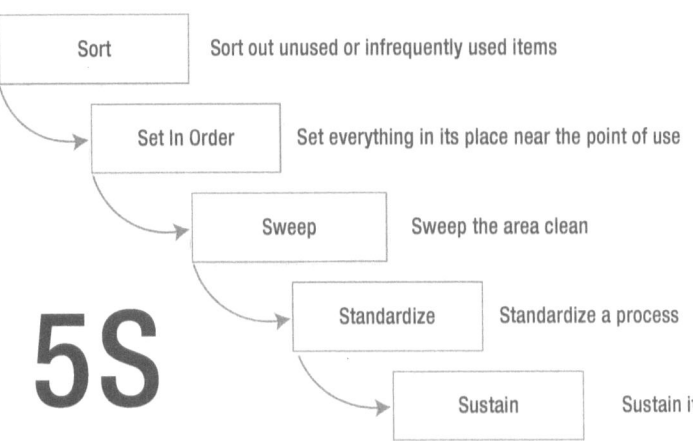

Figure 8-1. 5S Process

There are videos available online that show the effects of 5S. One in particular shows the use of 5S in an area as simple as an employee bathroom. There are pictures of what the room should look like. There are work instructions on how to clean the room after use. There is an audit and responsibility schedule

---

[2]Wisconsin Manufacturing Extension Partnership, "5S Offers Fast & Measureable Results," 2014, http://www.wmep.org/next-generation-manufacturing/systemic-continuous-improvement/lean-manufacturing-5s-visual-management-vsm-2?utm_expid=14996962-0._YuBIZBzR1qJ4cbWxWZQsA.1&utm_referrer=https%3A%2F%2Fwww.google.com%2F.
[3]Ibid.

that shows who is responsible for ensuring that cleanliness and organization is maintained. There are even inventory areas identified for cleaning supplies, with minimum and maximum quantities noted. 5S can be used almost anywhere.

The SMED Process

Another easy-to-use lean concept that will help with your workflow and layout is the concept of SMED, or Single Minute Exchange of Dies. This is the process of improving the time it takes to switch from making one item to making another. This concept got its roots from Shigeo Shingo in a steel fabrication factory, but is easily applied to many manufacturing, healthcare, or service industry operations.

The idea is to take activities that would be normally done while the equipment is not in use and convert them to being done without stopping the equipment. A simple example of SMED can be found in the activities to change a tire. I got in a minor car accident a few years ago. I was wearing my suit and had never changed a tire on my truck before. It took me 25 minutes to change the tire. Now consider Nascar. The tire change in Nascar takes about four seconds. There is a big difference between 25 minutes and four seconds. Pit crews have specially designed lug nuts and tools to remove the tire efficiently, there is a trained team who does the work, and everything is ready to go as soon as the stock car stops. The pit team utilizes the same techniques that Mr. Shingo developed. I have seen this technique reduce four or five hour changeovers into less than 30 minutes. The main benefits go back to 5S, which helps you analyze the workflow and layout to minimize wasteful motion or searching for tools. You also want to incorporate these methods with value-stream mapping (discussed in Chapter 4).

The Spaghetti Diagram

Although 5S and SMED help with layout issues that cause inefficiency and ineffectiveness, there is another tool—the spaghetti diagram—that you may use to implement these tools on its own or combine them with the other tools. Figure 8-2 shows an example of a spaghetti diagram. The lines represent three different people working in this area. The before picture shows excessive movement. By changing the layout and the job responsibilities, you can achieve the after layout and remove the wasteful movement.

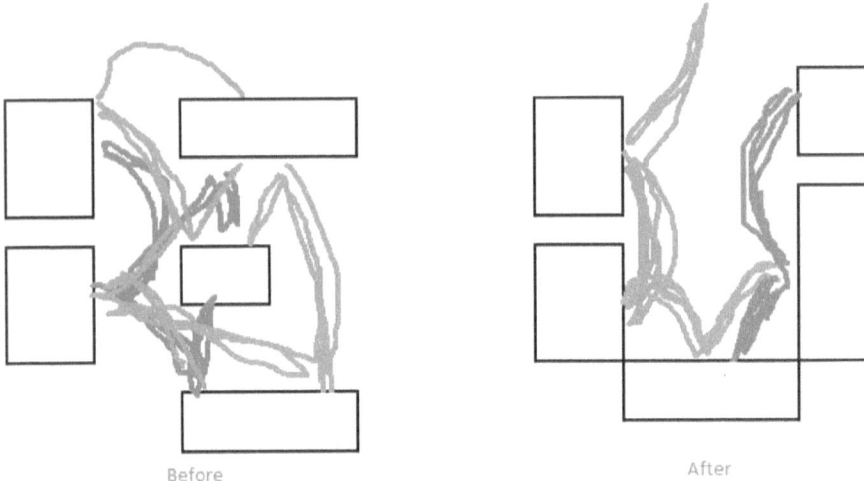

Before   After

Figure 8-2. Spaghetti Diagram

I have seen examples where the distance walked by employees is reduced by as much as 40 percent by using spaghetti diagrams to change the workflow and some work standardization. After some of my friends used these techniques, they have told me that they do simple things like prepare for the next day the night before so there is not as much to do in the morning or bring their coffee pot into the bedroom to reduce the walking distance. In our house, we pack all of the lunches for the family and set out the clothes for all of our children at night so that when we are getting everyone out the door in the morning, there is that much less work to do. There are simple things like having the drink station and bread warmer beside the salad station in restaurants, so that while a server is grabbing drinks and salads, she can also grab bread.

Something as simple as everyone using a centralized printer can create waste. This is because everyone has to run down the hall all day long. Poor layout design is a huge waste in most businesses, and you should be looking for these wastes around you. You might not think about where each employee's footsteps go every day, but if you do, you can save a lot of money.

Note Two of the eight wastes identified in lean operations are transportation and motion. Both of these wastes can be improved with a better layouts.

Poorly Designed Facilities

Having the right facilities for the job can help you avoid waste. The waste in facilities comes in part from the assumption that you have to use facilities a certain way. For example, many MBA programs teach you about improving distribution operations by analyzing your customers and establishing your business near them. There is truth to this, but it is not an absolute rule in business. We talked in other areas of this book about tactics such as telecommuting as a way to reduce business expenses. With the technology that is available today, you should be pushing for employees to work from home whenever practical (with clear expectations around productivity, of course). Remember, most studies show that working from home is more productive. One Harvard study found that when a company instituted a work-from-home policy, the workers increased productivity by 13.5 percent. These home-bound workers also quit at a 50 percent lower rate than the workers in the office, and had much higher job satisfaction.[4] (We discussed flextime and work at home time more in Chapter 5.)

Another source of facility-level waste is the way that your facility is organized, beyond just where people walk and get the things they need. The facility should be designed to optimize material and product flow. Figure 8-3 shows a simple factory design where the raw materials are received on one side of the building; the materials are manufactured into a product and then shipped out of the other side of the building. Similar material flow can be designed into any work environment and lead to efficiency in the operations. This is a simple concept but I have been in dozens of factories that aren't laid out in a way that makes material flow easy.

---

[4]Bloom Nicolas, "To Raise Productivity, Let More Employees Work from Home," *Harvard Business Review, The Magazine*, January-February 2014, http://hbr.org/2014/01/to-raise-productivity-let-more-employees-work-from-home/ar/1.

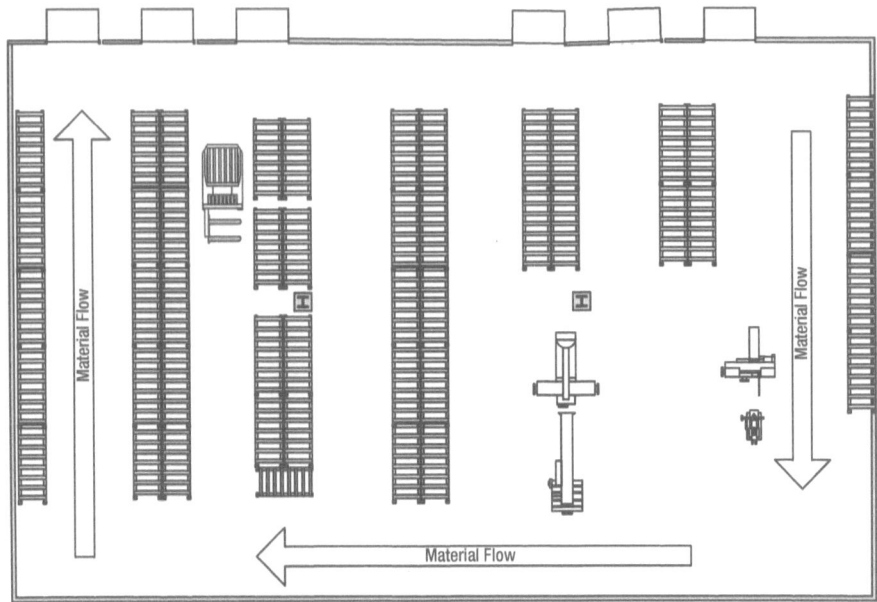

Figure 8-3. Factory Layout Example

■ **Note** If your facility expenses are high, look for creative ways to reduce your facility needs.

Over- or Under-serviced Equipment

Over the past 15 years we have worked with a variety of companies. Some choose to maintain their equipment very well while others choose to barely maintain their equipment at all. There is waste on both ends of the spectrum. Normally, the equipment manufacturers specify some maintenance requirements. When the equipment is under warranty, this should be the minimum requirement. Beyond that, how much you maintain your equipment depends upon a few factors.

How important is the quality of your product or service? If you rely on equipment to produce high-quality products or to test or measure something with a high level or precision and accuracy, then you should maintain your equipment as much as is necessary to ensure that it is performing well. You should also take the effort to test your equipment to ensure that your maintenance activities are successful.

How important is it to keep your equipment running all of the time? If the cost of not having your equipment running is greater than the cost to fix it, then you must keep it from breaking down. You can measure the overall equipment effectiveness (OEE) to look at the maintenance and productivity of your equipment. In the metrics section at the end of this chapter, we show you the calculation for OEE. It is a function of the time that the equipment is running, the speed at which it's running, and the quality level of your production. By maximizing OEE, you maximize the output of your equipment. You can also perform tests to predict equipment failures and proactively repair or replace components of the equipment to avoid downtime.

How expensive is the equipment? If the equipment is cheap enough, then it could be considered disposable. Look at the costs of maintaining the equipment versus replacing it frequently. Sometimes, it is cheaper to dispose of worn out equipment than it is to keep it running.

■ **Note** Maintain your equipment to the level that you need to meet your business requirements. Under- or over-maintenance can cause waste.

Unnecessary Supplies and Services

The profitability of some types of businesses depends upon the supply expenses. Supply expense often includes inventory costs (discussed later in this chapter). One of the biggest wastes in the workplace is the use of paper—which we have mentioned in this book a few times—because it is so unnecessary.

Last year, we calculated the cost of the paper used in the school for each of our kids. We simply used an estimate of six cents per page and counted how many sheets of paper were sent home each day. We found that it would actually be cheaper to buy electronic tablets, such as iPads or Surfaces, and load them with software than to use all of that paper. If we had included the other costs that accompany paper, then the costs would have been much higher.

In the business world, the average office worker uses 10,000 sheets of paper per year.[5] The costs of managing paper can be six times the cost of printing cost it. This means that the average office worker spends $3,600 per year due to paper use alone. Figure 8-4 shows the calculations used to come up with the $3,600 figure.

---

[5]Haggith Mandy, *Paper Trails: From Trees to Trash—The True Cost of Paper*, London: Virgin Books, 2009, p. xx.

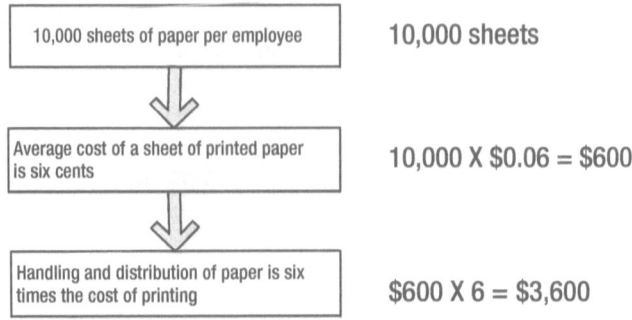

Figure 8-4. Paper Cost per Employee. (*Source:* Haggith Mandy, *Paper Trails: From Trees to Trash—The True Cost of Paper*, London: Virgin Books, 2009, pp 1-256)

We have all spent time in meetings watching packets of paper make their way around to the attendees while a presentation with the same information is projected on a screen. Or we have taken notes in our notepad only to review them later or copy them into a computer for safe storage. We cannot sit in the meeting with our iPad or laptop because it is considered rude since we might be doing something other than taking notes. So what do we do with all of those documents handed out in meetings? We write notes on them. Some of us doodle on them? Then, we either throw them away or put them in the confidential paper recycling bin. This is all waste. Of course, the cost of printed paper and its handling varies by business, and Figure 8-5 shows you how you can calculate these costs in your business.

Cost Source	Data	Multiplier		Answer
Annual Cost per Square Foot Cost			=	A
Number of Office Workers			=	B
Average Hourly Wage			=	C
Monthly Paper Cost		X 12	=	D
Number of Onsite Filing Cabinets		X 15.7 X A	=	E
Square Footage of Banker Box Storage		X A	=	F
Monthly Cost of Offsite Storage		X 12	=	G
Monthly Printer/Copier Rental Cost		X 12	=	H
Monthly Printer/Copier Maintenance Cost		X 12	=	I
Monthly Toner Cost		X 12	=	J
Monthly Supply Cost*		X 12	=	K
Daily Hours Managing Paper per Employee		X B X C X 250	=	L

Total Cost = D + E + F + G + H + I + J + K + L

Figure 8-5. Paper Cost Calculation Worksheet

Now imagine what you could do with that money besides using it to throw away paper. Why don't you take advantage of this opportunity? In order to reduce paper costs, you need to change the way you think about business and operate your business. You need to leverage technology in order to drive these costs out of your business. You do this by using shared document storage areas and avoiding duplication of business documents.

Also, consider how many office supplies you can get rid of when you eliminate paper: paper clips, staples, staplers, pens, pencils, sticky notes, folders, filing cabinets, shelves, binders, binder clips, page protectors, and so on. Go to your local office supply store and look at the costs of these items. Without paper, you don't need any of these. The space that you save can mean a smaller office space, which can improve your overall bottom line in addition to the basic paper and office supply costs.

Other supply costs include cleaning supplies such as trash bags. I have routinely seen janitorial staff take trash bags that are nearly empty and replace them on a daily basis. Now, because I do not use a large quantity of paper I generate a full trash can probably once every three to four weeks. So instead of one bag being used, 15 to 20 bags are being used. This is only $9 per year in material cost loss, but consider if this is done in a company with 1,000 employees. That is $9,000 per year. You may think that $9,000 per year is not a lot, but remember that this is only one small example. These small examples exist all around us and add up to significant expenses.

There are other supplies that are totally unnecessary: Styrofoam coffee cups, napkins, forks and other eating utensils that should be provided by the employee.

Then you need to think about all the possibly unnecessary services. At my place of employment, about 10 years ago, we went from having many janitors that were on staff 24/7 to having one. Each department has their own vacuum cleaner, bottle of spray cleaner, and rags. When each of us feels our office is a little dirty, we clean it ourselves. On the surface it seems like a bad decision (when you look at the hourly rate a professor makes vs. the hourly rate of a janitor), but faculty offices simply do not need cleaned daily. Really, at the amount they are used, they don't even need it monthly.

Some companies also pay for extremely wasteful services such as landscaping. If you use native, perennial plants and trees, you will not only save on landscaping, but also save on utilities. Native plants means possibly no watering needs, and native trees lower heating and cooling costs. We suggest you look around at all the services you are using to see what is really necessary.

■ **Note** Look at the routine operations supply and services costs and make sure that you still need to use those expenses. There is a lot of waste in paper.

Excessive Overhead Costs

There are lots of ways to cut down on overhead costs. With energy costs increasing, this can be a priority for many businesses. Manufacturers are large users of both electricity and fossil fuels. This is not a complex process. If you do the analysis on what it takes to cut energy costs, there is often a short payback when you make energy efficient changes. You can undertake large projects like changing out all of the lighting fixtures in your company or replacing natural gas burners. Depending upon the individual energy use of your company, these may be "no brainers."

Almost any company can justify the simple things to reduce energy costs. Installing motion detector lights and automatic and low-flow faucets are low-cost improvements that even smaller companies can undertake. An even lower-cost alternative is encouraging employees to turn computers off when they leave work or turning the lights off when they aren't needed. (Or, once again, introduce work-from-home policies.)

You can reduce your utility use by adjusting the thermostat up or down, depending on the season. (Of course, if you choose to do these things, you may negate any improvements if employees bring in space heaters or fans.) We had a horrible heat wave a couple summers ago, and some businesses instituted a four, 10-hour-day work schedule to keep their cooling costs down. This coincided with the first time gas spiked over $4.00 a gallon, so workers were happy to save on gas as well. For any improvement, you also need to look at the potential effect on employee productivity. You don't want your employees so uncomfortable or tired that they cannot work.

Another utility you can reduce is your phone service. You can utilize the voiceover Internet protocol (VOIP) instead of the standard telephone service to reduce your telephone costs. There is enough competition in this sector now that VOIP often makes more sense than using land lines. You should also consider whether your employees still even need phones. So much business is done through e-mail now, and many employees never use their desk phones. When they do make calls, they frequently use their cell phones. You are very likely paying for phone services that are not being used.

Although we are sure that large companies in part go after sustainability initiatives to be environmentally responsible, the main reason why they have adopted these practices is because they lower their costs. There are potentially thousands of dollars in lost revenue that could be gained by selling your recyclable materials rather than throwing them in the trash. Companies will pay you to come remove these materials from your facility, rather than you paying a trash company to remove them. The only effort that is necessary to take advantage of this opportunity is the time it takes to separate your trash according to type. You can also look for ways to recycle your own materials, limit your packaging materials, or purchase materials or packaging with recycled content. This is so simple to do. If you don't adopt some kind of internal recycle and reuse processes, you are throwing money away.

Note Save money and boost your company's reputation at the same time by becoming environmentally friendly.

Further, you should eliminate unnecessary entitlement costs. I can't count how many trade shows and conferences I have attended over the years. The majority of the time I spent at these events was wasteful. Now, that is not always the case—we discussed trade show benefits in the Chapter 4. There are other benefits such as educational opportunities. The point is that you need to look at each of these expenses and determine if there is a real return on investment.

You should also look for fixed costs, such as facilities, that can be eliminated. If you improve your operations in other facilities and use the available capacity to produce more products. Incorporating the inventory-reduction techniques that we talked about earlier may eliminate the need to have as many warehouse locations or allow you to reduce the size of your building. Work-from-home policies may eliminate the need for office space and office furniture.

You can also review all monthly or annual business dues, memberships, and subscriptions. If there is a true business benefit of these costs, they may be a good investment. Often they are just for personal enjoyment or to boost resumes. Many people sign up for LinkedIn premium or other similar sites and don't use them. I have worked in companies where one employee will get a subscription to a trade magazine and then pass it around to others. This is a simple way to keep subscription costs low while still providing benefit to all. If a database or publication is necessary to research the industry, then keep it, by all means, but don't be wasteful about such purchases.

Also, look at your company certifications. Certifications such as ISO 9001, TS16949, or AS 9100 often have a customer requirement tied to them. This means that because your customer wants you to have these certifications, you must have them in order to do business. One *huge* waste in quality-management systems certifications is getting them just because your customers ask you to. There can be real business efficiency and effectiveness gains from properly implementing these systems and using them as a foundation for your continuous improvement, supplier control, and quality control. But if your goal is to get a flag to hang in front of your building, then you are getting certifications for the wrong reason. If there is no process improvement from a certification and your customers don't care about the certification, then why are you doing it? We have seen companies spend tens or hundreds of thousands of dollars to get a certification that provides no real benefit, other than bragging rights. You should avoid these types of certifications. You need to identify all certifications you currently have, look at their costs and benefits, and then eliminate those without significant value.

> **Note** There are lots of ways to control overhead. Challenge every expense and determine if it is necessary.

Waste in the Product Development Process

Many businesses thrive on product or service development. Manufacturers develop products for sale in order to maintain their current size or grow the business. Service providers develop new services that customers want in order to do the same. If product development is so important, then why don't we do it well? To be fair, many companies develop products well, but the majority of companies don't. We drive waste into our businesses by doing a poor job of developing products. We discuss product development and market research in Chapter 3. Here we cover a few operational sources of waste in the process that many people don't think about.

Customer Requirements

As we began to discuss in Chapter 3 on marketing, misunderstanding or not taking the time to ask the customers what they want is a major driver of waste in the product development process. You obviously need to conduct and interpret proper market research. Having no or bad research can lead to building a facility to take care of customer needs that don't need to be filled or developing a product or service that doesn't sell. Just look at how many restaurants fail. Look at the products that are sold at closeout stores like Big Lots to see examples of not understanding customer requirements.

There are other issues around understanding customer requirements. In Chapter 4, we talked about the waste driven in sales. One major sales waste is not considering your sales job, engineering job, or customer service job as a job of gathering customer requirements. I have seen this multiple times in my career, where a custom manufacturer sells its services to a larger company without understanding the requirements of that company. These requirements may include open capacity, technical knowledge, quality control, specialized manufacturing processes, or even electronic communication for order fulfillment. If you don't understand these requirements up front, then you are likely to incur costs that you didn't budget on the project—if you are able to meet the requirements at all. If you cannot meet the requirements, you will probably lose the sales and never get another chance to get them back. You cannot assume that the way you have always done business will work for every customer. If you are not willing to do the work of gathering customer requirements and ensuring your capability to meet them, you are better off not getting the sale.

In my days of providing components to automotive suppliers, I developed price estimates for thousands of items. I quoted an item about 10 years ago at a price of around 40 cents. The buyer at my customer's business had two competitive quotations between 10 and 15 cents. Obviously, I did not get the sale on this part. I talked with the buyer and explained some technical issues with the part that would make it expensive to make and would drive the need for increased quality inspection. I knew my customer and knew what the requirements would be. Later, I found out that my customer was unsuccessful with the item using the cheapest supplier. With the second supplier, the costs ended up being close to what I had estimated after weeks of delay due to product development issues. This was a case where I felt good about the service that I gave to this customer. This, along with many other examples, built trust between this customer and my company that led to profitable growth using our capabilities as a manufacturer. You will save and make money long-term by understanding the customer's requirements, providing a quality product, and pricing appropriately.

Note You will save and make money long-term by understanding the customer's requirements, providing a quality product, and pricing appropriately.

Planning for Production

After gathering customer requirements, companies also tend to overpromise on delivery expectations. Still others frustrate their customers because they don't commit to deadlines that are aggressive enough. A primary reason for the variability in delivering on promises is that in the development cycle, the production or service operations are involved after the deadlines are established. Production personnel absolutely should be involved in establishing deadlines. This simple process can avoid product development waste by ensuring that promises are kept. Huge waste is created because sales and development departments don't talk to each other.

Customer Maintenance

I often tell a story of how we fired the third largest customer of the company where I worked as an example of how volume isn't the largest driver of profitability. When the company where I worked made the choice to eliminate this customer, its profitability almost immediately increased. The expense of taking care of all of this customer's service requirements exceeded the contribution to overhead. We were using profits made on other customers to subsidize this customer.

Not all customers are created equal. Not all customers are a good fit for your business. As we discussed in Chapter 4, you must know the CLV (Customer Lifetime Value) of each customer. If you have a mutually beneficial customer and supplier relationship, then you need to manage it. This includes ensuring that you continue to understand the requirements and your ability to meet them. In the product development cycle, you need to maintain your relationship with your customer to make sure that you are pursuing the right technology advancements to service your customer needs.

■ **Note** Not all business is good business. Not all customers are good customers. You need to maintain your relationships with your good customers and not spend all of your time courting new ones.

Waste in the Supply Chain

There are three major cost components to any business: labor, overhead, and materials. The distribution of these costs in any business varies depending upon the industry. Supply chain management includes the activities associated with the materials portion of this equation. Manufacturing companies have the largest percentage of cost from materials. Service companies, like restaurants and healthcare, have lower percentage of cost from supplies, but the costs are still significant. There are many places where supply chain operations can go wrong.

Managing Inventory Levels

One of the eight wastes identified in Lean Manufacturing is with inventory. In my days in the restaurant industry, I remember taking over the job of a Bar Buyer for a large restaurant. Unfortunately, I had taken over this job due to someone's sudden death, so I had no guidance to begin the job. There were very few records—another bad thing in the world of inventory control. I walked into the liquor storage room and just began to look around. I quickly realized that over half the bottles were covered in dust. This was an extremely busy restaurant with an extremely busy bar. We had as much as a two-hour wait every night, so the entire lounge area was full almost all the time. So why were there so many dusty bottles? I could go through many problems here: not using FIFO (first in first out), severe over-ordering, and ordering exotic liquors that were rarely used. The point here is that everywhere you carry inventory, even if it's just one stockroom of liquor, needs assessment.

Excessive inventory is wasteful because it can lead to obsolescence or product damage. Inventory also takes up space in your facilities, which keeps you from using that space for something productive. Inventory ties up your cash so it cannot be used for other purposes. Inventory's greatest waste is that it helps hide other issues in your operations or the supply chain. This is why "world class" companies work hard to minimize inventory. But sometimes inventory is a good thing because you have identified issues that you cannot control. If you have minimum order quantities, unreliable suppliers, or unpredictable customer orders, you should plan on having inventory to hide these problems. So even though having too much inventory is a waste, not having enough inventory can also be a waste.

Regardless of how much inventory you keep on hand, you should locate some of your inventory close to where it is being used. You should only locate a finite amount of the inventory here, because too much inventory will get in your way.

Note Make sure that your inventory levels are the right size and that an appropriate amount of inventory is stored near the work area.

During my career, I have witnessed various ways of managing inventory. One way to manage inventory is to review economic order quantities. This process looks at the costs associated with a purchase, including price, shipping, processing, and storage costs. You use this to figure out the lowest total cost for your inventory. This is a great idea in theory, but it can leave you holding onto inventory you don't need and may make you increase your warehouse space to accommodate the inventory because your inventory levels aren't based on your customer needs. Basing your inventory on purchase and shipping costs may drive you to buy inventory that you may never use.

Another method to manage inventory is by using a bin system and an electronic scanner. The "bins" are the locations in the warehouse. The scanners are like the ones you see at the grocery store. This bin system helps you maximize space utilization by allowing any inventory item to go anywhere in the warehouse since you are telling your computer system where items are stored rather than maintaining locations specifically designed for items.

This makes sense in some cases because of the space efficiency it offers. The other wastes, such as searching or transportation caused by this method, may be less than not maximizing your space utilization. In other businesses, the workflow is more important than the space utilization. You need to look at your own business to determine what is most important to you.

Another inventory management system is the Kanban system. In this system, you calculate the inventory buffer you need to ensure that you do not run out of inventory in operations. Then you order materials only when you reach your minimum inventory level. You then receive new inventory shortly before you run out of inventory. This is a great way to keep your inventory costs low, but you may pay more for the materials due to the smaller, more frequently needed order sizes.

Using the material requirements planning (MRP) method is very common as well. This is where you look at open orders or forecasts and order components in the quantities that are necessary to meet those requirements. This could leave you with inventory that you don't need if your forecasts aren't accurate or your customer orders fluctuate. Additionally, MRP relies upon production schedules and bills of materials (the recipe for the item) to be correct. Bills of material must be correct in any operation for accounting purposes but production schedules can change daily due to a variety of factors. MRP processes can drive up your inventory costs and leave you holding onto inventory that you may not use.

Consignment is another method that is used in inventory management. This is where you don't own the inventory until you use it. The materials are in your warehouse, but they belong to your supplier. You tell your supplier when you use the materials and pay for them at that point. This method of communication to the supplier may be through your own warehouse management system, a system supplied by your supplier, or a manual audit performed by your supplier. The downside to this method is that although you don't take ownership of the inventory, you take responsibility for it. You may also have to commit to some minimum use of inventory prior to entering into the deal. There is often some level of exclusivity that the supplier may expect as part of the deal. With exclusivity, there is a potential for abuse on pricing or other service costs. Consignment deals are great. But you need to be smart about how they are structured or they can drive waste.

Regardless of what the experts selling you software or hardware tell you, the best processes for inventory management are the ones that put the control of managing inventory as close to the user of the inventory as possible. Small and midsized businesses with only a few dozen or a few hundred inventory items don't need special software to manage inventory. A well designed spreadsheet to identify inventory needs and a Kanban system or visual signal to tell users to order material are the only tools that you need. Sometimes a pure Kanban system won't work well because of the issues mentioned earlier. You can get creative and work deals with suppliers that allow you to bundle different items to get volume discounts. You may also want to use a combination of the other tactics we mentioned earlier. Normally, the best solution is the one that uses the right tool for each situation.

If you have a larger company, there is no way to avoid using a MRP system to help you identify your material needs, but you can still use a combination of consignment and Kanban methods to minimize your inventory costs. Large manufacturers who utilize Lean manufacturing methods have been known to locate supplier facilities within a few hours of their facility to make daily shipments of materials easier. Using this combination allows companies like Toyota to use MRP to manage inventories but also keep only a few days of inventory on hand.

Note There is no single way to manage inventory that works for everyone. Fancy software is not necessary most of the time.

Managing Your Warehouse

Much like the process of managing your inventory levels, there is no one-size-fits-all way to run a warehouse. For operations with relatively low demand for supplies, a fixed location system where each supply has a home may be more appropriate than the bin-and-scanner method mentioned earlier. The waste in managing your warehouse generally comes from a combination of not doing some basic warehouse-management activities and from assuming that you should do it the same way as another company.

Just the Basics

If you are not doing some basic activities to manage your warehouse you should consider changing your processes. For instance, when you received components from suppliers, you should only have one unique component per box. We are not saying for instance that if you buy hamburger buns that you should only have one bun per box. What we are saying is that you should not mix your hot dog buns, hamburger buns, and napkins in the same box. If you receive multiple items in the same box, your warehouse workers have to separate them so they can be used. This may seem like a simple concept, but we have seen experienced warehouse leaders who didn't do this.

Along the same lines, you should have a maximum number of different types of items on a single pallet or skid. This is mainly important for companies that have a warehouse. Smaller companies may not buy items in enough bulk to be able to get skids full of supplies with only a few unique items on the skid. The efficiency lost in breaking down or separating the unique items sent on single skid or in a single box is substantial for larger warehouses.

Furthermore, you should have standard package sizes and quantities. For instance, every time you order hamburger buns, you should order 100 of them and they should come in the same size box every time. A key element of any warehouse management is standardization. Set yourself up for success requesting standardization from your suppliers.

Whether you have a single unique item on a pallet or multiple items, you should have your supplier label each pallet. This helps eliminate waste in figuring out what is on each pallet, making receiving of materials more efficient and effective. You should also standardize the labeling of your items. This includes the label format and location. By doing this, you know where your labels are on the boxes and you ensure that you are able to read or scan the label using barcode scanning.

If you are running a warehouse, you need to plan your space to maximize your effectiveness. Simple specifications around the size of the pallet that you receive from suppliers can help you optimize the storage locations. Most suppliers will meet your expectations, although there may be some extra expense associated with the request if you are asking for expensive materials. The size is not limited to just the pallet but also how your purchased supplies are stored. If you have storage racks, you need to make sure that your materials will fit in your racks. Again, this may seem basic, but many hours have been spent in warehouses repacking pallets from suppliers so that they would fit onto the storage racks.

You need to ensure your warehouse is optimized. Some warehouse managers choose to receive inventory into an area where the items are inspected and prepared to be put into the warehouse. If you set up standards with your suppliers, then you can eliminate this wasteful activity by receiving items directly into your warehouse and having any quality checks that are necessary concurrently with the receipt.

■ **Note** Minimize the waste in your warehouse operations by having standards in place. Your suppliers should be willing to help you with your standardization needs.

Movement or searching within the warehouse is a tremendous waste. I have personally spent hours in warehouses looking for items because the warehouse was not well organized. Whatever your organization method is, it should be clear and consistent. Your organization method should be simple enough that you can find things manually without a fancy system. As your warehouse management matures, you may decide to use fancier systems to maximize your space utilization, such as a bin system that allows you more flexibility on where you store items. I challenge you even at that point to try to keep some logic in your organization. Remember that if you can't make a process work manually and on paper, introducing an automated system will not make your processes any better. As we discussed in Chapter 6, you have to stop thinking about software as a solution and fix the basic processes first. Be organized and efficient.

Note Automation will not make a bad manual process any better. Organize first and automate later if needed.

Your Processes

Some warehouses operate through visual cues while others depend upon reports. The ones that depend on reports don't perform most warehouse activities unless there is a report that triggers them. The ones that use visual cues allow the warehouse workers to do the routine tasks needed to manage the warehouse based upon those cues. I have seen both methods work, but your processes should focus on execution of activities and your customers, instead of what you think is most efficient for your workers. Your customers want you to deliver your inventory to them in the most convenient manner possible. If any of your activities jeopardizes this, then you are generating waste by creating unhappy customers.

If you are counting on reports to tell you what to do within your warehouse, you should look for ways to use visual cues to tell you when to do an activity. For instance, if a supply is supposed to be stored in a location for use by your operation, it should be understood that when that supply gets below a certain level or depleted, someone is responsible for filling the location with new supplies. This is like the soda racks in a convenience store. There are slopes racks that always keep the inventory at the front of the shelf. The worker loads the soda from the back of the shelf to fill the available space. When I was in college, one of my jobs was to sell beer and malt beverages in a small shop attached to a bar in Pennsylvania. I went into each cooler, looked for shelf space that was not filled with inventory, and filled it with bottles of beer from cardboard cases stored within the cooler. I didn't have a report that told me that I needed to load a six pack of Molson Ice, a case of Woodchuck Hard Cider, and a few bottles of Bud Light onto the shelves. My eyes told me that I needed to do that work. Some warehouses become far too dependent upon reports and don't use the simple method of checking.

If you choose to have a dedicated receiving area rather than put all items directly into inventory, it should be understood that the receiving area is cleared before the end of the shift. Reports aren't necessary to tell the warehouse worker that there are items in the receiving area. Reports are necessary to alert workers to pull items if visual management is not in place or to send items to customers. Unless it involves an order to pull inventory for use, look for ways to get rid of the report-based process.

Your warehouse processes must be customer focused. This is true whether the customer is a third party buying items from your company or is another department in your company. Activities requested or needed by customers should always have priority. I couldn't believe the first time I saw a "kill or fill" order fulfillment process. This is when a request for inventory comes to the warehouse and triggers the warehouse to send inventory to a customer. If there is available inventory on hand then there is no problem. The warehouse fills the order. If there is no available inventory on hand, then the order is "killed," or not filled without any notice to the person who requested the item.

Needless to say, this process is used only with internal customers; if this process were used with external customers, you would not have customers for very long. The point is that this lack of customer service in a supply operation should never be accepted. At the very least, if a supply is not on hand, the customer should be notified with options such as a back order (a delayed order) or a replacement item. Any other process, although it may not cost the warehouse anything, costs the business dearly because a user of supplies is expecting them and doesn't get them. Even worse, the customer gets accustomed to this egregious lack of service and wastes precious time reordering items because they did not get the items the first time. This is another instance where departments should talk to each other. Sales should also know what is going on in terms of inventory.

Shipping

Companies frequently don't realize how much money is wasted due to poor planning. Expedited shipping costs are a large waste in many businesses. These can be avoided by eliminating common traps like delayed decision making or not managing your capacity well enough. These are the common root causes of high shipping costs.

You should spend time figuring out the best shipping methods for your company and negotiating fair rates. After you have done this, try to drive your overnight shipping costs to zero. This concept applies to the goods you ship to your customers as well. All logistics companies are in competition with each other and are happy to negotiate with you for better rates.

Vendor Management

We have talked a good deal about vendor management in regard to a warehouse. There are other considerations in regard to vendor or supplier management to avoid waste. For one, if the supplier supplies an item or service that is important to your product or service, you must evaluate that supplier to ensure that you get consistent quality and service. We have always supported developing long-term relationships with a few key suppliers, but it is frankly naïve to trust that your supplier is doing everything you need them to do. You should ensure that your supplier is delivering on time. Is he giving you consistent quality? Does the supplier follow through on promises? Are there technical skills or processes that you need that your supplier provides? If not, are they working on developing those skills or processes? Figure 8-6 shows an example of some criteria that you can use to evaluate your suppliers. The actual criteria that you use will vary depending upon your business needs, but the point is that where possible, you should develop objective criteria to measure your suppliers.

Criteria	Score				
	1	2	3	4	5
Quality Level	>1500 Parts per Million Defective	<1500 Parts per Million Defective	<1000 Parts per Million Defective	<500 Parts per Million Defective	Zero Defects
Delivery	<95% On Time Delivery	>95% On Time Delivery	>97% On Time Delivery	>99% On Time Delivery	100% On Time Delivery
Accuracy	>2% Undershipment	<2% Undershipment	<3% Overshipment	<2% Overshipment	Zero Deviations from Order Quantity
Technical Knowledge	Basic Technical Knowledge	Willing to Try New Technology	Invests in New Technology Occasionally	Actively Invests in New Technology	Innovative Technology
Cost Competitiveness	Lowest Cost < 40% of the Time	Lowest Cost > 40% of the Time	Lowest Cost > 60% of the Time	Lowest Cost > 80% of the Time	Lowest Cost > 90% of the Time

Figure 8-6. Supplier Ranking Criteria

Once you have developed and communicated the evaluation criteria, you can compute a weighted score. For instance, you may value quality, accuracy, and delivery more than the other criteria, so you give quality a weight of 30 percent, delivery and accuracy 25 percent, and the other two 10 percent. So your evaluation may look like the following:

$$Score = 0.3*Quality + 0.25*Delivery + 0.25*Accuracy + 0.1*Technical + 0.1*Cost$$

By giving each supplier a rating on each category, you can come up with a composite score. This score should influence purchasing decisions so the better performing suppliers are more likely to grow with you.

It is a good idea to ensure that you maintain a supplier manual to communicate your expectations to your suppliers. Failure to do this can lead to waste in areas where you depend upon your suppliers. In this manual you should cover various topics such as quality planning, product approval, certification requirements, quality control, problem solving, deviations from standards, and the performance rating system noted in Figure 8-6.

Companies either make the mistake of not doing this or they create manuals so complex that it is absolutely impossible for anyone to comply with the requirements. This is similar to a company policy and procedure manual that includes hundreds of pages of information that "every employee must know." This tactic of over-documenting requirements only creates red tape and slows processes. Much like your own quality and policy manuals, supplier manuals must be simple and only cover important points so they will be utilized.

Note Your suppliers are your partners. They want to make you happy to keep selling their products. Work with them to minimize your costs.

Purchasing Policies

Purchasing functions can often make or break the profitability of a company. This is especially true in manufacturing organizations with very high material costs. I once worked for a company that spent $30 to $50 per pound for a plastic material used in a process. Fluctuations in the material prices greatly influenced our overall costs. Vendor management is often done by the purchasing team so the purchasing team has a large influence over the quality of the supplied items. Companies often put in smart policies to avoid conflict of interest and govern how business is conducted. It would be a bad practice to allow purchasing decision-makers to accept kickbacks or gifts from suppliers. It would also be a bad practice to purchase items from family members or family-owned companies. You should have simple policies to avoid these types of unethical practices.

One of the most wasteful purchasing policies is looking for the lowest price. Now why do we say that the lowest price is bad? We are not saying that the lowest price is bad. Often the lowest price can be from the best quality supplier with the best service. More often, however, purchasers shop for the lowest price even though there are some quality, delivery, or service failures as a result. Your purchasing policies must be based on the total cost of purchasing. These costs include the ease of use of the products on the manufacturing floor, in the kitchen, on the nursing unit, or wherever those products are used. Another part of the total cost that is often ignored is the chaos caused by unpredictable service, quality, and delivery.

We have seen many times where the purchasing department is part of the finance team. The logic to do this is pretty good, right? Purchasing departments are supposed to control costs. Operations is a more appropriate place for purchasing departments. This is due to the need for the operations to use the purchased items. If the same person who is responsible for using the materials is responsible for keeping the costs low, you are likely to get the best balance of total cost. No chief operations officer worth his salt will allow the efficiency of his labor or quality of his product suffer because of cheaper materials. He also will not spend too much on materials with a limited return on efficiency or quality.

Another issue is supplier relationships. If you are requiring your suppliers to commit resources and technology to you, you should also commit to having a long-term relationship with those suppliers. It is not only the best thing for the supplier, but it also helps control your costs. As long as you have put in place a couple of competitive suppliers for key items to keep everyone honest, then the long-term relationship is based on trust and knowledge of customer needs. Having a committed group of suppliers who feel attached to your company eliminates the waste of monitoring multiple suppliers to ensure that they are doing the right thing. It eliminates the need to explain your standards every time you develop a new product. It eliminates the back and forth negotiation of deviations from standards because the supplier understands the questions to ask to ensure that he knows exactly what is important. We have seen both types of purchasing organizations. The overly cost-sensitive companies end up paying more in the long run. The companies with no supplier controls in place end up getting manipulated by the suppliers. There is a balance of fair pricing and respect for expectations of suppliers that benefits you and your suppliers.

Excessive Waste from Meetings

One of our favorite websites is despair.com. They make anti-motivation posters similar to the motivation posters that you see on office walls. A few years ago, despair.com created a poster that said, "Meetings: Because No One of Us is as Dumb as All of Us." An extremely large majority of meetings are very wasteful. In fact, most workers attend a total of 61.8 meetings per month.[6] Other studies show that half of the time in meetings is wasted.[7] This equates to about 31 hours a month of unproductive time spent in meetings for the

---

[6]A Network MCI Conferencing White Paper, "Meetings in America: A Study of Trends, Costs, and Attitudes Toward Business Travel, Teleconferencing, and Their Impact on Productivity," Greenwich, CT: INFOCOMM, 1998,
[7]Robert B. Nelson and Peter Economy, *Better Business Meetings,* Burr Ridge, IL: Irwin Inc, 1995, pp. 5.

average worker. If you assume the average salary of $68,000 for the average business manager, which was taken from Indeed.com, each company likely wastes $13,175 on each and every worker a year in unproductive meetings. For a company with 100 managers, this is $1,317,500 a year wasted in unproductive meetings! This figure does not even begin to include the money lost because the worker can't spend time on productive, money-making activities. Likely, the average company loses several million a year thanks to meetings.

Note Stop the wasteful meetings! They are most likely costing you millions.

There are many reasons why meetings have become such a large source of waste. The first is that many people haven't taken part in productive meetings, so they do not know how to have a productive one. We will discuss this is the following section. Another reason is that people fail to realize why they should have meetings. It's the "this is the way we have always done things" mentality again. We literally have over 100 years, maybe even 1,000 of thinking that if you need to get something done, bring people together into a meeting and discuss it. Partly based on our history, but partly based on faulty myths. For example, many of us believe in the concept of brainstorming.

Brainstorming is a good example of a business concept that doesn't work in actuality. In 1948, Alex Osborn, a partner in the advertising agency B.B.D.O., wrote a book called "Your Creative Power" about how he got the advertising executives at his firm to be more creative. In the book, which quickly became a best seller, Osborn talked about the concept he invented called brainstorming. Since 1948, hundreds of researchers have tried to replicate the concept. Instead of being productive, researchers have found that when people come together, fewer ideas are created and the ideas themselves are less innovative. By contrast, studies have shown that the more people involved in a project, the better the outcomes are.[8] The problems is not with people coming together to share ideas. Instead, the problem is in having people sit in a room and try to work out a problem during a specified meeting time. People are better off alone. Only after everyone has a solution or an idea should groups should come together and briefly share their contributions and outline a plan of action.

---

[8]Wuchty, Stefan, Benjamin F. Jones, and Brian Uzzi, "The Increasing Dominance of Teams in Production of Knowledge," www.sciencexpress.org, Kellogg School of Management, 12 April 2007.

> **Note** The effectiveness of brainstorming is an urban legend.

Since they are a necessary part of business, you should consider ways to make the meetings you do need more productive. There are some simple things that you can do to ensure that your meeting time is efficient. The first of these is to ensure that any meeting that you have has a real purpose. The scope of this includes other names for meetings such as committees or councils. Any time a group of people get together to discuss something, it is a meeting. If your meeting doesn't have a purpose, you shouldn't have it. An easy way to ensure that you have a purpose is to make agendas a requirement for all meetings. An agenda not only tells you what the meeting is about, but also gives you a clear timeline and some deliverable outcomes. When you insist on an agenda, you may realize that "quarterly" or "standing" meetings are not worthwhile. By agenda, we do not mean 1) Old Business, 2) New Business. We mean specific action items that need discussed. These must be issues that cannot be resolved via e-mail or through people working independently.

> **Note** If your meeting has a purpose, it should have an outcome.

Another core requirement for an agenda is a timeline. Meetings have a start and end time. Typically, any given meeting will last an hour. Meetings should operate on the college class schedule. That is, if the meeting is scheduled for an hour, then make it a 50-minute meeting. This not only reduces your time in the meeting by 18 percent, but it also gives you time to transition between meetings or other commitments. I once worked with an operations manager who would lock the conference room door no more than one minute after the start time of a meeting. Although this seems extreme (it is), any of you who have worked in a company that habitually runs late will appreciate this approach. This operations manager successfully changed the culture to having meetings that start and end on time over the course of a few weeks. With meetings that start and end on time and an agenda, you are more likely to get value from your meetings.

If your meetings have a purpose, there should be some decisions or actions that come from it. I have seen minutes from meetings that read like a long policy manual that nobody understands. I once heard a saying that when you write a five-page memo it is because you didn't have time to write a one-page memo. The reason this saying is true is because it takes more effort to be brief than to be verbose. Your meeting minutes should be brief. Often, meeting minutes may not be necessary. Simple documentation of the decisions that were made or actions to be taken prior to the next meeting are often enough.

The beginning of the next meeting on the same subject will be to review the actions that were to be taken and ensure that they were completed.

■ **Note** Meetings should follow a specified timeline. They should also have actionable outcomes.

The size of meetings is often a critical factor leading to their success or failure. Groups that are larger than six or eight are less likely to be productive. The challenge of structuring a team, a regular meeting, a committee, or work group is limiting the membership to the absolute minimum amount of people necessary. Think about departmental or company meetings, for instance. These types of meetings are not "meetings" because there are too many people in the room. What you end up with is one person lecturing and everyone else listening. If this is the case, the material can be typed up and sent out via e-mail or placed on the company's intranet. Managers rarely want to admit that these types of meetings don't have value, but they don't.

Once your group size is established, you need to set a frequency for the meetings. For any group, the frequency depends on the work to be done. Project-based teams should meet weekly or biweekly to help maintain momentum and finish the project on time. Committees or work groups need to set frequencies that ensure that the work is timely. If a committee's meeting schedule causes delays in other parts of the business, then the committee does not meet frequently enough. Much like the approval-process example in the Chapter 6, with lack of a decision or action from a committee, good employees will bypass the established structure to get the work done. Committees need to meet frequently enough to avoid this.

■ **Note** Meetings are very frequently a waste of time. Always have an agenda, never meet about things that can be resolved via e-mail, have measurable objectives, have a maximum of eight people, and meet no more than needed.

Waste by Not Using Process-Improvement Techniques

The operations management for healthcare course that I teach is almost entirely based upon process-improvement techniques. One of my students asked why the course focuses on this one aspect of operations management. The answer is that much of any business program is dedicated to operations management.

Another student felt that the operations management course "ties it all together." Operations management is about managing people, resources, finances, sales, inventory, technology, and basically anything this or any other business book discusses. When you get your MBA or business degree, you are lucky if you get one class period to talk about process improvement. Of course, every function in every organization can benefit from challenging the status quo and looking for ways to improve.

The waste in process improvement is in not actively pursuing process improvement in some way. I have seen multiple companies with issues with quality and profitability make huge improvements through process-improvement methods. We will go over many of these tools in the appendix of this book. The only wastes you can have from process improvement are not doing process improvement or not finishing it. What I mean by not finishing is a phenomenon I have seen in companies where resources are spent training employees who work on projects that aren't completed. There is often no requirement to continue improvements after the initial project. Process improvement is a company culture, not a short-term solution. It needs to be engrained into the fiber of your organization.

Leveraging Technology

While we talk a lot about technology in Chapter 6, we have a few comments to make here in regard to the operational use of technology. Over the last couple of decades, technology has improved at such a great rate that it's hard to keep up at times. Some of the greatest opportunities for improvement that we have seen are related to technology improvements. Plastic injection molding was revolutionized by the use of pressure transducers, temperature transducers, precise electric machines, and automated process changes based on feedback from the technology. Healthcare has had great improvements in imaging technology, which has allowed doctors to give more accurate diagnoses and improved care. Wireless warehouse management systems and logistics software has made possible some of the amazing order fulfillment that is done by companies like Amazon. There is no doubt that technology continues to help companies.

The waste in leveraging technology is caused by not properly evaluating when you should use the technology. Technology should be utilized to implement necessary quality improvements, meet customer needs, or improve the bottom line. Without the need, you should seriously consider if technology improvements are necessary.

On the other hand, you should evaluate some commonly used old technology to see if it is still necessary. There are still large companies in the United States who routinely use carbon paper forms or dot matrix printers to process customer orders. Fax machines and pagers are also commonly used in healthcare even though there are more efficient options. Other than when buying a house or working with healthcare providers, I have not used a fax machine since the 1990s. If I need to send a document to someone, I scan and e-mail it. You should look at your technology use and question if you are utilizing antique technology or if the technology is just fine for what you need. Use your technology to help your operations and make them more efficient.

> **Note** Utilize the correct technology for your business.

Waste from Magical Thinking

Magical thinking in business operations is the tendency for business leaders to think that there is unlimited capacity to do work. This includes not prioritizing work. Most people can handle a few (three to four) small projects effectively. When you ask your employees to do more than a few projects without proper prioritization, you set them up for failure.

The concept of magical thinking can be expanded to other areas, such as pursing new technology, facilities, or products without first having a customer need to do so. The research associated with understanding customer needs prior to investing in these things can avoid this magical thinking waste.

Magical forecasting is forecasting higher sales without real evidence that sales will increase. Magical budgeting is thinking that your financial performance will change without making changes to your operations to actually improve performance.

Magical thinking drives many forms of waste in companies due to the wasted resources pursuing unrealistic expectations. It frustrates workers who feel that they cannot accomplish all that is asked of them. It frustrates leaders who expect improvements that never seem to happen. The solutions to magical thinking are either prioritization or asking why. Prioritize work to ensure that employees have time to get projects completed. Ask why you expect sales to increase or supply costs to decrease. The simple 5 Why Lean tool that is designed for root cause analysis also works very well for decision making. For example:

1. We expect sales to increase six percent next year.
    a. Why?
2. Walmart is going to sell more of our products.
    b. Why?

3. We lowered our prices and committed to some promotions.

    c. Why do we think consumers will buy the product from Walmart?

4. Well, ummmm…

Obviously, if you go through the five whys here, you will realize this is probably a bad decision. Some retailers return goods that did not sell well back to the manufacturer. With conflicting priorities in companies and limited resources, it is the responsibility of leaders to avoid magical thinking. Make sure you always perform a complete analysis of your decisions.

Note Avoiding magical thinking will lead you to meet realistic goals.

Waste by Not Utilizing Your Workforce

Remember that the three major costs of operations are materials, labor, and overhead. Considerable waste also occurs when managing people. We talked about some of these in Chapter 5. We talked about the waste of not using your employees to develop improvements. You hired your employees. Now use them!

Your employees are experts because they are the people who do the work. They are not the people with the highest salaries or biggest titles. The experts are not a group of managers trying to figure out what the worker is doing wrong. Instead, the experts are the workers. No process-improvement team can hope to be transformational without the input of these experts. Without them, you are wasting your time.

Many of us have heard stories of continuous improvement goals that were never achieved. The reasons for failing continuous improvement initiatives are numerous, but one of the most prevalent reasons is because the frontline workers are not involved. Because the frontline workers are most familiar with the process, they are the ones most equipped to solve problems.

Note Which method you use is not as important as having a continuous improvement method in place.

Chapter 8 | Business Operations

Along with these wastes, another great waste is the way you interact with employees. Leaders need to understand the needs of each individual employee. Each manager tends to have her own style of management. It is entirely wasteful to think that even a good manager is the right manager in every situation. Certain management styles are ideal for certain employee types and business situations. Figure 8-7 shows some characteristics of six management types.

Management Style	Characteristics	When It Works	When It Doesn't Work
Directive	Close Control of Employees Uses Threats and Discipline	In a Crisis Actions Must Be Done a Certain Way	With Highly Skilled Employees Underdeveloped Employees
Authoritative	Firm but Fair Clear Direction Uses Persuasion / Feedback	Need Standards/Directions With a Credible Leader	Without a Credible Leader Underdeveloped Employees
Affiliative	People-First Focus Avoids Conflict Nurtures Relationships/ Happiness	Routine Tasks Responsible Employees	Poor Employee Performance Crisis Situations
Participative	Democratic Rewards Team Efforts	Employees Work Together Experienced Employees	Crisis Situations Lack of Employee Competence
Pacesetting	Leads by Example Sets High Standards	Competent/Motivated Employees When Managing Experts	Employees Need Developed or Coached Too Much Work for the Manager
Coaching	Develops Employees	Skills Need Developed Competent/Motivated Employees	Lack of Leadership Experience Poor Employee Performance In a Crisis

Figure 8-7. Management Types (Source: Cardinal, Rosalind, "Six Management Styles and When Best to Use Them–The Leaders Tool Kit", April 13, 2013, http://leadersinheels.com/career/6-management-styles-and-when-best-to-use-them-the-leaders-tool-kit/)

You should identify the type of manager you are and the types of managers you manage along with your employees and business situation. If the management style doesn't align well with the current situation, you should look for ways to modify your natural management style or get a different manager to help. Once you identify your management styles, you need to either maintain a group of employees that align with your style or learn how to adapt your style based on the needs of your employees.

Operations Metrics

In order to improve your operations, you need to identify opportunities, make improvements, and show some evidence of the improvement after the work is done. Since all businesses need to have continuous improvement, all businesses must also have good operational metrics.

Operational metrics have many manifestations. In call center operations, the primary metrics may be minutes on the phone calls, time that customers wait to get an answer, or some kind of output metric such as sales made or problems resolved. In manufacturing you probably have some throughput metrics such as pieces per hour and some quality metrics such as percent rejected. In a restaurant you may have an upsell rate telling you the percent of alcohol and dessert sales of the total or the food and labor cost percentage of sales. In healthcare, you have length of stay, mortality rate, and readmissions metrics to tell you how well you are taking care of patients. No matter what business you are in, there are operational metrics you should be examining in addition to your financial outcomes.

Performance Management

I once worked for someone who had a few areas of focus that he was looking at in order to "turn around operations." These included the usual suspects, such as labor, utility usage, quality, and safety. He established a bonus program where if the employees reduced the internal reject percentage and the number of safety accidents, every employee would get a semi-annual bonus. And it worked! Unfortunately, the warranty claims from external quality issues increased and employees who legitimately got injured failed to report their injuries (because rejects and injuries just weren't reported). Any potential savings that these improvements yielded were gobbled up by the warranty issues and lack of customer satisfaction. It was also not the right thing to do.

In process improvement we look at which inputs to our process drive the performance that we are seeing. Or $Y=f(X)$. The same is true for performance measurement. Focus needs to be on the behaviors or process metrics driving the performance that we want rather than measuring the end performance. For instance, for employee safety, improving the reporting of accidents that were avoided or potential safety issues will lead to a reduction in accidents. We should incentivize those metrics.

Labor Metrics

Labor metrics may vary depending on your industry, but all industries must manage labor. Your labor metrics must be based on a valid output per unit of labor. We talked about this in regard to sales productivity in Chapter 4. Sales productivity is not commonly measured because sales functions typically don't consider the sales person's time as variable labor that must produce an outcome. A few common metrics are applicable in most industries. The first is paid hours per unit. The unit may be a service, a sales dollar as a portion of market potential, or a product, but the basic metric is the same. You look at paid hours per unit to see how effective your labor expense is.

$$\text{Paid Hours per Unit} = \frac{\text{Total Hours Paid}}{\text{Total Units}}$$

Worked hours per unit is a similar metric. You should look at both paid hours per unit and worked hours per unit. The difference between the two is the non-productive time that is included in your labor expense, such as training, vacation, or sick time. Worked hours per unit tells you how efficient your people are. Paid hours per unit tells you how productive your total labor expense is.

$$\text{Work Hours per Unit} = \frac{\text{Total Hours Worked}}{\text{Total Units}}$$

Overtime is time that employees spend at work outside of the normal 40-hour week. Overtime is a critical measure to have because it should be kept to a minimum. Overtime cost can be one and a half to two times the cost of regular labor. Plus, people are rarely productive over a certain numbers of hours a week. If overtime is a regular occurrence, it may make sense to hire more employees. The formula of acceptable overtime will depend somewhat on your total new employee costs, including benefit costs. Overtime is normally measured as a percentage. Although it can increase your labor costs significantly, it is not always a bad thing. Overtime is often cheaper than hiring contract labor.

$$\text{Overtime \%} = \frac{\text{Overtime Hours Paid}}{\text{Total Hours Paid}}$$

Throughput is a measure of units or services produced per unit of time. Typically, this will be units produced per hour, but that may vary depending upon the industry. Many companies make their money by having high levels of throughput because if you can get the same people to make more money for you, then it is all profit. I once worked with a company that reduced labor expense by 10 percent while actually increasing production output. This was all because of throughput improvements.

$$\text{Throughput} = \frac{\text{Total Good Units Produced}}{\text{Total Hours Worked}}$$

Labor percentage of sales is another metrics used in all industries. The optimum level of this metric depends on the activity you are measuring, but it is a good metric to measure because you want to drive the three main costs of operations down.

$$\text{Labor \% of Sales} = \frac{\text{Total Labor Cost}}{\text{Total Sales Revenue}}$$

There are of course many other labor metrics that you can use. These are just the basic ones that you should be reviewing. Remember that there is little value in measuring these if you are not working on impacting the metrics. You must continually measure the metrics and look for ways to improve them, and then calculate the improvements and determine what caused them.

Equipment

Equipment cost is a significant expense in many industries. Equipment can cost hundreds to millions of dollars. Those expensive machines should be making you money as many hours of the day as possible. Therefore, you should be measuring how you are doing in managing your equipment productivity. A key metric that you can use is Overall Equipment Effectiveness (OEE). OEE is a product of the availability of your equipment, the performance of your equipment, and the quality of your equipment output. Equipment availability is how much time in the day your equipment is available to be used. Again, you should have this be as much time as possible but of course you need to plan some maintenance time and operate the equipment only when it is needed. For instance, if you need a machine eight hours per day, the available time is eight hours because you would not plan to run the other sixteen hours per day. This is also known as downtime, which is a common operational metric on its own.

$$\text{Availability} = \frac{\text{Operating Time}}{\text{Planned Production Time}}$$

Performance is the time lost by not achieving the optimum cycle for your machine. For instance, if you are supposed to run a cycle time of a product every 30 seconds but you actually get one every 34 seconds, you have lost four seconds of performance. In this formula, the ideal cycle time represents the 30 seconds.

$$\text{Performance} = (\text{Ideal Cycle Time}) / \left(\frac{\text{Operating Time}}{\text{Total Pieces}} \right)$$

Quality is the number of good pieces out of the total number of pieces produced. In some operations that don't have a quality element, the quality level is set artificially at 100 percent.

$$\text{Quality} = \frac{\text{Good Pieces}}{\text{Total Pieces}}$$

Once you have calculated all three parts for OEE, the calculation is simple.

$$OEE = Availability \times Performance \times Quality$$

A benchmarked OEE target would be at about 85 percent. When I have measured this in the past, I have typically seen the outcome between 40 and 70 percent. It is hard to realize just how much wasted equipment time you have until you calculate OEE.

Another key metric, which is a component of downtime or availability, is turnover time. This is the time between production runs or customers when the equipment is not being productive. This could include time to change tools in manufacturing, bus a table in a restaurant, or clean an operating room in a hospital. Services live by this number if they have any kind of wait. Wait may cause lost customers. This is a big reason why restaurants play fast music on the weekends. Fast music makes people eat faster and workers move quicker.

Because many businesses have some kind of turnover time, this is a universal metric that you should evaluate and improve. Improvements in turnover time will improve your equipment availability. This is a great thing when you can fill that capacity that is gained.

$$Turnover\ Time = (Time\ from\ the\ last\ produced\ to\ the\ first\ part\ of\ the\ next\ item)$$

Inventory

There are lots of options to evaluate your inventory and logistics functions. The first is fill rate. It is a measure of how much of your customer demand can be handled with inventory on hand. You typically want to aim at 100 percent for your fill rate.

$$Fill\ Rate = \frac{Customer\ Order\ Demand}{Inventory\ on\ Hand}$$

Out-of-stock rate is a way to measure how much of your customer's demand you are not able to fill with your inventory on hand. You want to aim for a 0 percent out-of-stock rate, but most companies experience some small percentage of out-of-stock items.

$$Out\ of\ Stock\ Rate = \frac{Orders\ not\ Fulfilled}{Total\ Orders\ Recieved}$$

Inventory turns is a measure of how well you are managing your inventory. Inventory takes cash to maintain. If your cash is tied up in inventory, you can't use it for other purposes. A restaurant would want to turn its perishable inventory on a weekly or even daily basis. Most manufacturing companies are happy with turning inventory 12 times per year.

$$\text{Inventory Turns} = \frac{\text{Sales Dollars}}{\text{Inventory Value}}$$

Or

$$\text{Inventory Turns} = \frac{\text{Cost of Goods Sold}}{\text{Inventory Value}}$$

Obsolescence rate is also called spoilage. It tells you how much of your inventory is obsolete and can't be sold. The definition of what is likely obsolete will change depending on the product and industry.

$$\text{Obsolescence Rate} = \frac{\text{Inventory Value of Unused Items}}{\text{Total Inventory Value}}$$

Physical inventory errors tell you how well you are managing your inventory. It's the total difference between the value of your inventory physically counted and your value that you have tracked in your accounting. A more accurate and frankly more meaningful measure is the difference from the inventory value, both positive and negative because it shows the full error opportunity.

$$\text{Net Physical Inventory Error} = (\text{Total Value of Inventory Accounted for}) - (\text{Total Physical Inventory Value})$$

$$\text{Absolute Physical Inventory Error} = \sum \text{Dollars Of Excess Inventory} + \left| \sum \text{Dollars Of Missing Inventory} \right|$$

So this is a complicated enough equation for an example. If your accounting method says that you have $1,000,000 of inventory and you count $1,000,000 of inventory, your net physical inventory error is $0. If you count your inventory and find that you have $100,000 too much of some items and $100,000 too few of other items, then your absolute physical inventory error is $200,000. You want both of these metrics to approach zero. Just looking at net psychical inventory error can be misleading.

Conclusion

There are multiple disciplines in business where wasteful activities persist. Even though operations management professionals have focused on continuous improvement activities for decades, you can still walk into almost any business and see basic operational inefficiencies. The challenge that you have is being able to use your frontline process experts to identify opportunities for improvement and implement solutions. We have given a few of the most common operations wastes in this chapter, but this is not a complete list.

You cannot afford to continue to do business as usual. All sectors of business continually become more competitive. The successful companies improve at a pace greater than their competitors, thus gaining a competitive advantage.

Operations Checklist

*All "no" answers identify a potential opportunity for improvement.

Workflow and Layout

Is your facility developed to optimize the flow of materials?	Yes ☐ No ☐
Is your facility designed to optimize the flow of the worker?	Yes ☐ No ☐
Have you implemented 5S activities?	Yes ☐ No ☐
Have you evaluated your equipment maintenance needs?	Yes ☐ No ☐
Have your evaluated your optimum inventory levels?	Yes ☐ No ☐

Office Supplies

Have you evaluated your paper waste?	Yes ☐ No ☐
Have you looked at alternatives to paper?	Yes ☐ No ☐

Product Development

Do you have processes in place to understand customer requirements prior to taking orders?	Yes ☐ No ☐
Are your operations employees involved in evaluating customer requirements?	Yes ☐ No ☐
Do you continually evaluate your customer relationships to ensure that you should keep all of your customers?	Yes ☐ No ☐

Operations Checklist
*All "no" answers identify a potential opportunity for improvement.

Supply Chain Management

Have you evaluated your inventory management method?	Yes ☐ No ☐
Is your inventory management method effective?	Yes ☐ No ☐

Warehouse Management

Do you control how your suppliers ship to your location?	Yes ☐ No ☐
Have you standardized your package sizes and quantities?	Yes ☐ No ☐
Do you have consistent labeling requirements for supplies?	Yes ☐ No ☐
Have you evaluated receiving inventory directly to stock?	Yes ☐ No ☐
Do your warehouse processes trigger your employees to do work without the use of a report?	Yes ☐ No ☐
Is your warehouse customer-focused instead of efficiency-focused?	Yes ☐ No ☐
Have you implemented shipping standards to minimize cost?	Yes ☐ No ☐

Vendor Management and Purchasing

Do you have a vendor-rating system?	Yes ☐ No ☐
Does your vendor-rating system influence your purchasing decisions?	Yes ☐ No ☐
Do you have a simple supplier manual to communicate requirements to your suppliers?	Yes ☐ No ☐
Is your purchasing department part of operations?	Yes ☐ No ☐
Is total cost more important than price?	Yes ☐ No ☐

Operations Checklist
*All "no" answers identify a potential opportunity for improvement.

Meeting Management

Do all of your meetings have a purpose and an agenda?	Yes ☐ No ☐
Do your meetings have a timeline that is followed?	Yes ☐ No ☐
Do you document decisions and actions to be taken before the next meeting?	Yes ☐ No ☐
Do you keep your meeting attendees to the minimum required?	Yes ☐ No ☐
Do your meetings occur frequently enough to avoid delays?	Yes ☐ No ☐

Process Improvement

Do you have a process improvement culture and method?	Yes ☐ No ☐
Are your frontline employees heavily involved in process improvement?	Yes ☐ No ☐

Operations Metrics

Do you have leading indicators of your process performance?	Yes ☐ No ☐
Do your metrics help you identify opportunities for improvement?	Yes ☐ No ☐
Do all your employees understand your operational metrics?	Yes ☐ No ☐

APPENDIX

Tools to Eliminate Waste

Throughout this book we have highlighted various wastes that we have found in companies and, where possible, we have suggested solutions to reduce or eliminate these wastes. In addition to using the ideas in this book, it is helpful to know how to use and implement Lean techniques in your organization, which is the purpose of this appendix.

The concept of "Lean" has become a bit overused and overhyped, sometimes touted by consultants and management professionals as a cure-all. Although not exactly a cure-all, the Lean concept does include a multitude of highly effective and proven tools to help you eliminate waste in your company. And when you use these tools correctly, you can rest assured you are cutting the appropriate waste, not services or anything else that is necessary to your company or customers.

A search of available books on Lean Six Sigma yields nearly 4,000 results, and we certainly are not going to attempt to replace these books with a short appendix on process improvement. We do, however, introduce some of the Lean and Six Sigma concepts so that you can research your areas of interest in order to address your wastes. We strongly suggest employing someone in your company, if your company is large enough, who is a true expert in the field of process improvement. No company needs to use all of the process improvement tools at once. In fact, in order to build a culture of continuous improvement, you should start small with simple changes that are easily adopted. Because many of these simple tools fall within the list of commonly used Lean tools, we will start by introducing them.

Lean Tools

Lean manufacturing is often known simply as "Lean" due to its applications outside of manufacturing. Representatives from Virginia Mason Health System, for instance, visited Toyota in Japan to see its Lean operations first-hand. When these representatives from Virginia Mason returned to the United States, they created the Virginia Mason production system. Lean is a great at producing efficiency. This is why it has its roots in manufacturing.

Production companies have struggled for decades with how to do more with better outcomes and fewer resources. The Japanese manufacturers, along with Dr. Edwards W. Deming, developed a series of tools and processes that became known as "Lean." We referenced a few of these tools in the workflow and layout sections of Chapter 8. As with any skill, even after reading and learning about these tools, you will need to practice them in order to become good at them. Lean creates efficiency by reducing and balancing the eight wastes shown in Figure A-1.

Waste	Description
Defects	Doing something wrong that will cause rework or trash.
Over-Production	Producing more than is necessary to meet customer needs.
Waiting	Waiting on materials or services because they are not available now.
Not Utilizing Talent	Not listening to your employees or utilizing their skills and knowledge.
Transportation	Moving inventory or customers to a resource because it is not located close to the work.
Inventory	Having excess materials and supplies.
Motion	Excessive reaching, stretching, bending, searching, twisting, etc.
Extra Processing	Doing too much to a product or customer, beyond expectations.

Figure A-1. Eight Wastes Identified by Lean (D.O.W.N.T.I.M.E.)

The process companies use to implement Lean is called *Kaizen*. Kaizen is a process where workers are removed from their regular duties so that they can analyze a process and improve it in 3 to 10 days. Figure A-2 shows the basic Kaizen process. Some of the improvements that are commonly implemented using Kaizen include changeover reduction, 6S organization, workflow reorganization, step reduction, and Kanban implementation. There are other times when Kaizen can be used; these are just a few examples.

Eliminating Waste in Business 305

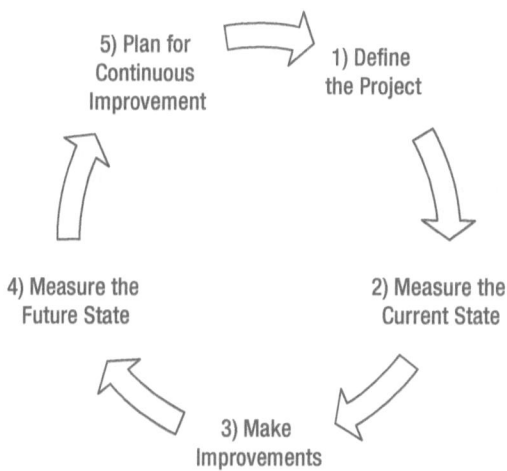

Figure A-2. Basic Kaizen Process

One major weakness of Lean is that it is not designed to address effectiveness issues. There are tools, such as poke-yoke, that will improve your ability to be effective, but the main effectiveness tools are from Six Sigma.

> **Note** Use Kaizen to implement the improvements from Lean tools.

Flowcharting

In other areas of this book we have used some flowcharting techniques. There are a few primary flowchart tools, as shown in Figure A-3. The selection of the right flowchart will depend on the process you are analyzing. The activity and deployment flowcharts are often the most appropriate.

Flowchart Type	What Is the Flowchart For?
Activity	To identify complexity in your processes and the overall process itself.
Deployment	To identify handoffs in the process. Handoffs are places where errors are easily made.
Spaghetti Diagram	To analyze travel and motion in a process to reduce distances traveled by workers.
Value Stream Maps	To reduce the overall time to fulfill customer needs by eliminating waste.
Value-Added Flow Analysis	To identify value-added (VA) activites and reduce non-value-added activities (NVA).

Figure A-3. Flowchart Types

Flowcharts are comprised of many different symbols, and the most common of these symbols are shown in Figure A-4. Programs such as Microsoft Excel, Word, and PowerPoint all have flowchart symbols included in their drawing tools, making it easy for you to quickly create flowcharts electronically. There are also many open source online tools that you can use to create flowcharts. Our favorite flowcharting tool is Microsoft Visio. In addition, you can find templates for almost any of these flowcharting tools.

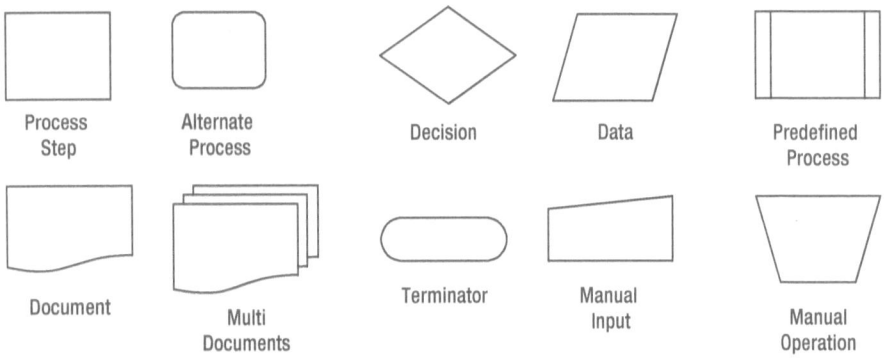

Figure A-4. Common Flowchart Symbols

In an activity flowchart, you can count the number of diamonds (decision points) to see how complex your process is. Figure A-5 is a simple version of an activity flowchart. This is a very simple example with only two decision points. We have seen many flowcharts with dozens of decision points. If you redesign your processes to reduce the number of decisions, you can save time and money by improving efficiency as well as improve quality due to a simpler process. Your goal should be to understand how any process is done so that you can eliminate all redundant, inefficient, or unnecessary tasks.

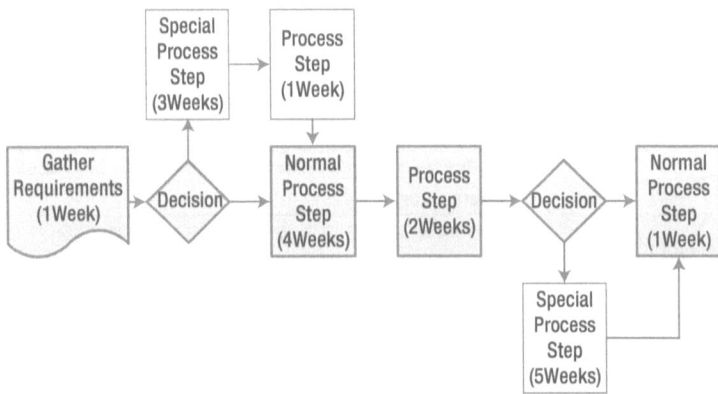

Figure A-5. Activity Flowchart

Figure A-6 shows a deployment flowchart. Each time the arrows between steps cross the lines between the lanes in the flowchart, there is a handoff. This process is like a relay race. Handoffs in a relay race are the points where the runners hand the baton to each other. This is when the baton is most likely to be dropped. Your business processes are the same as this relay race. It's when you hand off your processes between job functions or people that mistakes are more likely. You can use the deployment flowchart to look for ways to reduce handoffs, because every handoff creates an opportunity for an error.

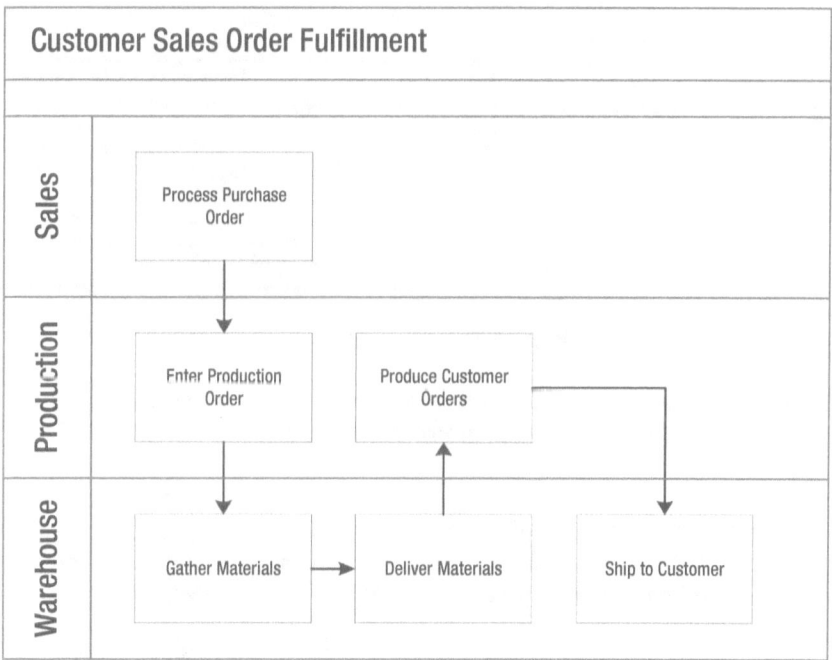

Figure A-6. Deployment Flowchart

As briefly described in Chapter 4, the value stream map is the flowcharting tool that evaluates how much time workers are actively working on filling customer needs versus the waiting time between stages. Figure A-7 shows a simple value stream map. By reducing the waiting time between steps and sometimes even reducing the value-added time through process improvements, you can reduce the time between customer request and delivery. There are many other techniques that can be used to document and improve a value stream map. Value stream mapping is a more advanced form of flowcharting. To do it effectively, you should get an expert to walk you through your first few value stream maps at a minimum.

Appendix | Tools to Eliminate Waste

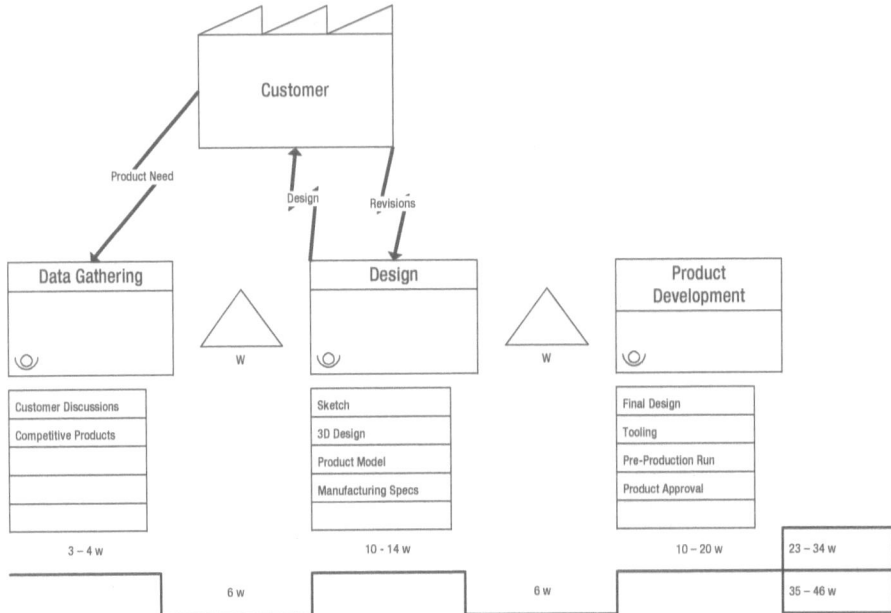

Figure A-7. Value Stream Map Example

Value-added flow analysis is the last flowchart type we discuss here. This is simply where you document each process step on a sticky note and put the notes on the wall in sequence. You then mark or pull out the value-added steps so that you can see how much of your process is value-added. Your challenge then is to eliminate as many of the remaining steps as possible. One variation of the value-added flow analysis has you put down the time for each step so that you could see how much you have reduced the process cycle time.

In Chapter 8, you can read about using the spaghetti diagram to streamline workflow in your business.

Note Use flowcharts to see your processes better and look for improvement ideas.

Tools to Improve

Once you have taken the time to understand your process through process mapping or by going to Gemba (the place where the work is done), you need to take action on the opportunities for improvement. The following sections describe a few of the simplest Lean tools to use. Companies that start a Lean journey usually start by implementing some or all of these tools.

5S

You can read about workplace organization (5S) in Chapter 8, where we talked about how to improve your workflow. Remember that this tool can help you organize just about any workspace, which can bring major savings to just about any kind of company. 5S is for workplace organization. By using 5S, you can make the workplace more pleasant and realize efficiencies by eliminating some of the eight wastes of Lean.

SMED

You can read about rapid changeover (SMED) in Chapter 8, where we talked about how to improve your workflow. SMED is the method that you use to reduce the time it takes to change from one production run to another or from one customer to another. This changeover time is wasteful, because your resources are not making you money.

Continuous Flow

Companies can service customers better and reduce waste by designing processes to avoid batching, or waiting to perform a task until it needs to be performed multiple times. This process helps avoid having a bunch of work that is partially done because each task is started and finished on a continuous basis. By creating continuous flow, you can often reduce the amount of time it takes to perform services or start delivering products to your customers.

Most of us have built assemble-your-own furniture or toys. When you assemble these items, you open the box and follow the step-by step-directions until the item is assembled. Now imagine that you buy five dressers for your home at once because you needed to replace your others due to some damage. Would you open all five boxes and then go through step-by-step on all five dressers at once? Or would you open one box and build the first dresser and then the second and so on? Of course, most of us would do that latter and build each dresser individually.

If this is the case, then why do so many manufacturing and service companies partially build many items at once, leading to what is called "work-in-process" inventory? Doesn't it make more sense to build one item at a time? This continuous flow process approach creates a continuous or one-piece flow. If you as a consumer build all five dressers at one time, it would take a long time until you finish one dresser. When you build one dresser at a time, you complete all the dressers a lot faster.

Now, you can make the argument that you can gain speed in each part of the assembly by working on five dressers at once, and you may be correct, but as with any other Lean tool, there is a balance to maintain. Continuous flow helps reduce the time to finish the first item. It also may improve quality because you focus on one item at a time. Regardless of whether you think this method makes sense in your organization, we challenge you to evaluate it in some kind of pilot test and let the results speak for themselves.

Cycle Time and Takt Time

The rate of production of a service or product is called its cycle time. Cycle times must be short enough to be able to meet the requirements of Takt time. Takt time is the rate of production of a service or product that is necessary to meet customer demand. It is calculated as follows:

$$\text{Takt Time} = \frac{\text{Available Work Time}}{\text{Customer Demand}}$$

For example, if your customers need to have 300 units per day (or product or service) and your productive work time for a 12-hour shift is 10 hours, your Takt time is 2 minutes per unit. Another way of saying this is that you have to produce a product or service every two minutes to meet customer demand.

$$\text{Takt Time} = \frac{10 \text{ hours} \times 60 \text{ minutes}}{300 \text{ units per day}} = \frac{2 \text{ minutes}}{\text{unit}}$$

This knowledge is important because if you know you are not able to meet the requirements of Takt time, you need to change something in your operation to meet customer demand.

Kanban

Kanban is used to help control inventory or the flow of process steps. It uses visual symbols or cues to pull inventory or work throughout the facility at the rate that it is being utilized by the customer. Kanbans are a very simple way to control inventory in a small to midsized business, where a complicated software system is not necessary and would cause extra waste.

Poke-Yoke

Poke-yoke is the concept of mistake-proofing. This is one of the areas where Lean can help you become not only more efficient but also more effective. There are two types of poke-yoke: warning and control.

Warning poke-yokes are like those red and green squiggly lines underneath spelling and grammar errors when you type a document in Microsoft Word. Another example is the beeping that your car makes when you leave your lights on. The warnings don't stop you from making a mistake, but they do notify you that you are about to make one. In the workplace, any machine that has warning lights or sounds is using a warning poke-yoke. In a healthcare setting, the various telemetry sounds end up becoming background noise and therefore lose their effectiveness. Pop-up warning messages that are common in software packages are also warning poke-yokes if you are allowed to proceed with the wrong action regardless of the warning.

Control poke-yokes prevent you from making a mistake. One example is the size of the diesel nozzle at gas stations. The diesel nozzle is larger than the gasoline nozzle. You can't put a diesel line into a car that runs on gasoline. If you look around your business and home, you will quickly find other examples of poke-yokes that have been designed to keep you safe. Your challenge is to design poke-yokes into your processes to keep your business from making mistakes.

These are just a few of the many Lean tools, and we have not gone into any depth on these tools. Lean has some tools, such as poke-yoke, that are for improving the *effectiveness* of your operations, as just described, but for the most part, Lean is about *efficiency*. In your business, you need to have both efficiency and effectiveness to be successful. For this reason, Lean is often combined with Six Sigma methods so that both efficiency and effectiveness are addressed through process improvement.

LEAN SIX SIGMA

> Just like the Lean weakness of not addressing effectiveness, Six Sigma is not designed to address efficiency. The marriage of these two methods has led to Lean Six Sigma, where workers utilize tools from both disciplines to make the maximum improvement in efficiency and effectiveness.

Six Sigma

Six Sigma was developed at Motorola as a way to improve quality, and it's a set of tools you can use to improve the effectiveness of your business. Effectiveness includes not only the quality of your products or services but also the customer requirements. For the most part, the Six Sigma tactics are simply a rebranding of previous quality-improvement methodologies. The rebranding and organization of these methods have improved the effectiveness of the tools, so Six Sigma has been a great success in business.

The goal of Six Sigma is for an organization to produce Six Sigma quality or at least pursue Six Sigma quality. This means that all product characteristics are within the expected dimension or performance within plus or minus six standard deviations from the mean. This level of performance produces 3.4 defects per million opportunities for a defect.

Appendix | Tools to Eliminate Waste

A Six Sigma project can be started when you need to develop a new process for producing a product or service or when you have an existing process that you need to improve. For example, if you have low customer satisfaction ratings, you would start a project to improve those ratings. This is process improvement. If you are opening a new service that you have not provided before, you would start a project to ensure that your new service is successful. This is process design. You work on each of these projects using tools for product or process design and a different set of tools for product or process improvement. Process improvement is a more common need, so we will focus on process improvement. But first, we'll take a brief look at the process for designing for Six Sigma.

Design for Six Sigma (DMADV)

Take a look at Figure A-8, which shows the process for designing for Six Sigma. Although we do not write about the details of designing for Six Sigma, we do want to introduce the steps.

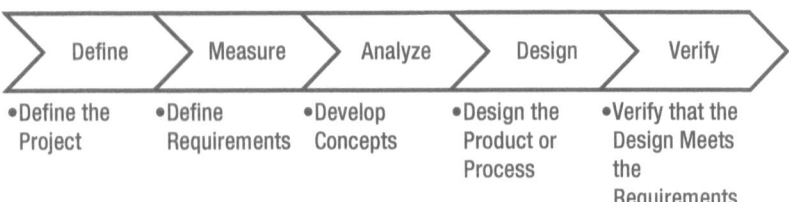

Figure A-8. Design for Six Sigma Methods (DMADV)

The tools for Design for Six Sigma include some of the same selection tools that we will discuss in the "Improve for Six Sigma" section. The rest of the tools are for requirement gathering, requirement ranking, and project management. Unless you are designing products, the depth of knowledge in DMADV is not necessary, so for brevity, we will go right into DMAIC.

Improve for Six Sigma (DMAIC)

Take a moment to review Figure A-9, which describes the process for process improvement. Each of these processes is discussed in more detail in the following sections.

Eliminating Waste in Business

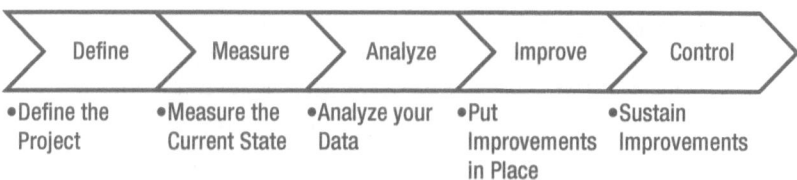

Figure A-9. Improve for Six Sigma (DMAIC)

Define

The define phase of the improvement process is used to specify what will be done during the project and what the customer requirements are. As with all of the phases of DMAIC, the define phase has multiple tools. Some of these tools you will use all of the time, and others you will use only when necessary. Experience with using these tools will help you know which one to use.

Charter

The project charter is one tool that you will use every time you have a project. It helps you define specific aspects of the project and keep focused on the problem that you set out to solve. We have seen various versions of project charters. However, there are a few fundamental portions of the charter that are common:

- **Problem statement:** The part of the charter that defines the problem in a way that shows how bad the problem is. This is to communicate why you want to work on this problem.

- **Business case:** Shows why your business would value this project. This value usually comes in the form of a financial gain. The gain may be related to cost reductions or avoidance, revenue increase, risk reduction, cash flow increase, or even capacity increase. At a minimum, the business case should show enough benefit to justify the effort associated with the project.

- **Scope:** A common issue that occurs in a project is scope creep. This is where you start to solve a specific problem but as your project moves forward, you find other problems to solve. Before you know it, your project is too big to finish quickly. The scope part of the project charter helps you keep to working on what is within scope.

- **Goals:** The goals section is where you document how you plan to measure the outcome of the project. It is best to have SMART goals. SMART is an acronym for specific, measurable, attainable, relevant, and time-bound. One example might be "Reduce our quality rejects from four to three percent by January 31, 2016."

- **Timeline:** A list of stages that includes checkpoints with your project sponsor to show what has been accomplished. Without specified "due dates," people tend to procrastinate. You could use the DMAIC phases for your timeline or any other method you find appropriate.

- **Team:** The final section of the charter is the team. This identifies who is working on the project, who owns the solution, and who is sponsoring the work. People need to be held accountable for every step to make sure tasks are accomplished.

Your project charter is a living document. That means that some of the information on the charter may change over time—as long as the project leader and project sponsor agree on the changes. Changes happen mostly because of things that you learn as you work on a project.

Note The charter is your contract with the team and the sponsor, but it can be modified as you learn during your project.

SIPOC

SIPOC is an acronym for suppliers, inputs, process, outputs, and customers. The SIPOC is a simple tool that helps you better understand your process and validate your charter. When you do a SIPOC, you start by identifying the customers so you know who to talk with regarding expectations of the process. As part of the customer identification, you should then start identifying the outputs of your processes in terms of what you provide for your customers. Then, you should identify your suppliers so that you can solicit help from them to identify and implement solutions. The inputs to your process should be your first set of inputs, which may be causing your poor performance. Finally, your process, which is limited to five to eight high-level process steps, helps you validate the scope. If the SIPOC and the charter don't match, one of them is wrong.

Figure A-10 shows a SIPOC for the owner of a hamburger restaurant. This idea is to improve the product and customer service. The owner can bring together a team of suppliers to determine what would improve the sandwich quality and the environment. By doing a SIPOC, the entire team has a better understanding of the project.

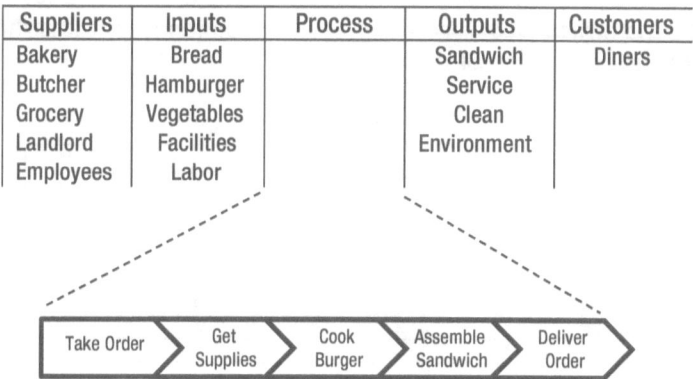

Figure A-10. SIPOC

Note Use SIPOC to validate your charter and to help understand your process.

Voice of the Customer

Voice of the customer is a set of tools designed to improve your understanding of the customer's needs. These tools are commonly used in market research and include surveys, focus groups, and data analysis. The point of the voice of the customer is that if your customer isn't telling you what her requirements are, you need to do work on your project to figure out these needs. We discuss market research in Chapter 3. These methods should be used as part of the voice of the customer work on your project.

Measure

The measure phase of the improvement process is about documenting the opinions of the experts and preparing to gather data to validate those opinions. The process experts are those frontline workers who perform the work in the process that you are improving. This is a fundamental concept of process improvement. Use the ideas coming from your workforce. These ideas are probably pretty good.

Prioritization Matrix

The prioritization matrix prioritizes the potential root cause(s) of the problem so that you can reduce the number of causes to analyze. This tool relies on the opinions of your workers. It uses a weighting system to define your prioritization criteria, with a rating scale of 0, 1, 3, and 9. Figure A-11 shows an example of the prioritization matrix. In this example, "lack of established process" gets the highest score, so the prevailing opinion is that it is the primary suspect of the root cause of the problem.

	Weights	Criteria			Score
		Influence by Personnel	Frequency	Critical to Quality	
Potential Root Cause		35%	40%	25%	
Lack of Established Process		3	9	9	6.9
Poor Attitude of Staff		9	1	9	5.8
Poor Quality of Materials		0	3	9	3.45
Machine Malfunction		0	1	9	2.65
Machine Too Slow		1	3	1	1.8

Figure A-11. Prioritization Matrix

You can use the prioritization matrix prior to the project kickoff (project prioritization) or in the improve phase (solution selection matrix). These are the same tool with different names.

Measurement System Analysis

If you are using a tool to measure something in order to collect your data, then your tool must be accurate and used consistently. There are two types of measurement system analysis: Gage R&R and Kappa studies.

Gage R&R stands for Gage Repeatability and Reproducibility. This is the method that you are using if you are collecting measurable data. Any measurement method used to measure continuous data, like weight, time, distance, or volume, uses Gage R&R as the way to validate that the measurements are reliable. The Gage R&R analysis typically will measure multiple people using the same piece of equipment and a variety of items to be sampled. Each sample is measured multiple times (typically three) by multiple people (typically three). Statistics are used to calculate the Gage R&R results. If the results are not sufficient, either a new tool or a process change is necessary to improve the results.

Kappa studies are used for measurement methods where a visual inspection is used, and the results are based on the opinion of the person doing the inspection. Typically, there more samples involved in a Kappa study because it uses discrete data (data that you can count and not logically divide). There are a few (typically three) people who are involved in the study, plus an expert

Eliminating Waste in Business

opinion who makes the final decision about the samples. The statistics used in a Kappa study look for the percentage of agreement between the people doing the inspection. A high percentage, such as 90 percent, means that the inspection method is acceptable. Lower agreement levels require more definition or tools to enhance visual perception.

Both measurement system analysis methods can be improved by improving the operational definition of how the measurements are to be performed and what the correct standards for good versus bad are.

■ **Note** Without measurement system analysis, you cannot trust your data.

Sampling

Because it is often impossible to look at all of the data for any given process, we rely on sampling to collect our data both for baseline measurements and measurements after we have implemented our improvements. Establishing a baseline is one of the more important aspects of any project because without a baseline, it is hard to prove that any real improvement is achieved. Along with a baseline, you need to understand how capable you are of meeting the customer requirements from your process. If your sampling method is faulty and your measurement system is not reliable, then your baseline data and data on the capability of your process is likely to be incorrect.

There are multiple sampling methods available, but we do not discuss these in this book. The most important aspect of any sample is that it be representative of the overall population of data for the process that you are studying. For sampling, the sampling method and size will have a great influence over the accuracy of your conclusions. Almost every reported data that you see on television or the Internet is a product of sampling. A common example is political surveys to show who is winning political races. These survey results normally come from asking questions of just a few thousand people, who then represent millions of voters. The accuracy of these surveys is based on the number of samples and the sampling method. As we talked about in Chapter 3, focus groups results are typically inaccurate. While focus groups have many faults, a large part of the error is due to sampling error. A sample of 8-12 people cannot adequately represent millions.

■ **Note** A reliable sample is necessary to establish baseline capability and the stability of your process.

Analyze

The analyze phase of the improvement process is where you look for patterns in your data and find ways to validate the opinions documented in the measure phase. The analyze phase is primarily completed using graphs, statistics, and analyses of flow charts. In the analyze phase, you are validating the root cause(s) of the problem and looking for trends or patterns in your data.

Time Series Plots and Control Charts

Time series plots, which are typically created in Microsoft Excel, are the line graphs that you see so often in business. Figure A-12 shows an example of a time series plot. Time series plots are taken over time and shown in chronological order. If the data shown on a line graph is not represented over time, then you cannot look for trends or patterns in the information.

Figure A-12. Time Series Plot of Sales Revenue

Control charts are basically time series plots with more data. This data helps you understand more about your process. There is an upper control limit (UCL) and a lower control limit (LCL) that are set by the variation in your process. For the purpose of determining if your process is stable, we set these control limits at three standard deviations from the average. In various industries where control charts are used, there are other criteria that define the control limits. There are also other tests that can be used to tell if the process is unstable when you use a control charts. Figure A-13 shows an example of a control chart for the same sales revenue data used in Figure A-12.

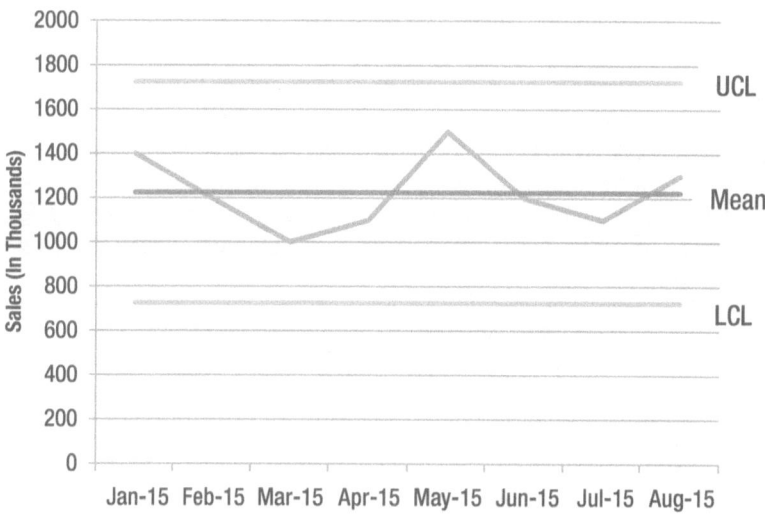

Figure A-13. Control Chart of Sales Revenue

When you look for a stable process, the primary characteristic is whether any of your data is outside of the UCL or LCL. You may also look for patterns in the data. The example shown in Figure A-13 would represent a stable process—that is, the amount of variation of sales revenue from month to month would be considered normal variation absent of any special events. Although this process is stable, it does not mean that it is capable of meeting your needs. For instance, if your requirement is that your sales revenue needs to be greater than $1.15 million, even if your process is stable, it is not capable of meeting your requirement. Given this information, you would have to take some action to increase your average sales each month.

> **Note** Use a control chart to look for stability. Stability, however, does not imply that the process is performing well enough.

Pareto

The Pareto chart is based upon the Pareto Principle developed by Vilfredo Pareto, an economist who said that 80 percent of the world's wealth was controlled by 20 percent of the population. This is more commonly known as the 80/20 rule. When you are trying to improve quality, this is a great tool to visualize your data.

Figure A-14 shows an example of some quality defects seen by a plastic injection molding company. Notice the "Other" category—in a Pareto diagram, the less frequent items can be grouped into a category to make the diagram simpler. In this example, there are five issues that are causing 80 percent of the quality rejects. By looking at this graph, you can see that excess plastic is the most frequent cause for a quality issue. Therefore, when working on reducing the overall quality rejects, it makes the most sense to focus on excess plastic as a cause of rejects. The tool helps you know which problem to address first.

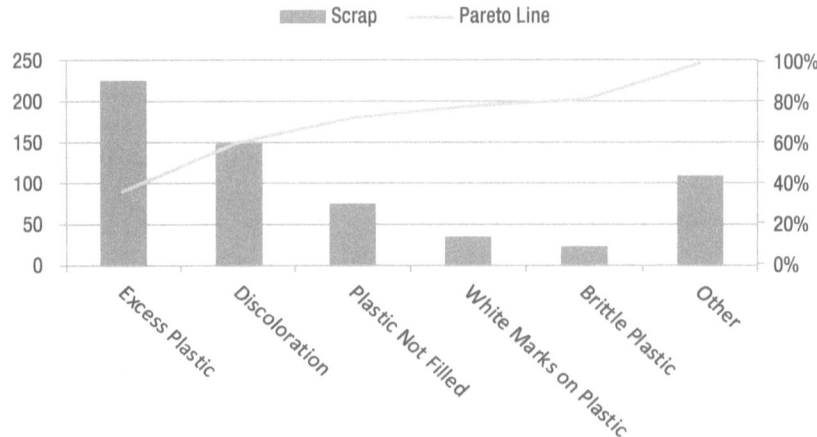

Figure A-14. Pareto Diagram of Defects in Plastic Injection Molding

As you work on the most frequent issue on a Pareto diagram, you should move to the next most frequent cause, making it necessary to focus on something else. In this example, once excess plastic is improved, discoloration would become the focus area for improvement.

> **Note** Use a Pareto diagram to prioritize the issues you will work on correcting.

Dot Plots and Bar Charts

Dot plots and bar charts are similar tools that look for the frequency at which something occurs. Typically, you need special software to create the dot plot easily, although it is possible with spreadsheet software. For this reason, we normally just use the bar chart function in Microsoft Excel or similar software when we want to create a simple frequency diagram. Figure A-15 shows a simple bar chart.

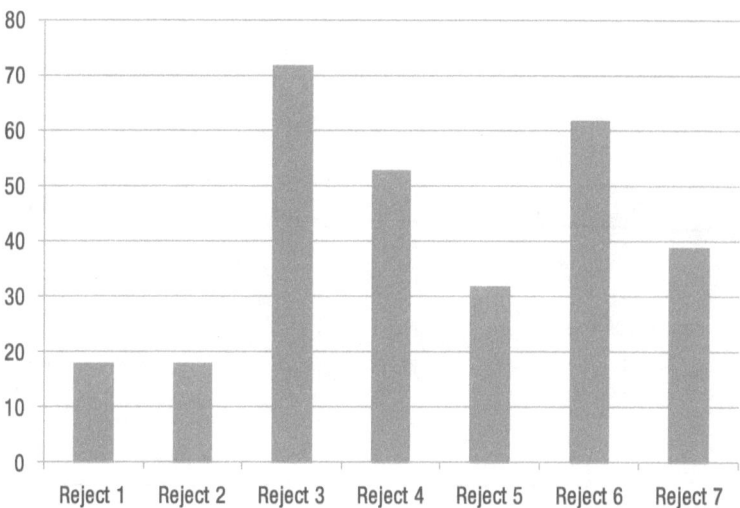

Figure A-15. Bar Chart

Although they are simple, bar charts convey more information than the raw numbers do, because the result is visual. If you have spreadsheet software, you can easily create a bar chart.

Note Use bar charts as a simple way of looking at data.

Box Plots

A box plot shows the range of your data. Figure A-16 shows an example of a box plot. In this example, you have a few weeks of information on how many rejects were created each day of the week. This tells you how much variation there is by day of the week and the total range within the day of the week. For instance, in this chart, Sunday has a lower median number of rejects than any day besides Monday because the centerline is the median value. The distance from the top of the top line to the bottom of the bottom line is the total range of the data over time. From this box plot you can conclude that Sunday is the most consistent and Tuesday is the least consistent day.

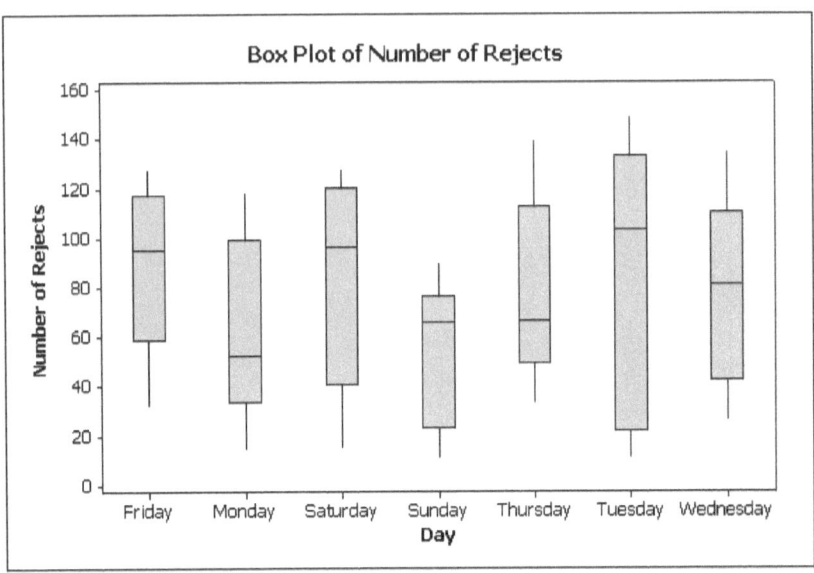

Figure A-16. Box Plot of Rejects by Day of Week

For such a simple graph, the box plot contains a lot of information. Unfortunately, it's not easy to create a box plot in a spreadsheet program; you may end up having to purchase special software to do this. The box plot is typically a part of the standard statistical software packages available for purchase. When you want to use hypothesis testing, you will need the same software. Therefore, if you use these statistical tools, make sure that the software your purchase is capable of meeting all your needs.

Hypothesis Tests

Hypothesis tests are the various statistical tests that you can use to determine if two or more characteristics of your data are statistically different. There are various tests, each of which has a specific purpose. These tests include a test for equal variances, which is used to determine whether the variation between two sets of data is similar. When comparing the averages of two sets of data, you can run the test for equal variances before running these tests.

The two easiest tests for comparing the averages of two sets of data are the analysis of variance (ANOVA) test and the t-test. You will need to consider your sample size and how accurate your results need to be in order to select the right test. In most manufacturing process-improvement projects, you will have the prerequisites to use ANOVA such as equal variances, no special causes, and normal data.

Tests such as Mood's Median and Kruskal-Wallace are used when you do not have the prerequisite data needed for ANOVA or t-test. In service industries like banking and healthcare, where you have a skewed distribution of data, these tests are very useful.

The steps of hypothesis testing are simple:

1. State the question that you are trying to answer.
2. Define the null hypothesis and alternate hypothesis.
3. Define the alpha value for the test, which is typically 0.05 or 0.01.
4. Compute the test and compare the P-value to the alpha. A P-value higher than the alpha value means that you cannot reject the null hypothesis.

The difficult part of hypothesis testing is choosing the right test for your situation. You also have to be careful to understand that just because you come to a conclusion the null hypothesis doesn't mean that you have proven anything. In fact, all you have done is shown how confident you are in your answer. In a company that is new to process improvement, the gains are often so big that the hypothesis tests are not necessary. If you plan to use hypothesis testing, we recommend that you bring in an expert to help you run the correct tests and interpret the results.

Note If you don't know how to use hypothesis-testing tools correctly, bring in an expert.

Ishikawa

The Ishikawa diagram (also known as the fishbone diagram) is typically used to determine the root cause(s) of a single problem. It is used when trying to brainstorm potential causes. Figure A-17 shows an example of an Ishikawa diagram. The Ishikawa diagram helps you narrow down to a potential cause. If you want to figure out the root cause, it is necessary to dig deeper.

Appendix | Tools to Eliminate Waste

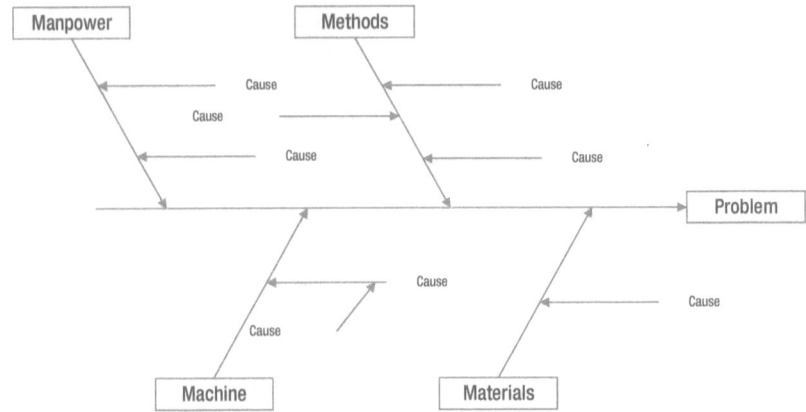

Figure A-17. Ishikawa Diagram

The Ishikawa diagram is a very useful tool that you may end up using frequently once you learn how to use it effectively.

Five-Why Analyses

When performing a root cause analysis, you often get to the apparent cause pretty quickly using a tool such a fishbone diagram. You can then use the five-why analysis to ask why until you get to the root cause. It is called the five-why analysis because you might ask "why" five times before you get to the root cause. The number of whys necessary depends upon the problem. For instance, you may get to the root cause by asking why only once or it may take more than five times. Once you have determined your root cause(s), it is time to improve your process. So let's look at an example.

1. Our sales are not high enough.
    a. Why?
2. Our sales people are not getting enough customer orders.
    a. Why?
3. Our sales people are not utilizing their time effectively.
    a. Why?
4. Our sales people aren't targeting which customers to focus on.
    a. Why?

5. Our sales people haven't analyzed the data.
    a. Why?
6. Our sales people do not have the necessary skills.
    a. Why?
7. We have not required these skills nor trained the sales people on these skills.

Improve

In the improve phase of the DMAIC process, you select solutions to the root cause(s) that you have identified. Along with this solution selection, you also must minimize risk and show that the changes drive the right amount of improvement. You should be careful to change one variable at a time so that you understand what is driving your improvements. If you change several variables at once, you may end up spending time and money implementing changes that are unnecessary.

You often start the improve phase by thinking of solutions and using the solution selection matrix. Remember that the solution selection matrix is the same tool as the prioritization matrix, but you're using it in a different way. Once you have identified your best solutions, it is time to minimize risk.

Failure Modes and Effects Analysis

Failure Modes and Effects Analysis (FMEA) is a tool that can help you identify process risks, propose improvements to your process, and put interventions in place to minimize those risks. You use FMEA to identify and rate risks on three scales. All three risk types are evaluated on a scale of one to ten.

The first scale measures severity. In this scale you are rating how bad the results of a failure would be. A ten could be life threatening. A one is not a big deal. All other numbers are relative between these two extremes. Typically, any failure with a severity rank of nine or ten should get more attention. You might need to use a poke-yoke to warn of this failure, for example.

The second scale measures occurrence. A ten means that this failure occurs every time, whereas a one means that it never happens. A high number may trigger you to put extra checks in place to ensure that you catch the failure before it reaches your customers.

The third scale measures detection. A ten signifies that you don't notice the failure until the customer has experienced the effects of the failure. A one means you that you always catch the failure before it reaches the customer.

Appendix | Tools to Eliminate Waste

After you have ranked all potential failures, you calculate a Risk Priority Number (RPN) to prioritize the issues to address. The RPN can be between 1 and 1,000. Many companies set a threshold of 100 to signify when an action needs to be taken—any RPN over 100 needs to be addressed. Obviously, you cannot modify how severe a failure would be so actions taken to reduce the RPN may include improved detection methods or occurrence reduction. Figure A-18 shows a basic version of FMEA. The Automotive Industry Action Group (AIAG) provides a solid format for FMEA that is universally accepted across industries.

Failure	Severity	Effects	Occurrence	Detection Process	Detection	RPN	Recommended Actions
Failure # 1	8	Effect #1	5	Inspection	3	120	Improve process to reduce occurance
Failure # 2	4	Effect #2	3	None	5	60	None

Figure A-18. Failure Modes and Effects Analysis

Once you have completed your FMEA, you can take the actions identified in the process that reduce the risk of failure. The FMEA can be used for DMAIC and DMADV work.

Design of Experiments

Design of experiments (DOE) is a fundamental skill necessary for a Six Sigma Black Belt to have. Many of the process-improvement projects don't require the use of DOE. This tool uses a structured experimental design. You change one variable at a time and then determine the effects of the change. You can also look at how changing multiple variables affects your process. This method is especially useful when you are pursuing an ideal recipe. In manufacturing, this tool is used extensively on machine settings and material formulations. You can often use this tool to make a process successful when traditional process-troubleshooting methods fail.

Piloting

Once you have designed your new process and put improvements in place, you can benefit from piloting your solutions. This is the process of testing your solutions to identify risks or issues caused by your improvements prior to full-scale implementation. Test-marketing new products is an example of a pilot. Test-driving new car designs before full-scale production is another example. Wherever possible, you should pilot changes to your process.

> **Note** In the improve phase, you need to minimize your risks and pilot your solutions.

Control

The final phase of Six Sigma process improvement is the control phase. This is where you do things to keep the new process in place after the project is completed. Without the control phase, you risk losing any gains that you have made over time. We encourage you to document your project so that others can learn from your work and implement similar improvements elsewhere in your organization.

In the control plan, you create policies, procedures, and training based on the new standardized process. Because most of these tools are common and easy to understand, we introduce only two of the not-so-common tools here.

Control Plan

The control plan, which is also known as the process-management plan, is a document that explains what actions you will take to monitor and control the process. It can include inspection or checkpoints at specified time intervals. It also includes what actions will be taken if the inspection is not favorable. It explains what, when, who, and how the new process will be controlled.

Visual Management

Visual management is the use of dashboards, displays, light trees, flags, and so on to differentiate the normal from the abnormal. Visual management is a key tool because it allows you to make close to real-time adjustments based on the feedback that you get. We have seen visual management done with whiteboards, chalk boards, LCD display monitors, light trees, line demarcations on the floor, signs, and even pictures. Control charts can even be a form of visual management if they're posted in the work area. The challenge behind visual management is ensuring that it affects the work being done and is relevant.

THE SIX SIGMA JOURNEY

Six Sigma users go through weeks of training and mentorship from a Master Black Belt to learn the Six Sigma tools and show practical application of those tools. These tools include brainstorming, prioritization, and root cause analysis activities as well as various statistical tools. The expectation of a Six Sigma Black Belt is knowledge of the tools, how to use them, and when to use them to implement breakthrough improvements.

Theory of Constraints

TOC is an acronym for the theory of constraints, a concept introduced by Eliyahu M. Goldratt when he wrote *The Goal* in the 1980s. The basic concept is that an operation is only as strong as its bottlenecks and weakest links. Goldratt introduced some methods to improve throughput by removing barriers to efficiency. TOC is a good set of tools to use in addition to Lean Six Sigma if there are process flow issues or bottlenecks in your operation, but it does not replace Lean Six Sigma.

Conclusion

There are, of course, other tools and methods used for process improvement, but Lean Six Sigma and Theory of Constraints are probably the most universal. Regardless of whether you use the ones that we recommended or you use other sets of tools, the point is that you need to have a structured continuous improvement process. If you do not have the resources in-house to implement process improvement, you should hire a consultant to introduce the techniques. You will also need internal champions who will continue the methods once the consultant has left.

Index

A

Areas of waste
  average business, 1
  average small business expenses, 2
  business operations, 18–21
  common growth strategies, 5
  departments, 3–4
  finance and accounting, 16–18
  human resources (HR), 10–13
  management and corporate strategy, 4, 6
  manufacturer, 1
  marketing and advertising, 6–8
  money, 1
  sales, 8–9
  small business owner, 2
  technology, 13–14, 16
  wages, 3
Audit and responsibility schedule, 266

B

Bosch Siemens Hausgeräte (BSH), 39
Budgeting
  forecasting
    accurate forecasts, 246
    bad forecasts impact, 246
    contingency plans, 247
    exponential smoothing, 249
    methods, 248
    qualitative methods, 249
    quantitative forecasting, 249
    statistician, 249
    unstable industries, 247
  simple budget process, 245
  zero-based (see Zero-based budgeting)
Business operations
  characteristics, management types, 294
  credit card processing process, 264
  excessive waste, meetings
    brainstorming, 288
    despair.com, 287
    documentation, decisions, 289
    timeline, 289
  lean manufacturing tools, 265–268
  leveraging technology, 291
  magical thinking, 292–293
  metrics, 294–295
  overhead costs, 274–276
  over-/under-serviced
    equipment, 270–271
  performance management (see
    Performance management)
  poorly designed facilities, 269–270
  process improvement wastes, 291
  root cause analysis, 292
  scheduling appointments, 263
  supply chain (see Supply chain
    management)
  unnecessary supplies and services
    confidential paper recycling bin, 272
    electronic tablets, 271
    inventory costs, 271
    paper cost calculation worksheet, 272
    paper cost per employee, 271–272
    types, 271
    wasteful services, 273

Index

Business operations (cont.)
  waste, product development process (see Product development process)
  workforce utilization, 293–294
  workspace layout, 265

C, D

CAC. See Customer acquisition costs (CAC)
Cloud computing
  average savings, 226–227
  benefits, 228–229
  legal contracts, 228
  PC/mobile device, 228
  responders percent, 226–227
CRM software. See Customer Relationship Management (CRM) software
Customer acquisition costs (CAC), 161
Customer lifetime value (CLV)
  assessment, 159
  CAC, 161
  calculation worksheet, 159–160
  churn rate, 161
  customer, 161
Customer needs and marketing research
  accurate information, 74
  cognitive biases and irrational consumer behaviors
    advertising slogan, 81
    decision-making processes, 80
    framing effect, 80
    gambler's fallacy, 80
    psychological principles, 80
  definition, 74
  outsourcing, 82–83
  rules, 84
  silos, 81–82
  statistical and analytical capabilities
    business intelligence (BI), 78–79
    Harvard Business Review (HBR) study, 77
    percent of projects, 78
    right talent, 77
  techniques
    biometric data, 76
    focus groups, 75
    Google Analytics, 76
    surveys, 75
    types, 74–75
  top-performing companies, 84–85
  U.S. companies, 73
Customer relationship management (CRM), 140, 155, 160, 215–217

E

Enterprise resource planning (ERP) system, 13

F

Finance
  budgeting (see Budgeting)
  business tax management, 255
  debt vs. equity, 253
  external funds, 252
  fake numbers, 252
  leasing vs. buying
    and taxes, 256–257
    technology, 256
    timeframe and industry volatility, 256
  loan/credit, 252
  metrics (see Metrics, finance)
  payment terms, 254
  small businesses, 253
  tiered approval processes
    control expenses, 242
    creative spending, 242
    manager, 242
    quotations, 242
  travel and business expense policies
    academic conferences, 243
    business lunches, 244
    conferences and trade shows, 243
    maximum amounts specification, 243
    travel expenses, company, 243
  waste checklists, 261–262

G

General Electric (GE)
  appliance, 25
  financial, 25
  transportation, 25

Index

H

HR metrics
    benefits and compensation, 194
    compensation and benefits programs, 193
    employee satisfaction, 195
    productivity, 193
    recruitment, 196–197
    workers' compensation, 196

Human resources (HR)
    activities, 168
    campus visits, 11
    description, 10
    employee evaluation process, 168
    employees, 10
    metrics, 193
    motivation, 180–181
    non-wasteful hiring, 172–173
    productivity analyses, 170
    productivity increment, 187
    recruitment personnel, 169
    support/business function, 168
    types of analyses, 169
    wasteful hiring processes, 170

I, J, K

Impact/effort matrix, 34

Internal recycle and reuse processes, 275

Inventory level management
    bin system and electronic scanner, 279
    consignment, 280
    economic order quantities, 279
    Kanban system, 280
    lean manufacturing methods, 281
    MRP, 280
    obsolescence/product damage, 279
    space utilization, 280

L

Lean manufacturing tools
    SMED process, 267
    Spaghetti diagram, 267–268
    5S process, 265–267

M

Marketing
    areas of waste
        award-winning show, 71
        customer needs (see Customer needs and marketing research)
        expenses, 73
        percentage of overall firm budget, 72
        product decisions (see Product development)
        product, place, price and promotion, 71
        warehousing, 72
    billboards and television advertising, 70
    checklist, 126–129
    customers, 202
    customer service and word-of-mouth, 69
    description, 69
    distributions, businesses and retail, 114
    HubSpot, 210
    Internet outlets, 70
    ISO-certified companies, 114
    measurement and accountability, 70
    metrics
        advertising, 124–125
        advertising department, 116
        brand preference, 120
        customer expectations, 118–119
        customer satisfaction, 117–118
        customer value, 119
        direct marketing, 123
        measurement method, 116
        net marketing contribution, 116
        price, 122
        product/service development, 121–122
        repurchase and recommend intentions, 120
    mobile apps (see Mobile apps)
    pricing
        company failure, 110
        discounts, 112–113
        low cost, 110–112
    promotional expenses and advertising effectiveness, 102

Index

Marketing (cont.)
  reputation management, 211–212
  shipping costs, 114
  supplier relationships, 114
  text messages, 212
  U.S. ecommerce sales projections, 114–115
Marketing and advertising, waste
  business misconceptions, 7
  effectiveness, 7
  statistical skills/sheer laziness, 7
Material requirements planning (MRP), 280
Mergers and acquisitions (M&As)
  management, 5
  organic growth, 51
  synergies, 50
  types, 49–50
Metrics, finance
  AP and AR days, 259
  contribution margin, 257
  current and quick ratios, 258
  net cash flow, 258
  pre-tax net profit, 257
  return on investment (ROI), 258
Mobile apps
  company spending vs. consumer behavior, 212–213
  usage growth vs. web usage, 214
Motivation, HR
  bonuses, 184
  celebrations, 183
  engagement, company outcomes, 180–181
  picnics and holiday dinners, 183–184
  positive management, 186–187
  rewards, 181–182
  team building, 182–183
  wage increase, 185
  wasteless, 185

N

Non-wasteful hiring
  assessment, 173–174
  candidates attraction, 175
  effective steps, 173
  filling gaps, 180
  gap assessment, 179
  job analysis, 174–175
  recruit selection, 175–178
  sound strategy, 172

O

OECD. *See* Organisation for Economic Co-operation and Development (OECD)
OEE. *See* Overall equipment effectiveness (OEE)
Organisation for Economic Co-operation and Development (OECD), 134
Overall equipment effectiveness (OEE), 297

P

Patient Protection and Affordable Care Act, 32
PDCA. *See* Plan, Do, Check, Act (PDCA)
Performance management
  equipment cost, 297
  inventory and logistics functions, 298
  labor metrics, 295–297
  obsolescence rate, 299
  physical inventory errors, 299
  turnover time, 298
Performance metrics
  infrastructure utilization percent, 234
  response time, 234
  unplanned downtime, 234
P.I.C.N.I.C., 14
Plan, Do, Check, Act (PDCA), 33
Product development
  brand personalities, 89–90
  companies, 97
  consistency, 92
  cost management, 101
  customer dissatisfaction, 87–88
  customer needs, 100
  expectations
    McDonald's, 90
    parents and providers, 90
    products and services, 91–92
  incremental profits, customer loyalty, 87
  initial process, 99
  mapping out, projects, 98
  overpaying, branding, 93–95

packaging, 101–102
premium executive furniture, 89
process with data, 99
referral programs and Facebook, 92
stage-gate process
   killing, projects, 96
   project-management method, 95
   "spaghetti-on-the-wall" strategy, 96
   "wishful thinking", 96
standard process, 98
statistics, 86
sustainable growth, 86
wasteful activities, 97

Product development process
and market research, 276
customer requirements, 276–277
maintenance, customer, 278
planning, production, 277

Productivity increase
administration positions, 190
contingent workforce, 192
education and training, 187–188
employee benefits, 192–193
employee evaluations, 188–189
employee surveys
   and suggestions, 189–190
flextime and working from home, 191
paid time off, 190–191

Promotional expenses and
   advertising effectiveness
brand loyalty, 102
buying decisions, 105
coupon/reward cards, 106
inefficiency, 106
percentage of purchases, 104
percentages, inefficient and efficient, 108
Procter & Gamble (P&G), 103
reasons, purchases, 104–105
searching and buying habits, 110
shopping, 106
slack analysis, 108–109
"sleeper effect", 103
"survey", 106
total spending, 107

Q

Quality-management systems certifications, 275

R

Recruitment selection
emotional intelligence (EQ), 177
methods, 175
personality characteristics, 176
personality tests, 176
pre-hire personality tests, 177
qualification, 179
qualification matrix, 178
reference checks, 178

Request for proposal (RFP), 144

Research and development (R&D)
Christine Moorman's study, 52
customers design, 58–59
description, 52
designers create dozens of
   concepts and pitch, 55
process mapping
   customer data, 52
   development process, 53–54
   information is gathered, 54
   information processing, 54
   inventory waste, 55
   transportation waste, 54
Product/service cannibalization
   eliminate bad products, 56
   innovation, 56
   natural inclination, 55
   new and old product sales, 56
   profitable product death spiral, 58
   profitable product death spiral, 57

Return on investment (ROI), 42

RFP. See Request for proposal (RFP)

S

Sales
area of business, 163
CRM systems (see Customer
   relationship management (CRM))
metrics
   CLV (see Customer lifetime
     value (CLV))
   pipeline analysis, 161–162
   sales executives, 159
   trade show metrics, 162–163
misconceptions, 131

Index

Sales (cont.)
   real-time buying and data, 217–218
   sales metrics (see Sales metrics)
   salespeople, 131
   "veteran reps", 131
   waste (see Waste)
Silos
   customer experiences, 59
   department acts, 59
   organizational structure
      customer design, 60
      functional design, 60
      geographic design, 60
      hybrid design, 60
      matrix design, 60, 62
      product design, 60
      pros and cons, 61
Social media
   consumers and companies, 203
   content marketing, 206–208
   definition, 202
   Facebook and Twitter, 203
   growth
      consumer profiles and data, 204
      efforts., 205
      networks, 204–205
   sales, 209–210
   "spaghetti-on-the-wall method ", 204
   waste, 208
Strategic planning process
   BSH, 39
   description, 38
   focus, 38
   Internal Revenue Service, 40
   no soft stuff, 39
   path forward, 39
   respect, 39
   Skype/Webex, 39
   small and medium-sized businesses, 39
   SWOT/multi-generation plans, 38
Strategy of waste
   and management
      accounting measures, 36
      Aneonline's strategy, 36
      growth and stock price, 35
      Lean Six Sigma methods, 35
      meet/exceed our customer
         requirements, 36
      organizational structure, 37
      payment methods, 37
      profitability and
         debt-to-equity ratio, 35
      SMART, 36
   benchmarking, 43–45
   capabilities view, 26
   China, 24
   commitment-stuck leaders, 42–43
   constant, tactics change, 26
   description, 25–26
   developments, 30–32
      initiative tracking, 32
      measurable and immeasurable
         strategies, 31
      straight line, 30–31
   enterprise, 25
   ever-changing/unattainable
      strategic plan, 25
   evolution, 27
   execution
      impact/effort matrix, 34
      implementation of Hoshin Kanri, 33
      PDCA, 33
   growth
      company identity dies, 46
      consumer market, 47
      control the market, 48
      Core Systems, 47
      customers benefits, 49
      equals profitability, 48
      General Electric (GE), 46–47
      leadership/lack of resources/
         capacity, 48
      mindset, 24
      organizational/leadership problem, 48
      perverse effect on strategy, 45
      sales, 47
   Hoshin Kanri process, 29
   implementing, metrics, 62–63
      balanced scorecard strategy, 62
      machine capacity, 63
   leadership, 40–42
   mergers or acquisitions (M&As), 49–51
   organic growth, 51
   organizational strategy, 28
   R&D, 52, 54–58
   resources-based view, 26
   silos, 59–61

Index

stock price, 23
strategic planning process, 38–39
SWOT, 30
understanding, 30
Supply chain management
   inventory levels, 278–281
   manufacturing companies, 278
   purchasing policies, 286–287
   vendor management, 285–286
   warehouse (see Warehouse management)
SWOT analyses, 30

T, U

Technology
   customer satisfaction, 234
   dot matrix printer, 230
   healthcare workers, 230
   higher-quality products, 230
   investment, 235
   marketing (see Marketing)
   metrics, social media, 232–233
   operational problems, 201
   performance metrics (see Performance metrics)
   project management, 235
   sales (see Sales)
   social media (see Social media)
   waste (see Waste technology)

V

Value-stream mapping, 267
Vendor management, 285
Voiceover Internet protocol (VOIP), 274
VOIP. See Voiceover Internet protocol (VOIP)

W, X, Y

Warehouse management
   customer focused, 284
   fancy system, 283
   fixed location system, 281
   movement/searching, 282
   repacking pallets, 282
   shipping, 284
   standard package sizes, 282

Waste
   assign territories, 156–157
   automated dialers and telemarketing firms, 158–159
   bad hiring and firing
      accuracy rates, 138
      candidates, 137
      company's sales force, 135
      cost, 136
      "gut instincts", 137
      recruiting/promoting, 138
      satisfaction with hiring practices, 136
      skilled professional sellers, 135
      unique characteristics, salespeople, 137
   checklist, 164
   company's budget, 132
   description, 8
   lack of value-stream mapping, 132
   productivity tracking and evaluation processes, 157
   sales expenses
      people and money, 149
      statistical and analytical skills, 152
      trade shows, 151–152
      travel and entertaining, 149–151
   sales performance, 132
   sales process
      cold calling, 148
      companies, 144
      CSO, 143
      customers, 147
      formalization, 144
      important, 148
      media vehicles and frequency, 148
      RFP quoting process, 144
      sales-management function, 142
      sales manager, 144
      sales rep, 147
      value-add and ROI, 147
      value-stream map with inefficiencies, 145–146
      worker, 147
   sales productivity
      academic research, 133
      companies, sales managers, 135
      customers, 133
      human resources, 132

Index

Waste (cont.)
    salesperson, 133
    sales productivity, 134
    sales rep, 133
    sales territories, 135
    the U.S. Bureau of Labor
       Statistics tracks, 132
    worker, 133
    worker productivity, 134
  territory management
    customers and markets, 154–155
    prior analytical skills and planning, 153
    salesperson's responsibilities, 153
    sales processes, 155
    territory design steps, 153
    workload, 155–156
  training
    candidates, 139
    CRM software, 140
    generic programs, 140
    just-in-time training, 141
    measure the sales force, 142
    product knowledge, 140
    rapid and constant evaporation, 141
    sales managers, 141
    sales reps, 141
    selling process, 140
    "stickiness", 139

Waste technology
  centralized/decentralized IT, 230–232
  cloud computing, 226–229
  data access and distribution, 224–225
  IT training and skills, 225–226
  reports, 222–223
  right software, 220–221
  sales presentation, 219
  software as solution, 219–220
  software potential, 221–222

Z

Zero-based budgeting
  activity-based costing, 250
  cost vs. revenue, 250
  data-based ROI calculation, 250
  sales forecast, 251

Get the eBook for only $10!

Now you can take the weightless companion with you anywhere, anytime. Your purchase of this book entitles you to 3 electronic versions for only $10.

This Apress title will prove so indispensible that you'll want to carry it with you everywhere, which is why we are offering the eBook in 3 formats for only $10 if you have already purchased the print book.

Convenient and fully searchable, the PDF version enables you to easily find and copy code—or perform examples by quickly toggling between instructions and applications. The MOBI format is ideal for your Kindle, while the ePUB can be utilized on a variety of mobile devices.

Go to www.apress.com/promo/tendollars to purchase your companion eBook.

All Apress eBooks are subject to copyright. All rights are reserved by the Publisher, whether the whole or part of the material is concerned, specifically the rights of translation, reprinting, reuse of illustrations, recitation, broadcasting, reproduction on microfilms or in any other physical way, and transmission or information storage and retrieval, electronic adaptation, computer software, or by similar or dissimilar methodology now known or hereafter developed. Exempted from this legal reservation are brief excerpts in connection with reviews or scholarly analysis or material supplied specifically for the purpose of being entered and executed on a computer system, for exclusive use by the purchaser of the work. Duplication of this publication or parts thereof is permitted only under the provisions of the Copyright Law of the Publisher's location, in its current version, and permission for use must always be obtained from Springer. Permissions for use may be obtained through RightsLink at the Copyright Clearance Center. Violations are liable to prosecution under the respective Copyright Law.

Other Apress Business Titles You Will Find Useful

When to Hire—or Not Hire—a Consultant
Orr/Orr
978-1-4302-4734-0

Improving Profit
Cleland
978-1-4302-6307-4

CFO Techniques
Guzik
978-1-4302-3756-3

The Employer Bill of Rights
Hyman
978-1-4302-4551-3

Reputation, Stock Price, and You
Kossovsky
978-1-4302-4890-3

The CPO
Schuh/Strohmer/Easton/Scharlach/Scharbert
978-1-4302-4962-7

Metrics
Klubeck
978-1-4302-3726-6

Industrial Problem Solving Simplified
Pawlak
978-1-4302-6577-1

Exporting
Delaney
978-1-4302-5791-2

Available at www.apress.com

GPSR Compliance

The European Union's (EU) General Product Safety Regulation (GPSR) is a set of rules that requires consumer products to be safe and our obligations to ensure this.

If you have any concerns about our products, you can contact us on

ProductSafety@springernature.com

In case Publisher is established outside the EU, the EU authorized representative is:

Springer Nature Customer Service Center GmbH
Europaplatz 3
69115 Heidelberg, Germany

www.ingramcontent.com/pod-product-compliance
Lightning Source LLC
LaVergne TN
LVHW091529060526
838200LV00036B/534